Cultural Authority
in Golden Age Spain

Parallax Re-visions of Culture and Society
Stephen G. Nichols, Gerald Prince, and
Wendy Steiner, Series Editors

Cultural Authority
in Golden Age
SPAIN

EDITED BY

Marina S. Brownlee and
Hans Ulrich Gumbrecht

THE JOHNS HOPKINS UNIVERSITY PRESS
BALTIMORE AND LONDON

© 1995 The Johns Hopkins University Press
All rights reserved. Published 1995
Printed in the United States of America on acid-free paper
04 03 02 01 00 99 98 97 96 95   5 4 3 2 1

The Johns Hopkins University Press
2715 North Charles Street
Baltimore, Maryland 21218-4319
The Johns Hopkins Press Ltd., London

Design by Christine Taylor
Composition by Wilsted & Taylor Publishing Services

Library of Congress Cataloging-in-Publication Data
will be found at the end of this book.
A catalog record for this book is available from the British Library.

ISBN 0-8018-4936-5
ISBN 0-8018-4937-3 (pbk.)

Contents

III
Historical Contexts

Translator's Note

When a preexistent translation is reproduced verbatim, the original translator's last name and the page number of the source are given. Modified translations resulting from a base English text are referenced in the same way, followed by "emended by Iarocci." Translations that are solely mine appear without further notation.

All references are to the following editions:

Anonymous. *The Life of Lazarillo de Tormes*. Translated by Robert S. Rudder and Carmen Criado de Rodríguez Puértolas. New York: Frederick Ungar, 1973.

Miguel de Cervantes. *Exemplary Novels III*. Translated by Michael and Jonathan Thacker. Warminster: Aris and Phillips, 1992.

———. *Don Quixote de la Mancha*. Translated by Tobias Smollett. New York: Farrar, Straus and Giroux, 1986.

Luis de Góngora. *Fourteen Sonnets and Polyphemus*. Translated by Mack Singleton. Madison: Hispanic Seminary of Medieval Studies, 1975.

———. *The Solitudes of Luis de Góngora*. Translated by Gilbert Cunningham. Baltimore: Johns Hopkins Press, 1964.

Lope de Vega. *La Dorotea*. Translated by Alan S. Trueblood and Edwin Honig. Cambridge: Harvard University Press, 1985.

Ovid. *The Love Poems*. Translated by A. D. Melville. Oxford: Oxford University Press [The Oxford World's Classics], 1990.

———. *Heroides and Amores*. Translated by Grant Showerman. Cambridge: Harvard University Press, 1977.

Francesco Petrarca. *Petrarch's Lyric Poems: The "Rime sparse" and Other Lyrics*. Translated by Robert M. Durling. Cambridge: Harvard University Press, 1976.

Fernando de Rojas. *Celestina*. Translated by James Mabbe (1631). Edited by Dorothy Sherman Severin. Warminster: Aris and Phillips, 1987.

Teresa of Jesús. *The Life of Teresa of Jesús*. Translated by E. Allison Peers. Garden City, N.Y.: Doubleday [Image Books], 1960.

Michael P. Iarocci

Introduction

Cultural Authority in Golden Age Spain
MARINA S. BROWNLEE

Over the past several years, a series of extraordinary developments have taken place in Golden Age Spanish studies. Important new issues have been addressed—and conceived—in innovative ways: questions of gender and sexuality; concepts of self and other; political and social contexts of literary production and reception. Whereas these investigations have already begun to have a significant impact on our current reconceptualization of culture in general and Spanish culture in particular, they have until now been somewhat overly dispersed, even fragmented—in large part because of their very nature as rethinkings, as experimental. There has been, in other words, no real forum for a collective examination of these kinds of key cultural issues within the historically specific context of Golden Age Spain. The present volume is meant to provide a first—and modest—step toward remedying this situation, that is, of bringing together for productive interaction some of the people who are doing this new work in such excitingly heterogeneous ways.

Within this overall context, the fundamental issue is the question of authority, conceived in cultural terms.[1] The present volume investigates this question, primarily by focusing on the phenomenon of literary continuation in Golden Age Spain.[2] Throughout history, different ages have responded to the issue of literary continuation in a variety of ways. At times, a given culture will be preoccupied with its origins, exploiting continuation as a way of celebrating the empowering myths that serve as its self-legitimation. At other times a given culture is obsessed by imitation in the opposite sense—as artificial, as imposture, even as forgery or plagiarism. Thus identity and counterfeit constitute the two mimetic extremes of continuation. And both of these extremes involve the question of cultural authority—that is, the ways in which a given culture both conceives of and represents its own authority, positively or negatively.

For our present purposes, the critical issue of cultural authority in Golden Age Spain involves, methodologically speaking, a tripartite division. First, there is political authority presented as cultural authority in the context of the central (and centralized) government of sixteenth- and seventeenth-century Spain. This is the "positive" side of the cultural authority problematic, in which myths of origin and legitimizing historiography play the crucial roles. Both the construct of "continuity" and the phenomenon of continuation figure as politically essential components in the official presentation of court culture and the monarchy as culturally legitimate and authoritative. The figure of genealogy—for the royal family, for the "Spanish people," for "Catholic culture," for Castilian literature—is consistently privileged in this context.

Second, there is what can be termed "negative" cultural authority, "subversive" responses to the official culture which themselves both require a cultural authority of their own and problematize that authority, as it were, by definition. In Golden Age Spain this "negative" dimension has two different, and complementary, sides. On the one hand, there are the subversive countertendencies built into the dominant cultural discourse. Especially relevant here is the concept of the baroque as both self-reflexive and distorting. On the other hand, there are subversive countertendencies—alternatives to the official discourse—clearly presenting themselves as such, clearly demarcated and "independent" in terms of their authority. Particularly relevant here are the categories of class (in, e.g., the picaresque), gender (in, e.g., María de Zayas and Garcilaso), and race (in both Inquisition and *Conquista* literature).[3]

There is also the key issue of the relation between cultural authority and the problem of the subject in Golden Age Spain. Several interrelated aspects of this problematic emerge, beginning with the fragile status of the authorial subject: where in Spanish culture does its authority lie?[4] Here again, continuity and continuation figure as empowering constructs, but with overtly ambiguous dimensions. The paradoxical double status of continuation results from the very condition of rewriting, of *rifacimento* as a process. For every continuation both utilizes and valorizes the authority of its model by the very fact of continuing it, while at the same time the rewriting process necessarily transforms, distorts, and redefines the model.

Directly related to, and part of the definition of, the Golden Age problematic of the authorial subject is that of the authority of the monarchical subject. The central politicocultural fact of the pan-Iberian (even pan-European) claims of the Castilian royal family involved myths of genealogy and lineage. In this context, a fundamental dialectic existed between heterogeneity and "*limpieza*" in both time and space. Cultural authority was thus conceived of as a dynamic struggle in which the threat of difference had to be first perceived and then resolved into identity, into sameness.

Finally, there is the problematic construction of the ideal ("pure") political subject, in both senses of the term, that is, the individual, civic self and the self as the servant to and extension of the Castilian crown. In this context, it is particularly important to view *limpieza de sangre* as a kind of continuation. The operative myth here is that the earlier "pure" race must be continued by breeding out heterogeneous elements. Cultural authority in this particular politicocultural setting appears as both justification and goal.[5]

With regard to both cultural authority and literary continuation, the *Siglo de Oro* constitutes a privileged case, in that it involves—and exploits—all of these problems simultaneously. For one of the most striking features of Golden Age Spain is its obsession with questions of authority, and one of the most characteristic features of Golden Age Spanish literature is its propensity for continuation. Thus many of the most important texts of the period, representing a wide variety of literary genres, are continued, thereby putting into question the status of closure. At the same time, this phenomenon of repeated continuation raises, in both historically specific and theoretically challenging ways, a number of other key issues: canonicity, ideology, history and literary models, textuality and intertextuality, the status of the authorial subject and his or her authoritative discourse(s).

The present volume is intended to provide a framework for exploring these interrelated aspects of the literary enterprise of Golden Age Spain: the double problem of cultural authority and literary continuation. It is, I think, a mark of the intellectual vitality of contemporary Spanish

Golden Age studies that the various responses to this double question are textually specific, historically aware, and theoretically informed in ways that open new perspectives for our continued reading of these culturally authoritative—and subversive—texts.

A Different Classical Age

HANS ULRICH GUMBRECHT

It may not be merely incidental that we seldom apply the adjective "classical" to the classical age of Spanish culture. The status of the *Siglo de Oro* is different from that of other classical periods. Unlike thirteenth- and fourteenth-century culture in Italy, it does not mark the emergence of a national language. Unlike seventeenth-century drama in France, it does not depend on a creative reception of Greek and Roman antiquity, and has never become strictly normative for the cultural production of the following ages. And unlike German literature and philosophy from the time around 1800, the aura of the *Siglo de Oro* is not grounded in the experience that, against an expectation of continuous historical change, it has maintained a relation of immediacy with the culture of the following centuries. The authority of Spain's classical age and the continuity of its presence have never needed to become programmatic.

As early as the middle of the sixteenth century, the highly conventional metaphor of the "Golden Age" became a standard form of self-reference for the Spanish state and the Spanish society.[6] It expressed the pride over the conquests and the political power of what had by then become the first modern empire, and it underlined, at least for a few decades, the empire's claim to fulfill a world-historical mission in the battle between the Reformation and the Counter-Reformation. Until the present day, *Siglo de Oro* as name for a period in cultural history has carried the connotation of its contemporaneity with the culminating moment in Spain's political history, and the reminiscence of such double greatness was certainly the initial condition for the canonization of texts and artifacts from the sixteenth and seventeenth centuries. Nevertheless, what we call "Golden Age culture" was certainly not "the culture of the empire" in any functional sense. Its most inspired religious poets and theologians were constantly under the suspicion of heresy. The lives of some of its most admired literary writers, such as Lope de Vega, Cervantes, or

Introduction

◆

Quevedo, frequently transgressed the borders of official legality, while other authors barely survived the persecution of the Inquisition. Many texts of the Golden Age thematized the darkest sides of social life, and some of its greatest works were far too esoteric to ever unfold a broad ideological impact. If, beyond their sheer contemporaneity, there is any relationship between the Spanish Empire and Spain's classical culture, it appears to be a relation dominated by tension and negativity.

Since the late seventeenth century the reception of the *Siglo de Oro* culture in Spain has always occurred in the style of a spontaneous gesture, although it was often highly selective. At any event, its popularity never needed to rely on explicit ideological programs or on strong institutional support. During the eighteenth century, the reference to authors from the Golden Age simply helped the country to maintain (and even to define) a national identity against the model of French culture which the new Bourbon monarchy was so eager to impose. In the age of Romanticism, Spain found itself becoming the object of a common European admiration (and, sometimes, even of international envy) on behalf of the medieval traces found in (or projected onto) its culture. While a reshaped Don Juan–figure fascinated the nineteenth-century bourgeoisie as evidence for the possibility of living a life in the style of ecstatic individualism without necessarily forgoing the hope for transcendental salvation, only a few decades later the main attention shifted to the figure of Don Quijote. In a moment of national humiliation, a new "philosophical" reading elevated Cervantes' protagonist to a status of exemplum in the role of a morally superior victim within an all too pragmatic world. In our own century it was the reevaluation of Luis de Góngora's extremely complex lyrical language that inspired Spain's specific contribution to the literature of high modernism. Each of these waves of reception provided a broad popularity and an almost unhistorical presence for the poets and the works on which it concentrated; given their extreme selectivity, however, none of them generated a totalizing view of the Golden Age as a period in cultural history.

If we speculate about the grounds that made such an uninterrupted chain of particular selections and reception forms possible—in the absence of any normative claim for continuity as it characterizes the "classical moments" in other national cultures—we encounter, as an inscription of their historical frame-situation, a peculiar oscillation and flexibility in the works of the Golden Age. They emerged out of a social situation in which, on the one hand, differentiated forms of subjectivity and anthropocentrism had found very early articulations, and in which, on the other hand, such subjectivity was restrained and repressed, from the middle of the sixteenth century on, by the newly institutionalized worldview of a Christian cosmology. Through this double-leveledness and the tension it created, a constant shifting between different spheres and styles of behavior became the dominating law of the quotidian; it brought forth an impressive capacity for creating and re-creating everyday situations with a high degree of "theatricality." The binarism "*engaño/desengaño*," the baroque gesture of denying immediate realities and of ontologizing the transcendental, and the never-ending mutual relativization of different world-constructions all go back to this historically particular—and perhaps even historically unique—situation. Therefore, the traces through which the *Siglo de Oro* inscribed itself into the texts and artwork of the Golden Age gave them a superior flexibility and adaptability for different frames of reception.[7] With the rise of a worldview of "multiple realities" from the late nineteenth century onward, the condition for such flexibility, inherent to many *Siglo de Oro* works, was progressively discovered and appreciated as an implicit philosophical quality. This change of perspective caused, for example, the decisive turning point in the reception-history of *Don Quijote*.

Surprisingly, such philosophical dignification did not immediately launch a rethinking of Golden Age culture. While it provided a new condition for its continued presence in everyday Spanish life, this transformation in the status of the *Siglo de Oro* was generally overlooked—at least until very recently. There was no impression of a breakthrough toward a new paradigm of reception, as had been the case, for example, with the redefinitions of German *Klassik* after 1945 or with the aggressive questioning, in the decade of the 1960s, of some leading premises underlying French classicism. The greatness of the *Siglo de Oro* remained a blind greatness, a greatness without intrinsic reflexivity.

From this perspective, the essays collected here seem to indicate a beginning of change. If there is nothing revolutionary in their suggestion of one further shifting in the long and complex reception-history of

Introduction

◆

Golden Age culture, their main importance may lie in the deliberate, even programmatic, nature of their further rethinking. But where could we find the reasons and the motivations for such a dramatic discontinuity in our relation with the *Siglo de Oro*? It is my hypothesis that this discontinuity may have to do with that very stage of transition within Western culture which we frequently label as "postmodernity." From the perspective of its socially constructed temporality, postmodernity can be characterized as the end of "historical time." Postmodernity therefore stages itself as the overcoming of a thought pattern according to which time was an inevitable agent of change, while past and future were experienced as being necessarily asymmetrical.[8] Instead of finding ourselves moving on a line of progress that constantly enters new horizons of the future and leaves behind itself the spaces of the past, we have become increasingly reluctant to cross (or to even mention) the threshold between present and future, and we are nostalgic enough to let our present be invaded by material and intellectual reproductions of past ages. Our postmodern chronotope is an increasingly broad space that substitutes the sequentiality of progress with a perception of simultaneity and a sharpened sense for contemporaneity; it is no longer the operating space of a strong Subject that chooses between different options of the future from a position of the present, but rather a sphere in which the Subject finds itself overwhelmed by the complexity of simultaneous possibilities. But while our discourses begin to cope with this new condition, we are—yet?—unable to leave the dimensions and notions of historical time, of teleology, of agency, and of subjectivity behind us. The new intensity in our relation with the Golden Age could therefore come from the impression that our (post)historical situation is also a situation of transition, of an overlapping and a tension between two different worldviews. It may be that we are facing manifold problems in leaving that very modernity that Golden Age culture was restrained from entering.

If such a perception of a double simultaneity approximates our own cultural situation to that of the *Siglo de Oro*, it could have made us more sensitive to the type of complexity that any sphere of simultaneity produces. We discover perspectives of intrinsic irony and problematization in Golden Age discourses; we enjoy their deconstructive play with institutionalized binarisms; we begin to pursue the margins, the ramifications, and the lateral moves of its worldviews, and we sympathize with the oscillations between its assertions and its dissolutions of Subjectivity. Altogether, it is a paradox that informs the reflexivity in our new approach to Spanish "classical" culture. As we try, perhaps for the first time, to think of the *Siglo de Oro* as a totality, we become increasingly aware that it will resist and ridicule any totalizing effort.

For more than half a century, from Walter Benjamin's "Theses on the Philosophy of History" to Jacques Derrida's *Carte postale*, we have been encouraged to disregard chronological continuity as a condition for cultural appropriation and for cultural authority. As I said at the beginning of this brief retrospective, as long as the *Siglo de Oro* remained within the dimensions of historical time, it never implied a programmatic claim of continuity and authority. This could be the reason why, instead of having to problematize and ultimately to break such claims, the postmodern moment has begun to set free, in its relation to the Golden Age, what one might consider as its equivalent to continuity and authority. It is a sense of intense proximity and of untamable complexity that characterizes our new confrontation with the *Siglo de Oro*.

Notes

1. For recent perspectives on the definition of culture and cultural history, see Lynn Hunt, ed., *The New Cultural History* (Berkeley: University of California Press, 1989), and Kevin Brownlee and Walter Stephens, eds., *Discourses of Authority in Medieval and Renaissance Literature* (Hanover, N.H.: University Press of New England, 1989).

2. In this context, see Wlad Godzich and Nicholas Spadaccini, eds., *Literature among Discourses* (Minneapolis: University of Minnesota Press, 1986), especially the editors' introductory essay, "Toward a History of 'Literature'" (pp. ix–xv), and the essay by José Antonio Maravall, "From the Renaissance to the Baroque: The Diphasic Schema of a Social Crisis," pp. 3–40. See also Peter W. Evans, ed., *Conflicts of Discourse: Spanish Literature in the Golden Age* (Manchester: Manchester University Press, 1990). For the wide-ranging semantic field of the term "Golden Age/Siglo de Oro," see Juan Manuel Rozas, "'Siglo de Oro': La acuñación del término," in *Historia de la literatura española de la Edad Media y Siglo de Oro* (Madrid: Universidad Nacional de Educación a Distancia, 1976), pp. 5–32.

3. For two fascinating recent volumes devoted to these aspects of the baroque, see Anne J. Cruz and Mary Elizabeth Perry, eds., *Culture and Control in Counter-Reformation Spain*, a special issue of *Hispanic Issues* 7 (1992), and Edward H. Friedman, ed., *"Otro cantará": Approaches to the Spanish Baroque*, a special issue of the *Indiana Journal of Hispanic Literatures* 1 (1992).

4. Significant contributions to the study of subjectivity are made by George Mariscal in his *Contradictory Subjects: Quevedo, Cervantes, and Seventeenth-Century Spanish Culture* (Ithaca: Cornell University Press, 1991), and by the collection of essays edited by Alison Weber, *Feminist Topics*, a special issue of the *Journal of Hispanic Philology* 13 (1989).

5. See Américo Castro's classic study, *De la edad conflictiva: El drama de la honra en España y en su literatura* (Madrid: Taurus, 1961).

6. See Fritz Schalk, "Das goldene Zeitalter," *Archiv für das Studium der neueren Sprachen und Literaturen* 199 (1963): 85–98.

7. For a broader development of this thesis (and its relation to processes of canon formation in Spanish culture), see my article "Klassik in Spanien," in Hans-Joachim Simm, ed., *Literarische Klassik* (Frankfurt, 1988), pp. 155–81.

8. For this definition of "historical time," see Reinhart Koselleck, "'Erfahrungsraum' und 'Erwartungshorizont'—zwei historische Kategorien," in *Vergangene Zukunft: Zur Semantik geschichtlicher Zeiten* (Frankfurt, 1979), pp. 349–75. I have tried to give a more detailed description of the postmodern time-construction(s) in my article "nachMODERNE ZEITENraeume," in Robert Weimann and Hans Ulrich Gumbrecht, eds., *Postmoderne—globale Differenz* (Frankfurt, 1991), pp. 54–70.

I

Questions of Authority

1

Tradition and Authority
in Lope de Vega's La Dorotea

LÍA SCHWARTZ LERNER

The function of *imitatio* in Renaissance culture has been redefined many times since Hermann Gmelin's famous codification of its diverse manifestations, beginning with Petrarch and ending with the close of the period.[1] *Imitatio* has been studied from the perspective of Renaissance treatises and in the example of literary works built on such a principle of composition. It is well known that imitation, which encompassed the re-creation of specific verbal models, was a basic artistic practice in the classical and early modern periods; hence the need felt in this century to understand its procedures and implications.

The study of the verbal sources of a text used to be a stronghold of positivistic philology. As it was practiced—and may still be, to a certain extent—it entailed discovering prior formulations of a given work, which were interpreted *lato sensu* as the origin of the text. Needless to say, too often this quest for origins made philologists forget the very text under scrutiny, while the enumeration of sources seemed to become an end in itself. Thus source studies were programmatically criticized by New Critics and other representatives of intrinsic approaches to the analysis of literary texts. However, the situation has changed in the last decade. The inquiry into the sources of a work can be now subsumed under the analysis of intertextuality as a specific mode of textual production. From some new theoretical perspectives, the identification of subtexts can become a search for clues leading to the reconstruction of a work's cultural context. Quotations and imitations indicate what was

3

read and to what had been conferred authority in a given culture, as well as, in a more general sense, which discourses were available for naming and interpreting reality.[2]

Renaissance writers shaped their subjectivity in the process of adaptation and imitation of texts that belonged to tradition.[3] At the threshold of the Renaissance, Petrarch described his engagement with the classical tradition as an ongoing conversation with the Ancients, a hearing of voices, which he quoted and emulated with reverence. It was a dialogical process, as Gerald Burns interprets it, in which the recovery of tradition enhanced the historical dimension of a reading-writing subject. Four centuries later Quevedo still paid homage to this topos and to Petrarch, portraying the life of the poet as an ongoing dialogue with deceased authors, whose voices he heard in solitude.[4] The citation of authorities was then a way of legitimating discourse. From the perspective of the writer, authority appeared to be, in many instances, a precondition of writing. From the perspective of the text, imitation and quotation make visible what has been defined by L. A. Montrose as "that interplay of culture-specific discursive practices, in which versions of the Real are instantiated, deployed, reproduced," and ultimately contested or transformed.[5]

Sources reworked in a new text give access to an author's *Bildung*, in Burns's words. A semio-philologist would say that sources offer clues to the reconstruction of the universe of ideological interpellations, in which the author's subjectivity and that of his reading subjects were constructed.[6] In the semio-philological theoretical project, therefore, the literary representation of human *subjects* is inextricably bound to the conception of subjectivity that was current in a given historical culture at a specific moment of its existence. Human relations were rationalized in Renaissance texts according to traditional models and materialized in a shifting *corpus* of *auctoritates*, sources of quotations that were imitated and resemanticized in the course of their appropriation. Thus the study of verbal models bridges the gap between our contemporary reception of a text, governed by modern or postmodern culture-specific structures of thought, and its reception by readers who were socialized in different modes of thinking, and in different imaginary constructs.[7]

The enactment of this new hermeneutic *Zirkel* can help to recover the historicity of a text. Yet acknowledging the inevitable historical position of the decoder, *pace* Schleiermacher, and the very textuality of history, this reconstruction can hold no claims to having found the "true meaning" of a work. As opposed to the assumptions of a traditional philologist, who thinks he recovered the "literal meaning" of a work by finding its sources, a semio-philologist scrutinizes them anew in the hope of actualizing *meanings* that have not been disclosed in former readings, or that have only become possible to perceive at the historical conjuncture in which he happens to work.

Genre and the Rhetoric of Love

Imitatio is the cornerstone in the production of that extensively studied *acción en prosa* that was either composed by Lope de Vega in the last years of his life or reworked from drafts he purportedly wrote before 1588, when he joined the expedition of the *Armada invencible*:

> Escriví *La Dorotea* en mis primeros años, y auiendo trocado los estudios por las armas debaxo de las vanderas del excelentísimo señor duque de Medina Sidonia, abuelo de V. Excelencia, se perdió en mi ausencia, como sucede a muchas; pero restituida o despreciada (que assí lo suelen ser después de auer gastado lo florido de la edad), la corregí de la lozanía con que se auía criado en la tierna mía.[8]
>
> [I wrote *La Dorotea* in my early years, and when I abandoned my studies to take up arms under the banners of the most excellent gentleman, the Duke of Medina Sidonia, Your Excellency's grandfather, Dorotea went astray in my absence, as often happens with such wayward ladies. But now that Dorotea has been restored, or misprized (a fate not infrequent when the bloom of youth has wilted), I have trimmed the rampant growth she flaunted in my own rampageous youth.] (Trueblood, p. 2)

While this *Ur-Dorotea* may perhaps be a matter of conjecture, there is no question that Lope "made literature" of this episode of his youthful affair with Elena Osorio. The result is a series of plays, novels, and poems, exhaustively studied since the nineteenth century, by, among others, *La Dorotea*'s editors, José Manuel Blecua and Edwin Morby, as well as by Alan Trueblood and by many other critics on both sides of the Atlantic.[9]

La Dorotea has been read from changing theoretical perspectives and, as might be expected, has elicited conflicting responses. We have learned to enjoy it in its *Literaturisierung des Lebens*—Vossler coined this expression that would later be adopted by Leo Spitzer—and as a *trattato d'amore*, in Alda Croce's perceptive commentary. We have read it as the culmination of the *comedia humanística* in the Celestinesque tradition, guided by María Rosa Lida's monumental study of its avatars in Spanish literature. We have reread it with Alan Trueblood in its inter-play of experience and literature, as a work in which tradition gives way to the expression of Lope's natural and very personal feelings. We have lately followed the actualization of some erotic subtexts in Márquez Villanueva's interpretation of the work as a story of the sordid love affair of a male character, cast as an idealized literary version of the young Lope, with a prototypical Renaissance courtesan.[10]

I would like to return to *La Dorotea* in an attempt to reexamine, once again, the *acción en prosa* in the context of its dialogical appropriation of the literary, philosophical, and medical tradition that helped to shape amorous discourse in the Spanish Golden Age. I read Lope's play as a continuation of *La Celestina*, which had, by the seventeenth century, become canonical. Thus I find it unnecessary to argue, for instance, about the go-between's function in the play. Gerarda, built in clear coun-terpoint to the character of Celestina in Rojas's work, is a satiric figure who has more than once been cryptically dismissed as superfluous to the development of plot, although she logically belongs in Lope's re-creation of a generic model.[11]

Yet *La Dorotea*'s poetics of *imitatio* is not limited to the re-creation of genre and the selection of characters. In fact, *imitatio* can be seen as an ongoing dialogue with cultural authorities that legitimate poetic dis-course. Thus the presence of authoritative dicta opens the path to a re-construction of ideological contexts. Moreover, Lope programmatically assimilated *inventio* and *imitatio* in his *acción en prosa*, referring to controversies of the Academici della Crusca. He makes this explicit in act 4, scene 2, where the character César, while discussing the satirical sonnet "Pululando de culto, Claudio amigo," a spoof on the aesthetics of *gongoristas*, elaborates a topic of Renaissance rhetorical theory, namely, that "L'imitazione e la 'nuenzione sono vna cosa stessa":

> *Cés.*—Sin passión digo que muchos dellos no son dignos de ala-
> bança, aunque yo lo quiero ser deste soneto. Porque como la inuen-
> ción es la parte principal del poeta, si no el todo, y *inuención y imi-*
> *tación sean también vna misma cosa,* ni lo vno ni lo otro se halla en
> el que comenta.[12]
> [Speaking dispassionately, I would say that many commentators are not
> worthy of praise, although I trust I'll be worthy of this sonnet. Because,
> while invention is the poet's main attribute, if not his whole stock in trade,
> and *though invention and imitation are one and the same,* you never find
> either in the commentator.] (Trueblood, p. 184)

Lope's identification offers further incentives to discover classical models upon which he developed a rhetoric of feelings and rationalizations of amorous relations. Lope's self-conscious display of sources fits in with the tradition of the chosen genre. It seems unnecessary, therefore, to dwell on the appropriateness of erudition in *La Dorotea*, a topic that has vexed many an interpreter.[13] The unrecognized tendency to privilege realistic discourse could make a critic forget that the play was composed within definite conventions, regardless of its autobiographical origins. To go back to the sources of the work now satisfies the need to identify traditional images and figures that inscribe characters in definite discursive spaces. There is no question that *La Dorotea*'s casuistry of love, though alien to our conceptualization of gender and sex, of love and of human relations, may be naturalized and assimilated to our own imaginary constructs. Yet, from my theoretical standpoint, it seems less important to read Lope's configurations of desire in their universal appeal, as anticipations of present psychological interpretations, than to stress their historical particularity. I take love to be mainly a cultural creation, the way Thomas Laqueur has convincingly defined sex.[14] If sexuality is "a way of fashioning the self in the experience of the flesh" and not "an inherent quality of the flesh that various societies repress or extol," love in *La Dorotea*, as well as in other works of the Golden Age, is a way of fashioning relations in the experience of authoritative models of behavior.

In his *acción en prosa* Lope represented a love affair that ends in separation and lovelessness, *desamor*. His representation is accomplished by imitating and referring to a threefold tradition in the transhistoric corpus of high love-literature: that of Roman erotic elegy, that of Renaissance Neoplatonic discourses, and that of Petrarchan love poetry. Some of these sources had already been imitated and adapted by Rojas in the composition of his *Tragicomedia*. There are many intertextual plays with *La Celestina*, which show the mediating function of the former in the transmission of a vocabulary of love and a rhetoric of self and sex. However, it is also evident that Lope drew anew on these traditions. His direct imitations of texts by Ovid, for instance, confirm that the classical love canon was not read in the same way a century later in Spain, which indicates that tradition itself is not immutable but is also subject to history. In fact, the Aristotelian-Galenic theory of love had been eclectically conflated with Neoplatonic and theological views in sixteenth- and seventeenth-century medical and philosophical treatises. In their 1990 edition of one of these treatises, Donald A. Beecher and Massimo Ciavolella traced the trajectory of the concepts of erotic mania and erotic melancholy, as it evolved from, say, Battista Fregoso's *Anteros sive tractatus contra amorem*, written before 1496, to Jacques Ferrand's *De la maladie d'amour ou melancholie erotique*, of 1623, and Robert Burton's *The Anatomy of Melancholy*, of 1621.[15] Françoise Vigier's examination of erotic madness in pastoral literature also showed that poetic conceptualizations of love in the sixteenth century were dialectically related to medical treatises in Spain.[16] Thus Lope's rhetoric of love resemanticizes literary tradition by reading it from the perspective of Renaissance scientific discourses.

The Construction of Subjectivity

The actors in Lope's play of love are constructed according to historically determined categories of male and female. It is well known that medical, legal, religious, and artistic discourses in the Golden Age privileged the male body. Women were thus conceived as imperfect notions of men: they were considered colder, weaker, and less stable. The gender system of the one-sex body, to quote Laqueur again, was based on the principle of hierarchy and reciprocity; the male was superior and the female inferior. The boundaries between male and female were thus of degree and not of kind. A man and a woman needed to unite sexually for conception, yet the male represented efficient cause, while the female represented only the material cause.[17]

In a paraphrase of Aristotle's definition of woman in his *De Generatione Animalium*, which had become a topos in the Renaissance, Gerarda is made to convey to Dorotea's mother, Teodora, the convenience of choosing a wealthy lover by reminding her of the inferior status of the female in their society:

> Los hombres en qualquiera edad hallan sus gustos, y son buenos para los oficios y para las dignidades; tienen entonces más hazienda, y son más estimados. Pero como las mugeres sólo servimos de materia al edificio de sus hijos, en no siendo para esto, qué oficio adquirimos en la república? Qué gouierno en la paz? Qué bastón en la guerra? Bolued, bolued en vos, Teodora. No acabe este moçuelo la hermosura de Dorotea, manoseándola.[18]
> [Now, men at any age discover ways of enjoying themselves. They find suitable occupations and positions of honor, increasing their means along with their reputations. But woman's only good is to furnish the stuff out of which men's children are made; once that function ends, what post do we acquire in the commonwealth, what governorship in peacetime, what command in time of war? Return to your senses, Teodora. Do not permit this miserable youth to finish off Dorotea's beauty by mishandling it.]
> (Trueblood, p. 13)

Regardless of their gender, characters in the play may be assigned a similar notion of the hierarchy male/female. Thus Dorotea's letter to Fernando, in act 3, scene 6, composed in imitation of two sources related in *contaminatio*, Dido's speech in canto 6 of the *Aeneid*, and Dido's letter 7 of Ovid's *Heroides*, develops the topos of male cruelty in line with this argument. Lope imitates here the traditional metaphor with which Ovid described cruelty by relating man to beast: "Te lapis et montes innataque rupibus altis robora, te saevae progenuere ferae"[19]

[Of rocks and mountains were you begotten, and of the oak sprung from the lofty cliff, of savage wild beasts (Showerman, p. 85)], which becomes, in Dorotea's words, "Qué coraçón de fiera con tan animosa determinación en vn instante executara, con cinco años de amor, tan gran castigo?" [What beast could be so hardhearted as to inflict in one instant and so implacably a punishment so great upon five years of love? (Trueblood, p. 141)]. Yet the metaphor is further amplified in another section with a reference to the traditional opposition courage/cowardice:

> Crueles fuimos entrambos, pero tú más conmigo como quien tiene más valor y entendimiento. Es la condición de las mugeres tan temerosa, y imprímese en su cobardía tan fácilmente la más mínima amenaça, que ella tuuo la culpa de mi atreuimiento. (p. 264)
> [Cruel as we both were, you were more so with me, in view of your greater strength and understanding. Woman's nature is so timorous, and the slightest threat so quickly uncovers her cowardice, that there the blame for my audacity must lie.] (Trueblood, p. 141)

Dorotea's answer to Fernando in 1.5 imitates another Aristotelian topos of similar filiation: "que la muger más fuerte al fin es obra imperfecta de la naturaleza, sujeto del temor y depósito de las lágrimas"[20] [for the strongest of women is but Nature's imperfect handiwork, a prey to fear and a well of tears (Trueblood, p. 26)].

Tears belong with the representation of the female; they are a sign of their *natural* weakness, but can also be a symbol of duplicity, another topos, which Fernando imitates in act 1, scene 5 when he characterizes women's tears as "entretelas de la risa," because "no hay tempestad en verano que más presto se enjugue"[21] [Women's tears are mere laughter turned inside out. No summer cloudburst dries so quickly (Trueblood, p. 29)]. Women are inconstant and fickle; Fernando compares them to *azoque* [mercury], in act 2, scene 4. Back from Seville, he finds out from his friend Ludovico that Don Bela is now Dorotea's lover. The friends' discussion of greed in women—defined by Fernando, in imitation of a Ciceronian sentence, as "género avarísimo"—develops scientific commonplaces on the nature of metals. Gold, silver, and others are children of sulfur and mercury, as characterized by Levinus Lemnius in his *Occulta naturae miracula*.[22] The learned reference to the origin of gold, however, elicits still another disparaging analogy between matter and women: "Ya me acuerdo de su inquietud y inconstancia, y juntamente de su prouecho, en que es parecido a la naturaleza mudable y bulliciosa de las mugeres" [I am well aware of its utter inconstancy and also of its usefulness, recalling both the fickle and garrulous nature of women (Trueblood, p. 126)].

Dorotea and Celia, in turn, also engage in defining the differences between male and female. Their rationalization of Fernando's behavior—he seems to have forgotten his love for Dorotea—will deal with man's inconstancy. Celia accuses him—"Mal conoces la inconstante naturaleza de los hombres" (2.2)—but Dorotea is made to state: "Do nosotros la tomaron," while she later reminds Celia once again of the traditional philosophical concept of female weakness: "No ves que está a su cargo nuestro sustento y vestido, y que corre por su cuenta nuestro amparo?" [Little do you understand men's inconstancy. . . . They learned inconstancy from us. . . . You forget that they are responsible for the feeding and clothing of us, and for our protection as well (Trueblood, pp. 54–55)]. The same Aristotelian dicta, incorporated into the patristic tradition, where they merged with biblical discourses and later crystallized in proverbial discourse, are similarly reworked in other definitions of female behavior in *La Dorotea*.[23] There is, for instance, the notion that women are slow at making up their minds but, once determined to do something, will be swift in executing it. Dorotea explains her decision to break with Fernando, at the end of her first monologue (1.4), with a sentence that imitates a statement in the *Ethica Nicomachea*: "Resuelta estoy. Qué aguardo? Iesús! Parece que tropecé en mi amor. O amor, no te pongas delante! Déxame ir, pues me dexaste determinar; que *en las mujeres la resolución es difícil, la execución es fácil*"[24] [My mind is made up. Why do I delay? Good Lord! Do I stumble over love? Ah, love, do not stand in my way. You let me make this choice, now let me leave, since *women find resolution difficult, though acting on it simple* (Trueblood, p. 18)].

The Illness of Love and Its Cure

Dorotea and Fernando are made to discuss their situation in scenes of confrontation that alternate with monologues and letters. Other characters also refer to the protagonists' plight, characterizing them from complementary or opposed perspectives. Love is seen, topically, as a disease, in the tradition of the "malattia d'amore," examined by Massimo Ciavolella and lately brought to attention by Aurora Egido in her study of Soto de Rojas.[25] "El amor es loco," in Dorotea's words (4.1), or in Julio's ironic comments on the poetical topos: "Pobre mancebo. Perderá el seso. Pero cómo puede perder lo que no tiene?" (1.5) [Poor fellow! He is losing his mind. But how can he lose what he does not possess? (Trueblood, p. 32)]. The poetic metaphor, as expected, finds confirmation in scientific texts. Julio himself is made to quote, not without irony, a medical opinion—that of Triverus's *Vniversae medicinae . . . methodus*, of 1592—to confirm the lovers' madness: "vn excelente calor vicia las operaciones, y este de tu amor desatinado no te dexa conocer la razón con la templança que en tales ocasiones tienen los hombres cuerdos"[26] [excessive heat warps its {the brain's} functioning, and this, brought on by misguided love, prevents your attaining the reasonable balance shown by sensible men on such occasions (Trueblood, p. 31)].

Triverus's quote, "Excellens caliditas operationes vitiat," reworked Hippocratic notions, systematized by Galen, in conjunction with an implicit reference to the doctrine of the passions. Love is a "harmful impulse" that deflects man from the road of reason and virtue. Lope makes "personal" in his characters what was common opinion in the medical tradition and in Petrarchist poetry.

Fernando's madness is also a function of his *imitatio Calixti*. His first words after the rupture, in act 1, scene 5, re-create Rojas's text:

Cierra la ventana y dexa la tiniebla acompañar al triste y al desdichado la ceguedad. Mis pensamientos tristes no son dignos de luz. O bienaventurada muerte aquella que deseada a los afligidos viene! O si viniéssedes agora, Crato y Galieno, médicos, sentiriades mi mal! O piadad celestial, inspira en el plebérico coraçón, por que sin esperança de salud no embíe el spíritu perdido con el desastrado Píramo y de la desdichada Tisbe![27]
[Shut the windows, and leave the darkness to accompany him, whose sad thoughts deserve no light. Oh death! how welcome art thou to those who

outlive their happiness! how welcome, wouldst thou but come when thou art called! Oh that Hippocrates and Galen, those learned physicians, were now living, and both here, and felt my pain! Oh heavens, if ye have any pity in you, inspire that Pleberian heart therewith, lest that my soul, helpless of hope, should fall into the like misfortune with Pyramus and Thisbe.] (Mabbe, p. 27)

This passage is the intertext of Fernando's

Muerto soy, Iulio. Cierra todas las ventanas, no entre luz a mis ojos, pues se va para siempre la que lo fue de mi alma. Quita de allí aquella daga, que el trato es demonio, la costumbre infierno, el amor locura, y todos me dizen que me mate con ella. (p. 101)
[I'm dying, Julio. Close all the windows, let no light reach my eyes, since the light of my soul is doused forever. Remove that dagger from my sight, for the flesh is a thing of the devil, habit of hell, love madness, and all are urging me to turn it on myself.] (Trueblood, p. 30)

Love, as an illness, is erotic mania, manifested in fury—Orlando's furor—but also erotic melancholy. It was described as such in Renaissance *polyantheae*, which perpetuated medical and philosophical opinion. Textor's *Officina* is the source for Ludovico's ironic diagnosis of Fernando's disease as *erotes*, "morbus est melancholiae, ex nimia amoris aegritudine proueniens": "Esta enfermedad, melancólica por amorosa inclinación o por la possessión perdida del bien que se gozaua, llaman los médicos *erotes*"[28] [This illness, which doctors call *erotes*, is a melancholia arising from amorous proclivities or from losing possession of a beloved whom one has enjoyed (Trueblood, p. 132)].

Lovers were conceived as living in a very special state of mind, in which there was no room for the laws of reason. Moreover, loving could be felt as a *psychomachia* of reason and passion, which constituted a vast space of suffering. Ovid's formulation in his *Heroides*, 4.154, was amply imitated: "Quid deceat, non videt nullus amans."[29] Don Fernando thus states: "Y yo [digo] con Ovidio, que ninguno que ama lo conoce [that is, what is important to know] y con Séneca, en su *Hipólito*, lo que tomó dél Garcilaso cuando dijo: *Conozco lo mejor, lo peor apruebo*"[30] [And I'll tell you what Ovid says, that nobody can recognize it, and what Seneca says in his *Hippolytus*, in that portion Garcilaso took from him: "*Albeit I know best, I but choose the worst*" (Trueblood, p. 115)]. As Morby indicates, Garcilaso imitated in line 7 of sonnet 6 not Seneca but a sentence from the *Metamorphoses*, 7. 20–21: "Video meliora proboque, / deteriora sequor," which, it should be added, was probably mediated by two lines in Petrarch's famous canzone 264, ll. 135–36:

> Cerco del viver mio novo consiglio,
> E veggio 'l meglio, et al peggior m'appiglio.[31]
> [I seek new council for my life / and I see the better but I lay hold on the worse.]   (Durling, p. 433)

The *Canzoniere* may have also provided sources for images in which lovers are described as lost in the labyrinth of love. At the least, it was an intermediary in their transmission. Some of Dorotea's words in her first monologue (1.3) show in palimpsest Petrarchan formulations, such as line 14 of sonnet 211 ("Nel laberinto intrai, né veggio ond'esca" [I entered the labyrinth, nor do I see where I may get out of it (Durling, p. 365)]) or line 4 of sonnet 214 ("Un lungo error, in cieco laberinto" [a long wandering in a blind labyrinth (Durling, p. 381)]), not indicated by Morby:

> Dónde me lleua este amor desatinado mío? Qué fin me promete tan desigual locura de lo que pudieran auer merecido las partes de que me ha dotado el cielo? Quando aya passado lo mejor de mis años en este laberinto amoroso, qué tengo de hallar en mí sino arrepentimiento para los que me quedaren, quando a los que desprecio les dé vengança?
> [Where is this perplexing love of mine leading me? What can be the end in store for this mad passion, so adverse to everything my heaven-sent gifts seemed to promise? Having spent my best years in this labyrinth of love, what shall be left me but the repentance for those that remain, as the years I have thrown away take their vengeance?]   (Trueblood, pp. 16–17)

What is clear, in any case, is that the image had become topical in other Petrarchist *canzonieri* of the seventeenth century. We are thus reminded of the persistence of what Augustin Redondo has defined as "des attributs, emblèmes ou symboles . . . souvent liés aux images de la folie (d'amour)" [attributes, emblems or symbols . . . often tied to images of (amorous) folly] in its recurrence in the poetry of Soto de Rojas, where he re-creates the topos of the labyrinth of love in at least one of his sonnets:

> Mas quando mas me aparto, mas me llego,
> Que es labirinto este tormento mio.[32]

[But the farther I go, the closer I am, / for this torment of mine is a labyrinth.]

The magnitude of the lover's suffering is thus related to his madness, an illness that controls conscience and will.[33]

Needless to say, the conceptualization of suffering in love was also perceived as coming from the coexistence of opposite feelings. The Catullian *odi et amo . . . et excrucior*, of *carmen* 85, had been reworked in the Ovidian tradition and in the philosophical-scientific one.[34] Thus it can be documented by Fernando with a quote from Aristotle:

Aristóteles escriue que la hermosa Hélide tuvo amores con vn etíope, y parió vna hija blanca; pero que el hijo de la hija nació negro. Y assí de la hermosura de Dorotea nace mi amor blanco; pero deste mismo, después, mi aborrecimiento negro. (3.1)[35]
[Aristotle writes that lovely Helis had an Ethiopian lover and bore him a white daughter, but afterward that daughter's son was born black. And thus Dorotea's beauty brings forth my love white, then from the same love later brings forth my hatred black.] (Trueblood, p. 106)

Another philosophical text confers authority to the poetic conceit that the lover, when separated from the beloved, leaves his soul in her, because, claims Julio, the south "está más donde ama que donde anima" (1.5). This time Ficino's commentary on Plato's *Symposium* confirms descriptions of desire in philographic treatises such as the *Diálogos de amor*, where it is explained that, "el amor y el deseo es medio que nos eleva desde el conocimiento imperfecto hasta la perfecta unidad, que es el verdadero fin del amor y del deseo"[36] [love and desire are a means that elevates us from imperfect knowledge to perfect unity, which is the true end of love and desire]. The Neoplatonic precept of the merging of souls as the goal of true love can, in turn, be ironically extended so as to postulate a true metamorphosis of the lover into the beloved, by which the first can lose his identity. Thus Dorotea reports Fernando's need to shed tears, when possessed by his passion: "Este era tan lisongero que dezía que ya él no era hombre; porque, transformado en su dama, auía perdido el ser" (2.3) [This one was so flattering he claimed that he had ceased to be a man; that, having turned into his lady, he'd yielded up his nature (Trueblood, p. 60)].

La Dorotea, however, does not represent an everlasting love relation, but precisely the dissolution of what Fernando redescribes, imitating Neoplatonic discourse as "Amor es nudo perpetuo y cópula del mundo" (5.3)[37] [Love is the eternal knotter and coupler of the world (Trueblood, p. 235)]. Yet, in spite of these and other references to Ficino and Leone Hebreo, Lope and his competent readers knew what kind of love was represented in the play. It was not a reworking of Plato's *Aphrodite Urania*, that pure love that saves the soul. It was a version of *Aphrodite Pandemia*, sexual love, that is, a disease—νόσημα—that destroys the soul.[38] In both cases, however, the obsessed lover was in chains. To get to the free state of a being who has liberated himself from the prison of love— again, topoi of Roman elegiac discourse re-created countless times in both the Petrarchist and emblematic tradition—Lope builds a sequence of events in the *imitatio* of Ovid's *Remedia amoris*.[39]

It is well known that Ovid's diptych—the *Ars amatoria* vis-à-vis the *Remedia amoris*—embodied the central rationalization of love as an illness that could be healed with a specific therapy. Ovid presents the poet of the *Remedia* as a physician who can help the suffering lover:

> Ecce, cibos etiam, medicinae fungar ut omni
> Munere, quos fugias quosque sequare, dabo.[40]
> [There's diet too: I'll end my doctor's duties / by telling you what to shun
> and what to pursue.]   (Melville)

After all, in the game of love, whoever pretends to be cured will anew feel healthy. Although a few passages of the *Remedia* have been pointed out as sources of *La Dorotea*, by Morby and Trueblood, I do not believe it has been sufficiently stressed that Lope's plot of disengagement from passion is basically an *imitatio Ovidii*. Fernando's decision to leave for

Seville, in order to forget Dorotea, as well as the rationalization of his departure, follows several recommended steps in Ovid's short poem.

> Tu tamtum, quamuis firmis retinebere uinclis,
>   I procul et longas carpere perge uias
>   (ll. 213–14)

[There's travel too: though you're held fast in bondage, / start a long journey and go right away.]   (Melville)

Fernando's need to remove himself from the city where the beloved lives is a painful need, as in Ovid; "porque estar adonde vea mi muerte, es sufrir tantas quantos instantes tuuiere el día" (1.5) [since to remain here where I behold my death is to suffer it every second of the day (Trueblood, p. 31)]. Once back, and after the reconciliation with Dorotea, when the desire to recover his freedom persists, the character is made to imitate other advice of the *Remedia amoris*:

> Yo, César, después de lo referido, como sé que el arte se haze de muchas experiencias, y la tenía tan grande por cinco cursos en la vniversidad de amor, peregrino estudiante, hize resolución de amar a Marfisa sin dexar a Dorotea, hasta que con el trato y el fauor de mi buen deseo conualeciesse de todo punto.   (5.3)
> [After what I have related, César, and considering that art is the result of much experience, and that I had had an abundant share of it, what with my five years as a prize student of the university of love, I determined to marry Marfisa without abandoning Dorotea, till the effect of the relationship and the desired consequence of my good intentions should bring about a complete cure.]   (Trueblood, p. 233)

The *Remedia*'s text recommends that a lover share two mistresses; the first obsessive passion will then purportedly weaken until it finally disappears:

> Hortor et ut pariter binas habeatis amicas;
>   Fortior est, plures si quis habere potest.
> Secta bipartito cum mens discurrit utroque,
>   Alterius uires subtrahit alter amor.

Grandia per multos tenuantur flumina rivos,
Saevaque diducto stipite flamma perit.

(ll. 441–44)

[I recommend you have a pair of girl-friends / (for having more it takes a
man who is braver); / Then each love saps the vigor of the other / and to
and fro the fissured feeling waver. / Great rivers are reduced by many
channels; / when fuel is dispersed the flame will die.]   (Melville)

Fernando's description of his process of detachment plays intertex-
tually with the above cited lines. Thus Marfisa can authoritatively be
presented as "el templo de mi remedio, la imagen de mi salud, y el último
asilo de mis desgracias" (5.3) [the temple of my salvation, the holy image
of my restoration, and the final refuge of my misfortunes (Trueblood, p.
239)]. One could point to other details that indicate the filiation of these
remedies of love. The point is not, however, to exhaust parallels, but to
suggest that the poetic fictions of Ovid, as in other instances, those of
Vergil or the poetic fabrications of self and of love that Petrarchan discourse disseminated in the Renaissance were appropriated to stage a
play of love and lovelessness, based on memories of Lope's youthful
affairs.

The reconstruction of Lope's amorous imaginary leads even to restrict semantically the meaning of the word *desengaño* in *La Dorotea*.
Desengaño is defined by *Autoridades* as "luz de la verdad, conocimiento del error con que se sale del engaño" [the light of truth, the
knowledge of error with which one escapes deceit/delusion]; *desenga-
ñarse*, in Covarrubias, is "caer en la cuenta de que era engaño lo que
tenía por cierto" [to realize that what one held as true was a delusion].
Often interpreted in our century as an expression of a generalized baroque feeling of disillusionment, of time and of solitude, I think it
should be construed here in relationship to the meaning it had in other
seventeenth-century works that developed the specific concept of *desengaño de amor*.[41] Suffice it to mention here María de Zayas's *Desengaños amorosos* (1647), or the above mentioned Soto de Rojas's *Desengaño de amor en rimas*, written between 1609 and 1614 and published
in 1623, which traces the fiction of a passion that ends in repentance.
Lope de Vega wrote an *Elogio* of the work, in which he extolled the work

of Soto, *el Ardiente*, as he was called in the Academia Seluage: "Lla-máuase en nuestra Academia el Ardiente, nombre que tomó para sí el excelente Portugués Luys de Camoens," says Lope. He then continues:

> Y vino bien este título a su ingenio, que en la lengua Latina Ar-diente es ingenioso, y como dixo Cicerón a Celio. *Ardor mentit ad gloriam.* En ella escriuió el discurso de la poética y perfecta medida del verso Castellano, imitando al Tasso en vna oración que hizo en la Academia de Ferrara. Los Poemas son varios, assí en la corres-pondencia de las Rimas, como en los sugetos, ofreciéndole Fénix las ocasiones, no menos honestamente, que al Petrarca Laura.[42]
> [In our Academia he was known as el Ardiente, a name that the excellent Portuguese gentleman Luys de Camoens took for himself . . . And this title fit his talent well, for in Latin Ardiente means ingenious, and as Cicero told Celius, *Ardor feigns gloriously.* In Latin he also wrote the treatise on the perfect, poetic measure of Castillian verse, imitating a speech that Tasso made in the Academia de Ferrara. The poems are as varied in rime combi-nations as they are in subject matter, and Fénix offers him opportunities no less sincere than those that Laura offered Petrarch.]

Soto de Rojas's last poems of part 1 redescribe the lover's liberation from the chains of love. Poem 163 is entitled "Libertad":

> Ya que apagado el fuego, y suelto el lazo
> Está, con que me vi, encendido, y preso,
> Alegre bueluo al primitiuo sesso,
> Mal grado del amor, y su embaraço:
> La dulce libertad amada abraço,
> Y en todo absuelto mi mortal processo,
> Quando el error que cometí confiesso,
> El pecho en penitencia despedaço.
> Mi vida presumió que acabaría
> Fénix cruel, y a otro se dio, burlome;
> Mas yo sané, no assí! mientras fue mía.
> Quando trató de amarme, aborreciome,
> Y quando se mostró que me ofendía,
> En vez de ofensa aborreciendo amóme.

[Now that the fire is extinguished, / and the knot is undone / (elements with which I had found myself ignited and bound) / I happily return to my earlier state of mind, / despite love and its entanglement. / I embrace sweet, beloved liberty, / and completely absolved of my mortal trial, / when I confess the error I made, / I tear at my breast in penitence. / Cruel Fénix presumed that she would end my life, / and she gave herself to another, she deceived me, / but while she was mine I did not heal. / When she tried to love me she shunned me, / and when it was plain that she was offending me, / in stead of offense, by shunning, she loved me.]

Poem 163, "Conocimiento," develops the topos of love's tyranny: "Ya dexé ya, tu vega amor tirano" [Tyrannical love, I've left, I've left your meadow]. It is followed by another sonnet, entitled "Conocimiento perfecto"; its first quartet reads:

> Dichoso aquel, que en apacible estado,
> Lejos de la vulgar y ciega gente,
> Con pecho firme, con serena frente
> Viue de amores de ambición purgado.

[Happy is he who in a peaceable state, / far from the lowly, blind masses, / lives with firm heart and calm mind, / purged of the ambition to pursue love.]

The last sonnet of part 1 sums up the new mental state of the lover:

Desengaño de Amor exortando

> O Tu que adoras miserable amante,
> Fantastica apariencia de belleza,
> Buelue mis hojas llenas de aspereza,
> Y en noche instable, aprende luz constante.
> Amor verás, si se creyó diamante,
> Frágil vidro después, que en su entereza
> Coronado de llanto, y de tristeza
> Brindó, al mejor de su campaña errante.
> Veneno entre christales emboçado
> Escusa, y solicita ya, sediento
> Cieruo, curso de fuente dilatado.
> Toma de tanto hydrópico escarmiento;

Más medra el abstinente, el recatado,
Que quanto el mundo ofrece es sombra, es viento.

[*An Exhortation to Awaken from Love.* Oh miserable lover, you who
adore / the illusory image of beauty, / turn through my harsh pages / and
find an unwavering light in the unstable night. / You will see that love,
thinking itself a diamond / became fragile glass, thoroughly crowned in
tears, / and offered sadness to the best {participants} in its errant
campaign. / Avoid the poison hidden among crystals; / search, thirsty
stag, for the long course of the stream. / Learn your lesson from so many
dropsical men; / the abstinent one, the modest one, profits most; / for
everything that the world offers is a shadow, is wind.]

La Dorotea may also describe the fictional process of liberation from
captivity in a deceiving relationship that could not lead to marriage, nor
to noble devotion. Perfect love in Golden Age texts, that is, love as it was
conceptualized in Neoplatonic discourses, was sealed with marriage in
plots of happy ending. Cervantes developed this configuration in many
of his *Exemplary Novels.* In love poetry, it was generally developed as a
constant spiritual feeling that could defy death. However, Fernando's
obsession with Dorotea was seen as a form of desire that eroticized the
mind and perverted the judgment. The last chorus of the *acción en prosa*
yields this reading, particularly when it is seen in relation to the four previous ones.

Quando del amor lasciuo
El trágico fin contemplo,
No sólo al deleite escriuo,
Pero sentencioso templo
La dotrina en lo festiuo,
Y en el engaño el exemplo.[43]

[When I think how wanton love / must always take a tragic turn, / even as
I entertain, / I would have my reader learn / how all appearances deceive, /
exemplify what he must spurn.]   (Trueblood, p. 267)

The exemplary lesson of this *trattato d'amore* is the victory of the protagonist who could finally disentangle himself from a pernicious relationship. Fernando's love for Dorotea disappears precisely after the famous reconciliation. In act 5, scene 3, he can tell his friend César:

Apenas, César, conocí que Dorotea me tenía el mismo amor que
antes que me partiesse a Seuilla, quando començó mi espíritu a so-
segarse, mi coraçón a suspenderse, y todas las acciones de hombre
cuerdo y prudente boluieron a la patria del entendimiento, de
donde las auía desterrado la inquietud de imaginarme aborrecido.
[César, scarcely had I discovered that Dorotea still loved me as she had before my departure for Seville, when I felt my peace of mind return, my
throbbing heart subside, as all the sensible ways a prudent man habitually
behaves came home to my mind, from which the anxiety of imagining myself abhorred had evicted them.]   (Trueblood, p. 231)

In parallel with Fernando's words, Dorotea's last monologue ends
with an exclamation of freedom:

O quién pudiera, como romper este retrato, hazer en el del alma el
mismo castigo! Iesús, qué fuerte se haze! Pues, perro, tú te resistes?
Pero no, que mi flaqueza es la que no tiene fuerça para romperle,
porque lo intentó con las manos de amor, y amor es niño. Desta vez
lo rompo; quiero boluer los ojos a otra parte. Rompíle. Vitoria! Lo
mismo haré con su exemplo del que tengo en el alma.
[Oh, if only, as I can tear up this portrait, I might punish the original en-
graved in my heart! Lord, how it defies me! Resist, then will you, you cur!
But no, it is only my weakness which lacks the resolve to tear it in two, since
the hands are hands of love, and love is a child. This time I *will* tear it—I'll
turn my eyes away! There, I have done it. Victory! This is but a token of
what I shall do to the one in my heart.]   (Trueblood, p. 245)

Lope's transmutation of experience into art, yet another topos, since,
at least Vergil's famous lines in the *Aeneid*, 8.387–92; 404–6, would
show that, while love is a transhistorical theme in art and literature, it is
historically actualized in different cultures with particular discourses.[44]
Cultures and their traditions shape man's emotions and the rhetoric of
their representation.

Notes

1. Hermann Gmelin, "Das Prinzip der *Imitatio* in den romanischen Literaturen der Renaissance," *Romanische Forschungen* 46 (1932): 83–173. The bibliography on imitation is vast; see among other titles, Bernard Weinberg, *A His-*

tory of Literary Criticism in the Italian Renaissance (Chicago: Midway Reprint, 1974); Feruccio Ulivi, *L'imitazione nella poetica del Rinascimento* (Milan: Marzorati, 1959); Marc Fumaroli, *L'âge de l'eloquence: Rhétorique et "res litteraria" de la Renaissance au seuil de l'époque classique* (Geneva: Droz, 1980); and Thomas Green, *The Light in Troy: Imitation and Discovery in Renaissance Poetry* (New Haven: Yale University Press, 1982).

    2. See the introduction to *Discourses of Authority in Medieval and Renaissance Literature*, ed. Kevin Brownlee and Walter Stephens (Hanover, N.H.: University Press of New England, 1989), pp. 1–19.

    3. G. Burns, in "What Is Tradition?", *New Literary History* 22 (1991): 18ff., addresses these issues by referring to well-known passages in the work of Petrarch.

    4. Quevedo developed the Petrarchan motif in one of his moral sonnets (no. 131 in J. M. Blecua's edition); see *Obra poética* (Madrid: Castalia, 1969), 1: 253, entitled "Desde la torre": "Retirado en la paz de estos desiertos, / con pocos, pero doctos, libros juntos, / vivo en conversación con los difuntos / y escucho con mis ojos a los muertos. / Si no siempre entendidos, siempre abiertos, / o enmiendan, o fecundan mis asuntos; / y en músicos callados contrapuntos / al sueño de la vida hablan despiertos. / Las grandes almas que la muerte ausenta, / de injurias de los años, vengadora, / libra ¡oh gran don Iosef! docta la imprenta. / En fuga irrevocable huye la hora; / pero aquélla el mejor cálculo cuenta / que en la lección y estudios nos mejora." I have already indicated his source in "Modelos clásicos y modelos del mundo en la sátira áurea: los *Diálogos* de Bartolomé Leonardo de Argensola," in the *Actas del II Congreso de la AISO*, Salamanca, 1993.

    5. L. A. Montrose, "The Elizabethan Subject and the Spenserian Text," in *Literary Theory / Renaissance Texts*, ed. Patricia Parker and David Quint (Baltimore: Johns Hopkins University Press, 1986), p. 305.

    6. The concept of subjectivity as a construction which results from the internalization of ideological discourses in a given culture is developed by, among others, Göran Therborn, *The Ideology of Power and the Power of Ideology* (London: Verso, 1980). See J. M. Lotman's classic studies, *The Structure of the Artistic Text* (Ann Arbor: University of Michigan Press, 1970) and *Tipologia della cultura* (Milan: Bompiani, 1975), as well as his *La semiosfera: L'asimmetria e il dialogo nelle strutture pensanti* (Venice: Marsilio, 1985). For the development of semio-philological theories of literature, see the works of Cesare Segre, *Semiotica, storia e cultura* (Padua: Liviana, 1977); *Semiotica filologica: Testo e modelli culturali* (Turin: G. Einaudi, 1979); *Avviamento all'analisi del testo letterario* (Turin: Einaudi, 1985), now translated by John Meddemmen as

Introduction to the Analysis of the Literary Text, by C. Segre, with the collaboration of Tomaso Kemeny (Bloomington: Indiana University Press, 1988), in which Segre reworks ideas already developed in other former studies.

7. See Stephen Greenblatt, "Psychology and Renaissance Culture," in *Literary Theory / Renaissance Texts*, for a critical examination of the limitations of a psychoanalytic interpretation of Renaissance texts, insofar as psychoanalysis is at once "the fulfillment and effacement of specifically Renaissance insights" (p. 210).

8. See Lope de Vega, *La Dorotea*, ed. Edwin S. Morby, rev. 2d ed. (Berkeley: University of California Press, 1968), pp. 48–49; all quotes are from this edition. Morby also published a modernized edition of the text for Clásicos Castalia (Madrid, 1980).

9. See Morby's introduction to his edition for Clásicos Castalia, pp. 15ff., and his earlier article "Persistence and Change in the Formation of *La Dorotea*," *Hispanic Review* 18 (1950): 108–25 and 195–217, as well as José Manuel Blecua's edition, *La Dorotea* (Madrid: Ediciones de la Universidad de Puerto Rico–Revista de Occidente, 1955), pp. 32ff. Alan S. Trueblood refers to this process of distillation of Lope's *Erlebniss* throughout his entire production in several articles and in his magnum opus, *Experience and Artistic Expression in Lope de Vega: The Making of "La Dorotea"* (Cambridge: Harvard University Press, 1974). See his list of "Principal Works Cited," pp. 635–49, for other contributions to the study of this issue.

10. Karl Vossler, *Lope de Vega y su tiempo*, 2d ed., trans. R. de la Serna (Madrid: Revista de Occidente, 1940); Leo Spitzer, *Die Literarisierung des Lebens in Lope's Dorotea* (Bonn: Ludwig Röhrschied Verlag, 1932); Alda Croce, *La "Dorotea" di Lope de Vega: Studio critico seguito della traduzione delle parti principali dell'opera* (Bari: Laterza, 1940); María Rosa Lida de Malkiel, *La originalidad artística de "La Celestina"* (Buenos Aires: EUDEBA, 1962), and Francisco Márquez Villanueva, "Literatura, lengua y moral en *La Dorotea*," in *Lope: Vida y valores* (Río Piedras: Editorial de la Universidad de Puerto Rico, 1988).

11. M. R. Lida described the character of Gerarda as "la mejor sátira de esta galería de alcahuetas elocuentes, moralistas y eruditas, de rigor en el género celestinesco"; see *La originalidad*, pp. 579–81.

12. See *La Dorotea*, p. 320. Morby relates this statement to the controversies of the Academici della Crusca, and gives its source in the *Apologia del S. Torq: Tasso in difesa della sua "Gierusalleme liberata": A gli Accademici della Crusca, con le accuse & difese dell' "Orlando furioso" dell' Ariosto* (Ferrara, 1586).

13. Vossler, Spitzer, Croce, Lida, and Trueblood dealt with the function of

literature and erudition in Lope's text; see now Márquez Villanueva's appraisal in *Lope*, p. 159, and Félix Monge, "*La Dorotea* de Lope de Vega," *Vox Romanica* 16 (1957): 60–145, and "Literatura y erudición en *La Dorotea*," in *Homenaje a J. M. Blecua* (Madrid: Gredos, 1983), pp. 449–63.

14. Thomas Laqueur, *Making Sex: Body and Gender from the Greeks to Freud* (Cambridge: Harvard University Press, 1990), p. 13. Laqueur quotes Foucault's well-known ideas on the nature of human sexuality, as a point of departure for his exploration of different concepts of sex and gender in the Renaissance and in the eighteenth and nineteenth centuries.

15. See Jacques Ferrand, *A Treatise on Lovesickness*, trans., ed., intro. Donald A. Beecher and Massimo Ciavolella (Syracuse: Syracuse University Press, 1990). In the extensive introduction (pp. 1–202) the editors deal with the reception of the classical medical and philosophical canon, and with Renaissance treatises on love. For another survey of these conceptions, see Massimo Ciavolella's early study, *La "malattia d'amore" dall' Antichità al Medio Evo* (Rome: Bulzoni, 1975).

16. Françoise Vigier, "La folie amoureuse dans le roman pastoral espagnol (seconde moitié du XVIᵉ siècle)," in *Visages de la folie (1500–1650)*, ed. Augustín Redondo and André Crochon (Paris: Université de Paris, 1981), pp. 117–29.

17. Laqueur, *Making Sex*, p. 29. Peter Dunn has dealt with this topos in his article "Materia la mujer; el hombre forma: Notes on the Development of a Lopean topos," in *Homenaje a William L. Fichter* (Madrid: Castalia, 1971), pp. 189–99.

18. *La Dorotea*, act 1, scene 1.

19. See Ovid, *Heroides and Amores*, ed., trans. Grant Showerman (Cambridge: Harvard University Press, 1977), letter 7, ii. 37–38, and *La Dorotea*, 3.6.

20. Its source is again Aristotle's *De Generatione Animalium*, 2.3.737a: see p. 95, n. 91, in which Morby evaluates its fundamental influence in Golden Age texts and in Lope's *corpus*. For a thorough examination of ideas about the female gender in theological, medical, ethical, political, and social writings during the Renaissance, see Ian Maclean, *The Renaissance Notion of Woman* (Cambridge: Cambridge University Press, 1980), and his earlier book, *Woman Triumphant: Feminism in French Literature* (Oxford: Clarendon Press, 1977).

21. See act 1, scene 5.

22. See p. 241, and Morby's article "Levinus Lemnius and Leo Suabius in *La Dorotea*," *Hispanic Review* 20 (1952): 108–22. Fernando reworks in "género avarísimo" a sentence from *De inventione* 1.1.94, which was certainly quoted as an example of a fallacious syllogism: "Mulierum genus avarum est." The

expression later became proverbial; see my *Mulier . . . milvinum genus*: la caracterización de personajes femeninos en la sátira y en la ficción áureas," in *Homenaje al profesor Antonio Vilanova* (Barcelona: Universidad de Barcelona, 1989), pp. 629–47.

23. Ian Maclean refers to the pervading influence of the Aristotelian notion of women until the end of the seventeenth century, as well as the extended idea of female inferiority in popular culture, which has an even longer history; see *The Renaissance Notion of Woman*, pp. 86ff.

24. See p. 81, n. 53: "Aiunt, cito agenda esse quae consultaveris, lente vero consultandum" (*Ethica Nicomachea*, 6.9.1142b).

25. See his above-mentioned *La "Malattia d' Amore"* and Aurora Egido, "La enfermedad de amor en el Desengaño de Soto de Rojas," in *Al Ave el Vuelo: Estudios sobre la obra de Soto de Rojas* (Granada: Universidad de Granada, 1984), pp. 32–52, included now in her *Silva de Andalucía (Estudios sobre poesía barroca)* (Málaga: Servicio de Publicaciones, 1990).

26. See 1.5 (p. 103, n. 109) for an appraisal of the success of these ideas in Lope's times.

27. F. de Rojas, *La Celestina*, ed. Dorothy S. Severin (Madrid: Cátedra, 1992), pp. 88–89.

28. See 2.4 (p. 251, footnote 107), for this source and further references in other works by Lope.

29. The line belongs to Phaedra's letter to Hippolytus, *Heroides*, p. 54.

30. Act 3, scene 1.

31. See E. L. Rivers's edition of Garcilaso, *Obras completas con comentario* (Madrid: Castalia, 1974), p. 81; Herrera indicated the Petrarchan source. I quote his poetry from Zingarelli's edition, *Le Rime di Francesco Petrarca* (Bologna: Zingarelli, 1964).

32. See his introduction to *Visages de la folie*, pp. 11ff. For Soto's poems, see A. Gallego Morell's edition, *Obras de don Pedro Soto de Rojas* (Madrid, 1950), sonnet 134, p. 125. A. Egido also analyzes these images: see *Silva de Andalucía*, pp. 132ff.

33. When Dorotea's complaint is related to *La Celestina*, however, it cannot fail to remind the reader of Pleberio's last monologue, in which the metaphor "laberinto de errores" describes the world, re-creating another Petrarchan voice, that of his *Familiaria*, 122, where it was defined as *Labyrinthus errorum* (cf. p. 338). Trueblood interprets Dorotea's *laberinto amoroso* as emblematic of a stage of *desengaño*, and as an expression of human suffering, without referring to Rojas. I think, however, that the two topoi have independent meanings in the seventeenth century.

34. See *Catull*, ed. W. Kroll (Stuttgart: Teubner, 1959), p. 259: "Odi et amo. quare id faciam, fortasse requiris. / Nescio, sed fieri sentio et excrucior."

35. See act 3, scene 1; Morby indicates Lope's reworking of a quotation from *De Generatione Animalium*, 1.18.722, in which he mistakenly interprets a geographical designation, *Hélide*, as a personal name.

36. León Hebreo, *Diálogos de amor*, trans. Carlos Mazo del Castillo, ed. José María Reyes Cano (Barcelona: Universidad de Barcelona, 1993), p. 141. See Morby's footnote on this notion, p. 11, with parallel passages in Fray Luis de León, Tirso and in Lope's *Arcadia*.

37. Act 5, scene 3. The passage is a mosaic of quotations from Marsilio Ficino's *Commentary to "The Symposium,"* as Morby has indicated. Don Fernando admits, however: "¡Qué metido estáis en el amor socrático! Ya de los platónicos me cupo el ínfimo."

38. *Phaedrus*, 244, a–b, and 265, a–b; see a discussion of Plato's definitions of love in Ferrand, *A Treatise on Lovesickness*, p. 44.

39. Trueblood refers to these literary antecedents, yet interprets Lope's characters from twentieth-century psychological perspectives; see pp. 267–323.

40. P. Ovidi Nasonis, *Remedia amoris*, ed. Henri Bornecque (Paris: Société d'édition "Les belles lettres," 1931), ll. 795–96.

41. See Trueblood's chapter 11, or, among other titles, Alban Forcione's "Lope's Broken Clock: Baroque Time in *La Dorotea*," *Hispanic Review* 37 (1969): 459–90.

42. See *Obras de Don Pedro Soto de Rojas*, pp. 13–15.

43. *La Dorotea*, "Coro del ejemplo," p. 458. The former ones are called: "Coro de amor" (p. 127); "Coro de interés" (p. 199); "Coro de zelos" (p. 286); "Coro de vengança" (p. 382).

44. Lawrence D. Kritzman analyzes this topos in his discussion of rhetoric and sexuality in Montaigne's *essai* 3.5, "Sur des vers de Virgile"; see *The Rhetoric of Sexuality and the Literature of the French Renaissance* (Cambridge: Cambridge University Press, 1991), pp. 133 and 138ff.

2

Textual Discontinuities
and the Problems of Closure in the
Spanish Drama of the Golden Age

JOSÉ M. REGUEIRO

La confusión de un retrato, Industrias contra finezas, El galán sin dama, La venganza en los agravios, La mujer de Peribañez, El desposado por fuerza, Contra el amor no hay engaños, La victoria de Norlingen y el Infante en Alemania,[1] all titles picked at random from the *suelta* collection at the University of Pennsylvania, represent brief but compelling signs of dramatic intertextuality.[2] They evoke worlds of gallant suitors, dignified *villanos*, witty *damas* at court, powerful kings, and arrogant nobles; all and one—from the mighty to the lowly, from the harmonious to the fractious, from the sacred to the profane—are contained in the *comedia.*

And yet, in spite of the multiplicity and diversity of the worlds portrayed in thousands of *comedias*, traditional criticism views the Spanish drama of the Golden Age as a monolithic enterprise and its most common practice, the *comedia de capa y espada*, as a typical comedy that strives to complicate situations in order to allow for a resolution that restores order and reaffirms traditional values. Social order (gender, for example) may be altered momentarily (woman dressed as man, for example), but conflicts must be resolved along the established generic code of "order disturbed to order restored."[3]

The emphasis placed on a mythic universal archetype—born more from a desire for an all-inclusive homogenization than a true relationship to a specific culture—does not allow for discordant and conflicting notes in the text. By highlighting the similarities among plays, the conventional approach strives to smooth out their differences, superimposing on them a predesigned structure of order disturbed returning to order restored so that they may conform to a balanced aesthetic vision.[4] As a result, the reader is compelled to arrange all the constituent parts into this universal configuration by discarding any element that does not correspond to this pattern. The reader's participation is therefore limited to the application of the prescribed formula under the assumption that this formula has a universal validity.

While admittedly many *comedias* follow the expected comic pattern and "produce in the reader a state of equilibrium and harmony,"[5] I would like to show that others resist the traditional generic classification: they allow for discordant and conflicting elements that disagree with the harmonious conclusion intended by the code. Before examining these plays, however, it is important to review some of the explanations formulated by the concepts of closure and reception aesthetics. Although originally developed for the study of poems and novels respectively, these approaches have much that is of value for the study of dramatic texts.

The basis for the study of the poetic text from its "closure" was established by Barbara Herrnstein Smith in 1968 from the following premise:

> Closure occurs when the concluding portion of a poem creates in the reader a sense of appropriate cessation. It announces and justifies the absence of further development; it reinforces the feeling of finality, completion, and composure . . . , and it gives ultimate unity and coherence to the reader's experience of the poem by providing a point from which all the preceding elements may be viewed comprehensively and their relations grasped as part of a significant design.[6]

For Herrnstein Smith the reader's experience of a text does not conclude with the reading of the last line but continues developing until it reaches a state of "finality, completion, and composure," allowing the reader to experience the text in its totality. For traditional criticism, closure is reached in the resolution of the play when a wedding, or any other act of social harmonization required by the generic code, takes place to justify all the preceding actions and complications—even when this solution does not restore order in all levels and situations. Comic resolution is viewed as a unifying concept which obviates the need for any further development since it is considered the stabilizing force that neutralizes previous disruptions and harmonizes prior conflicts.

Before continuing, another point needs to be clarified: the difference that exists between the written text, that is, the dramatic text, the text "composed *for* the theatre," and the performance text, the text "produced *in* the theatre."[7] The priority of one text over another has been a point of debate between literary critics on the one hand and actors, stage directors, and producers on the other. Keir Elam explains, however, that "the written text / performance text relationship is not one of simple priority but a complex of reciprocal constraints constituting a powerful *intertextuality*."[8]

In performance analysis, however, closure must take into account factors not present in the dramatic text. In a tragedy, for example, after the hero's death on stage, the actor rises in order to take a bow before the audience, thus subverting the tragic ending. How is the passage from illusion ("the second world") to reality ("the first world," in Harry Berger's terms) accomplished?[9] In a seventeenth-century *corral*, how does the spectator deal with the comic entertainment following the performance of a play, an entertainment which reaffirms life—such as the *zarabanda* or the highly erotic *chacona*—after having seen the hero die on stage? How do we approach closure in a "espectáculo totalizador," to use Díez-Borque's term, which embraces both the idealized fictional poetic "second world" of a *comedia* and the entertainment that follows, more firmly entrenched in the "first world" than in the "second"?[10] When the separation between the illusionary and the actual is blurred, when the "audience's shift from submission to mastery"[11] is not accomplished deftly by the curtain falling and the lights coming on (not possible in a *corral de comedias*) thus effectively closing the "second world," when does closure occur in these situations? These questions, having to do with the very nature of the theatrical act itself, require a separate answer than the one we are prepared to give in this essay. Our purpose here is limited to the examination of the indeterminacies and discontinuities present in some *comedia* texts and the difficulties of closure, accepting the written text as a legitimate object of study, as Elam suggests: "The basic action-structure and logical cohesion of the drama is accessible through analysis of the written text, which is of unquestionable value as long as it is not confused with performance analysis."[12]

Wolfgang Iser's reception theory is also a source of valuable ideas for the analysis of dramatic texts, although it was originally developed from the study of the novel. Iser considers the participation of the reader to be an indispensable function in the construction of the text. At each point throughout the reading process, the parts of the text, he explains, are re-arranged into new configurations guided by strategies contained in the text, in a continuing operation that is not concluded until a coherent configuration is achieved. For Iser an aesthetic object possesses only a virtual existence in its beginning, the final meaning being constructed by the reader when he or she is situated before certain cultural norms that have been "depragmatized" (i.e., defamiliarized)[13]—"depragmatized" in that these norms have been extracted from their daily ordinary con-text in order to be examined outside that context and allow the reader "to formulate that which has been unleashed by the text":[14]

> The fictional text makes a selection from a variety of conventions to be found in the real world, and it puts them together as if they were interrelated. . . . As a result, these conventions are taken out of their social contexts, deprived of their regulating function, and so become subjects of scrutiny in themselves. And this is where fic-tional language begins to take effect: it depragmatizes the conven-tions it has selected.[15]

All effective literature, Iser maintains, will generate new codes for un-derstanding by forcing the reader to recodify the signs implicit in the text in order to reconsider the premises on which it is based. Iser distin-guishes between a contemporary reader, reading literature at the time it is written, and a historical reader, reading a text removed in time from the time it was written:

> If the literary work arises out of the reader's own social or philosophical background, it [the literary repertoire, i.e., references to earlier works, social and historical norms, or the whole culture from which the text has emerged] will serve to detach prevailing norms from their functional context, thus enabling the reader to observe how such social regulators function, and what effect they have on the people subject to them. The reader is thus placed in a position from which he can take a fresh look at the forces which guide and orient him, and which he may hitherto have accepted without question. If these norms have now faded into past history, and the reader is no longer entangled in the system from which they arose, he will be able not only to reconstruct, from their recodification, the historical situation that provided the framework for the text but also to experience for himself the specific deficiencies brought about by those historical norms, and to recognize the answers implicit in the text. And so the literary recodification of social and historical norms has a double function: it enables the participants—or contemporary readers—to see what they cannot normally see in the ordinary process of day-to-day living; and it enables the observers—the subsequent generations of readers—to grasp a reality that was never their own. . . . For the contemporary reader, the reassessment of norms contained in the repertoire will make him detach these norms from their social and cultural context and so recognize the limitations of their effectiveness. For the later reader, the reassessed norms help to re-create the very social and cultural context that brought about the problems which the text itself is concerned with.[16]

The social conventions have been "defamiliarized" in the text, taken out of their social context, in order to be examined outside that context, so the reader will be able to formulate "that which has been unleashed by the text." This process of "defamiliarization" will deprive the social norms "of their regulating function" so they can be reinterpreted and recodified, allowing the reader to gain a new perception of the meaning of these norms. The discontinuities in the text (those elements that do not fit within the unifying pattern expected by a supposed transition of order disturbed to order restored) are then examined for their own importance as discordant elements thus shattering their original framework of reference. "The result," Iser explains, "is to reveal aspects (e.g., of social norms) which had remained hidden as long as the frame of reference remained intact," an assumed uncomplicated social order, in our case.[17]

In order to illustrate how difficult it is sometimes to reduce the *comedia* to the satisfying comic coherency proposed by traditional criticism, I have chosen for analysis three plays: Lope's *El arenal de Sevilla* and *La ocasión perdida* and Rojas Zorrilla's *Entre bobos anda el juego.*

El arenal de Sevilla is a typical *comedia de capa y espada* with the expected situations of intrigue, use of disguise, nocturnal duels, and lovers' trysts. It was published in 1618 in the *Oncena parte de las comedias de Lope de Vega Carpio* although it is believed to have been written fifteen years earlier, judging from contemporaneous historical events mentioned in the text. Of these, the most important one is the appointment on 29 January 1603 of the Conde de Niebla, Manuel Alonso Pérez de Guzmán el Bueno, as commander general of the Spanish fleet.[18]

The action is centered in and around the *arenal* of Seville, the stretch of land that extends from the old city walls to the banks of the Guadalquivir River, a harbor bustling with confused activity and busy commerce and teeming with people of different nationalities and languages. In the opening scene, Don Lope arrives in the *arenal* from Medina del Campo to arrange passage to the Indies at the request of his parents, who fear he will be sent to prison as a consequence of a duel in which Don Lope has seriously wounded his rival in love, Alberto. In the *arenal*, he meets Doña Laura, a *dama sevillana* whose beauty weakens his former resolve to stay away from love's snares. Don Lope is subsequently attacked by robbers in the *arenal* and badly wounded. Doña Laura gives him protection in her house, posing him as her cousin in order to avoid arousing the jealousy of Capitán Fajardo, her local suitor.

Five months go by. Don Lope, having recovered from his wounds, continues living in Doña Laura's home. Lucinda, the lady over whom Don Lope and Alberto had fought the duel, comes to Seville disguised as a gypsy to look for Don Lope. Alberto has heard that his rival is in Seville and also follows him there seeking vengeance. After a series of complications, Capitán Fajardo intervenes to bring about a reconciliation between Don Lope and Alberto and the play ends with a double wedding: Don Lope marries Doña Laura and Alberto marries Lucinda.

The use of the sonnet in this play—the poetic form privileged by the *comedia* to reveal internal conflict in the character[19]—is significant. Verse in the baroque theater creates linguistic hierarchies and separates scenic spaces, and—perhaps the most important function—it is used to separate emotional spaces. The change in meter does not necessarily imply a change of locale but it denotes a change of dramatic tone,[20] and the sonnet, given its confessional nature, explains the change from the character's perspective: "a sonnet in a play may become a moment of truth, a moment in which the reality beneath the fiction is brought into view."[21]

El arenal de Sevilla contains three sonnets. In the first, moments before being attacked in the *arenal* in the first act, Don Lope expresses his distress and affliction in view of the mutability and instability of his fortunes:

> Sembrando en tu arenal mis esperanzas,
> ¡oh Sevilla!, qué fruto será el mío,
> que ni del llanto bastará el rocío,
> ni del ligero tiempo las mudanzas.
>   ¡Oh tú, que del Ocaso al Norte alcanzas
> pensamiento menor que el desvarío,
> si en el arena siembras deste río,
> tu cosecha será desconfianzas!
>   ¡Si comparas tu arena con mis males,
> tú, ni la Libia, de montañas llena,
> tenéis bastante copia de arenales!
>   ¡Oh principio terrible de mi pena,
> si en él son las arenas desiguales!,
> ¿qué fin espero de sembrar tu arena?[22]

[In sowing my hopes in your *arenal*, / oh Seville! what will be my fruit, / for neither the dew of my tears / nor the changes of swift time suffice. / Oh

you, who span from West to North / should you sow a thought smaller
than a passing whim / in the sand of this river, you will reap a crop of
mistrust! / If you compare your sand to my misfortunes / neither you nor
mountainous Lybia / have enough abundance of sand! / Oh, terrible
beginning of my affliction, / if at the start the sands are unequal! / what
end can I hope for by sowing your sand?]

This sonnet serves the purpose of marking the change that takes place in
Don Lope's emotions as his intention to sail to the Indies is thwarted by
fate—the unexpected meeting with Laura causes him to abandon his resolve not to fall in love again.

In the second sonnet, Lucinda, dressed as a gypsy, laments her condition but finds, in the end, a moment of reconciliation and hope (albeit
unjustified hope). She pronounces the sonnet moments before meeting
Capitán Fajardo, who will take her to find Don Lope:

> Nace en Egipto el fiero cocodrilo,
> que al peregrino llama en voz humana,
> con que a su cuenta y boca el paso allana
> del que ha seguido su engañoso estilo.
>
> No lo es el llanto que por ti destilo,
> ni porque de tu vida soy tirana,
> que aunque traigo vestidos de gitana,
> nací en Medina y no ribera el Nilo.
>
> Peregrino del alma que te adora,
> Lucinda soy, que sin ventura vengo
> a decir a dos hombres la ventura.
>
> Dame, dame esa mano vencedora,
> que si ventura de tomarla tengo,
> su palma la vitoria me asegura.[23]

[In Egypt is born the fierce crocodile / that calls the pilgrim in a human
voice, / in that way clearing the path to his mouth / for those who follow
his deceptive style. / The tears that I shed for you are not {deceitful} / nor
is it {deceitful} that I am the tyrant of your life, / for although I am
wearing gypsy clothes, / I was born in Medina, and not on the banks of
the Nile. / Pilgrim of the soul that adores you, / I am Lucinda, who comes
with no fortune / to tell two men their fortunes. / Give me, give me that

victorious hand, / for should I have the fortune to take it, / its palm will assure me victory.]

This sonnet, marking the beginning of Lucinda's story (the first act was controlled by Don Lope, the second by Lucinda), separates the character's reflective individual feeling from the collective situation: it expresses the motives behind Lucinda's past actions and her determination to persevere in her intentions to reclaim Don Lope's affections.

The third sonnet, also spoken by Lucinda, marks the shift of the action to the streets of Seville away from the *arenal*. Moved by jealousy and Don Lope's rejection of her love, Lucinda has devised a ruse to play on Don Lope. Still dressed as a gypsy, she and her *criado* Florelo inform Doña Laura that Don Lope is not the person he pretends to be but Lucinda's own husband, a thieving gypsy. There is some truth in this because Don Lope had taken Lucinda's portrait from Alfredo after the duel, and their relationship, although it had not reached the point where a promise of marriage had been made, was interpreted by Lucinda to be directed to this end:

> Alarga riendas, pensamiento loco,
> si descansa el amor con la venganza,
> que cuando entre los males hay mudanza,
> yo pienso que los males duran poco.
>   Si con tus alas el remedio toco,
> no se anegue en la pena la esperanza,
> logre su pretensión la confianza,
> si al cielo con mis lágrimas provoco.
>   Mitigad, corazón, vuestros desvelos,
> esforzad el valor de mis porfías
> mientras os miran los piadosos cielos,
>   porque con celos estorbar los días
> que no se gocen los que le dan celos
> basta para templar las penas mías.[24]

[Loosen your reins, foolish mind, / if love rests on vengeance, / for when there is a change in misfortune, / I think that misfortune does not last long. / If with your wings I can reach the remedy, / let not hope be smothered with affliction, / let confidence reach its pretension, / if the heavens I move with my tears. / Mitigate, o heart, your concerns, / strengthen the valor of my struggle / while the kind heavens look on, / because disturbing the days with jealousy / so that those who provoke jealousy may not take pleasure / suffices to temper my sorrow.]

These verses speak of jealousy and the mutability of human affairs, including misfortune. Don Lope and Doña Laura's union is based on love—not on a passing whim, as is explained at the beginning of the play ("esto es amor, no es antojo")[25]—a relationship which is sustained by the lovers' mutual inclination. This is not the case with Lucinda: Lucinda does not love Alberto, although he loves her. Since Don Lope marries Laura, Lucinda's marriage to Alberto is dictated by the honor code (Alberto tells her, "A hacerlo estás obligada");[26] but the pangs of jealousy that she speaks about in the last sonnet give evidence that she still loves Don Lope. Honor does not play here the bewildering and baffling role that it does in the honor plays.[27] It is not mentioned in the sonnet; it belongs to the character's exterior social sphere, to an unbalanced exterior world; in the character's intimate world, expressed in the sonnet, love and jealousy constitute the disrupting elements.

The action of the play grants primary importance to the exterior space inhabited by a variety of people engaged in continuous and confused activity. The *arenal* symbolizes the disarray and polyphonic disorder caused by the multitude of voices and characters of diverse origins and social strata. It is the common ground, the microcosm, from and toward which a whole series of personal and national circumstances irradiate: the love entanglements of gallant suitors on the individual level, and on the national level the posting of the Conde de Niebla as commander general of the Spanish fleet. The moving sands of the *arenal* symbolize the mutability of the human condition in a disordered exterior space. The cacophony of voices in the *arenal*, the disjointed language of sailors, soldiers, "moros de galera," and harlots, creates a disequilibrium that leads to confusion, disorder, and alienation in the lives of the characters.[28]

In order to overcome these difficulties, the action moves from the *arenal* to the streets of Seville after it reaches the highest point of disarray and confusion as a result of the entanglements brought about by Lucinda's disguise. The resolution of the conflict may be said to start at the point when the action returns to the city streets, the characteristic urban milieu of the *comedia*. After Lucinda's subterfuge is uncovered and Don Lope and Alfredo have made peace at Capitán Fajardo's request, the play ends in a double wedding: Doña Laura–Don Lope, Lucinda-Alberto. Even though this double wedding is supposed to restore order on the personal level (as the appointment of the Conde de Niebla has restored order on the national level), the closing verses, summoning the assembled party to return to the shaky and unstable terrain of the *arenal* ("Vamos juntos a la orilla, / a ver al gran general, / dando fin en su Arenal / al *Arenal de Sevilla*"),[29] underline, on the other hand, the instability of human relationships and the uncertainty of the present moment, an uncertainty previously evoked in the sonnets. Although the reader may view the resolution in the double wedding from a unifying perspective that restores order, the potential outcome anticipated in the opening scenes in the *arenal* and reinforced by the return to the *arenal* at the end is one of disarray and confusion. The reader is confronted with the disquieting possibility that the resolution will not provide stability or will only in part and for a fleeting moment.

An even more disconcerting resolution is offered in *La ocasión perdida*, which was included in Lope's *Segunda parte* published in 1609.[30] Don Juan de Haro is exiled to the court of Brittany because he has incurred royal disfavor. The king of León disapproves of the affections of his sister, the infanta Armelinda, for Don Juan, and on the road to Brittany Don Juan's traveling companions attempt to kill him at the king's behest. Don Juan is rescued by Rosaura, princess of Brittany, who falls in love with him. Rosaura reveals her feelings to Doriclea, her lady-in-waiting, and asks her to pretend a feigned love for Don Juan so that he may visit Rosaura secretly in her chambers while pretending to look for Doriclea. Doriclea, as one might suspect, falls in love with Don Juan herself, to the distress of Feliciano, Doriclea's suitor at court. After the king of León's arrival (he has come to Brittany attracted by Rosaura's famed beauty), a series of deceptions and counter-deceptions, of foiled encounters and bungled nocturnal lovers' trysts ensue and result in frustrating the secret marriage arranged by Rosaura and Don Juan. The play ends with a triple wedding of mismatched couples in which at least one of the partners is in love with another: the king of León marries Rosaura, Feliciano marries Doriclea, and Armelinda marries Don Juan.

Love is portrayed as an unstable emotion and destabilizing force since the intended unions of Doriclea-Feliciano and Rosaura-Arnaldo (Rosaura's longtime suitor) are disrupted by the appearance of Don Juan and later by the king of León. Don Juan represents a threat to the established social order because Rosaura and Armelinda have both fallen in love with him in contravention of their noble station.[31] Don Juan's foiled attempt to marry Rosaura and become prince of Brittany shows that the power of love alone does not allow the character to rise in the social hierarchy.[32]

The "previous conditioning," the potential for a happy ending at the beginning of the play, a happy ending that does not materialize, ends in a labyrinth of love pairings in constant change.[33] The resolution—which brings the lovers together in pairs not united by love but by their social condition and contrary to their own inclinations—presents a happy ending as far as political harmonization is concerned ("obligación de estado") but not in accordance with the individual wishes of the lovers, a situation that Don Juan laments:

> Que quiso levantarme la fortuna
> a tan alto lugar y le he perdido.
> Quien nació para pobre, ¿qué importuna
> al cielo de sus quejas ofendido?
> ¿Habrá persona en todo el mundo alguna
> que a tan alto lugar haya subido
> y que tan presto dé tan gran caída?
> Tarde se cobra la ocasión perdida.
>
> Que subiesen los Césares romanos
> a la alta dignidad del cetro augusto
> después de tantos hechos soberanos,
> ya, en fin, tuvieron de gozarle gusto.
> Mas yo, engañado por amores vanos,
> ¿qué consuelo tendré de mi disgusto?
> si yerro de un papel erró mi vida,
> tarde se cobra la ocasión perdida.[34]

[For fortune deemed to take me / to such a high place and I have lost it. / He who was born to be poor, why does he importune / the heavens, offended by his complaints? / Is there a person in the whole world / who has climbed to such a high place / and who suddenly has taken such a great fall? / It is too late to redeem the lost opportunity. / The Roman Caesars climbed / to the high dignity of the august scepter / after so many deeds, / {and} had, in the end, the chance to enjoy it. / But I, fooled by false loves, / what consolation will I find in my grief? / If the mistake of {a piece of} paper made my life go astray, / {then} it is too late to redeem the lost opportunity.]

The baroque theme of fiction/reality is fully articulated in this play. Life is transmuted into theater and theater into life[35]—changing into reality (Doriclea's love for Don Juan) what had started in the beginning as a mere "artificial voluntad" (Doriclea's pretended love for Don Juan). Rosaura's ill-fated attempt to marry Don Juan and Don Juan's "ocasión perdida" position the reader before the indeterminate meaning of the text: the unifying perspective (the authenticity of love) is frustrated by the intention to disunite the solution at the end, and the centrality of the character's actions as a means to achieve an expected goal is impaired.

The third play that we propose to examine is Rojas Zorrilla's *Entre bobos anda el juego*, published in Madrid in 1645. It is considered to be one of the finest examples of the *comedia de figurón*.[36] The *comedia de figurón*, as indicated by the rubric, dramatizes the vicissitudes of a grotesque caricature of a wealthy bourgeois in his attempts to adapt to the life at court.[37] It is the conflict of two disparate worlds: at the center, Madrid, representing court and power, the world of elegance and courtly refinement versus the provincial world from which the *figurón* hails. The *figurón*, aware of his social status at the periphery of power and elegance, seeks to become a part of the aristocratic milieu of a decadent and impoverished court by marrying a woman of noble birth, who despises him for his lack of social grace, but whose parents approve of the union for the wealth that the *figurón* will bring to the family.[38] Two particular traits define the *figurón*: his absolute self-confidence and his inability to assimilate the courtly graces, "finezas del trato," which characterize the typical *galán* of a *comedia de capa y espada*.[39]

The plot of *Entre bobos anda el juego* revolves around the *figurón*

Don Lucas, an uncouth but wealthy *caballero* from Toledo, and his pretensions to marry into an aristocratic family. Don Antonio has decided to marry his daughter Doña Isabel to Don Lucas, whom Isabel despises not only for his lack of grace but also his physical deformities. Isabel favors the attentions of Don Lucas's dependent cousin, Don Pedro, a gallant and graceful *caballero*, the typical *galán* of the *comedia*, except for one essential aspect: he is poor. In the *comedia de capa y espada* wealth does not play an important role since it is assumed that the protagonist is rich, whether a *noble* or a *villano*. In the *comedia de figurón*, on the other hand, wealth is a motivating factor behind the action. Doña Isabel rebuffs Don Lucas's marital pretensions; he accepts her decision—thus excluding himself from the aristocratic sphere that he desires to become a part of[40]—but not before warning Don Pedro and Doña Isabel that he will not continue providing for Don Pedro's keep. Don Pedro and Doña Laura may be in love but:

> Pues, dalda la mano al punto,
> que en esto me he de vengar:
> ella, muy pobre; vos, pobre,
> no tenéis hora de paz;
> el amor se acaba luego,
> nunca la necesidad;
> hoy, con el pan de la boda,
> no buscaréis otro pan;
> de mí os vengáis esta noche,
> y mañana a más tardar,
> cuando almuercen un requiebro,
> y en la mesa, en vez de pan,
> pongan una fe al comer
> y una constancia al cenar,
> y, en vez de galas, se ponga
> un buen amor de Milán,
> una tela de "mi vida,"
> aforrada en "¿me querrás?"
> echarán de ver los dos
> cuál se ha vengado de cuál.[41]

[Then, give her your hand at once, / that in this I will take my revenge: / she, very poor; you, poor, / you won't have a moment of peace; / love is soon over, / need never {ends}; / today, with the bread of the wedding, / you will not look for another bread; / on me you take revenge tonight, / but tomorrow at the latest, / when you breakfast on an expression of love, / and on the table, instead of bread, / you are served faithfulness for lunch / and loyalty for dinner, / and, instead of fine clothes, you put on / a good love from Milan, / a cloth of "my love," / lined with "will you love me {forever}?" / then you both will see / who has taken revenge on whom.]

The indeterminacy of the text in this case prevents the typical spectator in a *corral madrileño*—who aspired to share the aristocratic values of a group that, although impoverished, continued to value elegance of manners as the most important social attribute—from embracing both concepts, love and wealth, within the unifying perspective proclaimed by the *comedia*. By disavowing the power of love—when impecunious—as an integrating force, Rojas Zorrilla cancels, with the *comedia de figurón*, the solution proclaimed by the *comedia de capa y espada*. If Lope de Vega in his *comedias de capa y espada* proposes "soluciones aristocratizantes"[42] albeit with disconcerting results in some instances, it may be said that Rojas Zorrilla in the *comedia de figurón* proposes "soluciones aburguesantes" that clash with the traditional *comedia* resolutions.

In the three *comedias* examined here, the love conflicts are ostensibly resolved by a series of concatenated acts, linked together by a cause-and-effect relationship, that lead to a comic resolution of order restored from order disturbed. The reader, however, cannot simply view the constituent elements of the play as forming part of a "significant design" which represents social harmonization. An attempt to accept the resolution of the wedding, or weddings, as the "appropriate cessation" of further developments for meaning discounts the possibility of deriving dissimilar interpretations from the text under a different set of strategies: the sonnets expressing mutability and change and the return to the shifting sands of the *arenal* (a return fraught with uncertainties and instability); the unsatisfactory love matches brought about by "obligación de estado" and not "amor correspondido"; impecunious love failing to provide a solution in a world guided by false courtly values—all these situations cannot be made to conform to the balanced aesthetic vision expected in a comic generic pattern.

By imposing upon the *comedia*—all *comedias*—an image of harmony that disregards the textual discontinuities present in individual plays (those elements that disrupt or contradict the expected progression from order disturbed to order restored) and conceals the instability of the presumed closure demanded by the large-scale adoption of a universal aesthetic formula, we run the risk of distorting a cultural reality. As we said in the beginning, following Iser, all effective literature will generate new codes for understanding by forcing the reader to re-codify the signs implicit in the text: expectations and hopes sowed in an *arenal* will reap "desconfianzas"; "la ocasión perdida" (love's purpose thwarted by the unequal social position of the lovers) will be lamented even after the pretended satisfying solution of the wedding; and love alone will not triumph over the impecuniousness of the lovers in a world sustained by an evanescent and courtly glory.

Closure, the "sense of appropriate cessation," that "feeling of finality, completion, and composure," of which Herrnstein Smith speaks, may be much more difficult to achieve in many *comedias* when they are freed from a universality of "order disturbed to order restored." Although not all *comedias* may resist being reduced to a single generic pattern as markedly as the plays examined here, the discontinuities manifest in these texts show how difficult it is to view the Spanish drama of the Golden Age as a homogeneous enterprise. If nothing else the sheer number of plays produced during the span of a century (ten thousand by some estimates)[43] frustrate our attempts to place one and all within a harmonious configuration. Textual discontinuities invite the reader to reassess the social and historical norms, the whole culture from which the text has emerged, and these "reassessed norms," Iser reminds us, will "help to re-create the very social and cultural context that brought about the problems which the text itself is concerned with. . . . The individual [i.e., historical and social] norms themselves have to be reassessed to the extent that human nature cannot be reduced to a hard-and-fast principle, but must be discovered, in all its potential, through the multifarious possibilities that have been excluded by those norms."[44] And so the panoply of the human condition presented in the *comedia* may be forever shifting in a polyphonic *arenal* of discordant voices "que siembran sus lamentos en la arena," resisting our best efforts to systematize literary expression into monolithic formulas.

Notes

1. See José M. Regueiro, *Spanish Drama of the Golden Age: A Catalogue of the "Comedia" Collection in the University of Pennsylvania Libraries* (New Haven: Research Publications, 1971), nos. 548 (732), 517, 591, 686, 568 (751), 596, 648, and 757.

2. Michael Issacharoff considers the title of a play to constitute the shortest theatrical text and to be the briefest sign of theatrical intertextuality, acting as a reading cue to the rest of the text. The dynamics of dramatic intertextuality are put in motion by the title, which acts as a hypotext (the earlier text), in relation to the dialogue and didascalia, which acts as a hypertext (the later text) (cf. Gérard Genette). See Michael Issacharoff, *Discourse as Performance* (Stanford: Stanford University Press, 1989), pp. 28–29.

3. See Arnold G. Reichenberger, "The Uniqueness of the *Comedia*," *Hispanic Review* 27 (1959): 303–16: 307; and "The Uniqueness of the *Comedia*," *Hispanic Review* 38 (1970): 163–73: 164. Influenced by the works of C. L. Barber and Northrop Frye, a similar view has guided Shakespearian traditional criticism. Jean E. Howard, in exploring the difficulties of closure in Shakespearian comedy, explains that "for both [Barber and Frye], these plays [Shakespeare's comedies] are primarily vehicles for testing and confirming social order and sexual difference by a purely temporary confounding of both. Turbulence, misrule, and Saturnalian confusion erupt within these plays only to give way before the reimposition of order and traditional values." See Jean E. Howard, "The Difficulties of Closure: An Approach to the Problematic in Shakespearian Comedy," in A. R. Braunmuller and J. C. Bulman, eds., *Comedy from Shakespeare to Sheridan: Change and Continuity in the English and European Dramatic Tradition. Essays in Honor of Eugene M. Waith* (Newark: University of Delaware Press, 1986), pp. 113–28: 113.

4. See Howard, "The Difficulties of Closure," pp. 113–14.

5. Ibid., p. 114.

6. Barbara Herrnstein Smith, *Poetic Closure: A Study of How Poems End* (Chicago: University of Chicago Press, 1968), p. 36. The concept of "closure" has already gained wide critical acceptance in the study of the novel (see Beth Wietelmann Bauer, "Innovación y apertura: La novela realista del siglo XIX ante el problema del desenlace," *Hispanic Review* 59 [1991]: 187–203; and Ha-

zel Gold, "Problems of Closure in *Fortunata y Jacinta*: Of Narrators, Readers, and Their Just Deserts/Desserts," *Neophilologus* 70 [1986]: 228–38). It has been applied recently to the analysis of dramatic texts (see Bernard Beckerman, "Shakespeare Closing," *Kenyon Review*, n.s., 7, no. 3 [1985]: 79–95; and Howard, "The Difficulties of Closure"). The study of literature has shifted its emphasis from the author-oriented criticism of the turn of the century to the reader-oriented criticism of the last few decades (see Terry Eagleton, *Literary Theory: An Introduction* [Minneapolis: University of Minnesota Press, 1983], p. 74; and James A. Parr, "La crítica de la comedia: Estado actual de la cuestión," in Manuel V. Diago and Teresa Ferrar, eds., *Comedias y comediantes: Estudios sobre el teatro clásico español*. Actas del Congreso Internacional sobre Teatro y Prácticas Escénicas en los siglos XVI y XVII, organizado por el Departamento de Filología Española de la Universitat de València, celebrado en la Facultat de Filologia, los días 9, 10 y 11 de mayo de 1989 [Universitat de València, Departament de Filologia Espanyola, 1991], pp. 321–28, 322–23). Parr recognizes three currents or approaches evident in *comedia* studies: the first one, starting at the end of the nineteenth century and continuing into the beginning of the twentieth century, is the scholarly-positivist current, which concentrated on the author as *creator* of his work; the second, the critical-literary current that concentrated on the study of language and the structure of the "message" as an independent entity of the author's intentions ("intentional fallacy") and the reader's reactions to the text ("affective fallacy"); and the most recent, the postmodern theoretical current which directs its attention from the reader-receptor to the text complemented by deconstruction and reception aesthetics. In most instances the advent of a new critical position does not entail a break with a previous one but rather the emergence of new tendencies that intermingle with former critical positions. With this article, Parr brings up to date his former study "An Essay on Critical Method, Applied to the *Comedia*," *Hispania* 57 (1974): 434–44. Eagleton detects the same three periods in the history of modern literary theory, noting: "The reader has always been the most underprivileged of this trio [i.e., author, text, reader]—strangely, since without him or her there would be no literary texts at all. . . . For literature to happen, the reader is quite as vital as the author" (*Literary Theory*, p. 74).

7. See Keir Elam, *The Semiotics of Theatre and Drama* (London: Routledge, 1988 [1980]), p. 3. María del Carmen Bobes Naves defines *texto dramático* as "la obra dramática en conjunto" composed of a *texto literario* and a *texto espectacular*. For Bobes Naves, the *texto literario* consists mainly of "los diálogos, pero . . . puede extenderse a toda la obra escrita, con su título, la relación de *dramatis personae*, los prólogos y aclaraciones de todo tipo que pueda incluir,

y también las mismas acotaciones, si se presentan en un lenguaje no meramente referencial" and the *texto espectacular* composed "por todos los indicios que en el texto diseñan una virtual representación, y que está fundamentalmente en las acotaciones, pero que pueden estar en toda la obra, desde el título, las *dramatis personae*, los prólogos y aclaraciones que incluya, etc." (María del Carmen Bobes Naves, *Semiología de la obra dramática* [Madrid: Taurus, 1987], pp. 24–25). In order to avoid confusion, I follow Elam's nomenclature of dramatic text (i.e., written text) and performance text, which is accepted by most critics. Jean Alter summarizes the prevalent opinion as follows: "In its most usual meaning today . . . , the dramatic text is handled as a literary work to be read (or heard), that is, as one of the possible forms in which a story is told with words, most usually in a book form," although the reader must bear in mind that the dramatic text demands "a different type of visualization than the literary text . . . [when] it is treated deliberately like a textual matrix of theatre, a text to be staged, a source of theatrical transformations" (see Jean Alter, *A Sociosemiotic Theory of Theatre* [Philadelphia: University of Pennsylvania Press, 1990], pp. 161, 164).

8. See Elam, *The Semiotics of Theatre and Drama*, p. 209. Elam maintains that "each text bears the other's traces, the performance assimilating those aspects of the written play which the performers choose to transcodify, and the dramatic text being 'spoken' at every point by the model performance—or the *n* possible performances—that motivate it."

9. See Harry Berger Jr., *Second World and Green World: Studies in Renaissance Fiction Making*, ed. John Patrick Lynch (Berkeley: University of California Press, 1988 [1990]), pp. 3–40, 111–29.

10. Díez Borque considers a *corral* performance as striving to present "un espectáculo totalizador" combining a *comedia*, structured on a "plano frecuentemente mítico y evasivo de la realidad," with "las formas más pretendidamente reales, alejadas de toda ilusión y de toda idealista deformación" embodied in the erotic and comic dances and skits which follow the presentation of a *comedia* (see José María Díez Borque, *El teatro en el siglo XVII*. Historia Crítica de la Literatura Hispánica. Dirigida por Juan Ignacio Ferreras, vol. 9 [Madrid: Taurus, 1988], pp. 38–39, 42). This superimposition of an idealized fictional world with a realistic satirical world closer to the spectators' own real world "aminoraban la *ilusión teatral* . . . buscando una complementariedad o nivelación" between the two spheres (Díez Borque, *El teatro en el siglo XVII*, pp. 39, 40). Marvin Carlson also speaks of "the semiotics of the entire theatre experience (as opposed to what happens on the stage or between the on-stage creation and the spectator). . . . When we begin to consider the audience experience of the the-

atrical *event* [emphasis added], we should soon come to realize that the actual performance of the play is only a part (and historically not always the most important part) of an entire social and cultural experience, and that the 'cybernetic machine' [Roland Barthes's definition of theater] by no means begins operating when the curtain rises [or ceases to operate when the curtain falls, we should add], assuming there is even a curtain" (see Marvin Carlson, *Theatre Semiotics: Signs of Life* [Bloomington: Indiana University Press, 1990], p. xiii).

11. See Beckerman, "Shakespeare Closing," p. 82.

12. See Elam, *The Semiotics of Theatre and Drama*, p. 99. Most critics nowadays agree that the study of the dramatic text and the performance text constitute different, although interrelated, tasks. Following Patrice Pavis, "we are concerned here solely with texts written prior to performance, not those written after rehearsals, improvisations or performances" as "one can certainly read a dramatic text in book form" (see Patrice Pavis, *Theatre at the Crossroads of Culture*, trans. Loren Kruger [New York: Routledge, 1992], pp. 24, 39). Issacharoff also finds that the dramatic text is "the sole constant element in what goes on in the name of theater. Consequently, [it is] preferable to speak of the verifiable rather than to offer hypotheses or speculation based on approximate memories of productions that may not have been seen by all readers" (see Issacharoff, *Discourse as Performance*, p. 4). See also Anne Ubersfeld, *Lire le théâtre* (Paris: Editions Sociales, 1977), pp. 20–22; and Alter's extensive and detailed discussion on the difference between dramatic and performance texts as objects of study, *A Sociosemiotic Theory of Theatre*, pp. 155ff.

13. See Eagleton, *Literary Theory*, p. 79; and Robert C. Holub, *Reception Theory: A Critical Introduction* (New York: Methuen, 1985 [1984]), pp. 18–20, 63, 70.

14. See Wolfgang Iser, *The Act of Reading: A Theory of Aesthetic Response* (Baltimore: Johns Hopkins University Press, 1978), p. 50.

15. Ibid., p. 61.

16. Ibid., pp. 74, 78.

17. Ibid., p. 109.

18. The Conde de Niebla was the oldest son of the famous Duque de Medina Sidonia, commander-in-chief of the famous foiled attempt by the Spanish Armada to invade England in 1588. The articles by J. H. Arjona and George Irving Dale contain extensive details of the events referred to in the play. See J. H. Arjona, "Apunte cronológico sobre *El arenal de Sevilla* de Lope de Vega," *Hispanic Review* 5 (1937): 344–46; and George Irving Dale, "'Periodismo' in *El arenal de Sevilla* and the Date of the Play's Composition," *Hispanic Review* 8 (1940): 18–23.

19. The use of the sonnet in the *comedia* has been studied by Peter N. Dunn and by Diego Marín. Dunn remarks: "By virtue . . . of its capacity to contain and relate within its frame a variety of meanings, it [i.e., the sonnet] can be used for putting into coherent speech the confusion of thoughts and feelings, the emotional conflicts within a character, and revealing motives to which he has shut his eyes" (Peter N. Dunn, "Some Uses of Sonnets in the Plays of Lope de Vega," *Bulletin of Hispanic Studies* 34 [1957]: 213–22: 221). Through the sonnet, "the speaker may reveal something which he does not intend and which he does not consciously put into words" (ibid., p. 222). Marín notes that "el soneto . . . combina las reflexiones generales con el sentimiento personal" (Diego Marín, *Uso y función de la versificación dramática en Lope de Vega*. Estudios de Hispanófila, 2 [Valencia: Castalia, 1962], p. 103).

20. Marín observes: "Con respecto a los cambios de metro, lo normal es que éstos sirvan para reforzar las mutaciones de escena (con su cambio usual de asunto, lugar o personajes), y cuando no ocurre así, ello puede deberse al deseo de resaltar el enlace temático de escenas distintas mediante la continuidad dramática. En el paso de una subescena a otra (es decir, al entrar o salir algún personaje), lo ordinario es conservar el mismo metro. Cuando se producen cambios métricos al comienzo de las subescenas suelen ir acompañados de un cambio en la forma (diálogo o monólogo), o en la situación (asunto o personajes), o en el tono dramático. . . . Lope no basaba el cambio métrico sólo en el cambio automático de subescenas, sino que atendía también al contenido y carácter de la situación" (*Uso y función*, p. 105).

21. Dunn, "Some Uses of Sonnets," p. 222.

22. I quote from the Colección Austral edition, Lope de Vega, *El perro del hortelano. El arenal de Sevilla* (Madrid: Espasa-Calpe, 1977), p. 115.

23. Ibid., pp. 121–22.

24. Ibid., p. 151.

25. Ibid., p. 115.

26. Ibid., p. 158.

27. See Antonio Rey Hazas, "Algunas reflexiones sobre el honor como sustituto funcional del destino en la tragicomedia barroca española," in Diago and Ferrer, eds., *Comedias y comediantes*, pp. 251–62. Rey Hazas views *honor* "como sustituto dramático del destino, como motor de acciones que se impone al mismo *fatum*" ("Algunas reflexiones," p. 262). He considers *honor* a "fuerza literaria motriz [que] es, en ocasiones, comparable a la del destino; más aún, es el sino de los personajes dramáticos barrocos, el sustituto funcional del destino antiguo en la nueva tragicomedia española seiscentista" (p. 253). Reichenberger, who viewed the *comedia* as "compact and coherent" ("The Uniqueness of

the *Comedia*" [1959], p. 315) and tragedy as "based on a strict, even rigid view
. . . as fifth-century Athens created it" ("The Uniqueness of the *Comedia*"
[1970], p. 168), discards the possibility that *honor* may be considered as a substitute of Fate: "Fate [in Greek theater] is supernatural, of divine origin, incom-
prehensible; the honor code is manmade" ("The Uniqueness of the *Comedia*"
[1959], p. 308).

28. Barbara E. Kurtz and Kay E. Weston study in detail the theme of the play
and the symbolism of the *arenal*, which I follow in part in my own analysis of the
play. See Barbara E. Kurtz, "*El arenal de Sevilla*: Circunstancialidad y simbol-
ismo analógico de una comedia lopesca," *Bulletin of the Comediantes* 37
(1985): 101–14; and Kay E. Weston, "Change and Essence in Lope de Vega's *El
arenal de Sevilla*," *Modern Language Notes* 86 (1971): 211–24.

29. Lope de Vega, *El perro del hortelano: El arenal de Sevilla*, p. 158.

30. This play has been intelligently studied by Mariateresa Cattaneo, whose
conclusions about the difficulty of closure in a "desenlace imperfecto" I follow
in general terms in my own analysis of the text. See Mariateresa Cattaneo, "El
desenlace imperfecto: En torno a *La ocasión perdida* de Lope de Vega," in
Diago and Ferrer, eds., *Comedias y comediantes*, pp. 109–17.

31. The instability of these love pairings produces a disquieting effect when
contrasted with the permanence and steadfastness of the relationship of the long
list of peasants in love who take part in the celebrations of the Feast of May (Cattaneo, "El desenlace imperfecto," p. 114). Even though this scene may only serve
a decorative purpose, there is an implicit irony in the distancing effect attained
by placing the urban spectator of the *corral de comedias* vis-à-vis rural life (the
corte/aldea theme).

32. Although the "tópico del amor igualador, por encima de las clases sociales" (see José María Díez Borque, "La obra de Juan del Enzina: Una poética
de la modernidad de lo rústico pastoril," in *Los géneros dramáticos en el siglo
XVI: El teatro hasta Lope de Vega*. Historia Crítica de la Literatura Hispánica.
Dirigida por Juan Ignacio Ferraras, vol. 8 [Madrid: Taurus, 1987], pp. 125–48:
137) sustains the character's transformation in Renaissance drama, the *comedia*
generally supports other solutions, such as the ruse contrived by Tristán in *El
perro del hortelano*. Lope's intentions, in maintaining such a blatant deception,
were "to ridicule the values of a society whose hollow properties could be so
easily satisfied" (see Melveena McKendrick, *Theatre in Spain 1490–1700*
[Cambridge: Cambridge University Press, 1989], p. 97). To the extensive bibliography on the subject of love in Renaissance drama cited by Díez Borque, the
following should be added: Robert L. Hathaway, *Love in the Early Spanish Theater* (Madrid: Playor, 1975); Anthony A. Van Beysterveldt, *La poesía amatoria*

del siglo XV y el teatro profano de Juan del Encina (Madrid: Insula, 1972); Bruce W. Wardropper, "Metamorphosis in the Theater of Juan del Encina," *Studies in Philology* 59 (1962): 41–51.

33. See Cattaneo, "El desenlace imperfecto," pp. 116–17.

34. I quote from Lope Félix de Vega Carpio, *La ocasión perdida*, in *Obras dramáticas*, n.e., vol. 8 (Madrid: Real Academia Española, 1930), p. 243a–b.

35. See Cattaneo, "El desenlace imperfecto," p. 111.

36. Although the general characteristics of the *comedia de figurón* are present in some earlier *comedias*, such as Lope's *La dama boba* (ca. 1613), Antonio Hurtado de Mendoza's *Cada loco con su tema* (ca. 1619), and Ruiz de Alarcón's *No hay mal que por bien no venga* (ca. 1623), Rojas Zorrilla's *Entre bobos anda el juego* is generally accepted to be the first true example of this type of drama (see Francisco de Rojas Zorrilla, *Entre bobos anda el juego*, ed. María Grazia Profeti [Madrid: Taurus, 1984], pp. 15–16). I quote from this edition.

37. In *Entre bobos anda el juego*, the focus of the main action is displaced from the "in" world of Madrid to the periphery of that world, the journey from Madrid to Toledo, to settle down in the end on the "outside," in the provincial world of Toledo, thus repudiating—or at least slighting—the values of the imperial court, the artificial illusion of the capital which sustains its courtly glory with an inarticulate, false, and ridiculous language (see *Entre bobos anda el juego*, p. 20).

38. Ibid., p. 17.

39. Ibid.

40. Ibid.

41. Ibid., vv. 2735–54.

42. See Joan Oleza Simó, "La propuesta teatral del primer Lope de Vega," in José Luis Canet Vallés, ed., *Teatro y prácticas escénicas. II: La comedia* (London: Tamesis, 1986), pp. 251–308: 254.

43. Charles V. Aubrun, *La comédie espagnole (1600–1680)* (Paris, 1966), p. v.

44. Iser, *The Act of Reading*, pp. 78, 76.

3

Creative Space

Ideologies of Discourse in Góngora's *Polifemo*

EDWARD H. FRIEDMAN

━━━━━◆ ◆━━━━━

There are a number of ways of looking at the question of continuity in literature, including a focus on discontinuity. To an extent, we have put aside—marginated—literary history in favor of difference. We look for markers of distance, of separation, of inexplicability. We seem to want meaning to elude us, yet we hope creatively to describe the indeterminacies, the scissions, the ungrammaticalities that defer and divert us as we read texts. The autonomous work that was the object of North American New Criticism and of other formalist modes has all but disappeared. Current approaches tend to stress the interplay and the interdependence of texts. The direct borrowing suggested by source studies has been superseded, or, one might say, subsumed, by the concept of intertextuality, which argues that every text is a response to previous texts and traditions and that the textual past is an inevitable presence in all literature. If New Criticism separates the author from the work, newer models show that invention is but innovative refurbishing, however ingenious the recasting may be. Michel Foucault's essay "What Is an Author?" relegates the author to "author-function," one of the numerous discourses in a text, a voice among many voices and many echoes. Despite the link to the past, the writer enjoys what may be termed a creative space, a space in which to express subjective thoughts, to become an artist, to rewrite history, to confront predecessors. In *The Anxiety of Influence* and other studies, Harold Bloom elaborates the mechanisms by which poets seek to surpass their predecessors. The dominant imagery in this case is death; the poet will kill off those who precede him by displacing and vanquishing them.

Creation is, above all, competition. Continuity in art is not only progression but rivalry, appropriation, change. The baroque period in Spain is a time of intense social, political, and religious conflict, and art reflects and becomes an arm of these struggles. Baroque cathedrals, for example, compete with outside, earthly distractions. Their adornments—more than the eye can see and more than the mind can capture in two or three or twenty visits—maintain the interest of churchgoers and bring them back to observe and to pray. Architects and artists thus join the theological establishment in fostering the faith. The Inquisition and other agents of censorship promote adherence to institutionalized thought, as does the studied conservatism of individual writers. Francisco de Quevedo makes Pablos, the protagonist of *La vida del buscón*, a more sinful, more delinquent picaro than Lazarillo de Tormes and Guzmán de Alfarache. As narrator, Pablos is more given to conceits, and he is more articulate, as well, in his ultimate acknowledgment of the hierarchical system of social justice. Expanding upon Lope de Vega's model, Calderonian drama reaches new conceptual and linguistic heights in the sphere of the court. Perhaps the most obvious form of literary competition is the writer's decision to tread familiar ground, that is, to retell a story attributable to another author or to a recognizable tradition. This is direct confrontation, in which the writer invites comparison through a dialectics of revision and rejection, reverence and disrespect, continuity and discontinuity.

No matter how brilliant the work of art or how impressive the victory over the past, there is no way to eradicate the predecessor. Like the picaresque antiheroes who cannot succeed in denying their bloodlines, the writer cannot sever ties with convention. The very act of emulation, albeit with an air of superiority, prohibits even the illusion of originality. The locus of inscription is not the tabula rasa, but the palimpsest. Competition, as contest, must refer—if not defer—to an ever-present "other" and must accept, however reluctantly, a lineage upon which it grafts itself and which finally becomes the graft. The "other" is part of the writing and part of the reading. The sense of alterity, of alteration, allows the reader to examine creation in context. It would be difficult to consider Luis de Góngora's carpe diem sonnet "Mientras por competir con tu cabello," whose opening verse is blatant in its competitive spirit, without glancing backward—if not to Ausonius—to Garcilaso de la Vega's "En tanto que de rosa y azucena" (and forward to Sor Juana Inés de la Cruz's "A su retrato"). Góngora does not merely force a contest between his love object and nature, thus breaking Garcilaso's balance of feminine beauty and the beauty of nature, but he breaks with the symmetry and tone of his predecessor. Garcilaso restates the carpe diem theme through the paradox of mutability: one can be certain only of the passage of time and of the changes time will bring. In the second tercet of his sonnet, Góngora goes beyond coaxing to remind the lady that after old age lie death, destruction, nothingness. Disjunction replaces equilibrium, in form and content. Góngora moves to obliterate the initial premise, challenging not only Garcilaso's poem but the poet, the movement he represents, and the historical moment over which he presides. Carpe diem is the medium, not the message. Góngora's sonnet is about competition, about composition. Competition is a key to the structure of the text and is its principal conceit as well. Rhetoric merges with ideology, a conventional topos with a metapoetic macrostructure.

Góngora's *Fábula de Polifemo y Galatea* offers an extended view of writing as competition. The baroque poet vies with a classical tradition and with Renaissance neoclassicism. The idea of writing as rewriting touches questions of subject matter, of form, and of language. Poetic skills notwithstanding, how does one contend with the authority of the classic text, and how can the vernacular triumph over the classical status of the mother tongue? How does one deal with the "perfection" attained by Renaissance masters and with the success of contemporaries? How does one establish a voice, within and beyond the poem? In the *Polifemo*, I would submit, Góngora addresses these points and defines his own creative space. Far from the disengaged, "absent" poet, he enters the text in order to exert control, to claim authority. He chooses a fable that he can use to replicate his situation as poet and that he can revise as a vehicle for his particular poetics.

The baroque in Spain, and in general, is notable for its resistance to a precise definition. The difficulty stems, in part, from the transference of the term from the plastic arts to other realms and from nation to nation. The baroque is often discussed as counterpoint to the Renaissance, the most apparent point of departure, and the classification covers the elements that we tend to place under the rubric of culture: the arts, society, and the institutions of the state. Designations such as mannerism and metaphysical poetry, together with attempts to subdivide the baroque into discrete categories, may yield fascinating results, but the groupings are nonetheless problematic. Every generality seems to lead to exceptions, to differences among the media and among artists who seek their distinctive signatures. How does one weigh the factors that link Góngora, Quevedo, Gracián, and Calderón against those that mark variation? The writers contribute to what may be called a baroque project, and it is relatively easy to indicate points of intersection within their writings. It is equally easy, and arguably more profitable from a critical perspective, to differentiate between the writings. Paradoxically, a common recourse of baroque artists is the use of binary oppositions (the technique of chiaroscuro, for example), which, by their very nature, foreground the dissimilar: *culteranismo* and *conceptismo*, diversion and didacticism, personal and professional rivalry.

Stephen Gilman finds in the artistic minority, the *cultos*, a rejection of shared values and beliefs and a consequent deviation from the various orthodoxies fostered by the state, which he sees as signs of a desperate search for individuality, as an assertion of "their own distinctive *soledad*."[1] José Antonio Maravall speaks of solitude as an aspect of the seventeenth-century "crisis of individualism," adding, "but let us not forget that it is always 'solitude' in the midst of 'competition.' "[2] The cultivation of individual talent in this period demands a willingness to isolate oneself from the mainstream and to defend oneself against detractors.[3] Góngora becomes a practitioner and defender of the new poetry. To justify his break from the norm, he needs to demonstrate the validity and, to a certain degree, the superiority of his creative method. In the center of the debate stands Góngora's poetry, complemented by his "Carta en respuesta," an open letter distributed in Madrid with manuscript copies of the *Soledades*.[4] The poet must account for the obscurity of his work on literary and ideological grounds. In an essay entitled "The Production of Solitude: Góngora and the State," John Beverley notes that the poet, coming from a titled but economically modest Andalusian family, is a marginalized aristocrat, who "must insert himself in the circles of power from the outside." As he proves himself to the community of literati, he may gain honor and status in society. Poetry is the means by which he can distinguish himself, that is, set himself apart from his literary predecessors and above those of his social class. He epitomizes an aristocracy of letters that seeks entry into the upper echelon of the sociopolitical hierarchy, the aristocracy of blood.[5]

Given the critical judgment which views Góngora's poetry as formally intricate but emotionally empty, there is an irony of sorts in the notion of a poet poised to climb the social ladder by virtue of his verbal ability. One is reminded of the prologue to *Lazarillo de Tormes*, which frames a hard-luck story with the Ciceronian adage that art brings honor, that the artist can cross social barriers. Or of Velázquez, as presented by Jonathan Brown in an essay on *Las Meninas*, whose aspirations to knighthood are intimately related to his commitment to the artistic enterprise. Velázquez imposes himself onto the canvas to show "the painter as worthy, because, not in spite of, his art."[6] Perhaps a more relevant analogy would be to the third chapter of Quevedo's *Buscón*, which describes Pablos's tutelage under the licenciate Cabra. The episode is noteworthy, among other reasons, for its remarkable juxtaposition of hunger and verbiage. The narrator satiates the reader with a richness of words and witticisms that depict gastronomical penury. The discourse is complex, but it signifies nothing, nothingness. It is insubstantial. The reader may fill up on words and then feel empty; the words are consumed, in the double sense. This is language that distances the reader, and, for some, it is empty language. Quevedo makes his presence known, but his own feelings seem to be absent. And this is precisely the detachment that directs critics to appraise Góngora as "the poet of personal absence."[7]

A major presupposition of Michael Riffaterre's *Semiotics of Poetry* is that a poem is a puzzle to be solved. The reader must overcome a series of linguistic and conceptual obstacles in order to capture the significance of the text. Spanish baroque poetry lends itself to the imagery of combat, in that the reader must struggle with the mysteries of the text and must use all resources available to decode and recode verbal messages. Góngora and his contemporaries carry rhetoric to extremes, and it seems clear that they relish the task of creating linguistic edifices that can be brought down only by an ingenious elite. Figurative language is the product of an active mind, and these minds are set on outdoing their predecessors. They employ an abundance of words. They make words work double- or triple-time in elaborate conceits. They elevate language through verbal play. They put language on display. They seem to say, with Eva Perón in the song "Buenos Aires" from *Evita*, "All I want is a whole lot of excess." Within this ideology of excess, baroque poets are open to objections based on the difficulty and on the vacuousness of their discourse.

The question of difficulty is at once an aesthetic and an ethical matter. The cultivation of obscurity can be rewarding for the creator and for the consumer; it can be, for both, mind expanding. The exercises in wit, in rhetoric, and in linguistic invention challenge the writer to explore subtleties of thought and of expression, which the reader must attempt to match, and to comprehend. Fueled by sixteenth-century Italian mannerism, the pursuit of expressive majesty and of verbal mastery helps to legitimize difficulty for its own sake. Baltasar Gracián and others document and dissect the process in their anatomies of wit. Mental sharpness and ingenuity serve as guidelines and as goals of the undertaking. The creative space seems to broaden, the result of a progressive shift from mechanical, prescriptive writing—and from passive, predetermined reading—to a spirit of openness. Ways of perceiving the world become more secularized, and the relation of *res* and *verba* becomes more flexible, less bound to a scholastic past.[8] When liberated from theology, the word may move in infinite directions. The figurative reading of the universe consists of a spiritual model, whose meaning is preordained, and a secular model, grounded in aesthetics. This is the difference between finding a path and forging a path, between a symbolic system and a self-defining system, between language as means and language as end. The signifier loses authority as the signified becomes more comprehensive in scope, more variable, and more dependent on an immediate context. Centralized authority is lost, to the advantage of the individual imagination. In short, the writer gains increased power over words.

The release of discourse from codified meaning may lead to a type of artistic freedom, but the openness of representation threatens not only the theological hierarchy but the didactic mission of literature as propagated by the Council of Trent, among other agents of faith. By endangering what one might call the allegories of reading, by daring to admit a manipulation of meaning, the new poetry places erudition and imagination above dogma. Emphasis on wordplay at the most elevated level suggests that the lessons—the utility—of fiction can be subordinated to aesthetic pleasure. For advocates of the liberated signifier, intellectual contortions lead to knowledge. For linguistic fundamentalists, creativity usurps a moral space. Freedom has a price, for the new discursive paradigm may be construed as distracting or atheistic.[9] What John Beverley refers to as "the exclusionary character of Góngora's defense of difficulty" becomes an ennobling gesture, a way of attaining nobility while requiring that the reader be equally honorable, that is, capable of honor, worthy of access to the text. This intense form of mental activity is the antithesis of manual labor, and only the most learned, the best educated, the cream of the cultured aristocracy will merit entry into the literary circle.[10] A counterpart to the intricacies of discourse is the self-consciousness of writers who become absorbed in the mirror images of art.

In *Trials of Authorship*, Jonathan Crewe detects in recent Renaissance scholarship, "often boosted by deconstruction," a desire "to produce large, synthesizing representations of counterontological innovation, displacement, gender-reversal, theatricality, positional mobility, power-shifting, dispersal, and cosmic remodeling." He notes that, in these representations of the Renaissance, Vergil and Ovid tend to overshadow Horace and Seneca, and he cautions us, in our revisionary zeal, "to recall that a good deal of Renaissance writing invokes the figure of the Stoic . . . and is thus by no means dominantly committed to translation and metamorphosis."[11] The admonition accepted, one may find an Ovidian thrust in the Spanish baroque, essentially a rewriting—revision, metamorphosis—of the Renaissance. The Renaissance search for symmetry, for equilibrium, for direct contact between the word and the world may lead to a faith in union—a oneness with nature, for example—which can never be achieved. Conscious of difference, of the misdirected attempt at mimesis, baroque literature faces the deceptive truth and finds a consolation of sorts in disillusionment. While abject depression is one response, a filling-in of gaps is another. At times, the world seems too much with the voices of the baroque; at others, the literary text seems to encompass the so-called real world, to bring the world into the text.

In *Don Quijote*, Cervantes manipulates the concept of historical truth in order to bring the real world into the literary text. Literature recreates life, in consummately ironic fashion, by inverting the traditional macrocosm/microcosm dichotomy. The historical record is a mediating factor in the story of Don Quijote. The knight-errant contemplates his role in history, that is, in the historical record. The reader is aware of several versions of that history, at least one of which has been projected into the real world (as contemplated within the fiction). A tangible version of the history validates the metafictional game. The battle between Alonso Fernández de Avellaneda's spurious sequel of 1614 and Cervantes' second part of 1615—and, most notably, the presence of the former in the latter—becomes an emblem of the reversal of fortune that incorporates the real into the imaginary, the world into the text. A few years earlier, Mateo Alemán avenges a literary theft in the pages of *Guzmán de Alfarache*. He punishes Juan Martí, the author of a false continuation, in print. He administers justice in the text when society will not come to his aid. In similar fashion, the baroque poet breaks the Renaissance balance by adding to the world what the world cannot do: represent itself figuratively, duplicate (and reduplicate) itself verbally, critique itself.

Pedro Salinas indicates the manner in which Góngora seeks to remedy "the poetic insufficiency of reality," a concern which dates from classical antiquity: "Telling and describing what one sees is not poetry. What must be done to convert it to poetry? Raise it, intensify its characteristics to an extreme degree, elevate it above its natural forms and extract from the latter all their esthetic content by means of the imagination and fantasy. Reality must be transformed, transmuted into another kind of poetic reality, material, sonorous, plastic."[12] Paul Julian Smith offers a variation on this reading by suggesting that "what we find in Góngora's career is not a progressive absenteeism, both cause and effect of an irresponsible excess of words, but rather the linguistic infilling or supplementing of a nature found increasingly to be lacking in substance."[13] Creation may be seen, then, as a double-edged sword. The poet supplements with words the deficiencies of nature, and, it may be argued, in order to find these words he moves inward, through mental deliberation and through a rewriting of the intertext. As he expands the field of vision and adds a poetic graft onto reality, he follows Cervantes (and, I would submit, the picaresque writers) in granting a privileged status to commentary on the creative process.

In *Culture of the Baroque*, Maravall notes that "the Spanish mentality of the baroque epoch had the general quality of deriving satisfaction from all artifice, from whatever ingenious invention that appeared, in terms of the novelty it offered."[14] The poet engages a literary past and a natural world in a search for a novel representation of the realm of shepherds and nymphs. Nature made artificial, artifice demands excess, in the best sense of a term that has positive as well as negative connotations in the period. The signifier is ever distant from the objects of nature as signified; the points of reference are words, not things. This is a dimension of what Elias Rivers calls "the pastoral paradox of natural art." In an attempt to clarify and to harmonize the forces of nature, poets resort to words, which may become increasingly unintelligible as their goals shift from explaining nature to outshining other words. The idealization of nature often produces a refinement of the bucolic world, and linguistic and rhetorical flourishes intensify this detachment. Convention overtakes—if not reality—a primary creative urge. Defining nature may be poetic, while poeticizing the lives of shepherds may not be natural, verisimilar. The cultured pastoral setting is a mediating factor between the harsh realities of nature and the artificial discourse of poetry. The literary pastoral is a metonymical center, evoking a visual presence and a verbal presence, both of which symbolically must be absented for the sake of novelty. If there is something akin to an original pastoral equation, the poetic history of that equation bears little nostalgia for the bleating of sheep and the smells of the countryside. The source, however real, is obscured by story, or myth, and by a defamiliarizing discourse.

Góngora's *Polifemo* is about nature and about the relation between nature and art,[15] but perhaps more than anything it is about the relation between words. The poem concerns the literary repertory and an implicit mandate to depart from tradition. It can hardly be coincidental that Góngora chooses to rewrite an episode from the *Metamorphoses*, which celebrates and reiterates acts of transformation, or that the bigger-than-life Polyphemus becomes a standard bearer for the aesthetics of excess. The course of literary development depends on the idea of movement, which Maravall considers to be "the fundamental principle of the world and human beings" in the culture of the baroque.[16] Time and change have always been with us, but the baroque gives special prominence to variety, restoration, modification, and disjunction. The impact is particularly strong with respect to processes of signification. The liberation of the word—of the signifier from a finite number of signifieds—offers a unique freedom of movement for the writer. Michel Foucault describes this phenomenon in *The Order of Things*: "At the beginning of the seventeenth century, during the period that has been termed, rightly or wrongly, the Baroque, thought ceases to move in the element of resemblance. Similitude is no longer the form of knowledge but rather the occasion of error, the danger to which one exposes oneself when one does not examine the obscure region of confusions."[17] The altered perception of the universe and of language affects the contiguity of the Renaissance and the baroque. The second may define itself not as an offshoot of the first, or even as an exaggerated continuation, but as the dark underside of a secure, controlled vision of the world. One would expect to find—and does find—an abundance of examples of antithesis, oxymoron, and catachresis, among other figures of opposition, in baroque poetry, but perhaps the most notable consequence of the ideological shift, from the perspective of rhetoric, is its impact on metaphor, conventionally a figure of similitude yet commonly regarded as the guiding trope of baroque poetry.

One way to divest metaphor of similitude is to convert the comparison into an unequal contest, as in Góngora's reworking of Garcilaso in "Mientras por competir con tu cabello." Another, more complex, more nuanced denial of similitude within a metaphorical framework is the metaphor derived from catachresis. Catachresis is a figure marked by the use of a term beyond its traditional contextual field, often in a paradoxical manner. In Góngora's sonnet which begins "En este occidental, en este, oh Licio, / climatérico lustro de tu vida"[18] [Lycius, in these most western years—these five / Climacteric—of your waning day (Singleton)], the phrase "¡Ciego discurso humano!" (v. 11) [Blind human speech!] is an example of catachresis. The roots of the word *discurso*, which means reason or judgment but which also means speech, lie in rhetoric, where rational discourse has persuasive powers. *Discurso* is on one level incompatible with the adjective *ciego* and on another level quite compatible; thus, the paradox. Beverley notes that enemies of the new poetry—"claiming to represent an orthodox Aristotelian discipline of the rules"—cite catachresis, associated with implausible connections, as the paradigm of Gongorism. The far-fetched analogies separate *res* and *verba*; they direct the reader toward the unraveling of conceits and away from meaningful content.[19] This would be obscurity without purpose. It seems, rather, that Góngora revises the figure of catachresis in order to establish more precise correspondences between elements.

In stanza 13 of the *Polifemo*, the poetic speaker describes Galatea as follows:

> Son una y otra luminosa estrella
> lucientes ojos de su blanca pluma:
> si roca de cristal no es de Neptuno,
> pavón de Venus es, cisne de Juno.
>
> [Stars be her eyes in lucent bold relieve / on pinion's white—such snow doth Beauty don, / for though of Neptune she is no milky reef, / Pavone she is of Venus, Juno's swan.]   (Singleton)

The brilliance of Galatea's eyes against her white skin inspires the imagery. As a daughter of the sea (metonymically evoked by Neptune, the father of Polifemo), her radiant complexion is crystalline, based on the implied metaphor of water as soft crystal. The stars are conventional metaphors for the eyes, and *pluma*, related to the skin by a two-tiered figure of metonymy (feather for plumage) and metaphor (plumage for the lady's complexion), inaugurates the interplay of peacock and swan. Identified as Venus's peacock and Juno's swan, Galatea enjoys the best of both worlds. As Dámaso Alonso and others demonstrate, the metaphors synthesize the whiteness of the swan, sacred to Venus, with the bright eyes set into plumage of the peacock, sacred to Juno.[20] Separately, "pavón de Venus" and "cisne de Juno" may be seen as catachresis, but the parallel structure and the earlier images allow these mixed metaphors (in the most positive sense) to maintain an internal logic. By the same token, *roca de cristal* suggests skin as soft as crystal in a nymph who is hard as a rock in disdaining her suitors, as the succeeding verses substantiate. When the poem reveals more about Galatea, catachresis is subsumed by metaphor.

In stanza 24, Acis arrives at the spring on a scorching summer day, "polvo el cabello, húmidas centellas,/si no ardientes aljófares, sudando" [dust in his hair—and limbs a sweat / of dripping sparks, if not pearls, indeed, on fire (Singleton; emended by Iarocci)]. The "A, if not B" construction unites the examples of catachresis that describe the beads of sweat running down his face and body. Fire and water become compatible. The "ardientes aljófares" are burning drops of dew and pearls set aflame. The catachresis-turned-metaphor stands between the heat of the dog-day afternoon and the promising coolness of the spring. If Sirius, the Dog Star, is (metaphorically) the sun's salamander, believed to live in fire, the sleeping Galatea is mute crystal, "cristal mudo," beside the resonant water, "sonoro cristal." The images of intense heat and refreshing water frame the central metaphor. The allusion to pearls links Acis to Galatea, associated with pearls in stanzas 14 and 47, for example. Galatea's element is now water, but Acis, with the aid of Cupid, will inspire her passion. What begins as catachresis, the joining of unrelated images, becomes the foundation of a linguistic deep structure, a unity built from difference.

Góngora is not denying meaning, or the meaningful, nor is he so absorbed in rhetoric that his images become empty displays of ingenuity. He turns to the dissimilar in order to redefine similitude. In his works, metaphor changes form—undergoes metamorphosis—as a means of moving beyond the poetic past. Góngora takes catachresis, the figure that rhetoricians at times refer to as "the wrenching of words,"[21] and practices a type of elision. He systematically removes the incongruities, by justifying the uncommon associations and by projecting a rational base for the paradox. No longer a misdirected or illogical metaphor, catachresis may be seen as the first stage of sustained and highly sophisticated metaphors. Despite their integration into the body of the poem, these metaphors never lose an air of difference, a consciousness of origin in the rhetoric of antithesis. In the *Polifemo*, Góngora reinvents discourse, just as he reinvents story.

In book 13 of the *Metamorphoses*, Ovid writes of Polyphemus and Galatea in 160 verses. R. V. Young observes that Pietro Bembo's "Galatea," one of many versions of the story, in 70 verses in Latin, "represents a clear effort to rival a classical poet in the treatment of a traditional theme in a conventional genre. Bembo creates another story like Ovid's in a style and tone reminiscent of his Roman original."[22] Although Young speaks here of rivalry, he recognizes that imitation of the classics takes a radical turn in the seventeenth century. Imitation, for Góngora, is dislocation: "Ovid's Latin style, however intricate and rhetorical, is marked by ease and fluency; when Góngora imposes Ovid's syntax on Spanish, he evokes a sense of strain and linguistic violence which matches the strain and violence of the one-eyed giant heaving the boulder on Acis."[23] Góngora's version of the story is three times longer than Ovid's. It intensifies what is already hyperbolic. It acknowledges the Latin source and the Latin diction as it disconnects itself from both. It adapts the Ovidian irony into new patterns of irony, and it reconstructs the narrative scheme. Bembo competes with Ovid in order to prove that the Renaissance can match its classical models. Góngora competes with Ovid in order to outmatch his rival.

The *Fábula de Acis y Galatea* of Luis Carrillo y Sotomayor, a poet, theorist, and decorated soldier who died at an early age in 1610, is remembered for its dedication to the Count of Niebla (to whom Góngora dedicates his poem) and for its difference in other respects from the *Polifemo*.[24] In his *Libro de la erudición poética*, Carrillo makes a distinction between the poet and the versifier, argues against the notion of pleasing the common reader, praises eloquence, and sees imitation as respect for tradition. The Romans copy the Greeks, with exemplary success, and there is no reason for the Spaniard to shy away from a similar competition. In the treatise and in his poetry in general, Carrillo exercises relative moderation, and, given his intermediate position, it is not surprising that critics laud him both as an early master of *culteranismo* and as an opponent of poetic excess. The *Libro de la erudición poética* maintains an interesting balance between the cultivation of difficulty and the dangers of excess, with classical masters as guides.[25] The appeal to discretion, to good judgment, and, most notably, to clarity of expression has points of contact with the arguments of Góngora's detractors. In his study of Golden Age preceptists, Antonio Vilanova refers, for example, to the somewhat ironic similarity between Carrillo's views on obscurity and the final chapter of the *Discurso poético* (1624) of Juan de Jáuregui, a bitter enemy of baroque innovation.

Scholars believe that Góngora had access to the *Fábula de Acis y Galatea*, since there are several cases of repetition of Carrillo's images in the *Polifemo*, but it seems evident that the influence is, at best, minor.[26] The *Fábula de Acis y Galatea* is written in ottava rima, as in Góngora's poem, and is exactly half the length of the *Polifemo*. Carrillo has Galatea narrate to Scylla (before her transformation) the story of Acis's death. The center and longest portion of the poem is the cyclops's lament as retold by Galatea, who in the final stanza mourns her loss alongside the stream into which Acis has been transformed. The borrowings from Ovid are numerous, as Rosa Navarro Durán's notes to the poem, in her recent edition of the complete works, make clear. Approaching Carrillo's text after reading Góngora, one may be struck by the smaller scale of the narrative. As would be expected, the poet takes frequent recourse to rhetorical figures, but the hyperboles seem mild by comparison and the metaphors are far fewer in number and far less audacious. Because Galatea gives her account after the fact, the poem does not create the tension of the *Polifemo*. Rather than a cyclops claiming to be reformed by love, Carrillo presents, following Ovid, a monster who seems more concerned that another suitor has triumphed. Within the multilayered rhetoric of Góngora's poem, there is an emotional range; the reader knows, to some extent, at least, how each of the main characters views the world, and each of them, if only momentarily, elicits sympathy. *Acis y Galatea* is, in every sense, Galatea's story, a story that rarely is encumbered, or unduly interrupted, by rhetorical devices. It would be hard to disagree with Dámaso Alonso's use of the adjective *sedoso* to describe the smoothness and even texture of Carrillo's verse.[27] Note, for example, the following passage in which a narrating voice describes Galatea, whose remembrance of an amorous tryst with Acis so fills her with tears that she is unable to continue her story:

> Venció, en fin, la memoria, y coronados
> de perlas Galatea entrambos ojos,
> sobre los hilos de oro derramados,
> de aljófar Scila vio varios despojos.
>
> (Carrillo, p. 205)

[Then memory was victorious / and Scila saw many nacreous spoils; / Galatea's eyes crowned by pearls / that spilled down veins of gold.]

The language is conventionally metaphorical; tears are pearls, locks of hair are veins of gold. Carrillo reiterates Ovid's image of the nymph too overcome with tears to speak, but changes the tears (*lacrimae*) of the Latin version to the figurative pearls. The words are affecting, but neither obscure nor radically removed from their source.

When Polifemo pleads with Galatea to accept his love, he is hyperbolic in his praise of her beauty and in his despondency over her hardheartedness. He tells Galatea,

> "Compite al blando viento su blandura
> —de cisne blanca pluma—y en dudosa
> suerte la iguala de la leche pura
> la nata dulce y presunción hermosa;
> en su beldad promete y su frescura
> del hermoso jardín el lirio y rosa.
> Y si mis quejas, ninfa hermosa, oyeras,
> leche, pluma, jardín, flores vencieras."
>
> (Carrillo, pp. 206–7)

[It {your countenance} competes in softness with the soft wind / —a swan's white feather—, and dubious / is the fortune of the pure milk's / sweet cream, which tries to equal it with lovely presumption; / in its beauty and freshness is the promise of the lily and rose of a lovely garden. / And if you were to hear my pleas, lovely nymph, / milk, feather, garden, and flowers would you surpass.]

The passage represents a middle ground between the symmetry of the Renaissance and the violent metaphors of the baroque. The softness, whiteness, and delicate beauty of the love object rival objects in nature, but there is no fierceness to the competition. If the metaphors are con-

ventional, there is something appealing, and revealing, in the repetition
of images at the end. Polifemo injects himself into the world of natural
beauty by suggesting that for Galatea to reach fulfillment—that is, to
"conquer" the opposition—she needs to hear his plaint, to accept him.
He is the supplement, the corresponding part that will justify the gifts
nature has bestowed upon her, for he is not only majestic but rich in the
fruits of nature. Self-absorbed and blinded by love, he cannot appreciate
the differences between them, nor can he comprehend the love of Galatea for Acis. He contrasts the signs of his manliness—his great height
and "el vello grueso y duro y barba espesa" (Carrillo, p. 212) [thick,
dark hair and abundant beard]—with "el tierno cuerpo de tu dueño
amado" (p. 214) [the tender body of your beloved].

One might use the phrase "creative emulation" to characterize Carrillo's achievement in *Acis y Galatea*. He is faithful to Ovid while developing his own discourse. He gives distinctive voices to Galatea and Polifemo as he articulates the grief of one and the arrogance of the other.
By working within the Ovidian frame, he limits himself to retelling, as
opposed to reinventing. He accentuates the self-deceptive attitude of the
cyclops, who, like a Narcissus bereft of aesthetic judgment, admires his
reflection in the water:

> No fue naturaleza tan avara,
> antes franca conmigo, de sus bienes;
> ni es tan rústica, no, mi frente y cara,
> ni son tan feas mis valientes sienes.
>
> (Carrillo, p. 211)

[Nature was not stingy, / but rather generous with her gifts; / my forehead
and face are not altogether rustic / nor are my bold temples so ugly.]

A unifying element of the poem is the sadness of Galatea, who nonetheless cedes over half the poem to Polifemo's song. In the discourse of the
cyclops, Carrillo expands the model through a symmetrically arranged
contrastive structure. Polifemo alternates between praise of Galatea's
beauty in one stanza and despair over her cruelty in the next, for example, leading to a balance of love and rejection, affirmation and negation, power and vulnerability. The formal elements of *Acis y Galatea*

produce order amid the chaos of the events narrated. Together with the compatibility of theory and practice in Carrillo, this order implies a respect for the classical model, for tradition in general, and for continuity.

Carrillo's version of the story of Polyphemus and Galatea, written only a few years before the *Polifemo*, is useful as a marker of what Góngora does and does not do. In essence, Góngora is a philosopher of language. He takes liberties with words and experiments with forms of signification. As in the case of Cervantes and *Don Quijote*, the new is intimately related to the old, to the intertext. Every innovation is a response to precedent, and every break from protocol is an acknowledgment of the norm. Góngora writes in the vernacular, but he re-creates aspects of Latin syntax. He moves away from Ovid's version of the Polyphemus story, but does not elect to write his own myth. He is an avid and perceptive reader of his Spanish predecessors, but he seems determined to implement a new semiotics. He does not reinvent rhetoric, but intensifies the standard tropes in unsurpassed fashion. The emphasis on rhetorical discourse—a discourse that mediates each stage of the reading process—must, in turn, mediate the message systems of the text.

One need not assume that highly figurative language in the baroque is an end in itself. Rhetoric informs the ideology of a text such as the *Polifemo*, and the rhetorical strategies of the text may be vital commentaries on the act of writing and, more comprehensively, on ways of perceiving the universe. Cervantes recognizes semiosis as plot material, and so, in his way, does Góngora. The fact that Góngora flouts his deviation from the intertext and from conventional rhetorical models—and the fact that whatever comprehension one may derive from the reading comes only after an exhaustive effort—must give the reader pause, in the double sense. Difficulty has a purpose, a purpose deeper than literary and social elitism. A presupposition of the obscure style is the challenge of reading, based on what would seem to be the writer's desire to have the reader reenact the trials of perception. The reader's battle with rhetoric is analogous to the competing narrative voices and variations of truth in the *Quijote*. The metaliterary devices of baroque texts display a special kind of self-consciousness, which preoccupies the reader and which becomes inseparable from the "content." The idea of rewriting the fable of Polyphemus bears on story and discourse, just as the purported history of Don Quijote involves a chivalric and writerly (and readerly) quest.[28] Góngora narrates the story in the competitive mode. Ovid, Garcilaso, and Polifemo, among many others, are his opponents.

Much of the artistry of the *Polifemo* stems from what one might call Góngora's traditional poetic skills. An example would be the sustained use of eye imagery and its connection with other images (light, the sun) and with sight (or insight) and blindness. Another would be the foreshadowing of Acis's death, not only in the description of Polifemo's destructive power, but also in the images of animals stalking their prey (the wolf in stanza 22, the eagle in stanza 33). The use of water imagery, linked to the three main characters and ultimately to the metamorphosis, offers an example of the ironic variation of a motif. What differentiates Góngora from other writers is his amplification of poetic recourses. Can there be a more appropriate—a more hyperbolic—subject for him than the cyclops? Or a more natural setting, both land and sea, to adorn with artifice, to remake through metaphor? The story deals with competition, with the pursuit of the exceptionally beautiful Galatea, worshiped by all mankind. The poem becomes an allegory of Góngora's pursuit of recognition, of authority over the material and over other poets.

In numerous cases, Góngora expands the structure of metaphor by inserting a third element, or mediating factor, into the equation. This is the element that makes sense of—rationalizes—the mixed metaphor; it is an interpretant, a word or idea that facilitates the making of connections.[29] Poststructuralism gives prominence to the middle ground between signifier and signified. It is in this space that the inner workings of fiction take shape, and it is in this space that we see the poet at work. In the *Polifemo*, the primary marker of the literary allegory is Galatea, caught between Polifemo and Acis. Polifemo has size, strength, and wealth on his side, while Acis has a splendid figure and Cupid on his. Galatea, like the young princess Margarita of *Las meninas*, may be an enigmatic center, an image that moves us to focus our glance elsewhere. In the Ovidian model, Galatea relates her story, with several brief passages from a third-person narrator. She reproduces Polyphemus's song from memory, as direct discourse. In the *Polifemo*, Galatea's voice is suppressed; the only speakers are a narrator and the enamored cyclops. Góngora's poem includes an account of the circumstances under which Galatea falls in love with Acis, who in Ovid is present only in his aquatic state.

Galatea is truly an object, a love object and an object of beauty. Her character is defined by disdain for all suitors; she is, ironically, "el monstro de rigor, la fiera brava" (31e). Her transformation is wrought by Cupid's arrow, which wounds her before she sees Acis. When she does catch sight of him, as he pretends to sleep, she is victim of a "deceptive rhetorical silence" ("mentido retórico silencio," 33c–d), an unknowing player in a plot invented by Cupid. The poem's narrator describes her as momentarily "mute" ("muda," 32a). The silence of Galatea is significant in light of her role as narrator in Ovid's story and the great attention given to the cyclops's voice in the *Polifemo*. Góngora's poem is rich in sensory images, as is baroque poetry in general, but aural elements have a special role in the *Polifemo*, through the frequent antithesis of sounds and silence, through references to musical instruments, and, most importantly, through the discordant oral performance of the cyclops. Polifemo's voice and music seem especially strong when the other members of the love triangle maintain silence. Although inspired by the cooing of a pair of doves ("trompas de Amor," 40h), Galatea and Acis are ruled by the visual, by physical attraction and the implicit promise of internal beauty.

Polifemo, in contrast, could hardly be louder, or more cacophonous, and he accompanies himself on crude, untuned pipes. The narrator calls his voice thunderous ("el trueno de la voz," 45g) and horrendous ("su horrenda voz," 59a). If man and nature cease to function in order to worship Galatea, they are made immobile out of fear of Polifemo. His appeal to Galatea in stanzas 46 through 58 is an extraordinary mix of self-praise and self-deception. He calls her "sorda hija del mar" (48a) [deaf daughter of the sea] and pleads with her to listen to his voice "por dulce, cuando no por mía" (48h) [if not because it is mine, because it is sweet]. The song is a paean to his possessions, to his lineage, to his imposing stature, and to the eye ("un sol en mi frente," 53e) [a sun in my forehead] that he has seen reflected in the water. At the end of the song, Polifemo calls attention to his new-found sensitivity. Love has taught him to respect life, he declares; his cavern no longer boasts human trophies, but has become a shelter for the wayfarer. Offering Galatea a magnificent bow and quiver from his bounty, he alludes to Venus and to Cupid, as the sound of goats interrupts his song and sets in motion the events that lead to Acis's death. Polifemo's actions disprove his rhetoric. The professed reformation through love is an illusion. The destructive force cannot be contained, nor can violence be averted. Their silent harmony invaded, the lovers invoke divine assistance. The narrator alludes to these cries for help without reproducing them. Sea deities transform the bleeding, lifeless Acis into a stream, where, in a spiritual yet pyrrhic victory, he will dwell at the side of Doris, mother of Galatea. Polifemo, for his part, speaks no more. The figurative conversion, negated by wrath, is overshadowed by the metamorphosis of Acis.

In stanza 4, the narrator describes a huge rock that serves as a gag to the mouth of the cavern inhabited by Polifemo. A far more accurate association is the depiction of Galatea as "mute crystal." Why would Góngora deprive Galatea of discursive space? The nymph, like the upper nobility, is graced by birth. She haughtily disdains her suitors. Her beauty is distracting; she causes work to go undone, and what is produced is placed as an offering before her. She stands at the center of the poem's conflict, but she does not play an active role in the conflict. Her love for Acis—her metamorphosis—comes at the hands of Cupid as deus ex machina. One could say that love puts Galatea in her place, as the contested object whose fate is determined by those vying for her. Although the suppression of women's voices is common in the Golden Age—the male-inflected discourse of picaresque antiheroines is but one example[30]—the *Polifemo* seems to be less about sexual politics than about authority in the realm of art.

With the aid of Cupid, Acis exerts a certain control over Galatea. Proud of his natural gifts, he "shows off his person" ("la persona ostenta," 38b) during the brief courtship ritual in which he is as much the object of beauty as is Galatea. In the condensed temporal frame of the poem, the courtship progresses to union, in a natural setting transformed into nuptial couch by the love deities. When Polifemo discovers the couple, they are defenseless, and their only recourse is to flee. The cyclops is the outsider, the intruder, unlike anyone around him. He is of exaggerated proportions, and the world appears smaller in his presence. When, moved by love, he strives to follow social decorum, that is, to subdue his destructive instincts, the combative urge wins out. He seeks to blot out, to erase, the enemy. In allegorical terms, Acis may represent Renaissance poetry, or the more comprehensive intertext, and Polifemo the new poetry, a hyperbolic reinscription of the old. Góngora fights for supremacy, but he knows that erasure of the intertext is impossible. Acis dies, to be reincarnated in another form, in another medium, and his presence is a reminder that one cannot escape the traces of the past. Polifemo is defined, in part, by Acis, by the act of competition. Change does not come without sacrifice. Within this scheme, Galatea may represent the public, forced to recognize the inevitability of change and the superiority of the more substantial model. Like the *infanta* of *Las meninas*, she directs us to the mirror in the work of art—to the work of art as a mirror—and ultimately to our own reflection as judges of the creative process.

There is another symbolic contest in the *Polifemo*, a competition between two poets: the narrator, representing Góngora, and Polifemo as "author" of the entreaty to Galatea. Samuel Guyler and Anthony Cascardi see the cyclops's song as a parodic imitation of Góngora's verse, and the result is, of course, a poetic composition of lesser merit. Góngora gives Polifemo a distinctive voice, as playwrights give voices to their characters and novelists to first-person narrators. Just as figures in the *comedia* speak in verse and a narrator such as Pablos in the *Buscón* employs the language of *conceptismo*, Polifemo's discourse both resembles his master's style and forms its peculiar idiolect. The cyclops, distracted by love, avails himself of a harsher, more earthy lexicon and on occasion breaks with literary protocol. If he is inferior to Góngora, however, that does not mean that he is not a most accomplished poet. Some of Polifemo's verses reflect the more straightforward approach to poetic diction. He describes his impressive height as follows:

Edward H. Friedman

♦

¿Qué mucho, si de nubes se corona
por igualarme la montaña en vano,
y en los cielos, desde esta roca, puedo
escribir mis desdichas con el dedo?
        (52e–h)

[Is it surprising that the mountain / crowns itself with clouds in vain in
order to equal me, / and that from this peak, I can / write my grief in the
heavens with my finger?]

The narrator writes,

Un monte era de miembros eminente
este (que, de Neptuno hijo fiero,
de un ojo ilustra el orbe de su frente,
émulo casi del mayor lucero).
        (7a–d)

[An enormous mountain of limbs was / he who—wild son of Neptune—, /
illuminates his browed sphere with one eye, / virtual rival of the brightest
star.]   (Singleton; emended by Iarocci)

It is fascinating to observe that passages of great beauty, spoken by Polifemo, dim beside analogous passages of the narrator. Consider, for example, the delicacy of the cyclops's use of pearl imagery:

Pisa la arena, que en la arena adoro
cuantas el blanco pie conchas platea,
cuyo bello contacto puede hacerlas,
sin concebir rocío, parir perlas.
        (47e–h)

[Step on the sand, for in the sand I adore / the shells that your white foot
makes silver; / by its beautiful contact with them, / without conceiving a
drop of dew, they bear pearls.]

The narrator says of Galatea,

De su frente la perla es, eritrea,
émula vana. El ciego dios se enoja,

y, condenado su esplendor, la deja
pender en oro al nácar de su oreja.
(14e–h)

[With her brow the pearl of Eritrea / rivals in vain. The blind god angers /
and condemns its splendor to gold, / dropping it from the pearl which is
her ear.]   (Singleton; emended by Iarocci)

Góngora places Polifemo in the discursive center of the text, between silenced, or remade, traditions and the major advocate of the new poetry.
The giant is powerful enough to defeat his symbolic enemy, but he must
defer to the artistry of his creator. There is consistency in difference, and
therein lies a paradox of the *Polifemo.* In portraying the hyperbolic,
magnified world of the cyclops, who hurls boulders the size of pyramids
and who can almost touch the sky, Góngora holds back, reserving for
his poetic alter ego—the narrator—the creative extreme, the definitive
hyperbole, the competitive edge.

Cascardi finds in the murder of Acis a convergence of the two artists,
one as performer and the other as bard. He notes that "as Góngora has
Polifemo brutally kill Acis, the destruction of the pastoral world that
was begun in the grandiose delusions of the cyclops' song is brought to
completion."[31] Observing the preponderance of sea imagery throughout
the poem, Kathleen Dolan calls the metamorphosis of Acis an inversion
of neoplatonic mysticism through affirmation of a marine rather than a
celestial source of all forms. Thus, "it is not Acis but Polifemo who is finally effaced by the ecstatic poetics of the fable," in a fusion of figure and
ground.[32] Rather than viewing Polifemo as merging with his author or
as erased from the text—the true object of metamorphosis, the self-
consuming artifact—one may argue, I believe, that the cyclops remains
the same; that is, paradoxically, he is a sign of difference, of determination, of overdetermination. Erasure is impossible, and, what is more,
erasure is undesirable. In order for creation to take place, the "other"
must be present. Acis needs Polifemo. Polifemo needs Góngora's narrator. Góngora needs Ovid, Garcilaso, and Carrillo, and he needs his detractors. Cupid and the sea deities in the *Polifemo* control, respectively,
the amorous feelings of Galatea and the metamorphosis of Acis. They
are markers of the presence of the intertext, markers of Góngora's

shared authority in the text. The poet must fight tradition and expand upon tradition, must deconstruct in order to reconstruct, must know the enemy. Harold Bloom makes the point that poets "need to know that the dead poets will not consent to make way for others. But, it is more important that the new poets possess a richer knowing. The precursors flood us, and our imaginations can die by drowning in them, but no imaginative life is possible if such inundation is wholly evaded."[33] Góngora builds into his bellicose text an acknowledgment of the rigors of creation and of the loving and hateful relation between alterity and interdependence.

The *Polifemo* is, in many ways, an overdetermined text. The fable, however modified, is a known quantity. Even when narrated in the present of experience, the story is perhaps more ironic than suspenseful. Polifemo's song repeats much of the narrator's account; what is new—the professed conversion—turns out to be false. The repetition is hardly superfluous. The cyclops's lament shows us his perspective, his perception of the state of events, his rhetorical strategies. Stephen Gilman remarks that "conceptist tongues do not talk from the heart which feels intuitively the oneness of all things, but from the mind, only concerned with its own advantage, with its own individuality. Thus the desperate artist played with the forms and words of a disjointed world, a world he disjoined further."[34] Góngora gives his monster a heart and a cultured, if bucolic, artistic sensitivity. Polifemo is alterity hyperbolized and hyperbole made relative, a killer and a poet. He exists in the margins, but he is master of what lies between the margins. For all his material wealth and lofty claims, he is willing to settle for less; he is willing to settle for being Acis. Difference mediates and undermines his desire, and he must destroy the antithetical double, who now inhabits the margin. Góngora, recognizing that he cannot be Garcilaso, attempts to overpower his predecessor with words and fights to relegate him to the margin, where he will survive as a trace of the Renaissance.

Góngora's principal mechanism—his strongest arm—is the open signified. Paul Julian Smith refers to a "constantly shifting sign system," "an unregulated circulation of signs, and, indeed, of sexes" in the *Polifemo*.[35] Malcolm K. Read depicts a Góngora "in battle with the body, his body, his poetic predecessors." And, he says, in the Baroque, when

the parental figure assumes the size of Polifemo, the poet must rise to unknown heights, . . . violating language beyond all permissible limits."[36]
Smith and Read have brilliantly defined the bodily politics of the *Polifemo*. The poem seems to fit the pattern of what Terence Cave calls the
cornucopian text, in which sexuality certainly comes into play. I would
suggest that the most evident "cornucopian" aspect of the *Polifemo* is its
link with rhetoric. This would include the duality of the Erasmian *copia*,
both elegant speech and copy, and *cornucopia*, abundance, productiv-
ity. For Cave, "the phrase *copia dicendi*, or even *copia* alone, is a ubiquitous synonym for eloquence [and] suggests a rich, many faceted discourse springing from a fertile mind and powerfully affecting its
recipient. At this level, its value lies precisely in the broadness of its figurative register: it transcends specific techniques and materials, pointing towards an ideal of 'articulate energy,' of speech in action."[37] The
cornucopian design of the *Polifemo* may, in the end, encompass its ideology. Sicilian abundance, abundance in nature, abundant beauty and
exaggerated ugliness, abundance of possessions, mercantile abundance,
an abundance of words, of images, of figures, of connections, of linguistic and semantic metamorphoses: this is what the poem is about. It is
about the means by which the poet reads the world and other texts and
about how he can leave his mark—his signature—on the world. It is
about what happens when the writer's world expands and about how
the expansion orients both story and discourse. It is about the trials of
authorship and about the role of the public. It is about profusion and
lack, and about the relative nature of signs. It is about change. It is about
competition, in the most violent and admiring sense.

Notes

1. Stephen Gilman, "An Introduction to the Ideology of the Baroque in
Spain," *Symposium* 1, no. 2 (1946): 82–107.

2. Antonio Maravall, "From the Renaissance to the Baroque: The Diphasic
Schema of a Social Crisis," trans. Terry Cochran, in *Literature among Dis-
courses: The Spanish Golden Age*, ed. Wlad Godzich and Nicholas Spadaccini
(Minneapolis: University of Minnesota Press, 1986), pp. 3–40.

3. For discussion of polemics regarding the new poetry, see, among other
studies, those of Dámaso Alonso, *Góngora y el "Polifemo,"* 7th ed., 3 vols. (Ma-

drid: Gredos, 1985); Eunice Joiner Gates, "Sidelights on Contemporary Criticism of Góngora's *Polifemo*," *PMLA* 75 (1960): 503–8; Colin Smith, "On the Use of Spanish Theoretical Works in the Debate on Gongorism," *Bulletin of Hispanic Studies* 39 (1962): 165–76; Andrée Collard, *Nueva poesía: Conceptismo, culteranismo en la crítica española* (Madrid: Castalia, 1967); David William Foster and Virginia Ramos Foster, *Luis de Góngora* (New York: Twayne, 1973); Ana Martínez Arancón, *La batalla en torno a Góngora* (Barcelona: Antoni Bosch, 1978); Emilio Orozco, *Introducción a Góngora* (Barcelona: Editorial Crítica, 1984); and Angel Pariente, ed., *En torno a Góngora* (Madrid: Júcar, 1987).

4. John R. Beverley, *Aspects of Góngora's "Soledades,"* Purdue University Monographs in Romance Languages, 1 (Amsterdam: John Benjamins, 1980).

5. Ibid., pp. 27 and 29.

6. Jonathan Brown, "On the Meaning of 'Las Meninas.'" In *Images and Ideas in Seventeenth-Century Spanish Painting* (Princeton: Princeton University Press, 1978), p. 109.

7. Paul Julian Smith, "The Rhetoric of Presence in Poets and Critics of Golden Age Lyric: Garcilaso, Herrera, Góngora," *Modern Language Notes* 100 (1985): 239.

8. John R. Beverley, "The Production of Solitude: Góngora and the State," *Ideologies and Literature* 3, no. 13 (June–August 1980): 24; Terence Cave, *The Cornucopian Text: Problems of Writing in the French Renaissance* (Oxford: Clarendon Press, 1979), p. xi.

9. Beverley, "Production," p. 24; Lorna Close, "The Play of Difference: A Reading of Góngora's *Soledades*," in *Conflicts of Discourse: Spanish Literature in the Golden Age*, ed. Peter W. Evans (Manchester: Manchester University Press, 1990), pp. 184–98.

10. Beverley, "Production," p. 25.

11. Jonathan Crewe, *Trials of Authorship: Anterior Forms and Reconstruction from Wyatt to Shakespeare* (Berkeley: University of California Press, 1990), p. 9.

12. Pedro Salinas, *Reality and the Poet in Spanish Poetry*, trans. Edith Fishtine Helman (Baltimore: Johns Hopkins Press, 1966), p. 140.

13. Paul Julian Smith, *The Body Hispanic: Gender and Sexuality in Spanish and Spanish American Literature* (Oxford: Clarendon Press, 1989), pp. 70–71.

14. Antonio Maravall, *Culture of the Baroque: Analysis of a Historical Structure*, trans. Terry Cochran, Theory and History of Literature 25 (Minneapolis: University of Minnesota Press, 1986), p. 233.

15. Addressing Colin Smith's "Approach," M. J. Woods comments that "it is

interesting . . . that Góngora should describe the perfection of his natural setting in terms appropriate to civilized life—carpets, canopies, blinds, and four-
poster beds . . . Góngora sees the beauty of nature as a kind of artifice, which
means that he cannot be said to be seeking to establish an antithesis between the
untamed natural world on the one hand, and the creations of artifice on the
other." M. J. Woods, *The Poet and the Natural World in the Age of Góngora*
(Oxford: Oxford University Press, 1978), p. 156.

16. Maravall, *Culture of the Baroque,* p. 175.

17. Michel Foucault, *The Order of Things: An Archeology of the Human Sciences* (New York: Random House, 1970), p. 51.

18. Elias L. Rivers, ed., *Renaissance and Baroque Poetry of Spain* (Prospect
Heights, Ill.: Waveland, 1988), pp. 157–58.

19. Beverley, "Production," p. 24. Paul Julian Smith (*The Body Hispanic*)
points to a "linguistic surface which refuses to be anchored safely to the solid
materiality of a pre-existing referent" and notes that "Góngora's catachreses
(metaphors deprived of primary terms) . . . point to an absolute attribute
(beauty, femininity) which they necessarily fail to embody" (p. 64).

20. See Alonso, *Góngora y el "Polifemo,"* 3: 97–100, and Miroslav John
Hanak, trans., *"The Fable of Polyphemus and Galatea": A Bilingual Version
with a Critical Analysis* (New York: Peter Lang, 1988), pp. 39–41. See also
Alonso, *Poesía española,* pp. 370–77.

21. Edward P. J. Corbett, *Classical Rhetoric for the Modern Student,* 3d ed.
(New York: Oxford University Press, 1990), p. 445.

22. R. V. Young, "Versions of Galatea: Renaissance and Baroque Imitation,"
Renaissance Papers, ed. Dale B. Randall and Joseph A. Porter (Durham: South-
east Renaissance Conference, 1984), p. 62.

23. Ibid.

24. Carrillo has been studied by Dámaso Alonso, Justo García Soriano,
Emilio Orozco Díaz, and Fernando de Villena, as well as by Vilanova. An edition
of the *Libro de la erudición* by Angelina Costa appeared in 1987, and Rosa
Navarro Durán's edition of the complete works (cited here) was published in
1990 (Luis Carrillo y Sotomayor, *Obras,* ed. Rosa Navarro Durán [Madrid:
Castalia]).

25. See Carrillo, esp. pp. 345, 364–65, 368, 380–81, and Navarro Durán's
introduction, pp. 67–90.

26. See Navarro Durán, pp. 55–56, and Antonio Vilanova, *Las fuentes y los
temas del "Polifemo" de Góngora: Revista de Filología Española,* Anejo 66
(Madrid, 1957), 1:237 and 2: 523–24. Melinda Eve Lehrer, in *Classical Myth
and the "Polifemo" of Góngora* (Potomac, Md.: Scripta Humanistica, 1989),

devotes a chapter of her study of the *Polifemo* to a comparison of the two works (pp. 36–51).

27. Alonso, *Góngora y el "Polifemo,"* 1: 205.

28. For a presentation of the concept of *le scriptible*, or of the dichotomy *lisibilité/illisibilité*, see, for example, the introductory sections of Roland Barthes' *S/Z*, trans. Richard Miller (New York: Hill and Wang, 1974).

29. The term *interpretant* is used by Charles S. Pierce to denote the necessary third element that links a sign to its object. See Winifried Nöth, *Handbook of Semiotics* (Bloomington: Indiana University Press, 1990), pp. 43–44. Michael Riffaterre incorporates this term and the concept in *The Semiotics of Poetry* (Bloomington: Indiana University Press, 1978).

30. See Edward H. Friedman, *The Antiheroine's Voice: Narrative Discourse and the Transformations of the Picaresque* (Columbia: University of Missouri Press, 1987).

31. Anthony J. Cascardi, "The Exit from Arcadia: Reevaluation of the Pastoral in Virgil, Garcilaso, and Góngora," *Journal of Hispanic Philology* 4 (1980): 135.

32. Kathleen Dolan, "Figure and Ground: Concrete Mysticism in Góngora's *Fábula de Polifemo y Galatea,*" *Hispanic Review* 52 (1984): 232.

33. Harold Bloom, *The Anxiety of Influence: A Theory of Poetry* (London: Oxford University Press, 1973), p. 154.

34. Gilman, "An Introduction to the Ideology of the Baroque in Spain," p. 107.

35. Smith, *The Body Hispanic*, p. 66.

36. Malcolm K. Read, *Visions in Exile: The Body in Spanish Literature and Linguistics, 1500–1800.* Purdue University Monographs in the Romance Languages, 30 (Amsterdam: John Benjamins, 1990), p. 45.

37. Cave, *The Cornucopian Text*, p. 5.

4

Góngora and the Footprints of the Voice

MARY MALCOLM GAYLORD

Vox tu es, et nihil praeterea.

———◆——

Few readers of the *Soledades* fail to note Góngora's linking, in the poem's striking first lines, of his pilgrim's physical footsteps with the movement of verse itself:

> *Pasos* de un peregrino son errante
> cuantos me dictó *versos* dulce Musa
> en soledad confusa,
> perdidos unos, otros inspirados.

[Such *verses* as my muse may grant / are *steps* upon a wandering pilgrim's way; / while some may go astray, / in lonely mazes, others live inspired.]
(Cunningham, p. 3)

Maurice Molho's extraordinary reading has illuminated the semantic density of this passage's (con)fusion of the *peregrino*'s steps with the wandering ways of his verses (classically endowed with metric *feet*) and with the labyrinthian space-time of his *Soledad*.[1] Now lost, now inspired—but most important of all fused together—the physical figure of the protagonist, the physical shape of verse form, and the dictates of poetic inspiration march and meander their way through the poem. For Molho, Góngora's formal achievement is epic: "El genio de Góngora supo llevar a cabo la peligrosa empresa que consiste—*aventura sin precedentes* ... —en conferir una estructura a la misma libertad, un orden al desorden, una coherencia a la incoherencia"[2] [Góngora's genius

79

found the way to undertake the dangerous endeavor—an adventure without precedent—of giving a structure to liberty itself, an order to disorder, a coherence to incoherence]. Out of the treasure troves of his literary predecessors, that is to say, he creates a poem without precedent and without equal: the monumental *silva/Soledad*.[3]

This formidable formal triumph, however, is not had without a price. Even as Góngora celebrates the visit of the muse and her double gift of *pasos/versos*, even as he makes the love pilgrim's progress a figure for the poem itself, he elides—as Molho stresses[4]—the figure of the poet (evoked only obliquely in "cuantos *me* dictó versos") and thereby effectively foreshadows his own subsequent "absence" from the long poem. Molho rediscovers this same move in the 1615 sonnet offered in the early editions as "Alegoría de la primera de sus *Soledades*,"[5] where poetic *foot* and *poem* are once again fused, this time in the allegorical figure of *Soledad*: "Restituye a tu mudo horror divino, / amiga Soledad, el *pie* sagrado" [Soledad my friend, restore your holy foot to your divine, mute horror]. The first verses of this later piece would indeed seem to seal the marginalization of the poet, subordinating his figure to the literary ideal realized in his magnum opus. When the sonnet's tercets bring the poet back into view (or hearing) with the image of the "voz doliente" [pained voice] of the "tórtola viuda" [widowed turtledove], Molho acknowledges fully that figure's currency in the sixteenth-century lyric ballad as quintessential image for the voice of pure sentiment. Yet he interprets the turtledove's solitary voice here as the solitude of poetry, as a unique, self-made aesthetic solitude, and reads the allegory as a defense of the elitist poetry for which Góngora was so often attacked.[6] Abstract interpretation of the sonnet's figure for voice, then, by subordinating voice to message, serves to confirm once again the studied impersonality of the poet of the *Soledades* and the elusiveness of his voice.[7]

But does displacement of the poetic voice necessarily signify its disappearance? Do these tropological metamorphoses of the lyric persona—into the poem *Soledad*, into the *tortolica*, into the poet-lover-pilgrim—work only to make that voice more philosophical, and thereby less personal and less lyrical? Concretely, when the poet uses figures of the voice of feeling as allegorical embodiments of his poetic journey, can we afford to conclude that aesthetic theory has overwhelmed, diminished, or even eliminated the discourse of sentiment that gives these tropes their energy? If the love lyric, as it emerges in the European Renaissances and in the Spanish Golden Age, serves indeed as one of the chief breeding grounds for the emerging self-consciousness of the modern subject, then it seems ill-advised to limit the significance of these figures, and particularly that of the poet-lover, who is perhaps *the* central figure in Góngora's verse for the mysterious experience of poetic creation.[8]

In order to get closer to that elusive lyric subject and perhaps to understand better his subsequent appearances in Góngora's verse, I propose to look at another, earlier poem in which *verses* or *(voices)* and *feet* once again find themselves in poetic proximity. The sonnet, "Descaminado, enfermo, peregrino"[9] ["Wayward, sick, and wandering"], happens to be, moreover, a poem many readers including Salcedo Coronel have connected, via the outlines of its argument ("De un caminante enfermo que se enamoró donde fue hospedado" [Of a sick traveler who fell in love in the place he had been lodged]), to the later *Soledades*. I want to use the 1594 sonnet to pose the question of the nature and the role of voice—the voice of feeling, the voice of the poet—in Góngora's poetry and in poetry like Góngora's that, for whatever reasons, conspicuously eschews transparency of feeling and of meaning. This essay asks, in the case of a poet so committed to many-layered imitation of his predecessors as well as to the cultivated difficulty of learned language, what is at stake in such commitments. And it asks too whether there is any evidence that Góngora pondered these stakes as in each new poem he not only renewed but escalated his devotion to difficulty and to artifice. Did he meditate on what his elaborately wrought language stood to imperil or even lose, as well as what it hoped to gain? Or did he perhaps find in the labyrinth of controversial *culterano* rhetoric itself a powerful metaphor for the dilemmas and the limits of lyric self-expression?

I am aware that my title may for some have Derridean overtones, and that I might therefore be expected—by virtue of pressing *feet* and *footsteps* into *footprints*—to invoke supplementarity and the figure of the trace, written language as the leftovers of the work of signification in its restless movement from signifier to signifier. That theoretical shoe might indeed be made to fit Góngora's poetic foot, but that is not my project here. Instead, by shifting the focus from Góngora's literal *verse/ steps* to their *prints*, I want to call attention to the poetic utterance as a physical itinerary, one whose verbal markers (rhetorical, lexical, grammatical) point the way not only toward sense but also inevitably toward that framing speaker who is always—whether or not he "speaks," no matter how successful his disappearing acts—at least implicitly present in his poem. It is on this very material path, a path paved with words— new or used, familiar or foreign, sometimes bearing the conspicuous imprints of earlier travelers—that the poet and his readers must inevitably meet as they chart (or contest) the route to meaning.

The trope of the poet's path is, of course, no newcomer to the Renaissance lyric. Before Góngora made his several versions, it had served Petrarch, Dante, Garcilaso, and countless others very well. Fernando de Herrera's look at the figure is particularly suggestive. For the author of the 1580 *Anotaciones* to Garcilaso's verse, the central image of his first sonnet ("Cuando me paro a contemplar mi estado" [When I pause to contemplate my present state]) conjures up the position of poets in general. Herrera's commentary moves metonymically from Garcilaso's survey of his sentimental *camino* to a far-reaching meditation on the shared literary itinerary of all poets. The sonnet becomes the commentator's pretext for an essay on poetry as imitation. He makes this poem, and the sonnet as a form, an Ur-scene for the poet, one in which he must gather up a great mass of material (by implication inherited), then condense and enclose it in a tiny, rigidly defined space, a space he must *deserve* (by comparison with his predecessors) to occupy. Like Garcilaso's lyric persona, the poet portrayed in the *Anotaciones* is poised between retrospection and prediction: as he looks back on the legacy of his predecessors and forward to an uncertain future, he too stands stopped. In short, Herrera thematizes the *pasos* of the Toledan poet's sentimental itinerary *as poetry*. And he helps us to see that many other poems that hang on the same well-worn geographical image also do just that. As a venerable figure for both writing and reading, then, the foot-printed poetic path may offer to us as well a powerful trope for conventional (that is, imitated) poetry and thus for the complexity of cultural continuity as it is acted out in the journeys through language and through time of poet-imitators and scholar-readers, who struggle to identify telltale footprints, who strain to hear echoes of their owners' voices.

Góngora has been, since the time of the first generations of his readers, the supreme figure of poetic difficulty. Pedro Salinas sees difficulty as the very essence of his "poetical way of being."[10] That quality has traditionally transformed the poet into either an angel or a demon. In his own time he was adopted as angel of the erudite elite, while for more fundamentalist readers his work provided definitive proof of Quintilian's gloomy prediction about the wages of runaway metaphor: too many metaphors lead to allegory, and allegory leads to enigma—that is, beyond the realm of meaning and of truth.[11] In the eyes of the most offended, Góngora's poetry appears finally to fall into nothingness. For these readers, Góngora's poetic revolution sins by subverting the traditional subordination of unit to whole (fable to episode), figure to ground, sound to sense, senses to intellect. By placing metaphor, sound, linguistic unit on top, Góngora becomes either the champion of poetic language for its own sake, or the emblem of nonsense. While readers in the seventeenth, eighteenth, and nineteenth centuries found his subversion to be alarming, obscene, sacrilegious, or simply in poor taste, the twentieth century has revindicated Góngora as the quintessential poet of metaphor. Lorca rhapsodized about the centrality in his verse of the figure and of the moment. For poets of the Latin American neobaroque, as for Barthes and Lacan,[12] Góngora's practice and even his name open poetry up to the vast spaces of *non-sense*, freeing the signifier from the binary prison of sense, setting it loose in the utopia of purposeless free play.

On one subject, enthusiasts and denigrators of the Cordovan poet concur: in Góngora the verbal vehicle, in its aestheticizing, hedonistic complexity, predominates over message; *dulce* completely eclipses *utile*. In the limit case, Góngora becomes a poet of pure language. And virtually all readers from both camps subscribe to the general principle that as language becomes more preeminent, meaning grows fainter, soon becomes superfluous, and finally disappears altogether. Yet even among the apologists of Góngora we find traces of a nostalgia for meaning. Paul Smith remarks that "the significance of the *Soledades*, then, is primarily, *if at all*, self-reflexive. . . . Góngora's text, motiveless and inconsequential, embodies the virtue of pure spectacle."[13] And Dámaso Alonso, to whom several generations of readers owe a large part of their wonder at Góngora's technical virtuosity, openly rues the superficiality of the linguistic surface and the wornness of what lies beneath it. For the father of modern critical *gongorismo*, the imitative practice that underwrites the poet's difficulty implies a loss of direct, *original* vision. Alonso places the blame for this loss squarely on the accumulation in the poet's language of inherited perceptions: "Constantemente, entre la imagen vista y la imagen pensada se le está interponiendo un recuerdo. Poco hay de original en el mundo de su representación"[14] [For him, memory constantly interpolates itself between the image that is seen and the image that is thought. In his world of representation, very little is original]. It is a sad conclusion: Góngora has nothing new to say; his poetry, therefore, is in some sense not his own. In the cultivated linguistic confusion, the poet himself gets lost.

So widespread is this sense of the ephemerality of Góngora's verbal wonder show that issues that first haunted only readings of the longer and later poems, chief among them the *Soledades*, inevitably spill over into the earlier, more accessible poems. The introduction to the most recent edition of the *Sonnets*, for example, makes Góngora a poet of language and of technique to the *n*th power, his verses overflowing with the violence of *encabalgamiento* and *hipérbaton*, accumulation of words chosen for their musicality or plastic beauty, daring metaphors that pile up or invert terms of comparison, mythological allusions that eclipse reality. Góngora's stock of themes, typically baroque, are presented as hackneyed, almost beside the point. For the editor, Biruté Ciplijauskaité, the "tendencia de convertirlo todo en metáfora" announces a downhill slide: "la metáfora se lexicaliza" then becomes "tópico" and finally dies of stagnation.[15] In short, the rampage of the signifier, briefly responsible for stylistic "dynamism," soon becomes language's dance of death. And the most serious loss is that of the poet's emotion. Ciplijauskaité speculates that suppression of emotion is the price paid for formal perfection: "Casi se le ve [al poeta] luchar con sus sentimientos por obtener una obra más perfecta"[16] [One can almost see the poet fighting his emotions in order to obtain a more perfect work]. So it would seem that perfection, Góngora-style, must be bought at the expense of meaning *and* of feeling. The love sonnets, with their "perfecta hechura arquitectónica," are almost a contradiction in terms: "es difícil . . . clasificarlos como tales" [it is difficult to classify them as such].

Sí corresponden al tema, pero son completamente *impersonales, fríos, puramente descriptivos,* inspirados en modelos petrarquistas. *No logramos imaginar detrás de ellos al poeta.* . . . Ninguno de los sonetos amorosos ni de lejos se acerca a *la pasión directamente transmitida* por Lope o por Quevedo . . . , y si tuviéramos que juzgar por los sonetos, nos inclinaríamos a afirmar que el poeta nunca estuvo enamorado.[17]
[They correspond in theme, but they are completely *impersonal,* cold, purely descriptive, inspired by Petrarchan models. *We cannot imagine the poet behind them* . . . none of the love sonnets even begins to come close to the *passion conveyed directly* by Lope or by Quevedo . . . , and if we had to judge by the sonnets, we would be inclined to state that the poet had never been in love.]

Octavio Paz, in an essay on the long poem, echoes these very complaints: the *Soledades* are "una pieza de marquetería sublime y vana"[18] [a sublime, empty exhibition of marquetry]. And, although the Mexican poet takes a somewhat more modern view of the products of pure aestheticism, the vanity of Góngora's verse consists for him precisely in the same *human* emptiness lamented by the editor of the sonnets:

El mundo de Góngora no es el teatro de las pasiones humanas o el de las batallas y amores de los dioses. Es un mundo estético y sus criaturas, tejidas por las palabras, son reflejos, sombras, centelleos, engaños adorables y efímeros. ¿Qué queda después de la lectura?[19]
[Góngora's world is not a stage for human passions or for the battles and desires of the gods. It is an aesthetic world, and its creatures, woven out of words, are reflections, shadows, glimmers, adorable and ephemeral tricks. What is left after the reading?]

It is ironic indeed that what Foucault could applaud as the modernity of *Don Quijote*—Cervantes' discovery of the mystery of representation—

should be judged inexcusable in the *culterano* poet, inescapably type-cast as an unrepentant, empty aestheticist.

Thus praise for technique does not succeed, or even want to succeed, in disguising a general disappointment. With Góngora, we can't imagine the poet behind the poem; we can't take his pulse, hear his voice. And that is, clearly, what is foremost in the minds of readers, whose fundamental expectation is that the lyric poem will speak or sing as though from an authentic, individual voice, and that its language will validate itself by reference to that voice. Even the classificatory activity of the editors of Góngora's sonnets constitutes a tacit confession of frustration. In José María Chacón, we find the sonnets categorized and separated as "Sacros, Heroicos, Morales, Fúnebres, Amorosos, Satíricos, Burlescos, Varios,"[20] whereby they become a kind of anthology of the topoi of their time, a repertory of depersonalized rhetorical stances, certainly not an image of the poet. Here we are a far cry from Petrarch, whose *Rime sparse* get their coherence from the illusion at least of their origins in life, or even from the *cancioneros* of Garcilaso or Lope de Vega, where that same illusion, even when frustrated, has nonetheless exerted a strong force on our readings.[21]

Góngora's voice, then, to the extent he is perceived to have one, is seen caught in a web of words, and worse still, in a web of other poets' words. What readers like Ciplijauskaité, Robert Jammes, Paz, and perhaps even the rest of us miss is a *yo*, like the one that presses itself on us in Garcilaso's first sonnet ("Cuando *me paro* a contemplar *mi estado* / y a ver los pasos por dó *me* han traído, / *hallo* . . ." [When *I pause* to contemplate *my current state* / and to look over the places *my* steps have brought *me* / *I find* . . .]), one that speaks insistently of its thoughts, feelings, experience, and of itself *as voice.*

In a subgenre like the love sonnet, linked as it is by convention to sentimental autobiography, elusiveness of voice is understandably vexing. And in Góngora's love sonnets, the poetic voice *is* in fact hard to get hold of. Although the mention of a *you* (*tú, vosotros, vuestro*) lets us know that an *I* is speaking, we rarely hear that *I* call himself by name. By contrast to the poetry of Petrarch or even Garcilaso, where first-person pronouns and verb forms dominate, in very few of Góngora's sonnets do we hear a *yo* call himself *yo* or even *mí/me*. While of course implicitly present in a lyric discourse that describes, admires, urges, or admonishes, he usually does not speak of himself, but rather stands aside like the *mirón* of the *Soledades*. The case of sonnet 80 appears to be the exception that proves the rule.

De un Caminante Enfermo que se Enamoró Donde Fue Hospedado

Descaminado, enfermo, peregrino
  en tenebrosa noche, con pie incierto
  la confusión pisando del desierto,
  voces en vano dio, pasos sin tino.
Repetido latir, si no vecino,
  distincto oyó de can siempre despierto,
  y en pastoral albergue mal cubierto
  piedad halló, si no halló camino.
Salió el Sol, y entre armiños escondida,
  soñolienta beldad con dulce saña
  salteó al no bien sano pasajero.
Pagará el hospedaje con la vida;
  más le valiera errar en la montaña,
  que morir de la suerte que yo muero.

[*Of a Sick Traveler Who Fell in Love in the Place He Had Lodged*

Wayward, sick, and wandering / in the dismal night; stepping through / the confusion of the desert with uncertain foot; / he cried out in vain, taking senseless steps. / A repeated beating-barking—nearby / if not at a distance—, he heard from an ever wakeful dog, / and in a poorly covered pastoral shelter / he found pity, if not his way. / The sun came up, and hidden in ermine furs, / a sleepy beauty, with sweet anger / assaulted the yet healed voyager. / He will pay for his lodging with his life; / he would have been better off wandering in the mountains / rather than dying of the fate of which I die.]

A number of previous readers have found the poem tantalizing as a potentially juicy autobiographical tidbit.[22] Yet if we ask the question of *who* is the principal figure of the sonnet, simply on the level of language (grammar, syntax, lexicon), we get very different results. Even if we come to the poem without preconceptions about Góngora's impersonality, or any particular desire to know about his historical personality, carrying only the conventional expectations we would bring to any lyric poem, we still are likely to suppose that the verses represent the utterance of an implied *speaking subject*. In Petrarchan sonnets, convention causes us to expect that the speaking subject is quite likely also to be the *grammatical* subject of the utterance, probably identified not by a noun but by a first-person pronominal or verbal form. Alert for signs of his presence (convention tells us it is not *her*), listening in time, waiting for him to speak, we enter the textual space of this sonnet.

We are drawn into that space by the three words of the poem's first hendecasyllable, three terms in apposition—qualifiers, adjectives, or participles that could be nouns but here are suspended, referring beyond themselves, deferring meaning along a syntactic chain. To whom do they refer? We don't know. They might even constitute an apostrophe; that is, they might even refer to us, to the reader(s). But we are led on, first to a physical and affective time-space ("tenebrosa noche"); to a body ("*con* pie incierto"), implied owner of the foot who participates physically and perhaps mentally in its uncertainty. This might be the subject we are looking for; yet revelation is again deferred, while another abstract noun ("confusión") holds out the hope that we may at least be about to find some personification of humanity. As the poem's first verb form ("pisando") describes a physical action, we wonder if indeed a personified Confusion is treading with uncertain foot. Yet the prepositional phrase "del desierto" obliges us to revise that expectation and sends us back to the beginning of the line, to recognize "confusión" as *object* of the gerund "pisando." If the concreteness of that verb, placed at the very center of the poetic line, seems to let the poem touch ground, as it were (we are still, after all, right to suppose that *someone* is taking steps), the same word destabilizes reading once again. For the action of stepping takes place in the sliding verb time of the unconjugated gerund, unattached to tense, still unconnected to any visible subject, even a personified one. And the ground being touched is, moreover, anything but terra firma. It is the shifty terrain, suspended between abstract and concrete, of "la confusión del desierto": not even the desert itself but the vaguer aura of its confusion.

We thus arrive at the poem's fourth verse (noting that the poem's first complete sentence will end with the quatrain), to be confronted in the conspicuous accented first position with another noun (*voces*), which might be a candidate for the position of the grammatical subject, although its feminine plural conflicts with the expectations created by the masculine singular forms of line 1. The mystery doesn't last much longer: "Voces en vano" (ringing almost like a joke on our readerly impatience) is followed at last by a conjugated verb—*dio*—that falls squarely on the central, accentuated syllable of the quatrain's closing verse. At last we have a grammatical subject, the implicit third person contained in the form *dio*, which sends us back not only to the beginning of verse 4, to confirm *voces* (as well as the *pasos* that follow) as grammatical objects, but also to anchor the gerund *pisando*, the disconnected, wandering *pie*, and the first verse's three qualifiers to *his* organizing presence in the whole. Now we are prepared to recognize his mysterious figure as the grammatical subject of the three third-person preterite verb forms (*oyó, halló, no halló*) that follow in the second quatrain: it is "*he*" who hears the dog, who finds mercy at least, if not his way.

But who is making his way in sonnet 80? The poem's language still has not let us know with certainty where he is going, even who he is. Problems of identity and direction are compounded as the poet tampers with the syntax of ordinary language. So insistent are constructions that invert usual subject-verb-object word order (e.g., "la confusión pisando," "voces . . . dio," "latir . . . oyó," "piedad halló"; even in "si no halló camino," a possible pun lurking in "si no"—*sino*[*destino*] or *signo*—would give "sino/signo halló") that Góngora here comes nearly to the point of normalizing the inversion. In the sonnet, this nearly systematic inversion of transitive verbs is only turned around following the standard colloquial "Salió el Sol" (v. 9) when the sun's intransitive appearance is succeeded metonymically by the somnambulent beauty's physical assault on the "no bien sano pasajero" (v. 11). This is the first unambiguous appearance (i.e., the first time he is named, designated by a noun, albeit a generic noun) of the figure who was grammatical subject of the quatrains. Thus, paradoxically, the first straightforwardly reported actions belong not to that subject but to the new grammatical

subject(s) of the first tercet (Sol / soñolienta beldad). After all his mean-
derings, the mysterious *subject* of the quatrains is named only after he
has become, in grammatical terms, an *object*.

But we still have not resolved the question of *who* is the subject—the
speaking subject—of sonnet 80. We have only succeeded in tracking
down a grammatical subject, and only at the point where he metamorphoses into grammatical object at the hands of the *serrana*. And, although he is a look-alike for the ill-fated poet-lover, exiled to misery or
absence, of the poetry of Dante, Petrarch, the Spanish *cancioneros*, and
Garcilaso, he is not the traditional lyric subject. Rather he is a third person: belatedly named, repeatedly modified, dismembered by synec-
dochic evocation, scattered in abstract time-space; in short, *descaminado*, nearly lost. This displaced person is the non-person of Benveniste,
who denies the third person of Western morphology the status of true
person, because he or she never speaks as an *I* to a *you*, from a present
place and moment, from a here and now. The same verses that have
withheld from the poem's ostensibly central figure his syntactic preeminence have also exiled him from the present of the poem's discourse.
And now, in the poem's penultimate line, the traveler passes from this
temporal exile to the multiple displacements of "más la valiera errar en
la montaña": he is returned figuratively to the mountains, to atemporal
wandering (via the conditional value of the imperfect subjunctive *valiera*); and he is relegated to the grammatical position of indirect object.
Scarcely an improvement, though better, the speaker assures us, than his
own (the speaker's) death.

And here at last, the lyric pact is honored. A person—a first person—
speaks, as an *I*, in a here and now. The original lyric subject, or persona,
of the sonnet's first three sentences turns out to be not their grammatical
subject but the implicit speaker who defines the entire poem's enunciation. And in the sonnet's very last breath, that speaker, having described
what happened to another *him*, back *then*, over *there*, now turns to
speak of himself (*yo*) in the moment of his speech and to sum himself up
in the powerful first-person present "*yo muero*." Something of a *tardón*,
like the Pyramus of Góngora's romance, this *yo* comes at the end of a
long syntactic line. He is not even the subject of the poem's final sentence: "que yo muero" is a relative clause, modifying a noun ("suerte")

in a prepositional phrase modifying "morir," a nominalized infinitive. Furthermore, the poem's syntax seems to place the speaking subject at the very limit of meaning. The phrase "morir de la suerte que yo muero" is part of a comparative structure: *A* ("errar en la montaña") would be better ("más le valiera") than *B* ("morir de la suerte que yo muero"). But the introduction of *B* here creates a perfectly circular structure. Contrary to the expected function of a comparative term, *B* clarifies nothing: we know nothing about the manner (*suerte*) of the subject's death. The fate of his fate is to remain unspecified, intensified to be sure by semantic (*suerte = destino*) and phonetic (*suerte/muerte*) reverberations, referred to only by the grammatically relative but subjectively absolute standard of "*yo muero*." So our journey through the utterances of the lyric voice brings us finally to the moment of utterance and to the voice itself, whose *yo* can only announce its own death.

Robert Jammes becomes uneasy at this point in the poem, when the figure of the traveler he wants to cast as the poet is eclipsed by a different speaking *yo*. How, he puzzles, can *él* be *yo*?[23] The problem is not trivial. Not only do *he* and *I* part grammatical and logical company in the sonnet's final line: it is the manner of their disjunction that is unsettling, particularly in its implications for the status of the lyric subject. If indeed *he* were summoned as a figure for *I*, then the gist of this poem (as in countless love sonnets and Vergilian similes) would be "As *he* is, so am *I*." *He* would exist for the sake of *I*; the protracted, proleptic comparison would serve to prepare the emergence, however brief, of the speaker he images. In Góngora's sonnet, that expectation is thwarted by syntax: when *yo* makes his brief appearance at the end of the poem, it is in the role of the comparative term, in the service of *él*. Consequently the project of verbalizing the manner of the *yo*'s own death is deferred indefinitely.

In characteristic fury over *culterano* unintelligibility, Francisco Cascales asks at one point whether Góngora is one of those writers Cicero mocked for affecting obscurity in order to deceive others and even themselves into thinking they possess some superior knowledge, out of reach of the common man. Does Góngora know something his reader does not? Is he teasing us, armed with a library of authorities, with riddle-poems that could be turned inside out or right side up at will to reveal what "he" or his *yo* "really means" to say? Or would he simply like us to assume he knows something, when he really means to say nothing? Sonnet 80, with its overwrought narrative foreground that all but eclipses the poem's speaking subject, might be read in this light, as the perfect figure for authorial teasing, or as early evidence for the willful disappearance of the poet from his poem that Molho finds in the later work.

Yet neither of these possibilities seems sufficient to explain the importance of the speaking subject in the poem we have been looking at. Syntactically contingent though he may be, the appearance he makes in the sonnet's final lines is nonetheless highly dramatic. And for all that he is made, by the logic of grammar, to serve as comparative term for the *descaminado peregrino*, whose story dominates the poem's foreground, his final words turn the comparison inside out, revealing the pilgrim's tale as part of a narrative hyperbole in the service of the lyric subject himself. The sonnet slyly uses the figure of one possible subject as displaced reflection of the other. The mute pilgrim who, rather than speak intelligibly, only cries out in vain (*voces en vano dio*), appears in the end as trope; his suffering fades into a pale copy of the pain of the speaker who pleads, "yo muero," before he too falls silent. In that doubling alone is ample confirmation of Góngora's preoccupation with the fate (*suerte/ muerte*) of the lyric subject and his voice. Yet it is still eminently worth asking why Góngora places so many obstacles between us and his lyric persona, why he chooses to hedge him about with linguistic difficulty. Another way to pose the question would be to ask why we as readers have been so slow to find Góngora's poetic voice, and what we can learn about that voice as we make our way through the thicket of his words.

Much of Góngora's difficulty, I believe, is bound up with the question of time. For all that twentieth-century readers subscribe to Antonio Machado's celebrated axiom about poetry as "la palabra en el tiempo," Góngora's difficult syntax still tends to detemporalize our readings of his texts. It can push us to the extreme of actually diagramming sentences, as we would with Latin, in order to "normalize" them. This normalizing is straightforward enough in the typical case of *hipérbaton*, but it is less simple in the area of subject-verb-object positions. When we claim to normalize, furthermore, we do not only mean that we are re-

producing "normal" sequences, but that we are excluding from the poetic text ambiguities or uncertainties that are often present in ordinary
language, where objects are commonly made to precede verb and/or
subject, and where prolepsis creates multiple possibilities that sometimes can only be sorted out with reference to context. In the first quatrain of sonnet 80, interpretive normalizing of syntax is likely to obscure
the particular way the passage's grammatical subject makes his appearance haltingly, mysteriously, *in time*.

That personal appearance takes places, of course, not in abstract time
but with reference to the time of reading apprehended by the reader.
Central to recent critical and theoretical meditations on the nature of
lyric is the idea that the single most important convention of that genre
is its link with the speaking voice, its implicit status as "speech overheard."[24] Yet, while much Renaissance and some later poetry cultivates
its ties with speech and with song (countless *cancionero* poets, the traditional lyric, romances, Garcilaso, Cetina, and others were all being set
to music), Góngora's texts seem to carry us far away from the immediacy of either speech or song. The poet himself, in the famous letter in defense of the *Soledades*, suggests that his work should be read like that of
a Latin poet, that is, *textually* (as opposed to aloud).[25] And he recommends for its understanding the standard technique of medieval textual
exegesis: "quitar la corteza para descubrir lo misterioso que encubre"[26]
[remove the outer shell to discover the mysteries it hides]. The traditional trope of *corteza/meollo* turns the texts into an object (visible, pal-
pable) that can be looked at, touched, contemplated, one that remains
stable and can be examined and reexamined by a reading subject who is
free to shift his position in the act of contemplating it. It is a startling fact
of Góngora criticism that our sense of his texts as objects has kept all
manner of readers—philological, stylistic, New Critical, semiotic—focused on his poems as products. We look at individual linguistic signs—
sometimes only at signifiers, sometimes at signifieds, sometimes at
both—as though they were exquisitely crafted museum pieces, often
scrutinizing them at the expense of the discourse that produces and
frames them.

On the other hand, the very same emphasis on the text as object can
be turned around to focus on this reading subject who engages in exe-

gesis as a kind of adventure, as heroic exercise of *entendimiento* and *voluntad*, moving as in a quest or a hunt toward discovery ("el fin de el entendimiento es hacer presa en verdades"[27] [the object of understanding is to capture truths]). With the restlessness of Augustinian consciousness and the effort of an act of valor ("vacilando el entendimiento en fuerza de discurso" [the understanding wavering with the strength of reason], he strives to overcome obstacles and reach satisfaction, conviction, content, repose. What Góngora describes as the heroic activity of understanding spells out the narrative of an active itinerary of reading, a distinctly *temporal* journey of the mind through time, toward a truth—or a mystery—that is invoked in subjunctives of readerly discovery and delight: "en tanto quedará más deleitado, cuanto, obligándole a la especulación por la obscuridad de la obra, fuera hallando debajo de las sombras de la obscuridad asimilaciones a su concepto"[28] [he will be more pleased to the extent that, obliged to speculate by the work's obscurity, under the dark shadows he find similarities with his concept]. The itinerary reaches toward, assimilates, approximates, but never quite reaches the atemporal clarity of *concepto*. Like Augustine's confessional self, the reader and reading are irrevocably situated *in time*. Indeed, this later evocation of the journey of exegesis makes the "descaminado, enfermo, peregrino" of the sonnet as much a literary cousin of the reader of Góngora as of the pilgrim protagonist of the *Soledades*. (Perhaps, after all, the sonnet's first line is also an apostrophe.)

In any case, before we stumble upon the sonnet's elusive grammatical and thematic subject, before we know its first words refer to him and not to us, the poem's first itinerary is *our itinerary* as readers, through the temporal sequence that unfolds as word follows word, verse follows verse, stanza follows stanza. The organization of poetic discourse in verses or lines, with meter (counted syllables or feet) and rhyme, has a paradoxical relation to the temporality of poetic language. For if meter and rhyme keep time with the sonorous march of words, they also produce a stop-and-start effect. With and without the aid of punctuation marks, we are continually made to wonder whether the formal end of the line is actually the end, whether sound is meant to stop or pause with scripted or printed sign, and whether sense is meant to stop with sound. Few poets have had a more acute sensitivity to this paradox of poetic meters than Góngora. What he does, I believe, is to use syntax to disrupt absolutely the regular march of meter, at the same time that he uses meter to confound the ordering power of syntax. The result is what Cascales uncannily called (apropos of the *Soledades*) a "modo de hablar peregrino" [wandering way of speaking] that moves like a wolf ("camina como el lobo, que da unos pasos adelante y otros atrás, para que, así confusos, no se eche de ver el camino que lleva"[29] [he moves like a wolf, taking some steps forward and others backward so that, in this confusion, his path should not become apparent]). The philologist laments that in the confusion of its steps the poem's path is obscured; amid all the backtracking, words and even thoughts become unrecognizable.[30]

And, as though Góngora's relentless subversion—via Latinate syntax and the artificial demands of meter—of the expected march of speed were not enough, the difficulty they create is intensified by yet another factor. Not only does the poet's idiosyncratic word order do violence to familiar patterns of speech; he very often plays as well with the precarious logic of ordinary language. In the famous "Carta en respuesta," Góngora tells his critic in a loud whisper a "secret" about the victims of the mythic disaster of Babel, alleging that "no los confundió Dios a ellos con darles lenguaje confuso, sino en el mismo suyo ellos se confundieron, tomando piedra por agua y agua por piedra"[31] [God did not confuse them by giving them confused languages; it was rather in their own languages that they became confused, taking stone for water and water for stone]. The brunt of confusion falls not simply on rocks and water: sonnet 80 shows the lyric subject himself in equal peril. Many of the candidates for grammatical subject of the sonnet's first two sentences (ones that turn out to be objects—*confusión, voces, latir, piedad*) in fact denote what we might call operations of subjectivity or of being: feeling, cries, speech, heartbeats. Because of their semantic nature, they seem to press their claim, already made tentatively by syntax, to the status of grammatical subject or even, allegorically, for the position of speaking subject.

The Spanish expression *dar voces* offers a telling example of language's built-in confusions: one (a speaker or subject) apparently *gives voice*, utters cries or words, produces sound as the voluntary, physical act of the subject. Yet it is also cries, words, and voice that point to, identify, give voice to the speaker himself. "*Repetido latir . . . oyó*" is another such case. By way of syntactic translation, the *latir* turns out to belong to the "can siempre despierto" of line 6. But with its double semantic reach—to the dog's barking *and* to the heart's beating (the primary sense of *latir*, which resists the pressures of context)—*latir* is pulled between the beast and the deepest seat of human feeling and consciousness. Whether or not it occupies the grammatical position of subject of the sentence, *latir* is a powerful center from which sound, sense, and finally being radiate. The qualifiers "si no vecino, / distincto" report that the subject of *oyó* hears that sound (reversing order) as "distincto si no vecino." The Gongorine "si no" adds an option without either confirming or denying it. Is the sound near or far away? Does the subject hear the dog's barking or the beating of his own heart—a speaking heart? Moreover, to limit the reference of the qualifiers "siempre despierto" would be to restrict their possible senses arbitrarily: the masculine subject of *oyó* (*he*) could as easily be "ever wakeful" as the dog, attentive to the animal's barking or to the pulsing of his own heart.

In the context of this sonnet, *voces dio* and *latir . . . oyó* are not simple instances of mechanically inverted word order but rather highly charged syntactic signs of the troubled connection between speaker and speech, between cries and words, and between both of these and the voice from which they issue and to which their reference keeps returning. "*BOZ*" is given in Covarrubias[32] as "propiamente el sonido que profiere el animal por la boca" [the sound that an animal utters through its mouth]—primordial sound, shouts or cries, related to animals, to musical instruments and other inanimate objects. "*Dar vozes*, exclamar y hablar descompuestamente" [*to call out*, to exclaim and to speak without composure]. The *Tesoro* inexplicably (along with many modern dictionaries) fails to register the secondary meaning of *voz* as *palabra*, clearly present in the Latin *vox*, and so widespread in Golden Age usage that it cannot be doubted that so active a Latinizer as Góngora would have cultivated the word's multiple resonance, especially in the poem at hand, whose speakers teeter precariously, with their words and cries and barks, on the threshold of meaning.

If words are next of kin to cries, then we may now want to risk pressing one step further the autonomy of units of sound from the organizing lexical, morphological, and syntactic forces of sense. When we try to read these verses blind, to hear their *voces* first not as already formed words, but as sounds still unfettered by graphic signs, then these lines produce some astonishing results. Inside the labyrinth (or the super-order) of Góngora's Latinate syntax, when sounds are allowed to move apart and merge together once again under the pressure of voice, then what we get is this: "Voces en va*no dio, pasos sin tino*" (v. 4) could also give "*pasos sin ti, no*" or even "[él] *no dio pasos sin ti, no.*" "Repetido latir *si no vecino*" (v. 5) could yield "*sino[= destino] vecino*" or "*sino[= signo] vecino,*" or even "*si [él] no ve [= verbo] sino [o signo].*" And finally, "*Distincto oyó*" (v. 6) could give the simple, but dazzling "*Distincto YO.*"

Is it legitimate, someone is sure to ask, to violate the integrity of language's organizing units when we read poetry? In the case of Góngora, I think the answer has to be a resounding yes. Although Herrera would undoubtedly have cast a disapproving eye on the consequences—both the verses and the possible readings I suggest here—, I suspect that Góngora is in part heeding precisely his fellow Andalusian's challenge to poets who would find a voice of their own in order to break, to open up, to distance language from itself.[33] Herrera loved the Castilian tongue, because the virile solidity of its forms resists the poet ("ni añade sílabas, ni trueca ni altera forma" [it doesn't add syllables, nor does it switch or change form]), unlike a softer, effeminate Italian, which virtually collapses under the force of speech ("muda i corti i acrecienta los vocablos" [mutes, shortens, or increases the words]). Yet Herrera insisted at the same time that, in verse, form should not dictate (i.e., force) content, but rather that content should exert pressure on form.[34] Góngora takes that principle to its limit, forcing the resistant morphology, syntax, and lexicon of Spanish to yield under his poetic pressure.

What seems most remarkable to me about the pressure of poetic will on form, as it appears in these examples from sonnet 80, is that Góngora first forces Spanish into neo-Latin contortions, obliging it to take a form other than its own, making it all but unintelligible, and then—as if by magic—he pulls a simple, almost diaphanous marriage of sound and sense out of the very same verbal hat. Bruce Wardropper[35] has observed "the complexity of the simple" in the *Soledades*' subtle attention, via the poetic image, to the imposing beauties of the natural world. Indeed, in Góngora, the complex and the simple regularly coexist as interfaces for one another; but not only does the simple turn out to be complex. Here in the brief verses of "Descaminado, enfermo, peregrino," the other side of complexity yields a dazzling simplicity: *"sin ti no"* ("no dio pasos sin ti no"); *"si no ve si(g)no"*; *"Distincto yo."* By pushing (with the poet) the unity of sound and sense to the very limit, even beyond, we come around, through the thicket of difficulty, to a kind of *claro de bosque*—the clarity of conventional, direct utterance. Góngora's game rests, I think, on the intuition that the passage from sound to sense is always a troubled one, and that it always involves doing a kind of violence to both.

The surprise appearance of simple, direct usage in the thicket of complexity may well be a "joke" Góngora enjoyed more than once in complicity with, and at the same time at the expense of, learned readings of his work. It is inscribed, I think, in as conspicuous a place as the first line of the *Soledades*, where our critical pilgrimage began: *"Pasos de un peregrino son errante."* In order to glimpse the inscription, however, we must first suspend our eagerness to complete the utterance by reading *"son"* as a verb and pursuing the likelihood that the copula will produce a metaphorical equivalent to *"pasos."* We must also, paradoxically, suspend our learned expectations of pervasive *hipérbaton* in Góngora's syntax. If we do this, letting the end of the metric line arrest our reading, we then hear the verse by itself: *"Pasos de un peregrino son errante,"* with *"son"* functioning as a *noun* with two modifiers (*peregrino, errante*). The result—in English, "the *steps* of a strange and wandering *sound*"—would then give precisely the figure for the utterance's deferral of grammatical logic and of meaning. It is an unsettling reading, though, because it separates the *pasos* (partly at least) from the body of the pilgrim and associates them with the much more elusive movement and imprint of *sound itself* on the senses, and ultimately on sense. Like Cascales' critique (and even like Herrera's reading of Garcilaso's poetic *pasos*), it makes us wonder whose steps we see/hear, and therefore whom we are following, on what *camino*. Do sounds or words or images have a life of their own? When we hear voices in a poem, what or whom are we hearing? Does a speaker give voice to a poem, or does the poem give its voice to him? As the poet and the reader tread the path of poetic tradition, are they leading or following?

Centuries of readers who have struggled with, tried to embrace, or rejected Góngora have come back again and again to the familiar vision of his brilliant, difficult, obscure, blinding language in the foregound, at the expense of the speaker. That often invisible framing voice of discourse, his intentions and meanings, even his very status as speaking subject, have in general been pushed into the shadows. It is a mystery indeed that a scholarly tradition which has celebrated the poet's great linguistic and formal achievements should have—sometimes conspicuously, at other times imperceptibly—deprived him of nothing less than his poetic voice. This critical impasse brings us back to the poetic mystery that, as Salinas maintained, is also a key to Góngora. Difficulty— the difficulty of pure language—*is* that mystery key, though in a way that I believe has not yet been articulated. For me, the meaning of Gongorine difficulty is this: the route through the twisted path of verse form is the route of and to his poetic persona. Leading through morphology and syntax and semantics, through the space-time of utterance that warps and folds constantly back on itself (like Cascales' wolf or perhaps for us like the spaces of Einsteinian relativity) before lurching forward, we know not where, that route belongs not only to the deciphering reader but to the speaking subject who gives voice both to meaning and to himself. *His voice* delivers him from the labyrinth of words, a prison which also paradoxically offers him the only way out.

Far from rejecting clarity, meaning, feeling, so as to inhabit a neutral space of language, Góngora takes up precisely—as his principal poetic subject—the journey of language: the pilgrimage of the speaker (and the reader) *through* language, his efforts to make himself heard, and our struggle to understand ("vacilando el entendimiento en fuerza de discurso"). That journey takes him—and us with him—into the heart of all the old linguistic orders: grammar, syntax, lexicon; canonical genres and their codes; classical mythology; the idiolects of great poets; Spanish popular tradition. Góngora invokes their authority, then tests their limits, but bears steady witness to the fact that we can only speak, can only communicate with inherited, shared language(s). And Góngora's journey "ends"—in the sonnet we have been reading, and in his work generally, I am convinced—*not* by writing the epitaph of the Western poetic tradition but by voicing a very modern intuition about the relation of the subject to the languages through which she or he speaks, about the unsayability of feeling and intent and self, and by offering a profound insight into the troubled relation between the subject and the world.

What have emerged in our readerly journey through complexity to clarity are precisely utterances of and about the subject latent in the poem. The possible reading "si no *ve sino* [or *signo*]" intensifies the sonnet's focus on the third-person grammatical subject's imagined interiority, otherwise only faintly visible, and suggests that much more than we thought may be at stake in his perceptions. And, in the midst of the distance that appears to separate the poem's implied speaker from this mute figure who is seemingly the protagonist of his poem, sequences like "pasos sin *ti* no" and "distincto *yo*" cause the controlled preterites of historical narrative to erupt without warning into the powerful present of Benvenistian discourse. These unexpected eruptions underline dramatically the status of the love-pilgrim's figure as displaced version of the poet, who speaks—or does not speak—in and through his wandering other self.

Yet the poem goes way beyond simply doubling the poet's image: the poem's voices themselves, in the layered jumble of their discourse, are made to serve as signs of poetic speech itself. Its words, cries, sounds—produced all at once by the poet, his pilgrim double, a wakeful watchdog, the beating of a heart—together bespeak, give voice to the difficulty of utterance and understanding. They bear troubled, sometimes semiaudible witness to the agony of the lyric subject and indeed of all human subjects. And together they constitute an eloquent sign—a *signo* that is also a *sino*—of the risks, the near-impossibility, and yet the urgency of speaking about consciousness, about self, about death. Even the poem's final words, apparently its most direct—"*yo muero*"—unmask themselves too as displacement, as still figured. For the death of the body, used here as trope for emotional or physical suffering *in vita*, cannot logically say itself directly in words. In the end, then, the poem's subject (is it truly a *distincto yo?*) is never quite distinct, never wholly extricated from the language of its figures; because the moment when all of metaphor's debts are paid, when the subject's self-images finally collapse into self-sameness, is not only the moment of the death of imagination. It is the moment of death itself.

Once, thinking to scoff at *culterano* language, Lope told the story of a man who "quitaba . . . las plumas a un ruiseñor; y descubriendo tan débil carne, dijo: *Vox tu es, et nihil praeterea*"[36] [was removing . . . the feathers from a nightingale, and on discovering such paltry meat exclaimed: *You are sound, and nothing else*]. Although he undoubtedly meant to chide his contemporaries for making verses out of meaningless, insubstantial *sound* (the first meaning of *voz* in the Golden Age), the Latin adage of his punch line gives an uncanny portrait of Góngora, in a sense Lope probably did not intend.

My recent readings persuade me that Góngora was concerned, throughout his career, to the point of obsession, with the category of voice.[37] If Chacón's dating of "Descaminado, enfermo, peregrino" is right, then in 1594, nearly twenty years before the writing of the *Soledades*, Góngora was mapping—or erasing the map of—the itinerary of the speaking, writing, reading subject. And he gave it a series of problematic representations, beginning with the sonnets and *romancillos* of the early period, such as "Lloraba la niña" (1590),[38] continuing through his maturity in the *Soledades* and the *Polifemo*, and finally culminating in the extraordinary *Fábula de Píramo y Tisbe* ("La ciudad de Babilonia" [1618]), which he considered his crowning achievement. This long meditation on voice gets its energy in part, as sonnet 80 suggests, from the tenacity and the tensions of the lyric tradition of Petrarchism. In the *Soledades*, Góngora launches the Petrarchan lyric subject onto a landscape that hovers between pastoral and epic, that even threatens to become a transatlantic, imperial landscape, in search of a place from which to speak; and then watches him settle, reluctantly, for the role of *mirón* ("muda la admiración, *habla callando*" [wonder, though mute, in silence speaks (Cunningham, p. 19)]), speechless witness to the world and to other speakers that silence him and perhaps speak metaphorically for him. In part the energy comes from mythology, as in the *Poli-femo*, where the silence of perfect lovers, and their rhetoric of mute signs and speaking bodies, contrasts with the horrific "music," natural and monstrous, destructive and self-destructive, of Polifemo's voice. And in the *Píramo*, the text in which the poet most clearly makes audible his own voice in the face of mythopoetic tradition, Góngora remakes the fable of erotic communication or noncommunication into a story of the fate of voices. Here his energy comes not only from the same mythological and lyric sources: it comes in addition from the traditional Spanish *romances*. In the old ballads, Góngora found poems made not of events but of their telling, not of physical acts but of speech acts, not of narrated history but of narrating voices. And he exploited the complex relation of the *romance*'s organizing speaker and its audience to the times both of the poem's historical subject and of its utterance. Above all he found a principal speaker who constructed his own speaking voice out of both the *ellos* of his story ("non-persons" from the past) and the *vosotros* of his audience, present in formulas like "Bien *oiréis* lo que *decía*." In these poems, the absence of a single voice signals not the absence of voice altogether, but rather the presence of many voices.

In that plural may lie a "secreto a voces" about Góngora's (or his poems') speaking subject. During a recent discussion of resonances of authorial voices within and between other Spanish Renaissance texts, my colleague Roland Greene asked whether we might not gain something by suspending, at least temporarily, our concern with the unified subject positions of singular authors. That question resonates forcefully with the nature of voice in Góngora's verse. What do we gain if we stop asking Góngora to speak with one voice—that is, with "his own" voice? Or what do we lose? What we have to give up, I believe, is the fiction that because we don't hear one clear, distinct, unique voice, it must be that Góngora either couldn't or didn't want to produce one. When we accept that he does speak with many voices, we may also be able to imagine that his syntactic and metaphorical dances with voices (or with wolves) constitute a profound engagement with language—*not* with a rarified language he alone can understand, but with the mystery of all language and the self that must inevitably speak through it.

But it is not so easy for us as readers of lyric, I think, to welcome plural voices as warmly as we do the singular voice. In a four-line fragment of a poetics, titled "Contra los recitales," José Emilio Pacheco protests:

> Si leo mis poemas en público,
> le quito su único sentido a la poesía:
> hacer que mis palabras sean tu voz
> por un instante al menos.[39]

[If I read my poems in public, / I remove poetry's one meaning: / to make my words be your voice / at least for an instant.]

It is likely, precisely because the first person of lyric *is* so inviting, because it insists that we stand momentarily in its place, that for this very reason we have chosen to give Góngora's speaker(s) a wide berth. For to occupy the shifty, murky locus of his poetic persona, even for a moment, is not only to risk the analytical "objectivity" of our critical business-as-usual, but to endanger the integrity of that personal voice—beyond poetry and criticism—by which we try to know ourselves.[40]

Notes

1. Maurice Molho, *Semántica y poética. Góngora, Quevedo* (Barcelona: Editorial Crítica, 1977).

2. Ibid., p. 81. Italics mine.

3. For a recent, still more radical view of the generic novelty of the *Soledades*, see Nadine Ly's "Las *Soledades*: 'Esta poesía inútil . . .'," *Criticón* 30 (1985): 7–42.

4. Molho, *Semántica y poética*, p. 60.

5. Luis de Góngora, *Obras completas*, ed. Isabel and Juan Millé y Jiménez (Madrid: Aguilar, 1943), no. 341; *Sonetos completos*, ed. Biruté Ciplijauskaité (Madrid: Castalia, 1987), no. 159.

6. "La *soledad* del Poeta es, para Góngora, la consecuencia de su singularidad, que le lleva a concebir una poesía hermética, reservada a unos pocos elegidos" (p. 77).

7. "El poeta, por el hecho de su genio extraordinario y singular, es un ser solitario entre los hombres que lo rodean, y no se mezcla con ellos sino como expectador de su indiferente existencia. ¡No hay rastro de melancolía en la soledad de Góngora! La ha elegido y no existe más que para ella: ella es su orgullo y la razón de su vida" (pp. 78–79). Implicit in what follows in the present essay is my conviction that melancholy cannot be so neatly scripted out of Góngora's poetic voice.

8. Antonio Vilanova, "El peregrino de amor en las *Soledades* de Góngora," in *Estudios dedicados a Menéndez Pidal* (Madrid: Consejo Superior de Investigaciones Científicas, 1952), 3:421–60.

9. Millé, no. 258; Ciplijauskaité, no. 80. I refer hereafter to this poem as sonnet 80, since Millé's numbering includes compositions of all forms.

10. Pedro Salinas, *Reality and the Poet in Spanish Poetry* (Baltimore: Johns Hopkins Press, 1940), p. 137.

11. Quintilian, *Institutio oratoria* 8.6. 14–15; Joel Fineman, "The Structure of Allegorical Desire," in *Allegory and Representation*, ed. Stephen J. Greenblatt (Baltimore: Johns Hopkins University Press, 1981), pp. 26–60.

12. See Paul Julian Smith, "Barthes, Góngora, and None-Sense," *Proceedings of the Modern Language Association* 101 (1986): 82–94.

13. Ibid.

14. Dámaso Alonso, *Estudios y ensayos gongorinos* (Madrid: Gredos, 1960), pp. 71–72.

15. Ciplijauskaité, *Sonetos completos*, pp. 16–17.

16. Ibid., p. 18.

17. Ibid., p. 21.

18. Ibid., p. 22.

19. Ibid., p. 23.

20. Ibid., p. 126.

21. The autobiographical illusion, widespread in much interpretation of lyric, is discussed in John Freccero, "The Fig Tree and the Laurel: Petrarch's Poetics," in *Literary Theory/Renaissance Texts*, ed. Patricia Parker and David Quint (Baltimore: Johns Hopkins University Press, 1986), pp. 20–32; Guiseppe Mazzotta, "The *Canzoniere* and the Language of the Self," *Studies in Philology* 75 (1978): 271–96; Inés Azar, "Tradition, Voice, and Self in the Love Poetry of Garcilaso," in *Studies in Honor of Elias Rivers*, ed. Bruno Damiani and Ruth El Saffar (Potomac, Md.: Scripta Humanistica, 1989), pp. 24–35; and Mary Gaylord, "Proper Language and Language as Property: The Personal Poetics of Lope's *Rimas*," *Modern Language Notes* 101 (1986): 220–46.

22. Chacón, Dámaso Alonso, and R. O. Jones (all cited by Ciplijauskaité, p. 145) all claim to glimpse life experience behind its lines. Robert Jammes ties the sonnet to Góngora's travels, then uses the short poem to ground the more abstract landscape of the *Soledades* in an "authenticité poétique" made up of the poet's sentiments and memories (Robert Jammes, *Etudes sur l'oeuvre poétique de don Luis de Góngora y Argote* [Bordeaux: Institut d'Etudes Ibériques et Ibéro-Américaines, 1967], p. 587). Bruce Wardropper in "Góngora and the serranilla," *Modern Language Notes* 77 (1962): 178–81, links the composition

primarily to the traditional Castilian *serranillas*, but at the same time points to the explicitness of its reference to a sexual encounter, as if by way of rescuing Góngora from abstraction.

23. Jammes, *Etudes*, p. 587.

24. Northrop Frye, *Anatomy of Criticism* (Princeton: Princeton University Press, 1957), p. 249; Chaviva Hosek and Patricia Parker, eds., *Lyric Poetry: Beyond New Criticism* (Ithaca: Cornell University Press, 1985), pp. 17, 38, and passim.

25. Margit Frenk, who has expanded immeasurably our awareness and appreciation of orality in Golden Age literary culture, has now gathered convincing evidence that even Góngora's most difficult verse was regularly read aloud during the poet's time. I am much indebted to her for sharing this idea with me in conversation, for it has pressed me to rethink his verse from the standpoint of its oral reception.

26. John Beverley, ed., *Soledades* (Madrid: Cátedra, 1980), p. 172.

27. Ibid., pp. 172–73.

28. Ibid., p. 173.

29. Francisco Cascales, *Cartas filológicas*, ed. Justo Garía Soriano (Madrid: Espasa-Calpe, 1959), 1:188.

30. Ibid., 1:220.

31. Beverley, *Soledades*, p. 173.

32. Sebastián de Covarrubias Horozco, *Tesoro de la Lengua Castellana o Española* (1611) (Madrid: Turner, 1979), pp. 232–33.

33. "Pero cuando quiere alguno acompañar el estilo conforme con la celsitud i belleza del pensamiento; *procura desatar los versos*, i muestra con el deslazamiento i particion cuanta grandeza tiene i hermosura en el sugeto, en las vozes i en el estilo." Fernando de Herrera, *Obra Poética*, ed. José M. Blecua (Madrid: Anejos del Boletín de la Real Academia Española, 32, 1975), p. 69.

34. Ibid., pp. 75, 74, 68.

35. "The Complexity of the Simple in Góngora's *Soledad primera*," *Journal of Medieval and Renaissance Studies* 7 (1977): 35–51.

36. Herrera, p. 280; cited by Wardropper ("The Complexity," p. 37).

37. This reading had its origins in my preparation for a Harvard graduate seminar on "Góngora and the Poetics of Reading" in the fall of 1990 and in the intensely rewarding discussions of that group, which devoted nearly three long sessions to sonnet 258. I am grateful to the members of that seminar—Michael Armstrong-Roche, Mark De Stephano, Fernando Espejo-Saavedra, Carmen Hsu, Julieta Muñoz, and Juan Silva—for their insights and for their extraordinary enthusiasm.

38. Gaylord, "The Grammar of Femininity in the Spanish Traditional Lyric," *Revista/Review Interamericana* 12 (1984): 115–24.

39. José Emilio Pacheco, *Tarde o temprano* (Mexico City: Fondo de Cultura Económica, 1980), p. 145.

40. I want to acknowledge the presence, in my thoughts, throughout the latest remaking of this piece, of my treasured friend Ruth El Saffar, who always spoke in so strong and so personal a voice, and who emboldened others of us to follow that example.

5

Postmodernism and the Baroque
in María de Zayas

MARINA S. BROWNLEE

*P*ostmodernism acknowledges that all cultural practices have an ideological subtext which determines the parameters of their production of meaning. It may be seen, in part, as a corrective to the belief in textual autonomy that dominated literary studies in the sixties and seventies. It is, by all accounts, a self-reflexive attitude that interrogates our institutions, intellectual as well as aesthetic—the media, the university, museums, and so forth. As a result, the postmodern condition in which we currently find ourselves has been aptly termed a "crisis of legitimation."

In terms of literary production, postmodernism concerns itself very centrally with the power and constraints of mimesis. It is committed to metafictional self-reflexivity in order to address extratextual issues of politics and history. García Márquez's *Cien años de soledad* is often invoked in this context as a paradigm of the *contradictory* features that define postmodern fiction. As Larry McCaffery observes: "[*Cien años*] . . . has become a kind of model for the contemporary writer, being self-conscious about its literary heritage and about the limits of mimesis . . . but yet managing to reconnect its readers to the world outside the page."[1] Linda Hutcheon further specifies a second feature, namely that postmodern literature is "an art of shifting perspective [inscribing narrators who are] either disconcertingly multiple and hard to locate or resolutely provisional and limited."[2] Rosalind Krauss offers a third definition of the postmodern text by coining the neologism "paraliterary"—a type of text that challenges "both the 'work of art' and the separation of that concept from the domain of the academic critical establishment: the paraliterary space is the space of debate, quotation, partisanship, betrayal, reconciliation; but it is not the space of unity, coherence, or resolution that we think of as constituting the work of art." This is the space of the postmodern—"the paradoxes of continuity and disconnection, of totalizing interpretation and the impossibility of final meaning."[3]

I mention these descriptions of the postmodern because they bear a striking resemblance to descriptions of the literary baroque. In spite of those critics who view the postmodern phenomenon as an unprecedented moment in Western culture, I maintain that it bears a strong resemblance to the cultural climate of the baroque. Like the baroque, postmodernism is both a chronological and a theoretical construct— both historical and typological in conception, both a period and an assembly of transhistorical features. In an unintentionally provocative remark, Ihab Hassan juxtaposes postmodern and baroque, stating that postmodernism is "an ongoing cultural process or activity," one that eludes definition "except as a shifting matrix of ideas, a moot consensus, which may or may not *harden* some day into a term like 'baroque.'"[4] To my mind, however, it would be just as erroneous to view the baroque as a homogeneous cultural movement as it would be to misrepresent the polymorphous nature of the postmodern. I would like to enumerate a few striking similarities shared by these two cultural currents in order to illustrate that they, in fact, have a lot in common. Moreover, this configuration of shared features—far from being a unique phenomenon—recurs periodically in literary history. In this context Nietzsche insightfully "recognizes a baroque stage after the Renaissance, which he, however, conceives also as a recurrent phenomenon in history, occurring always at the decadence of great art as a decline into rhetoric and theatricality."[5]

Postmodernism, like the baroque, is the cultural expression of a society that critically reappraises the myths of the preceding era which viewed itself as paradigmatically "modern." Both movements undermine a humanist vision, be it that of Erasmian humanism or secular humanism. Both movements, likewise, overtly discredit utopic cultural structures, be they imperial or Marxist. In other words, both demythologize—that is what the "crisis of legitimacy" is all about. Postmodernism, like the baroque, is much more form-conscious than the age that preceded it and to which it is responding. The existence of these two movements, in addition, was first perceived in the plastic arts and only thereafter in literature. Both exploit the same literary figures: antithesis, oxymoron, paradox, catachresis, hyperbole, and—of particular importance for my purposes here—example.

I would like to explore this theoretical affinity between the two cultural movements in a concrete textual corpus, and the text I have chosen is one of María de Zayas's *Novelas amorosas y ejemplares*. What will emerge from my analysis of her text as it relates to narrative exemplarity is an illustration of the fact that her writing exhibits all the aforementioned features attributed by McCaffery, Hutcheon, and Krauss to postmodern fiction. At the same time, the framework for my close reading of Zayas provided by this set of preoccupations concerning literary periodicity and cultural authority will serve to reveal both the irreducible historical specificity of her literary enterprise and its resistance to easy systematization with regard to strategies of literary or ideological analysis.

Let me begin by suggesting—in general terms and with a purposefully polemical slant—the usefulness of viewing the contrast between periods of literary or cultural history in terms of a contrast between privileged or dominant rhetorical figures. More specifically, I would like to suggest that both High Renaissance and high modernist culture privilege metaphor, while both baroque and postmodern culture privilege metonymy—and, in particular, the metonymic figure of example. Interestingly, Roman Jakobson has argued very persuasively for the "alternative predominance of one or the other of these two processes."[6] In the case of baroque Spain, however, his distinction must be qualified, for a simultaneity is operative whereby metaphor is privileged in the realm of poetry and metonymy in the sphere of prose. Nonetheless, they are both exploited in order to undermine logocentrism.

The cultural authority exerted by a given rhetorical figure varies markedly from one age to the next. Witness, for instance, the twentieth-century fascination with metaphor. The bibliography devoted to this subject is voluminous. By contrast, interest in metaphor's "forgotten sibling"[7]—the exemplum—has been largely relegated to the periphery by modern criticism. It is important to note that it is not simply a matter of aesthetic taste that accounts for such deprivileging of a particular rhetorical figure. Rather it is a phenomenological issue—namely a given culture's perception of the cognitive process itself—that is at stake. As a result, it is not difficult to understand why example poses a threat to certain movements in intellectual history. As John Lyons observes:

> For a positivist or a realist, the basis of all assertion is shaken when examples of laws and rules are revealed as discursive constructions like any other rhetorical figure. A more sophisticated approach of the deconstructionist type, however, might well be embarrassed by its need to use examples (if only in the form of textual reference) for the kind of appeal for support it requires from an "outside." Every example can be deconstructed, and, in an approach that moves forward by selecting and deconstructing exemplary texts, the whole critical movement could be derailed by an excessive attention to its initial gestures. (p. 4)

Indeed, despite efforts to the contrary, we as literary critics cannot escape example. For when we produce a critical text that attempts to situate a literary text within a broader context (be it ideological, tropological, stylistic, etc.) we necessarily exploit the literary text as example.

In spite of this reluctance to consider example as an object of literary-critical study, recent interest in discourse analysis has led to a marked increase in critical attention devoted to it. And, among the results obtained by this methodological perspective, is a realization that example often presents itself in a deceptively simple light. Although example, unlike metaphor, explicitly proclaims a particular pedagogical function, let the reader beware. Writers of exempla, particularly during the Renaissance, exploited the exemplum as a metacritical tool to comment on the deceptive nature of language itself. We are coming to realize, as several key Renaissance writers did, that exempla can in fact be exploited for their powerful "ability to . . . suspend the apparent speech acts that constitute their situation of enunciation."[8]

María de Zayas—often referred to as the "Spanish Boccaccio"—is a case in point. As I hope to show, her rewriting of *Decameron* 10.5 illustrates her interest in the potential of the example as commentary on the performative ambiguity of language. Moreover, my claim for Zayas's linguistic skepticism constitutes a departure from the three prevailing views of her work: either as realist, as exemplar, or as an exclusively feminist apologist.

Known primarily as a writer of two novella collections published in 1637 and 1647, Zayas was highly esteemed during her lifetime for her literary talents. Lope de Vega refers to her in *El laurel de Apolo* as "la inmortal doña María de Zayas,"[9] while Castillo Solórzano praises her as follows:

> En estos tiempos luce y campea con felices lauros el ingenio de doña María de Zayas y Sotomayor, que con justo título ha merecido el nombre de Sibila de Madrid, adquirido por sus admirables versos, por su felice ingenio y gran prudencia, habiendo sacado de la estampa un libro de diez novelas que son diez asombros para los que escriben deste género, pues la meditada prosa, el artificio dellas y los versos que interpola, es todo tan admirable, que acobarda las más valientes plumas de nuestra España.[10]
>
> [It is very daring in these times when I see that such brilliant people give birth to creations as admirable as they are witty, and not only men who profess to know humanity; but in these times the wit of Doña María de Zayas y Sotomayor sparkles and shines with happy laurels. She has justly deserved the name of Sibyl of Madrid, acquired thanks to her admirable verses, her felicitous mind, and great prudence, having published a book of ten novellas [her first collection, the *Novelas amorosas y ejemplares*] which are ten wonders for those who write in this genre, since the meditated prose, the artifice, and the verses that she interpolates are all so admirable that they intimidate the most valiant pens of our Spain.] (Garduña)

Virtually no biographical details are known about Zayas, except that she was born at the turn of the seventeenth century, that she lived in Madrid, and died in the 1660s. Her fiction, however, reflects her profound knowledge of the European novella tradition (Boccaccio, Bandello, Salernitano, Sercambi, Marguerite de Navarre, Cervantes, among others) as well as a highly innovative approach to the exemplary form.

The first of her framed novella collections (published in 1637) is entitled *Novelas amorosas y ejemplares* (Exemplary Love Stories), the second, published ten years later, she calls *Desengaños amorosos* (The Disillusionments of Love). These two collections had a notable impact in Spain and beyond, as Patsy Boyer explains:

> Zayas' novellas became instant best sellers in Spain and remained so for two hundred years, rivaled only by Cervantes' novellas in popularity. During the 1650's Scarron and Boisrobert translated and adapted them into French without attributing them to Zayas. Consequently, the widespread diffusion of Zayas' novellas in France and England has redounded to the fame of her French adapters. Often her works were attributed to Cervantes, but never, outside of Spain, have they achieved recognition as hers.[11]

The first ten novellas (narrated by five men and five women) are imbedded within a frame during the course of five lavish Christmas soirées designed for the entertainment of Lysis, who is convalescing from quartan fever. Although the second ten tales are planned for a New Year's Day celebration of Lysis's marriage to Diego, they are postponed for more than a year. When the group reconvenes, we find a structural repetition of the first part in that there are ten stories narrated by characters from the original frame story. However, Lysis redefines the rules in thematic terms and in terms of gender. For, unlike the *Novelas*, where both male and female narrators relate tales of adventure and deception, the *Desengaños* must be narrated only by women and are, she indicates, designed to expose the intolerable cruelty of men. Once she has heard these narratives, Lysis decides not to marry her adoring suitor, instead withdrawing from the world to live a secular life in the convent, joined by four other ladies.

That the *Desengaños* offer a more vivid exposé of male brutality than the *Novelas* is evident in their outcome. As Boyer observes, "six of the ten [*Novelas*], for example, end in ostensibly happy marriage, two women enter the convent, and the two satires end with the death of the foolish male protagonist. In contrast, six of the ten [*Desengaños*] end in vicious wife murder, and the other four depict traumatic torture and persecution of the female protagonist before she takes refuge in a convent" (p. xix).

Before turning to *Decameron* 10.5 and Zayas's *Jardín engañoso*, I would like to offer a brief consideration of the critical reception accorded to Zayas's work. As I have indicated, modern critical assessments of her work view Zayas according to one of three broad interpretive categories. The first interpretation, represented by such critics as Agustín de Amezúa and Eduardo Rincón, considers Zayas to be a writer of realist fiction, a faithful portrayal of life in seventeenth-century Spain.[12] Such a view, however, is undermined by the abundance of excessively grotesque behavior and supernatural phenomena in her prose. Amid descriptions of daily life we encounter, in *La inocencia castigada*, for instance, a necromancer who hypnotizes a faithful wife so that she will comply with her would-be suitor's wishes. When her totally unwilled capitulation is discovered by her brother, husband, and sister-in-law, she is imprisoned in a room for six years. And this is no ordinary room, but a room so painfully small that it prevents her from even standing upright. Her torture is magnified by the fact that she is immobilely encased in her own bodily waste. The prevalence of this type of detail provoked the eminent German critic Ludwig Pfandl to write in 1929: "Can there be anything more gross and obscene, more nonaesthetic and repulsive, than a woman who writes lascivious, dirty, sadistic, and morally corrupt stories?"[13] Nonetheless, by the depiction of this type of grisly brutality, not to mention necromancers and even the Devil himself, it is clear that Zayas is not interested in replicating on paper a realistic slice-of-life depiction of everyday Spain.

As we now admit, all interpretations are political—that is, based on specific a priori values. In Amezúa's case it is his reverence for "realism" as the highest form of art that leads him to classify Zayas's *novelas* as such, despite their profusion of unrealistic details. In fact, the gory and demonic aspect of her prose has led some critics to regard Zayas instead as a precursor of the gothic novel.[14]

The second critical perspective seeks to portray Zayas as the author of exemplary narratives designed to celebrate establishment values (the sanctity of female chastity, the incompatibility of love and honor, and the status quo of Christian marriage). This view continues to be represented by some critics. Among them Patsy Boyer, who recently published an English translation of the *Novelas*, where she indicates that

"Zayas' novellas are in no way unorthodox and were lauded as exemplary by the censors, yet they treat moral issues and present material (rape, battering, murder) with a frankness that seems shocking to us. The spirit of the novellas is secular and the language is conventional" (p. xxv). Despite her many fine observations concerning the *Novelas amorosas y ejemplares*, I disagree with Boyer in terms of Zayas's language; it is anything but "conventional." Indeed, Zayas has been taken to task for her prose style, for her unfortunate ungrammaticality at various points in her novellas.

This stylistic idiosyncrasy can be viewed as either willed or unwilled—as a mark of female "spontaneity" (i.e., ingenuousness, lack of intellectual rigor) or as a calculatedly willed device. Of this double perspective Paul Julian Smith writes:

> The same men who praise Zayas for her simplicity and naturalness chide her for the inclusion of irrelevant detail and the failure to conform to grammatical precept. Disrupted syntax is the same "fault" found by critics of St. Teresa. [Fray] Luis de León complains that Teresa begins a new topic before she has finished the old one, mixes up arguments and breaks the thread ("rompe el hilo") of logical discourse (*Vida*, p. 15). In both Teresa and Zayas the lack of grammatical linking (known technically as anacoluthon) is said to contribute to the spontaneity of the style. Yet there is an alternative reading of this phenomenon, a "womanly" one. [Luce] Irigaray calls for a text that will overturn syntax ("boulverser la syntaxe") and suspend teleology through the breaking of linguistic threads ("la rupture des fils").[15]

Zayas acknowledges that seen in this light, as a willed device, "woman's experience cannot be spoken in a man-made language without gaps and discontinuities; and that the utopia of a purely female space must be a break or threshold in a dominant male order."[16]

The gaps and discontinuities evidenced in Zayas's *un*exemplary style echo the *un*traditional nature of her exempla, as borne out by textual detail. It is true that several of her stories celebrate the importance of fidelity in wedlock. But, at the same time, other stories depict the unwarranted brutality of husbands toward faithful wives. Such discrepancy between what Fredric Jameson calls the "semantic" and "syntactic" dimensions[17] of the narratives makes it impossible to view Zayas simply as an establishment author. A further qualifier must be pointed out in connection with the stories that offer a celebration of marriage and its virtues. Namely—as we will see in her rewriting of *Decameron* 10.5— the frame of the story is crucially important, as important to interpretation as the story itself.

What is very telling in terms of any traditional exemplary intent is the fact that she advocates withdrawal into a convent—even for married women. Although this type of ascetic flight is part of a long tradition of female behavior, here the motivation is dramatically different. Renunciation of the world is advocated by Zayas *not* as a way of avoiding worldly vice and temptation, but rather to escape the cruelty of men.[18] At the end of her second collection, Lysis (the principal frame character) retreats in precisely this way. The anonymous, omniscient narrator comments on her action by saying: "No es trágico fin, sino el más felice que se pudo dar, pues codiciosa y deseada de muchos, no se sujetó a ninguno" (*Desengaños*, p. 670) [This end is not tragic but rather the happiest that one could have asked for, because she, wanted and desired by many, did not subject herself to anyone (Boyer, p. xvii)].

The third critical assessment views Zayas as feminist.[19] In the nineteenth and early twentieth centuries, especially in a country like Spain, to call someone a "feminist" was a way of summarily dismissing her from serious consideration. Such is no longer the case and, indeed, Zayas's literary output is now a topic of substantial critical activity from the perspective of feminist theory. This is understandable given her outspoken defense of the intellectual merits of women. As she indicates, it is history, not biology, that accounts for the notable lack of women authors. By way of introducing her first collection, Zayas writes:

> Quién duda, lector mío, que te causará admiración que una mujer tenga despejo, no sólo para escribir un libro, sino para darle a la estampa, que es el crisol donde se averigua la pureza de los ingenios; porque hasta que los escritos se rozan en las letras de plomo, no tienen valor cierto, por ser tan fáciles de engañar los sentidos, que la fragilidad de la vista suele pasar por oro macizo lo que a la luz del

fuego es solamente un pedazo de bronce afeitado. Quién duda, digo otra vez, que habrá muchos que atribuyan a locura esta virtuosa osadía de sacar a luz mis borrones, siendo mujer, que, en opinión de algunos necios, es lo mismo que una cosa incapaz.

(*Novelas*, p. 21)

[Oh my reader, no doubt it will amaze you that a woman has the nerve, not only to write a book but actually to publish it, for publication is the crucible in which the purity of genius is tested; until writing is set in letters of lead, it has no real value. Our senses are so easily deceived that fragile sight often sees as pure gold what, by the light of the fire, is simply a piece of polished brass. Who can doubt, I repeat, that there will be many who will attribute to folly my audacity in publishing my scribbles because I'm a woman, and women, in the opinion of some fools, are unfit beings.]

(Boyer, p. 1)

Zayas further justifies her literary enterprise by citing illustrious female predecessors: Lucan's wife Argentaria, who according to him not only revised his three books of the *Pharsalia* but even wrote many passages assumed to have been penned by Lucan himself; Pythagoras's sister, who wrote an admirable book of maxims; and many other women (both ancient and modern) as well. The issue of witchcraft and magic that recurs in Zayas is related to her feminist ungrammaticality. As Boyer rightly observes, "magic and witchcraft are significant feminist issues in that the persecution of witches was, in fact, a persecution of women, and the phenomenon points out women's lack of power in posthumanist societies" (p. xviii). Zayas's interest in witchcraft is all the more striking given that in Spain there were notably few witch trials, as the energy of the Spanish Inquisition centered on heretics rather than witches and magicians.

   In addition to this self-conscious feminist stance articulated by Zayas in her prologue, several of her ten storytellers often deliver equally staunch feminist discourses. However, on several occasions these discourses conflict with the characters' personalities. Even more blatant is the fact that they themselves will sometimes disavow in an unambiguous way the validity of their own feminist message. When Lysis instructs the women to speak ill of men in the *Desengaños*, some of them complain. As a preface to her narration of *La más infame venganza*, Lisarda says, for instance:

> Mandásteme, hermosa Lisis, que fuese la segunda en dar desenga-
> ños a las damas, de que deben escarmentar en sucesos ajenos, para
> no dejarse engañar de los hombres. Y cierto, que más por la ley de
> la obediencia me obligo a admitirlo que por sentir que tengo de
> acertar. Lo primero, porque aún no ha llegado a tiempo de desen-
> gañarme a mí, pues aún apenas sé si estoy engañada, y mal puede
> quien no sabe un arte, sea el que fuere, hablar de él y tengo por ci-
> vilidad decir mal de quien no me ha hecho mal. Y con esto mismo
> pudiera disculpar a los hombres; que lo cierto es que los que se que-
> jan están agraviados, que no son tan menguados de juicio que di-
> xeren tanto mal como de las mujeres dicen.   (p. 377)

[You order me, beautiful Lysis, to be the second in disenchanting the ladies by means of the adversities suffered by others so that they will not permit themselves to be deceived by men. In fact, I do this in order to comply with (your) rule rather than the conviction that I can succeed. Firstly, because I have not yet been disenchanted myself; indeed, I don't think I have ever been deceived. And one who has never experienced something cannot speak of it convincingly. In addition, I consider it rude to speak disparagingly of those who have done me no harm. For this reason alone I could excuse men; for certainly those who complain have been mistreated since they are not so deficient in judgment as to fabricate all the evil they claim about women.]

By way of introduction to her *desengaño* (*Tarde llega el desengaño*), Filis states that "ni los hombres deben ser culpados en todo, ni las mujeres tampoco" (pp. 457–58) [neither men nor women should be blamed for everything]. From this she proceeds to a rather pointed criticism of female vanity: "Si no se dieran tanto a la compostura, afeminándose más que Naturaleza las afeminó, y como en lugar de aplicarse a jugar las armas y a estudiar las ciencias, estudian en criar el cabello y matizar el rostro, ya pudiera ser que pasaran en todo a los hombres" (p. 458) [If (women) would give up obsessing so much about their physical appearance, turning their attention instead to the martial arts and the study of science, they would surely surpass the accomplishments of men]. Isabel qualifies the song she sings to introduce the narration of *La perseguida triunfante* by explaining: "Yo he cantado lo que ha de ser, no lo que es. Y tengo por sin duda que no todos los poetas sienten lo que escriben; antes imagino que escriben lo que no sienten" (p. 579) [I have narrated things as I had to, not as I myself see them. And, furthermore, I believe that not all writers believe what they write; I imagine, rather, that they write things that they do not believe]. In diegetic terms, it is also important to qualify a strictly feminist reading. It is, after all, not a man but a woman who sets in motion the martyrdom that Elena suffers in *Tarde llega el desengaño*. Likewise, the six-year torture endured by Inés in *La inocencia castigada* stems from the greed of another female— a procuress. To give a final example, in the *Jardín engañoso* it is also a woman's perfidy that results in death and destruction, for which she goes unpunished.

Lysis herself offers the most incriminating evidence that calls into question the validity of her unambiguous defense of women. While she always defends the cause of women, showing how they are the innocent victims of men, the story she narrates (*Estragos que causa el vicio*) centers upon a very unexemplary woman (Florentina) who cruelly mistreats another woman. If, as the storyteller claims, this tale is intended to instruct women on how to defend themselves from cruelty, then it is female cruelty that is at issue here. Beyond this contradictory example, Lysis shows herself to be operating according to motives that are equally unexemplary in terms of her professed feminism. That is, in the course of the frame-narrative she manipulates Diego (a devoted suitor) in order to take revenge on Juan (who has rejected her). As a result, she emerges as the proverbial cunning female, a victimizer of men. This revenge motif, spread out among the many hundreds of pages of the *Novelas*, serves to further undermine the truth status of her discourse. Or rather, it functions to remind the reader that one must proceed with caution, that the gap separating *histoire* and *discours*—for women as for men—may be considerable.

If the interpretation of Zayas as an establishment proponent of wifely virtues has its dangers, claims that she is a modern-day feminist (like Lysis—with whom she is often mistakenly conflated) are equally troublesome. The presence of exemplary feminist narrators in tandem with unexemplary, hypocritical ones complicates interpretation substantially. As Hans-Robert Jauss remarks on a somewhat different but related topic, "one puts a princess in a fairy tale next to a princess in a novella, and one notices the difference."[20]

I would suggest that it is *not* Zayas's desire to invalidate the feminist perspective professed by several of her narrators (and this includes occasional males as well). Susan Griswold concludes that Zayas's feminism is "a topos which responds to an established literary tradition," and it is, she claims, "balanced by an equally vigorous use of the topos of anti-feminism."[21] From this observation Griswold reasons that the two discourses—the feminist and misogynist—cancel each other out, being reduced thereby to the status of "pure rhetoric" with no transcendent value. I strongly disagree with this view, finding the presence of both discourses to be meaningful indeed.

In the context of Zayas's work, I would suggest the appropriateness of Julia Kristeva's relational definition of feminism, that is, the study of "that which is marginalized by the patriarchal symbolic order"—a relational feminism which is "as shifting as the various forms of patriarchy itself, a definition which can argue that men can also be constructed as marginal by the symbolic order."[22]

Zayas offers several examples of such oppressed male subjectivity—at the hands of male and female oppressors alike. *El prevenido engañado* (Forewarned but Forestalled) is a bold case in point, in which a black slave is relentlessly exploited as sex object by a beautiful European woman of "vicious" sexual appetites. Clearly, this narrative does not offer an exemplary perspective on gender or race. By contrast, many other of Zayas's narratives do. How, then, are we to account for this discrepancy? Zayas, I believe, is committed to exploring perspectivism in all its complexity—biological, racial, social, and intellectual—with a degree of intensity that is hard to equal. Moreover, this project does not diminish her undeniably gendered reading of society. Instead of an exclusive focus on the gender of the speaker or character, she undertakes an analysis of the many discourses (sexuality and gender as well as socioeconomic status and racial identity) whose conflicting imperatives collectively define the unstable boundaries of the individual subject of baroque culture. This perception of human subjectivity is at the center of the baroque aesthetic.

While not wishing to devalue her feminist belief, Zayas calls attention to the power of language, to its complex performative function. She presents a variety of potentially exemplary, totalizing discourses—feminist and masculinist—in their power both to represent legitimately and to manipulate illegitimately. By her metalinguistic critique of the most venerable cultural institutions such as marriage, honor, religion, and the justice system, Zayas, in my view, seems remarkably postmodern.

Lyotard, in defining the postmodern author, writes as follows:

> A postmodern artist or writer is in the position of a philosopher: the text he writes, the work he produces are not in principle governed by preestablished rules, and they cannot be judged according to a determining judgment, by applying familiar categories to the text or to the work. Those rules and categories are what the work of art is itself looking for. The artist and the writer, then, are working without rules in order to formulate the rules of *what will have been done*. Hence the fact that work and text have the characters of an *event*; hence also, they always come too late for their author, or, what amounts to the same thing, their being put into work, their realization always begins too soon. Postmodern would have to be understood according to the paradox of the future (*post*) anterior (*modo*). [Thus] the essay (Montaigne) is postmodern, while the fragment (*The Athaeneum*) is modern.[23]

Bearing in mind Zayas's critical legacy, let us now turn to a consideration of *Decameron* 10.5 and the last novella of her first collection, *El jardín engañoso*.

Decameron 10.5 is, like all of Day 10, devoted to the theme of magnanimity. More precisely, this tale offers a dramatization of the power of language. In order to protect her virtue, the married woman makes an impossible request of her suitor—that he create a splendid garden in the dead of winter. When, with the help of a magician, he accomplishes the request, she must yield to him. As the distressed wife explains this problem to her husband, he indicates that she must *keep her word* and comply with her suitor. The suitor is so impressed by the husband's commit-ment to *linguistic integrity* that he annuls their verbal contract. Indeed, he and the husband further illustrate their reverence for the word by their mutual admiration, becoming the best of friends. Variations on this theme can be found in Boccaccio's *Filocolo*, Chaucer's *Franklin's Tale*, and Boiardo's *Orlando innamorato*, as well as in a variety of an-cient sources. What is important to note is that, despite the particular test involved, in each case what is being tested is the power of language. In each case the tale concludes with a celebration of referentiality. Keep-ing one's word leads to reward; an unproblematic, prelapsarian view of language is imposed.

Like Boccaccio, Zayas is similarly interested in the power of language. But unlike him, Zayas, I would argue, focuses on the darker, labyrin-thine possibilities of the garden. The *Jardín engañoso* tends to be inter-preted as a lighthearted conclusion to Zayas's first collection. E. B. Place, for instance, sees it as "rival[ing] some of the most brilliant passages in the French burlesquing *nouvelles*."[24] This is due, in part, to the fact that Zayas replaces the magician with the Devil himself. The suitor makes a pact with the Evil One in order to furnish the required garden. And, like Boccaccio's magician, the Devil ultimately grants the suitor freedom from his contractual perdition. This is uncharacteristic behavior, to say the least. In fact, Zayas is credited with having written the only known example of such diabolical magnanimity.

Yet, why, we may rightly ask, does she emphasize this atypical behav-ior? In attempting to ascertain who has been the most magnanimous—the husband, the lover, or the Devil—she writes: "Principiaron a dis-putar [y] cada uno daba su razón: unos alegaban que el marido, y otros que el amante, y todos juntos, que el demonio, por ser en el cosa nunca vista el hacer bien" (p. 327) [Some favored the husband, others the lover, and everyone agreed that the devil had outdone himself because it's un-heard of for the Devil to do a good deed (p. 312)]. Is it magnanimity, the sin of pride, or—more likely—weakness verbally disguised as its oppo-site that motivates this extraordinary behavior? The Devil exclaims: "Toma don Jorge: ves ahí tu cédula; yo te suelto la obligación, que no quiero alma de quien tan bien se sabe vencer" (p. 326) [Take back your pact! I don't want the soul of a man who's learned to conquer himself

(p. 311)]. If one has learned to conquer himself, then he cannot be conquered by the Devil.

Zayas understands the paradigmatic function of the Boccaccian narrative in terms of pre- and postlapsarian language. That is why she makes the linguistic dimension explicit by transforming Boccaccio's magician into the Devil. That is also why she entitles her story *El jardín engañoso*, meaning the deceitful or deceptive garden. Boyer, in my opinion, mistranslated it as *The Magic Garden*, presumably because the *Novelas* are traditionally—and to my mind erroneously—viewed as largely unproblematic stories of connubial coexistence.

Textual specificity belies such an unproblematic reading. Zayas renames Boccaccio's wife-figure (Dianora) Constanza, at the same time inventing for her a sister (Teodosia), who will, in fact, eclipse Constanza's role as female protagonist. And in a move that is characteristic of the exemplary narrator, both women are presented as being paradigmatically perfect in every way. Their names are carefully chosen as well— "constancy" and "a divine offering" lead us to expect an illustration of the semantic value indicated for each woman.

But Zayas is not interested in following the path of predictable exemplarity. Instead her interest lies in the power of words to deceive— and in deceivers who triumph. She offers a superficially exemplary narrative that uncovers a sinister truth. Speaking of the exemplum and its highly controlled nature, Lyons writes:

> The example is a dependent statement drawing its meaning from the controlling generality. As dependent statements grow into complex narratives, however, the number of other concepts that can be illustrated by the narrative begins to threaten the control of the generality. The dependent statement may bring details that cast an entirely new light on the apparently simple generality being illustrated, or both writer and reader may be carried away by the richness of the concrete instance to the neglect of the concept being illustrated. (p. 34)

It is precisely this *threat* that Zayas dramatizes in her narrative.

Briefly stated, Zayas complicates Boccaccio's basic plot by giving the wife a sister and the suitor a brother. Teodosia falls in love with her married sister's suitor (Jorge) and tries to turn his attention away from Constanza to herself. As a result of her lies, the suitor secretly kills his brother, thereafter fleeing the country. For over two years Constanza remains faithful to the inexplicably absent Jorge, at which time a new suitor (Carlos) tricks her into marrying him. He pretends to be dying and to have chosen Constanza to be the executrix of his substantial estate. This is his last wish. She is so moved by it that she marries him, at which point he recovers from his feigned illness. And, although he discloses his double deception (in terms of his health and his estate) to Constanza, they live happily thereafter. The narrator indicates that "era Constanza tan discreta, que en lugar de desconsolarse, juzgándose dichosa en tener tal marido, le dió por el engaño gracias" (p. 318) [instead of ruing the deception, she considered it a stroke of fortune (p. 303)].

Meanwhile, four years after his disappearance, Jorge returns and attempts to woo Constanza once again. She refuses and, in order to rid herself of him, tells him that she will favor him only if he produces a splendid garden overnight:

> Hagamos, señor don Jorge, un concierto; y sea que como vos me hagáis en esta placeta que está delante de mi casa, de aquí a la mañana, un jardín tan adornado de cuadros y olorosas flores, árboles y fuentes, que ni en su frescura ni belleza, ni en la diversidad de páxaros quien él haya, desdiga de los nombrados pensiles de Babilonia, que Semíramis hizo sobre sus muros, yo me pondré en vuestro poder y haré por vos cuanto deseáis. (p. 321)
> [If, between now and tomorrow morning, you will make for me in the square in front of my house a garden with flowerbeds full of perfumed flowers, trees, and fountains that, in all its beauty, freshness, and diversity of birds, surpasses the famous gardens that Semiramis had built on the walls of Babylon, then I shall place myself in your hands for you to do with as you please.] (p. 306)

With the Devil's help he produces the fabulous artifact and, struck by the husband's magnanimity when he insists that Constanza keep her word, Jorge frees her from her promise and marries Teodosia in accord with her sister's wishes. The narrator ends by relating: "Vivieron muchos años con hermosos hijos, sin que jamás se supiese que don Jorge

hubiese sido el matador de Federico, hasta que después de muerto don
Jorge, Teodosia contó el caso como quien tan bien lo sabía. A la cual,
cuando murió, le hallaron escrita de su mano esta maravilla" (p. 327)
[They all lived for many years and had lovely children. No one ever
found out that Jorge had murdered his brother, until after his death,
when Teodosia told the story she alone knew. When she died this narrative was found written in her own hand (p. 312)].

As a result, Teodosia, Carlos, and Jorge (each one guilty of uncon-
scionable verbal deception) go unpunished (indeed, they are rewarded
with great happiness). Carlos (a fraud) and Jorge (a fratricide) are literally hailed as "exemplars" of nobility and virtue by the assembled lis-
teners. Even more shocking is the fact that the storyteller's motivation
in telling the tale is completely forgotten. Laura had introduced her tale
by observing:

> Matar un hermano a otro, ni ser una hermana traidora con su her-
> mana, forzándolos al uno celos y al otro amor y envidia, no es caso
> nuevo; pues desde el principio del mundo ha habido hermanos trai-
> dores y envidiosos, como nos dicen dos mil ejemplos que hay escri-
> tos. Pues que la pobreza enseña ardides, y más si se acompaña con
> ciega afición, tampoco es cosa nueva. Ni lo es que un amante aven-
> ture la perdición de su alma por alcanzar lo que desea. Ni menos lo
> será que una mujer, si quiere guardar su honor, busque ni haga im-
> posibles . . . pues el decir [mi maravilla] yo no es más que para dar
> ejemplo y prevenir que se guarden de las ocasiones. (p. 311)
>
> [It's nothing new for a brother to kill a brother or for a sister to betray a
> sister if they're driven by jealousy, love, and envy. From the very beginning
> of the world there've been invidious and treacherous brothers and sisters,
> as we see in a thousand stories that have been written down. Neither is it
> new for poverty to produce ingenious trickery. . . . Nor is it novel for a
> lover to risk his soul to get what he wants, or for a woman trying to protect
> her honor to ask a lover to do the impossible. . . . I'm telling this story only
> to make a point and to warn people to be careful.] (p. 295)

The inscribed audience interprets this last tale of the collection in the
opposite way—as an exemplum of magnanimity—having entirely forgotten Laura's motive. Thus the "intricate labyrinths" ("tan intricados

laberintos") of the Devil's garden may well be construed as the *verbal labyrinths* that stem from the original Garden—that of Eden. Etymologically, *exemplum* meant a "clearing in the woods." Zayas, while ostensibly clearing the woods, points to their unredeemed darkness. By her dramatization of totalizing discourses—feminist, masculinist, canonical, and uncanonical, all vying for power—Zayas reveals her literary project to be both paradigmatically baroque and strikingly postmodern.

Notes

1. Larry McCaffery, *The Metafictional Muse* (Pittsburgh: University of Pittsburgh Press, 1982), p. 264.

2. Linda Hutcheon, *A Poetics of Postmodernism* (New York: Routledge, 1988), p. 11.

3. Rosalind Krauss, "Poststructuralism and the 'Paraliterary,' " *October* 13 (1980): 37.

4. Ihab Hassan, "On the Problem of the Postmodern," *New Literary History* 20 (1988): 23.

5. René Wellek, *Concepts of Criticism* (New Haven: Yale University Press, 1963), p. 116.

6. Roman Jakobson, "The Metaphoric and Metonymic Poles," in *Fundamentals of Language*, ed. R. Jakobson and Morris Halle (Paris: Mouton, 1971), p. 92.

7. John D. Lyons, *Exemplum: The Rhetoric of Example in Early Modern France and Italy* (Princeton: Princeton University Press, 1989), p. 3.

8. Ibid., p. 25.

9.   ¡Oh! dulces Hipocrémides hermosas,
        las espinas pangegeas
        aprisa desnudad, y de las rosas
        tejed ricas guirnaldas y trofeos
        a la inmortal doña María de Zayas,
        que sin pasar a Lesbos ni a las playas
        del vasto mar Egeo
        que hoy llora el negro velo de Teseo
        a Safo gozará Millenea,
        quien ver milagros de mujer espera.
        (*Laurel de Apolo*, 1630)

10. Alonso de Castillo y Solórzano, *La garduña de Sevilla* (Madrid: Clásicos Castellanos, 1957), p. 66.

11. Patsy Boyer, trans., *The Enchantments of Love: Amorous and Exemplary Novels of María de Zayas* (Berkeley: University of California Press, 1990), p. xii.

12. See, for example, the introduction to Agustín de Amezúa's edition of the *Novelas amorosas y ejemplares de Doña María de Zayas* (Madrid: Aldus, 1948) and Joaquín del Val, "La novela española en el siglo XVII," in *Historia general de las literaturas hispánicas* (Barcelona: Barna, 1953) 3:xliii–lxxx.

13. Ludwig Pfandl, *Historia de la literatura nacional española en la Edad de Oro*, trans. Jorge Rubió Balaguer (Barcelona: Sucesores de Juan Gili, 1933), p. 370.

14. See, for example, Kenneth Stackhouse, "Verisimilitude, Magic, and the Supernatural in the Novellas of María de Zayas," *Hispanófila* 62 (1982): 65–76.

15. Paul Julian Smith, "Writing Women in Golden Age Spain: Saint Teresa and María de Zayas," *Modern Language Notes* 102 (1987): 239.

16. Ibid., p. 239.

17. Fredric Jameson, *The Political Unconscious: Narrative as a Socially Symbolic Act* (Ithaca: Cornell University Press, 1981), p. 107.

18. For example, see Agustín de Amezúa, ed., *Novelas amorosas y ejemplares de Doña María de Zayas* (Madrid: Aldus, 1948), p. 246. All quotations from this text by Zayas refer to Amezúa's edition. His subsequent edition of her *Desengaños amorosos, Parte segunda del sarao y entretenimiento honesto* (Madrid: Aldus, 1950) is also cited.

19. Several recent studies treat this issue in a variety of interesting ways. See, in this regard, Sandra Foa, *Feminismo y forma narrativa: Estudio del tema y las técnicas de María de Zayas y Sotomayor* (Valencia: Albatros, 1979); Patricia Grieve, "Embroidering with Saintly Threads: María de Zayas Challenges Cervantes and the Church," *Renaissance Quarterly* 44 (1991): 86–105; Susan Griswold, "Topoi and Rhetorical Distance: The Feminism of María de Zayas," *Revista de Estudios Hispánicos* 14 (1980): 97–116; Elizabeth Ordóñez, "Woman and Her Text in the Works of María de Zayas and Ana Caro," *Revista de Estudios Hispánicos* (1985): 3–15.

20. Hans-Robert Jauss, *Toward an Aesthetic of Reception*, trans. Timothy Bahti (Minneapolis: University of Minnesota Press, 1982), p. 82.

21. Griswold, "Topoi and Rhetorical Distance," p. 113.

22. See, in this connection, Toril Moi's chapter "Marginality and Subversion" in her *Sexual/Textual Politics* (London: Routledge, 1985), p. 166ff.

◆

23. Jean-François Lyotard, "Answering the Question: What Is Postmodernism?" in *The Postmodern Condition: A Report on Knowledge*, trans. Geoff Bennington and Brian Massumi (Minneapolis: University of Minnesota Press, 1984), p. 81.

24. Edwin B. Place, "María de Zayas, an Outstanding Woman Short Story Writer of Seventeenth-Century Spain," *University of Colorado Studies* 13 (1923).

II

Representations of the Self

Homographesis in Salicio's Song

PAUL JULIAN SMITH

———➤ ◆———

> No soy, pues, bien mirado,
> tan difforme ni feo,
> que aun agora me veo
> en esta agua que corre clara y pura,
> y cierto no trocara mi figura
> con esse que de mí s'esta reyendo;
> ¡trocara mi ventura!
> Salid sin duelo, lagrimas, corriendo.
>
> (First Eclogue, 175–82)

[Given a good look, I am not / so deformed or ugly, / for even now I see myself / in this water that flows clear and fresh, / and I would certainly not trade my features / with the man who is laughing at me. / I would change my fortune! / Come forth unhindered, my tears, flow.]

In his critical edition of Garcilaso's works Elias Rivers cites, after the sixteenth-century commentators, a number of precedents for this stanza.[1] The most authoritative, as is acknowledged by both El Brocense and Herrera,[2] is Vergil's Second Eclogue, which treats the hopeless love of Corydon for his master's lover Alexis:

> Nec sum adeo informis, nuper me in littore uidi,
> Quum placidum uentis staret mare: non ego Daphnim
> Iudice te metuam: si nunquam fallit imago.

Herrera gives a Spanish version:

> Ni soy tan feo, que ha poco en la ribera
> me vi, cuando quieto sin los vientos

estaba el mar, no temeré yo a Dafnis
a tu juicio, si es la imagen cierta.

(p. 461)

[Nor am I so ugly, for shortly ago, on the shore, / I saw myself, when free
of the winds / the sea was still; I will not fear {a comparison to} Daphnis /
in your judgment, if the image is true.]

Rivers goes on to cite the debate that had raged since the earliest commentaries on Vergil, as to whether it was indeed possible to see one's reflection in the sea. He also cites a comic version of the motif[3] (from
Lope's *Gatomaquia*), which testifies to its wide diffusion:

Pues no soy tan feo,
que ayer me vi (mas no como me veo)
en un caldero de agua.

(p. 281n)

[Well I am not so ugly, / for yesterday I saw myself (though not the way I
look now) / in a kettle of water.]

In his *Critical Guide to Garcilaso de la Vega: Poems*, Rivers places
this fragment in context: "Salicio does not hesitate to praise his own
wealth, musical ability and handsome figure. He has simply been unfortunate, the victim of an irrational 'ventura'; . . . Galatea can have no
possible objective reason for abandoning Salicio."[4] Earlier Rivers has
stressed the dependence of the eclogue on a pastoral narrative other than
the Vergilian: Ovid's account of the jealous Cyclops Polyphemus and his
unrequited love for another Galatea: "Garcilaso expected his reader to
recognize this tradition which he was elaborating on, in quite a different
way, in Salicio's song" (p. 66). Like the shepherd, the Cyclops also
claims to see himself reflected in the ocean.

Of the two competing pre-texts, Vergil's is clearly the more prominent: in his *La trayectoria poética de Garcilaso*, Rafael Lapesa has no
hesitation in identifying Salicio with Corydon, the homosexual lover of
the Second Eclogue.[5] And the reference to "el mantuano Týtero" by
Garcilaso himself in the previous stanza has always been taken as an
homage to Vergil. However, in his study of the eclogues, *The Lyre and
the Oaten Flute: Garcilaso and the Pastoral*, Dario Fernández-Morera
cites as a precedent Vergil's Eighth Eclogue, in which Damon laments

the marriage of his female beloved, while contrasting the absence of women in Vergil with their presence in Garcilaso's pastoral world.[6] It is surprising that Fernández-Morera should neglect the homosexual precedent here; for elsewhere he claims that "the pastoral may be considered a masculine mode, in which songs to male friends or lovers have usually elicited the finest lyrics." Once more, he contrasts this classical and Italian tradition with the "narrowness" of Garcilaso, who strips the genre of many of its characteristic themes, such as the love of men (pp. 117–18). In this essay I would like to work back into the homosexual pretexts that are occluded by Garcilaso's text, but which return constantly to haunt it.[7] I will argue for a reading informed by homographesis;[8] that is, an awareness of the textual splitting of the word even where it appears to remain the same.

We may start by looking more closely at the Latin commentaries on Vergil that accompanied the text in sixteenth-century editions.[9] These reprint the traditional assertion that in the figure of Corydon, the jealous lover, Vergil chose to represent himself; and that Alexis, the scornful youth, was a slave whom Vergil had met at dinner and had received from his host as a gift: "For Virgil is said to have possessed a love for boys: and he loved him [the slave boy] not dishonorably [*nec . . . turpiter*]" (fol. 9r). This narrative is confirmed at greater length by the biographical sketch attributed to Donatus reprinted at the start of the *Opera*:

> Rumor has it that he was more prone to youths in his desire, but wise men thought that he loved them in the same way that Socrates loved Alcibiades and Plato his [youths]. Of all of them, he loved Cebes and Alexander best. The latter, whom he calls Alexis in the Second Eclogue, had been given to him by Asinius Pollio. He left the youths not unlearned [*non ineruditos*]. For Alexander became a grammarian and Cebes a poet. (fol. *iir)

What interests me here is the curious movement by which homosexual desire is simultaneously affirmed and denied. Servius and Donatus clearly take it for granted that it is the nature of some men to love their own sex; and that this love is integrated into the social structures of the day (friendship, slavery, and pedagogy). They also take it for granted that such love will be more or less directly expressed in pastoral elegy.

But they are anxious nonetheless to deny that homosexual love is dishonorable or that it might harm its object. And here we find a curious coincidence of phrasing: for Servius and Donatus use the same double negative we have seen in Garcilaso and Vergil: "nec turpiter . . . diligebat"; "non ineruditos dimisit."

Herrera writes on Garcilaso's "ni feo": "Es figura litote, cuando se dice menos y se entiende más; porque quiere parecer muy hermoso, pero huyó el odio de la jactancia" (p. 462) [It is the figure of litotes, when less is said and more is understood; because he wants to appear to be beautiful, but he fled from the hatred that boastfulness induces]. Litotes is here the figure of modesty: avoiding boastfulness by hinting at greater things while saying less. Here, once more, the sixteenth-century commentator coincides with his Latin antecedent. Servius notes of Vergil's "nec . . . informis": "he bashfully [*verecunde*] invokes his good looks [*pulchritudinem*]" (fol. 10v). However, Servius's example reveals a contradiction in litotes unstressed by Herrera. Servius cites a passage in Cicero where a man who claims to be "not bad-looking" ("non deformem") clearly meant to say that he was "most handsome" ("pulcherrimum"). Litotes, then, is a slippery figure: as an example of meiosis or rhetorical diminishing, it affirms by modestly negating the contrary. But it can also serve as a means of amplification, of boastfully asserting that which the speaker holds to be self-evident. The deceptive simplicity of litotes (from *litos*, meaning "smooth" or "plain") can thus serve as a model for the representation of homosexuality in the pastoral: it is at once asserted and denied, transparently obvious and wholly unacknowledged.

It may be no accident that this figure should occur in a passage where men seek an image of themselves reflected in nature. And once more there is a famous polemic around these lines. Thus Servius claims that to see oneself in the ocean is denied by the very nature of the world ("per rerum naturam") (fol. 10v). Vergil followed Theocritus's description of the Cyclops here. However, what was excusable for the inhuman monster ("because he had a giant eye and was the son of Neptune") is not appropriate for the mortal shepherd. Perhaps, Servius suggests, Vergil was referring to water the waves left behind in a pool on the beach.[10] But he goes on to state that the scene took place when "the sea was calm and still." Servius complains that a reflection ("imago") cannot be perceived in the sea, because the latter is not still; and that even if it were still, it would not have the power to return the image to the observer. This is part of a general mistrust of the reflection. Servius goes on to claim (against Vergil's "si numquam fallit imago") that nothing deceives more than the image: "for in a mirror we see everything back to front; and in water we see an undamaged oar as if it were broken" (10v).

This argument may seem pedantic; but it raises important questions about representing the self which are taken up by Garcilaso's commentators. Thus Herrera (p. 463) argues, against Servius, that when the wind is low reflections can indeed be perceived in the sea. After citing a number of classical and Italian authorities, he appeals to experience: "Cada uno puede haber hecho experiencia que en la agua del mar se ven los rostros, pero aunque la agua sea muy clara, si tiene hondura, prohibe y impide la vista, que no podamos ver las piedrecillas en el asiento de ella" (p. 463)[11] [Each of us may have learned by experience that one can see faces {reflected} in the sea's waters, but though it may be very clear, if it is deep it hinders and impedes one's sight, so that we are not able to see the small stones in its bed]. Here, as so often, in his attempt to resolve the question at hand the commentator raises a new problem that had not been anticipated. If the nature of water is to be transparent as well as to reflect, there is always the danger that it will display not the desired reflection of the self but the chaotic accidents of nature (the little stones on the bottom of the sea).

Thus if litotes is at once assertion and denial, then water is at once image and the negation of image. And the controversy around both of these areas (the ability of language and the world to represent the subject) is provoked by a rare moment in which a man seeks to picture himself but in order to do so must appeal to a pastoral tradition whose homosexual ethos dare not be acknowledged. We can now look more generally at that tradition and its relation to the First Eclogue.

In *The Constraints of Desire*, John Winkler has suggested a new approach to pastoral.[12] He reads the genre in the context of a "constrained life" in which resources must be husbanded and social intercourse be subject to restraint and control. For example, in Greek pastoral romance the gender of the love object is less important than the manner in which the courtship is conducted. Here as elsewhere, it is profligate expenditure of goods or words that is reprehensible and prudent economy of expenditure and diction that is praised. The pastoral is thus the space not of natural desire but of cultural negotiation: of the socialization of love. And at the center of its apparently harmonious enclosure is an institutionalized violence which enforces male dominance by repeatedly insisting on female vulnerability.

Winkler is writing on a classical text. But much of what he says holds good for Garcilaso, as it does for Vergil. Thus the motif of the gifts from shepherd to beloved (rehearsed by both Salicio and Corydon) can be read within a context in which respect for frugality imposed an awareness of the value of foodstuffs. Likewise, the disordered discourses of both shepherds signify a wasteful and chaotic mode of love, one which neglects the proper protocols. The question of the differing genders of the love objects does not apply here. The rejection of the shepherds by their respective love objects suggests the socialization of desire: the disorder that results in the pastoral landscape is not natural but is rather produced by the lovers' neglect of their social and economic responsibilities. Finally, there is the violence of their love, a violence that is wholly naturalized: neither shepherd can understand why the beloved dares scorn him. Whatever the gender of the object, she or he is denied as a matter of course the right to free choice and independent agency. Critics of Garcilaso have often read Galatea's rejection of Salicio and the latter's angry tirade against her as proof of the "unnaturalness" of her negative response. However, rather than colluding with the text in the perpetuation of these violent hierarchies (of male and female, nature and culture), we might do better to adopt Winkler's attitude to pastoral, and read "against the grain" of an androcentric genre (p. 126).

At one point Winkler cites Longus on pastoral romance as "ta tôn allôn": "the [experience] of others" (p. 107). The eclogue takes place in the locus where others have been before; the genre has an originary relationship to art. And it is clear that we find in the pastoral not just a dense play of learned allusion but also a male genealogy or pedagogy: Garcilaso cites Vergil, but he in turn cites Theocritus. And Garcilaso plays a vital role in the reproduction of a Spanish literary tradition that is naturalized as male. Thus eighteenth-century commentator José Nicolás Azara aims in his prologue to "renovar los escritos de los Patriarcas y fundadores de la Lengua Castellana"[13] by holding Garcilaso up to his readers as an example worthy of imitation. Azara complains that the current decadent state of letters in Spain is shameful. In the past the "seed" of the fifteenth century led to the "harvest" of the sixteenth, a time of "fecundity" for the Spanish mind. The works published in Philip II's time, however, were merely the "fruits" of the literary labors of the "fathers and grandfathers" of those who wrote in the period. Later, Spanish culture was "corrupted" by French translations and the introduction of "halfbreed words" (*voces mestizas*).

Here the agricultural metaphors that describe the development of a national culture coincide with the pastoral locus of Garcilaso, that culture's first "patriarch" and its unchanging model of pure diction. But more important than this coincidence between the pastoral genre and the Spanish cultural tradition is the appeal to images of generation that exclude any female agency: the reproduction of male writing is presented as parthenogenetic, an endless chain of self-generating males.

This leads us back to the question of gender in the First Eclogue. We have seen that Fernández-Morera, for one, has contrasted the absence of women in Vergil with their greater prominence in Garcilaso. But while women are much invoked in the First Eclogue, they never actually appear: Galatea is absent and (later) Elisa is dead. And Salicio's song has a further parallel with Vergil's homosexual antecedent. This is the triangular structure of desire. Thus both Salicio and Corydon rage against their male rivals. And in the lines we have examined in this essay, each invokes another male as witness to his own self-image: Salicio would change not his face but his fortune for the nameless man who has bested him; Corydon will not fear his fellow shepherd Daphnis, if the image shown to him by the sea does not lie.

I would suggest that here, as in the male genealogy of great Castilian writers, we find a homosocial relationship which, while claiming to be heterosexual, effectively works to exclude women. We can thus uncover a hidden bond between men. As Eve Kosofsky Sedgwick puts it: "In any erotic rivalry, the bond that links the two rivals is as intense and potent as the bond that links either of the rivals to the beloved."[14] The vehemence of Salicio's lament would tend to bear this out, as does his reliance on a male rival to confirm his own sense of self. To cite Sedgwick once more, this time on Shakespeare's sonnets: "My point is not that we are here in the presence of homosexuality (which would be anachronistic) but rather (risking anachronism) that we are here in the presence of male heterosexual desire, in the form of a desire to consolidate partnership with authoritative males in and through the bodies of females" (p. 38). In the First Eclogue the relationship between the various male figures (and indeed their very identities) remains vague. For example, the two shepherds are simply juxtaposed in time and space ("Salicio juntamente y Nemoroso"). But there is little doubt that this discursive space between men (which need not be described, which is wholly taken for granted) exists only at the cost of the definitive exclusion of (absent or dead) women from that same space.

Salicio compares his face to his rival lover and his song to his rival poet, the Mantuan Vergil. In this traffic of homosocial reproduction the imaging of the self in water seems to have a particular significance. The history of the pastoral is quite literally one of displacement: the locus shifts from Greece to Italy to Spain. And in its density of reference to past authorities (to "the experience of others"), the pastoral poses the threat of an uncontrollable metonymic contagion in which the same fragments of amorous discourse are endlessly repeated. In "Homographesis" Lee Edelman argues that the ceaseless metonymic movement of desire is curtailed by a logic of metaphoric identity.[15] The latter imposes a frozen, specular image of the self on the random contingency of events. To take a characteristic example, the "fact" of sexual object choice, which was felt in antiquity to be contingent and devoid of meaning, came in the nineteenth century to be (mis)recognized by subjects as the hidden truth of their being, the essential key to their identity. There can be no more violent scene of the imposition of identity over the contingencies of the world, no more transparent attempt to halt metonymic contagion, than the shepherd's claim to recognize himself in the sea, an act the earliest commentators claim to be "against nature." It seems possible, then, to read this "recognition scene" as a symptom of homosocial panic: it testifies to an attempt to break the chain of proliferating male images, to stop the movement of a desire which might well lead on or back to improper relations between men.

Homographesis is at once the constitution of the homosexual as a body to be "read" and interpreted and the investiture of writing itself by the logic of the same. Its figure is the homograph, a word that looks identical to another but whose meaning and derivation are quite different. I would suggest that the homograph is a way of approaching the vexed question of the autobiographical reading of Garcilaso's eclogues. In spite of the rhetorical bias of classical and Renaissance poetics, commentators of both Vergil and Garcilaso seem happy to identify their respective shepherds biographically with the poets themselves and their friends. But in both cases the identifications are disputed. Thus, as is well known, "Salicio" is a partial anagram of "Garcilaso" but is also derived from *salex*, the willow. And "Nemoroso" clearly derives from *nemus* or wood but could refer to either his friend Boscán ("bosque") or once more, Vega himself. Herrera claims that the latter refers to Isabel's husband, but gives no etymological evidence to support his theory (p. 423). The multiple derivations of Garcilaso's names thus suggest not only that the single word is open to many interpretations but that those interpretations are wholly arbitrary, based on the contingencies of pun and polyglot coincidence. Onomastics (the naming of the self) leads to homographesis (the dispersal of that self in writing).

Garcilaso's practice of imitation might also be read as homographesis. Imitation has always implied a dangerous confusion of the same, an inability to distinguish between self and other. Even in the eighteenth century Azara still finds it necessary to defend Garcilaso from charges of plagiarism. By reproducing almost exactly (as he does in our stanza) the words of an authoritative homosexual precedent, Garcilaso cannot prevent the literate sixteenth-century reader from calling that precedent to mind.[16] Indeed, he himself signposts that identification through the reference to "el mantuano." However, by placing those canonic words within an unambiguously heterosexual context, he renders them the same, but different, cleft down the middle. The irony, then, is that a scene of self-recognition, of the violent imposition of identity on the world, should at the same time raise questions about the constitution of that identity and the role of sexual object choice in its production.

A final example will further illustrate the pleasures and the dangers of male relationships in the period. When Castiglione's courtiers discuss friendship, they take it for granted that the most intimate relationships are between men.[17] Federico stresses how important it is to choose friends wisely, because of the dangers of sameness or identity: since like attracts like, everyone assumes that a man will have the same character as his indissoluble companion. Bembo answers that care should also be taken because there are so few true friends to be found nowadays. Couples such as Pylades and Orestes, Theseus and Pirithous, or Scipio and Laelius no longer exist. Federico replies that, in spite of this, men cannot be happy without a perfect friendship that will endure until death. But that bond should not involve more than two people or it may become dangerous: harmony is easier to achieve between two instruments than between many (pp. 137–38).

The connection between Castiglione's prose dialogue and Garcilaso's pastoral verse may not seem evident. But we find in this passage the same homosocial mechanisms we saw in the eclogue. On the one hand, there is the logic of identity or reflection: men see themselves in each other's eyes, in the mirror image of their own sameness. On the other hand, there is the danger of proliferation: beyond the narcissistic dyad of subject and reflection lies chaos, an endless displacement of uncontrollable relationships or dissonant melodies. We see also once more the constant reference to a classical world which was at once the experience of others and the confirmation of the same (of the fragile continuity of relations between men).

To read Garcilaso (or Castiglione) as homographesis, then, is not to seek some homosexual identity or tradition secreted within or behind their texts. Rather it is to explore homosexuality as (in Lee Edelman's words) the "ambiguous intersection of the metaphorical and the metonymic"; and hence to interrogate "the repressive ideology of similitude or identity itself" (p. 204). Salicio's song thus helps to disclose the historical constraints of that homosocial desire that exists between men but cannot be recognized by them.

Notes

    1. Garcilaso de la Vega, *Obras completas con comentario*, ed. Elias Rivers (Madrid: Castalia, 1981).

    2. Antonio Gallego Morell, *Garcilaso de la Vega y sus comentaristas* (Madrid: Gredos, 1972).

3. Two later examples of the motif show the variety of expression it provoked. Thus Quevedo in a love sonnet ("Esforzaron mis ojos la corriente") sticks closely to the original: "no es tan fiero el rostro mío" (*Poesía original*, ed. José Manuel Blecua [Barcelona: Planeta, 1974], no. 318). Góngora's version in the *Polifemo* is much more elaborate: "que espejo de záfiro fue luciente / la playa azul de la persona mía" (cited by Antonio Vilanova with a number of other versions in *Las fuentes y los temas del "Polifemo"* [Madrid: Revista de Filología Española, 1957], 2:595).

4. Elias Rivers, ed., *Garcilaso de la Vega: Poems* (London: Grant and Cutler, 1980), p. 68.

5. Rafael Lapesa, *La trayectoria poética de Garcilaso* (Madrid: Istmo, 1985), p. 125.

6. Dario Fernández-Morera, *The Lyre and the Oaten Flute: Garcilaso and the Pastoral* (London: Tamesis, 1981), p. 39.

7. Another example of the occlusion of a homosexual pre-text by Garcilaso and his critics is the treatment of Orpheus. Thus critics have called attention to the reference to Orpheus's dismembered body in the Third Eclogue without mentioning the cause of the hero's death: Anne J. Cruz, *Imitación y transformación: el petrarquismo en la poesía de Boscán y Garcilaso* (Amsterdam: Benjamins, 1988), p. 103. Suzanne Guillou-Varga also fails to refer to this aspect of the myth in *Mythes, mythographies, et poésie lyrique au siècle d'or espagnol* (Paris: Didier, 1988). For a recent account of homosexuality and Renaissance literature outside Spain, see James M. Saslow, "Homosexuality in the Renaissance: Behavior, Identity, and Artistic Expression," in *Hidden from History: Reclaiming the Gay and Lesbian Past*, ed. Martin Duberman, Martha Vicinus, and George Chauncey (New York: Penguin, 1990), pp. 90–105.

8. See Lee Edelman's major article "Homographesis," *Yale Journal of Criticism* 3 (1989): 189–207.

9. I cite from *P. Virgilii Maronis opera cum Servii, Donati, et Ascensii commentariis* (Venice, 1542). Translations from Latin are my own.

10. Ascensius suggests that the reflecting surface may be a puddle of rainwater (fol. 11r).

11. Garcilaso, of course, is not referring to the sea but to running water; but Herrera must defend him from the same charge made against Vergil.

12. John Winkler, *The Constraints of Desire* (New York: Routledge, 1990). In the paragraph that follows I paraphrase Winkler's chapter on Longus: "The Education of Chloe: Hidden Injuries of Sex" (pp. 101–26).

13. José Nicolás Azara, ed., *Obras de Garcilaso de la Vega ilustradas con notas* (Madrid, 1765). The "Prólogo del editor" is unnumbered. Although Azara's

annotations are few in number, he does cite Vergil's Second Eclogue as a precedent for the reflection scene in Garcilaso.

14. Eve Kosofsky Sedgwick, *Between Men: English Literature and Male Homosocial Desire* (New York: Columbia University Press, 1985), p. 21.

15. In *Poesía y reflexión: la palabra en el tiempo* (Madrid: Taurus, 1980), Manuel Ballestero writes of a "principle of identity" in Garcilaso exemplified by the use of pleonastic adjectives (p. 58). This is comparable on a rhetorical level to the thematic motif of reflection in water that I treat here.

16. Spanish poets were clearly aware of the homosexual background to classical verse. Thus Quevedo claims, unconvincingly, that the reader can discriminate between Anacreon's male and female portraits: "Cuando Anacreón pinta a Batylo en sus obras, no dijo más de que pintasen su hermosura; y tratando en la pintura de su señora ausente . . . , pintando sus labios, dice que inciten y persuaden a besarlos. . . . Y en todas las obras suyas se ve que amó mujeres claramente, y que fue perdido galán suyo." Quevedo goes on to note that Greek writers who favored "the illicit Venus" made no secret of their preference. *Obras completas*, ed. Luis Astrana Marín (Madrid: Aguílar, 1932), p. 674. I have written elsewhere on Spanish reluctance to praise male beauty, so different from the Italian amplifications of the topic: "*Descriptio pueri*: Praise of the Young Hero in Some Poets of Renaissance Spain and Italy," *Studi Secenteschi* 24 (1983): 57–66; *The Body Hispanic: Gender and Sexuality in Spanish and Spanish American Literature* (Oxford: Clarendon, 1989), p. 52.

17. Baldesar Castiglione, *The Book of the Courtier*, trans. George Bull (Harmondsworth: Penguin, 1987).

CHAPTER

7

Literary Continuity, Social Order,
and the Invention of the Picaresque

HARRY SIEBER

In the exploration of various interrelations between literature and history in the second half of the sixteenth century in Spain, my main interests are those points of contact between literature as a process of imitation and renewal, of "new" texts re-creating "old" texts on the one hand, and historical tradition on the other, or rather, tradition as a cultural force in history. "For the literary historian and critic"—and here I intentionally abuse a quotation from Robert Weimann in order to make it my own—the problem "is not whether to accept both worlds and points of reference, but rather, since each is so inevitable and necessary, how to relate them so as to discover the degree and consequences of their connections."[1] José Antonio Maravall's *La literatura picaresca desde la historia social* is a recent example of an attempt to articulate such relationships through the language of a social history of *mentalités* in an age of crisis and decline and in a world, defined in another context by Theodore K. Rabb, "where everything had been thrown into doubt, where uncertainty and instability reigned."[2]

For the purposes of this essay I focus more narrowly on Spain's cultural preoccupation with its origins in the process of exploiting continuation as a way of celebrating the empowering myths that serve as its self-legitimation. The manifestations of this reappropriation of the past are contingent with Pierre Bourdieu's general observation in *Outline of a Theory of Practice*: "If all societies that seek to produce a new man through a process of 'deculturation' and 'reculturation' set such store on

143

the seemingly most insignificant details of dress, bearing, physical and verbal manners, the reason is that, treating the body as a memory, they entrust to it in abbreviated and practical, i.e., mnemonic form the fundamental principles of the arbitrary content of the culture."[3] Bourdieu's remarks seem especially relevant to the literature, history, and culture of late-sixteenth-century Spain when translations, adaptations, and imitations of Italian treatises of courtly conduct—of manners—coincided with debates over honor, status, and identity.

Courtesy literature, as Frank Whigham has written, must be viewed as "having an intricate social purpose combining poetry and politics, philosophical speculation and social combat, ritual pageantry and ambition," because the "court was simultaneously an arena of conflict and a mart of opportunity as well as a radiant center of order."[4] Whigham refers to Elizabethan England, but much of his argument can be applied to late-sixteenth-century Spain as well. Spain, like England, had its own "educational revolution," producing a surge of educated men in search of social mobility and ladders of opportunity in law, the church, the military, and governmental administration.[5] And as in England, "movement across the gap between ruling and subject classes was becoming increasingly possible, and elite identity came to be a function of action rather than of birth—to be achieved rather than ascribed."[6] In addition, Ruth Kelso (again writing of Elizabethan England) also reflects the Spanish scene: "Those who lacked the title [of gentlemen] were busy trying to acquire it . . . those who had it were anxious to resist encroachment."[7] One of the paths toward the achievement of such status was to embrace courtesy books as perceptive manuals, which Stephen Greenblatt has characterized as "handbooks for actors, practical guides for a society whose members were nearly always on stage, . . . offering an integrated rhetoric of the self, a model for the formation of an artificial identity."[8]

The extent to which the translations and adaptations of the works of Castiglione and his descendants—Guazzo, della Casa, Riminaldo— played a comparable role in the Spanish court is still unknown.[9] We do know that Castiglione's *Book of the Courtier* was reprinted at least fourteen times in Spain after being translated by Juan Boscán in 1534,[10] and that by 1591 Juan Benito Guardiola's *Tratado de la nobleza* had transformed Castiglione's *gentiluomo* into a Spanish *caballero*. By the late 1580s, strategies for advancement in the court had become a parlor game. Alonso de Barros's treatise *Filosofía cortesana moralizada* (1587), first introduced to its readers with a sonnet by a relatively unknown Miguel de Cervantes, was actually an instruction manual that accompanied a board game not unlike Monopoly, in which, with the throw of the dice and the right moves, one could land on a space called Good Fortune, arrange a meeting with the king's favorite, and win the pot. However, one could also land on spaces—called "casas"—such as the *Mudanza de ministros* or *La muerte del valedor* and lose what had been gained and be forced to begin the game again at the *Puerta de la opinión*.[11] For many at court, such activity was no trivial pursuit but rather a matter of life or death, as the famous case of Rodrigo Calderón would later attest.

It is also important to note that the historical situation in Spain had prepared the way for the reception of such treatises. Charles V, for instance, continued the practice of his predecessors by elevating those not born to nobility who rendered military and financial service to the crown. "Government service," as John Elliott has written, "could lead to dramatic social advancement, as the career of Charles V's secretary, Francisco de los Cobos, spectacularly demonstrated."[12] Some merchant families gained noble status through entry into the military orders, and by marriage into the ranks, as Ruth Pike has pointed out in her study of Genoese traders in Seville, and as Henri La Peyre has argued with regard to the Ruiz family of Medina del Campo.[13] While Philip II seems to have cast a suspicious eye on the nobility and their proximity to the sources of power in government service, the demand for honor and a place near the king reached a critical juncture at the end of his reign, perhaps as the result of increasing taxes levied throughout the century, taxes from which only those of noble status were exempt. Becoming a nobleman from mid-century on implied more than acquiring honorable status. Even with the introduction of the "Servicio de los millones" in 1590, a consumer tax placed on basic foodstuffs, those landowners of noble descent who lived in Madrid could import their own supplies of food without having to pay taxes, thus providing for themselves some financial buffer from all taxation policies imposed by both royal and local governments by the end of the sixteenth century.

After the king's death in September 1598, Francisco Gómez de Sandoval y Rojas, the Marquis of Denia who would soon become the Duke of Lerma, quickly began to consolidate his power over the new king and the court. Some three months later, in January 1599, the contemporary court historian Cabrera de Córdoba was able to report that "la privanza y lugar que el marques de Denia tiene con S.M. desde que heredó, va cada día en aumento sin conocerse que haya otro privado semejante, porque son muy estraordinarios los favores que se le hacen"[14] [the favor and position the Marquis of Denia has gained with His Majesty from the moment he became king is increasing every day unchallenged, as evidenced by the extraordinary favors with which the king showers him]. Patronage, status and honor, lineage and wealth became matters of immediate concern and debate in a court in which a favorite held power. Lerma and the men he had appointed around him would virtually become the source of "royal" patronage as Philip III removed himself from the day-to-day affairs of government. Antonio Feros has recently demonstrated that "monopolio del favor, lisonja, interés privado y compraventa fueron . . . prácticas que socavaron la distribución del patronazgo real"[15] [monopoly of favor, flattery, personal interest, and venality were . . . practices that undermined the distribution of royal patronage] and characterized the regime of Lerma and his favorites. Thus Philip II, often distant and isolated at the Escorial monastery but obsessively in charge of his government, was succeeded by Philip III, who left government to others and whose court in Madrid provided a larger, more public space in which status, identity, and former codes of courtly conduct were subjects of debate.

Many of Philip II's ministers and court functionaries were exiled or expelled from service, and new men with relatively unknown backgrounds and experience, such as Pedro Franqueza (secretary to the queen), Rodrigo Calderón (secretary to the Cámara del Rey), and Silva de Torres (alcalde de casa y corte; corregidor of Madrid), found themselves with new power and authority. At the same time these men actively sought to control access to their ranks by neutralizing those who questioned their power. More significant for us is the fact that it was precisely at this moment that a little novel first published almost fifty years previously, *La vida de Lazarillo de Tormes*, was reprinted as an appendix to Lucas Gracián Dantisco's Spanish translation of Giovanni della Casa's *Galateo*.[16] Why the *Lazarillo*, principally known for its subtle irony and biting satire of a cruel beggar and priest, proud nobleman, fraudulent pardoner, hypocritical chaplain, and venal archpriest, reappeared at this moment to become part of such a volume is the question I hope to answer by placing it in the context of the literature of manners, the formation of a new court, and the invention of the picaresque novel.

Claudio Guillén has pointed out that *La vida de Lazarillo de Tormes* has been made an integral part of the history of the picaresque novel at the turn of the seventeenth century primarily by publishers and readers, and more specifically through Ginés de Pasamonte's famous reference to its title in *Don Quijote*.[17] The 1554 edition was placed on Inquisitor Valdés's 1559 *Index of Prohibited Books*. There is no evidence of the novel's being reprinted in Spain until 1573, and only then in the censored version of Juan López de Velasco, Philip II's cosmographer and principal chronicler, whose primary fame today is based on his authorship of *La geografía y descripción universal de las Indias*. Because Velasco's edition was most likely the version of the *Lazarillo* available to readers at the turn of the seventeenth century, I would like to identify him briefly and to outline the role he may have played in resurrecting the novel.

Juan López de Velasco was recommended for his position at the Escorial library by Juan de Ovando y Godoy, one of Philip II's trusted advisors and president of the Council of the Indies in the late 1560s.[18] Ovando was also a member of the Council of the Inquisition. Both Ovando and Velasco corresponded with Benito Arias Montano, who was in Antwerp during these same years on official business, presiding over a committee charged with compiling an updated list of prohibited and expurgated books.[19] The exchange of letters between Ovando, Velasco, and Montano also reveals that Montano was involved in the book market in general, buying and shipping great quantities of material for

Ovando's personal library as well as for the library at the Escorial. Montano was thorough in his work. In his letter to Ovando, dated August 2, 1571, he was able to assure his superior that "el libro o índice expurgatorio se está imprimiendo: será una cosa de grande provecho; porque, de cuantos libros admitían expurgación no se ha dejado de ver y examinar cosa y darse sentencia sobre cada lugar dellos con toda equidad"[20] [the book, or index, of expurgated works is at press. It will be of great benefit, for among the books that could be expurgated, nothing has been left unscrutinized or unexamined, and the books have been judged with the utmost fairness]. It is possible that the *Lazarillo* was one of these "cuantos libros."[21]

Velasco for his part had a number of interests beyond writing and copying letters and compiling data for his history of the Indies. He was particularly fascinated with spoken and written Spanish, publishing his *Ortografía y pronunciación castellana* in 1582, and with educational reform, as indicated by his *Instrucción para examinar los maestros de escuela de la lengua castellana y enseñar a leer y escribir a los niños.*[22] His sensitivity to matters of language and style no doubt accounts for his interest in the *Lazarillo* and other Spanish texts that had already appeared in Valdés's catalog of prohibited books. The fact that Velasco's version is based on the 1554 Antwerp edition of the novel rather than on the Burgos or Alcalá editions of the same year suggests that communication between Ovando and Montano may have played an important role in supporting Velasco's efforts to obtain permission or even with the text that was printed in Madrid two years later, by itself or with other previously prohibited works,[23] as Velasco's prologue indicates:

> Aunque este tratadillo de la vida de Lazarillo de Tormes, no es de tanta consideración en lo que toca a la lengua, como las obras de Christóbal de Castillejo y Bartolomé de Torres Naharro, es una representación tan biva y propria de aquello que imita con tanto donayre y gracia, que en su tanto merece ser estimado, y assi fue siempre a todos muy acepto, de cuya causa *aunque estaba prohibido en estos reynos, se leya, y imprimía de ordinario fuera dellos.*[24]
> [Even though this short treatise on the life of Lazarillo de Tormes is not, when it comes to language, as worthy of consideration as the works of

Christobal de Castillejo and Bartolomé de Torres Naharro, it is such a lively and fitting representation of what it charmingly and wittily imitates, that as a whole it is deserving of esteem; and as such everyone always found it appealing, which is why *despite being prohibited in this kingdom, it was commonly published and read outside of it.*]

Velasco's rescue of three Spanish "classics" coincided with the Inquisition's strategy: his newly available *Lazarillo* would eventually replace the relatively few surviving 1554 originals (if any) or manuscript copies made from them. Given the tone of mid-sixteenth-century Spanish censorship, it was more acceptable to have a "corrected" *Lazarillo* circulating at the time than to allow the continued reading of its original prohibited version.

After 1573—with the possible exception of a Tarragona edition of 1586—there is, according to Claudio Guillén and others, no explicit reference to *Lazarillo* the novel in Spain until 1599. It seems that perhaps earlier, however, our novel acquired new life as it began to circulate with the *Galateo español*.[25] Miguel Martínez, a Madrid bookseller with a somewhat tarnished reputation, added an anonymous translation from Italian of another courtesy book, Oracio Riminaldo's *Destierro de ignorancia*, obtaining permission to print and sell all three works in one volume "que *otras veces* con su licencia han sido impressos" (Medina del Campo, 1603) [which *on other occasions* have been printed with his license], indicating that the novel reached its audience perhaps earlier and was more widely distributed at the end of the century as part of a trilogy.[26] Here it is important to note that the project was initiated and financed by Martínez ("a costa de . . . ," the title page informs us), who would have hired Luis Sánchez to print all three *tratados* together. Martínez, then, was the one who clearly perceived a common thread linking the *Lazarillo* to the *Galateo*, and then to the *Destierro*: together they constituted a courtesy book aimed at a specific group of readers. Martínez's marketing strategy is revealing in this regard: the second edition containing all three treatises was published in Valladolid in 1603 and the third in Medina del Campo the same year.

These locations coincided with the movement of the court of Philip III at the beginning of the century. Despite considerable public protest, the court, through the Duke of Lerma's influence, was moved from Madrid to Valladolid in 1601. And to make room for the large bureaucracy that accompanied the court, nearby Medina del Campo was chosen as the place for the royal tribunal and its various judges, lawyers, and secretaries.[27] Only when Madrid regained royal favor with bribes and special real estate deals for Lerma, his family, and the men he had placed in office did the court return in 1606.[28] It seems evident that the readers Martínez had in mind were those literate courtiers, government bureaucrats, merchants, and hangers-on who followed the court and who, according to Madrid's city fathers, numbered in the hundreds.[29] Martínez's own travels during these years followed the same itinerary. He had operated a bookshop in the Patio of the Alcázar as early as 1591; in 1601, soon after pirating an edition of Mateo Alemán's *Guzmán de Alfarache*,[30] he too moved to Valladolid, where he opened another shop to serve his recently departed clients.

Without detailing all the appropriate forms of courtly behavior listed by Lucas Gracián, many of which are direct translations from della Casa's treatise, it is enough to point out that his manual is designed to communicate to his readers one of the potential sources of honor and privilege in the court: the art of winning the goodwill and favor of others through the use of proper language and behavior. Acceptable speech, forms of address, table manners, topics of conversation, dress, and ceremony are illustrated, often through negative examples. At one point Lucas Gracián seems to recall an incident that takes place in the squire episode of the *Lazarillo*:

> Muchas veces acaece . . . venir a reñir y enemistarse, . . . quando un ciudadano dexa de honrar a otro como es costumbre, no quitándole la gorra, ni hablándole con crianza. . . . Y ansi quien llamasse de vos a otro, no siendo muy más calificado, le menosprecia y haze ultrage en nombralle, pues se sabe que con semejantes palabras llaman a los peones y travajadores. (Morreale, p. 132)
>
> [Many times it happens that citizens fight one another and become enemies . . . when one fails to honor the other as is customary, refusing to tip his hat or to speak properly. . . . And thus one who addresses the other as "vos," not being of higher rank, insults him and commits an outrage in re-

ferring to him in this way, because it is known that with such words one refers to common peasants and laborers.]

Then there is advice related to bearing and dress: "Y hay algunos de tal manera que ponen todo el gusto y su felicidad y cuidado en sus vestidos y compostura exterior . . . son fríos, inútiles y de poca sustancia en su trato y conversación, que no son más que para mirados, o topados en la calle" (p. 114) [There are some who put all pleasure, happiness, and care in their clothing and exterior demeanor . . . {but} are cold, useless, and of little substance in their behavior and conversation; they only want to be seen or encountered in the street]. He also refers to clearly unacceptable behavior when he narrates the following scene, again taken from della Casa, which would later be associated with the court satire of Quevedo:

Hase visto . . . otra mala costumbre de algunos que suenan las narizes con mucha fuerça y páranse delante de todos a mirar en el pañizuelo lo que se han sonado, como si aquello que por allí han purgado, fuesse perlas o diamantes que le cayessen del celebro.   (p. 109) [You have seen another evil custom of those who blow their noses with great force and then stop in front of everyone to look in their handkerchiefs at the results, as if what they discharged were pearls or diamonds that have fallen from their brains.]

Unfortunately, searching for pearls or diamonds in the discharge of one's nostrils was not the place where wealth and power would be found in the court of Philip III.

It may be useful at this point to describe briefly some of the main differences between the *Lazarillo* of 1554 and Velasco's censored text because, as I have noted elsewhere, it was López de Velasco's version of the novel that was most likely read by Cervantes, Mateo Alemán, and Francisco de Quevedo, as well as by other writers of picaresque fiction during the first years of the seventeenth century. The excised fourth and fifth chapters and various sentences and words may seem at first glance to reflect little damage, but the sharp scissors wielded by the censor and approved by the Inquisition weakened the novel's anticlerical tone and suppressed central episodes, one of which, according to Raymond Willis, is artistically necessary for our modern understanding of the final half of the book.[31] Seventeenth-century readers learned that Lazarillo's father confessed but was not allowed to deny his crimes, and while his father is still located in "heaven" ("la gloria") he is not called one of the "blessed" ("bienaventurados"). A paragraph that compares Lazarillo's stepfather to "clerics and friars" who steal from the poor to support their religious houses is conspicuously absent. The third chapter with the squire is left intact. The Mercedarian friar and the fraudulent pardoner in the fourth and fifth chapters never make an appearance. The structure of the novel also changed. The episode of the blind beggar was extracted to become a separate chapter, "Assiento de Lázaro con el ciego," and Lazarillo's adventures as a water seller, paint grinder, constable's assistant, and town crier are collapsed into one: "Lázaro assienta con un capellán y un alguazil y después toma manera de vivir" (fol. 278r).[32]

By the end of the sixteenth century, the *Lazarillo* would have been for its original author a different book, emphasizing primarily the lessons learned by Lazarillo about how to manipulate others through language, the lack of charity as exemplified by the episode with the priest, the shame of poverty and importance of honor of the squire, and the ironic success Lazarillo claims at the end of his life as he boasts of his position as town crier. The centerpiece of the new *Lazarillo* is the squire episode, which clearly attracted the attention of Miguel Martínez and the court with its critique of ritualized manners, proper speech, courtly dress, distinguished lineage, and powerful role of honor. We are told, for instance, that the squire was born in Valladolid. After he arrives in Toledo, he is described by Lazarillo as he leaves his rented house "con un paso sosegado y el cuerpo derecho, haciendo con él y con la cabeza muy gentiles meneos, echando el cabo de la capa sobre el hombro y a veces so el brazo, y poniendo la mano derecha en el costado"[33] [walking slowly, holding his body straight and swaying gracefully, placing the tail of the cape over his shoulder or sometimes under his arm, and putting his right hand on his chest]. When he attends mass, Lazarillo continues, his master wishes only to be seen by others, remaining through "los otros oficios divinos, hasta que todo fue acabado y la gente ida. Entonces salimos de la iglesia" (p. 73) [the other holy ceremonies very devoutly until they had ended and the people had gone. Then we left the church]. The squire carefully straps on his sword, proudly displaying it as if it were a fine piece of jewelry—and just as useless, Lazarillo implies, because it is used only as decoration. The squire embodies the proud and mannered nobleman whose rhetoric of courtly manners fails to provide him with that artificial identity to find a place in Toledo's closed society, an example that was unlikely to be lost on those who sought honor and privilege in the court of Philip III.

The Velasco/Martínez *Lazarillo* is "picaresque" in the narrowest historical sense because it is the version mentioned in all probability by Cervantes in the "Galley Slaves" episode of *Don Quijote* and is closely associated with the word *pícaro* in Mateo Alemán's *Guzmán de Alfarache*. Recall that Guzmán becomes a *pícaro* in Book 2 after he arrives in Madrid ("Trátase cómo vino a ser pícaro y lo que siéndolo le sucedió"[34] [{This second book} deals with how he became a *pícaro* and what happened to him]). The story continues through Chapter 8 with his journey to Toledo. Guzmán enters the city at night, but before appearing in public the next morning he quickly changes his attire, "vistiéndose muy galán" (1:329) [dressing like a gentleman]. More importantly, these chapters are shot through with references to honor, the same subject that obsessed the squire in the *Lazarillo de Tormes*. In Alemán's text Guzmán sermonizes against the vanity of honor: "¿Qué sabes o quién sabe del mayordomo del rey don Pelayo ni del camarero del conde Fernán González? Honra tuvieron y la sustentaron y dellos ni della se tiene memoria. Pues así mañana serás olvidado" (1:281) [What is known or who knows about King Pelayo's majordomo or of Count Fernan Gonzalez's servant? They acquired honor and lived by it and no one remembers them or their honor]. But it is not only honor that Guzmán criticizes; he also attacks its trappings and rituals. Attempting to sustain honor is self-effacing because it precludes the possibility of individualizing one's identity; instead the self is invented and sustained by others. "¡Oh . . . lo que carga el peso de la honra y como no hay metal que se le iguale! ¡A cuánto está obligado el desventurado que della hubiere de usar! ¡Qué mirado y medido ha de andar! . . . y cuán fácil de perder por la común estimación!" (1:266–67) [Oh . . . how heavy is the weight of honor and how no metal equals it! How obligated is he who uses it!

How he must look and walk! . . . and how easy it is to lose it in the esteem of others!]. Honor demands a rule-governing form of behavior: costume, manners, proper forms of address, gaining the friendship and favor of others, and avoiding the appearance of poverty point to an imprisoned existence. This is precisely the problem of the squire in the *Lazarillo*: the artificiality of his studied manners and ostentatious dress are emphasized by his claims to be able to lie, flatter, laugh, and serve "titled gentlemen" better than anyone else despite his poverty and new identity.

Such mannered behavior for Guzmán, then, is seen as a form of imprisonment; he speaks of the "freedom" he has by not joining those who choose to live by the strict rules of honor. Like Lazarillo, he too becomes a beggar to feed himself and refers to crop failures as the reason for lack of charity in Toledo: "Dábase muy poco limosna y no era maravilla, que en general fue el año esteril y, si estaba mala la Andalucía, peor cuánto más adentro del reino de Toledo y mucha más necesidad había de los puertos adentro" (1:263) [Very few alms were given because of crop failures everywhere, and if it was bad in Andalucia it was worse in the kingdom of Toledo and even worse in the city itself]. Despite his use of flattering language, his dress and behavior broadcast his poverty and reputation and determine the role he will play in Madrid: "Viéndome tan despedazado, aunque procuré acreditarme con palabras y buscar a quien servir, ninguno se aseguraba de mis obras ni quería meterme dentro de casa en su servicio, porque estaba muy asqueroso y desmantelado. Creyeron ser algún pícaro ladroncillo que los había de robar y acogerme" (1:263) [Seeing myself in such rags, although I tried to gain confidence and look for someone to serve, no one could be certain about my deeds nor wanted to place me in his house as servant, because I was filthy and ruinous. They believed I was a thieving *pícaro* who would rob them and escape].

The more freedom he seeks, the further he alienates himself from the social hierarchy he hopes to join, until he becomes a "pícaro de cocina" (1:287). He is told by his master, however, that someday he might become a magistrate and enter "la casa real y que, sirviendo tantos años, . . . retirarme rico a mi casa" (1:287) [the royal household, and after serving a certain number of years . . . retire a wealthy man to my estate]. When he returns to Madrid after his journey to Italy, he initiates his strategy to gain admittance to the court in order to sell his stolen jewelry by choosing and wearing the proper clothes in order to associate with his gentlemen clients: "Comencé mi negocio por galas y más galas. Hice dos diferentes vestidos de calza entera, muy gallardos. Otro saqué llano para remudar, pareciéndome que con aquello, si comprase un caballo, que quien así me viera, y con un par de criados, fácilmente me compraría las joyas que llevaba" (2:320–21) [I began my trade with finery and courtly dress. I made two different outfits with long stockings, very elegant. I took out another pair to change into, appearing to me that if I were to buy a horse whoever would see me (and with a couple of servants) would readily buy the jewelry I had].

These hurried references to the *Guzmán* and the *Lazarillo* suggest an intertextual reading that announces the origins of the picaresque and its association with the court. Alemán closely follows the historical definition of the *pícaro* given to us by sixteenth-century texts: "pícaro de cocina," "pícaro vagabundo," that is, the *pícaro* who formed an integral part of the growing urban population that contributed to Madrid's demographic explosion at the end of the sixteenth century. He combines historical, immediate experience with the central problem of honor and its rituals as explored in the *Lazarillo*. His master tells him: "Aquí verás, Guzmán, lo que es la honra, pues a éstos la dan. El hijo de nadie, que se levantó del polvo de la tierra, siendo vasija quebradiza, llena de agujeros, rota, sin capacidad que en ella cupiera cosa de algún momento, la remendó con trapos el favor, y con la soga del interés ya sacan agua con ella y parece de provecho" (1:278) [Here you see, Guzman, what honor is, because to these it is given. The son of a nobody who raises himself up from the dust of the earth is like a leaking vessel full of holes, without the capacity to contain anything of substance; favor patched it with rags, and with the rope of interest others are able to bring it up filled with water and with profit too]. The shift from worthlessness and poverty to material gain and success through the "patchwork" of favors is a movement from the historical *pícaro* inherited by Alemán to the redefined *pícaro* of the court: the basic "vessel" remains the same. The power of goodwill and favor to win and maintain a position at court with flattering words and proper dress and behavior, central to Gracián Dantisco's project in the *Galateo español*, is the target of Alemán's critique of what he perceived to be the arbitrary nature of honor and privilege at the end of the sixteenth century in Spain.

In order to demonstrate how and why the *Galateo*, the *Lazarillo*, and the *Guzmán* found an enthusiastic audience in the first years of the seventeenth century, I must turn briefly to another novel—described variously as the zenith or nadir of the picaresque genre—Francisco de Quevedo's *La vida del Buscón*, written about 1604, according to the most recent authorities,[35] but not published until 1626. Quevedo's novel tells a story, a simple but grotesque story, about the son of a thief and a prostitute who seeks to deny his blood by falsifying his lineage in order to become a gentleman and to gain admittance to polite society, that is, to live an honorable life in the court. To use Alemán's metaphor, Pablos, the "son of nobody," a "broken vessel" made up of "dust of the earth," seeks honor and profit in the court through special favor and connections. He hopes to become part of Madrid's society by acting like a gentleman, by associating with others of rank, and by marrying into the right family. Quevedo's readers discover that Pablos's efforts to adopt the style of the court fail, that his true identity is discovered, that he abandons Madrid, traveling to Seville, where like many of his kind in the sixteenth and seventeenth centuries, he escapes to the Indies in the hope of improving his fortune.

But Pablos is not the only character who seeks to break through social barriers by speaking, behaving, and dressing like a gentleman. All characters in the *Buscón* pretend to be of higher rank than they are. Pablos's reputed father is a barber who insists that he be called a "tundidor de mejillas y sastre de barbas" ("shearer of cheeks and tailor of beards"). His mother is a prostitute whose surnames—"hija de Diego de San Juan y nieta de Andrés de San Cristóbal" [daughter of James of St. John and granddaughter of Saint Christopher]—are mentioned to prove that she is descended from the Litany of the Saints (pp. 73–74).[36] The licentiate Cabra, Pablos's schoolmaster, puts bacon in the soup "por no sé qué que le dijeron un día de hidalguía allá fuera" (p. 98) [for something they said to him one day out there about nobility], alluding to the purity of blood statutes that traditionally defined noble old Christian lineage. Pablos's uncle, the hangman from Segovia, refers to the "ocupaciones grandes desta plaza en que me tiene ocupado su Majestad" (p. 131) [the weighty affairs of this employment in which it has pleased His Majesty to place me]. In Madrid Pablos carefully dresses according to the style of the court and names himself "don Ramiro de Guzmán," telling others that he is "un hombre rico, que hizo agora tres asientos con el Rey" [a rich man, who has already gained three contracts from the king]. Nearly everyone in the *Buscón* except Don Diego de Coronel y Zúñiga, Pablos's childhood friend, appropriates courtly language and manners to create new identities to survive in Madrid, searching for honor and profit, the philosopher's stone that will transform them as if by magic from the margin to the center, from the fringes of the court to a place in its society.

Maurice Molho has noted that the narrator of the *Buscón* could just as easily have been Don Diego Coronel de Zúñiga.[37] When Quevedo writes in the first words of the novel that Pablos is from Segovia, his statement applies to Don Diego as well. And when he refers to Pablos's attempts to disguise his lineage and deny his blood, Quevedo cleverly alludes to Don Diego's family too. The name "Coronel" was taken by the converted Segovian Jew, Abraham Senior, in 1492 for himself and for his descendants.[38] Don Diego's second surname, "Zúñiga," may have made him doubly suspect to Quevedo's contemporary readers because in some minds it would have linked him to various noble families or even to Diego de Zúñiga, the first son of the president of the Council of Castile under Philip III, Pedro Manso de Zúñiga, whose meteoric rise to power was described at the time as an "estallido tal que a todos pareció de los milagros de la naturaleza"[39] [such an explosion that everyone thought it was a miracle of nature]. The major difference between Don Pablos and Don Diego, however, is that the latter appears in the novel already the son of a gentleman (no matter how tainted), whereas the former will never attain such status. Both apparently descend from converted Jews, but Quevedo allows Don Diego to remain at court as a *caballero* of a prestigious military order while he condemns Pablos to the life of a hardened criminal. If Don Diego is not as worthy a character as some have argued, why is he not exiled along with Don Pablos? Why is he perceived to be part of the dominant elite in the court of Philip III?

It is possible to begin to answer such questions by first going to another of Quevedo's works, written at about the same time that he was composing his novel. I refer to his satiric poem "Poderoso caballero es don Dinero."[40] Sir Money is the subject of a daughter's confession to her mother: "Madre, yo al oro me humillo; / él es mi amante y mi amado" [Mother, I humble myself before gold; / he is my lover and my beloved]. His genealogy is of supreme importance:

> Son sus padres principales,
> y es de nobles descendiente,
> porque en las venas de Oriente
> todas las sangres son reales;
> y pues es quien hace iguales
> al duque y al ganadero
> *poderoso caballero es don Dinero.*[41]

[His parents are illustrious, / and he is descended from noblemen, / because in veins {of gold/of blood} of the East / all blood is royal; / since he is the one who makes equals / of the duke and the rancher / *a powerful knight is Sir Money.*]

That Don Diego is meant to be perceived as a wealthy nobleman Quevedo leaves little doubt, locating his house on the Calle del Arenal, one of the most prestigious streets in early-seventeenth-century Madrid.[42] His neighbors would have been the Count of Oñate, the Count of Fuente Ventura, the Marquis of Salinas, and the Duke of Arcos, among others.[43] The power of Don Dinero, then, has no limits, and it is the relationship between money and power that turns profit into honor, rustic into nobleman, *converso* into *caballero*.[44] The language and manners of the court for Quevedo, when driven by ostentatious—if not illegitimate—wealth, were forms of deception that allowed those of questionable birth and tainted blood to live nobly and among noblemen in Madrid. Writers of picaresque fiction, if we base their role on Quevedo's example, were morally bound to expose through the language of satire the threat to social and political order that such behavior disguised.

The Coroneles were examples of noblemen by concession and not by blood: "de privilegio y no de sangre," a traditional pathway to nobility that suddenly was perceived to threaten the exclusivity and legitimacy of those who considered themselves to constitute the high elite and who were already in power. Within months of Philip III's accession to the throne, Cabrera de Córdoba reported that "hánse dado más hábitos de las tres órdenes, después que S. M. heredó, que no se dieron en diez años en vida del Rey su padre; porque pasan de cincuenta personas a los que se han dado, y que los más lo han alcanzado con poca diligencia"[45] [more military habits of the three orders were given after the king inherited {the throne} than were given in ten years during his father's reign, because there are more than fifty persons to whom they were given, and most of them obtained them with little effort]. The worst was to come. By 1605, the son of Rodrigo Calderón, less than a year old, was admitted to the prestigious Order of Alcántara. Reaction was swift against the king's wholesale creation of *caballeros*. The Order of Santiago met in 1603 and approved new entry qualifications: "Ordenamos que el que hubiere de tener el hábito de nuestra orden sea hijodalgo de sangre de parte de padre y de parte de madre y no de privilegio"[46] [It is ordered that whoever joins our ranks must be of pure blood on both the father's and mother's side; nobility based on concession is not allowed]. This and other restrictions came too late, and in the final analysis—as we have noted with regard to Rodrigo Calderón's son, and certainly with Don Diego Coronel—had little impact. Don Diego and his kind point to that powerful elite, already too entrenched and powerful to be attacked directly and by name. In sum, Don Diego, despite the tainted blood of his ancestors and his questionable behavior in the novel, is identified as the legitimate son of a Segovian nobleman, whereas Don Pablos is unmasked as the bastard son of a Segovian barber whose *oficio mecánico* alone was sufficient to deny his family noble status.

Quevedo was intimately aware of the strategies adopted by Don Diego and Don Pablos at the beginning of the seventeenth century. Those who would get ahead had to live nobly, forge strong political alliances, and be connected to the right families. Quevedo's own success was assured when he attached himself to the Duke of Osuna, who was appointed viceroy of Sicily in 1609, a year after he arranged the marriage of his oldest son to the second daughter of the Duke of Uceda, Lerma's son. Quevedo profited handily by associating himself with *hombres de bien*; he insisted on maintaining the exclusivity of the legit-

160

Harry Sieber

♦

imate elite through his picaresque novel by exiling Don Pablos and by
pointing a finger at those like Don Diego who would falsify their lineage
and deny their blood.[47]

Claudio Guillén is correct when he writes that the invention of the picaresque took place with the almost simultaneous publication of the re-
discovered *Lazarillo* and the *Guzmán de Alfarache*. However, it may
not have been because an enterprising printer named Luis Sánchez
wanted to cash in on the popularity of a new literary genre, but rather
because a politically and financially astute book publisher named Miguel Martínez had detected the signs of a new court, a court within
which the values of the picaresque found a responsive audience. The social and political worlds of the *valido* both engendered and resisted the
picaresque novel, a literary genre that questioned and sustained the arbitrary nature of identity, the power of money and courtly manners,
family networks, and political favoritism.

Notes

1. Robert Weimann, *Shakespeare and the Popular Tradition in the Theater:
Studies in the Social Dimension of Dramatic Form and Function* (Baltimore:
Johns Hopkins University Press, 1978), p. xiii.

2. José Antonio Maravall, *La literatura picaresca desde la historia social*
(Madrid: Taurus, 1986); Theodore K. Rabb, *The Struggle for Stability in Early
Modern Europe* (New York: Oxford University Press, 1975), p. 33.

3. Pierre Bourdieu, *Outline of a Theory of Practice* (Cambridge: Cambridge
University Press, 1977), p. 94.

4. Frank Whigham, *Ambition and Privilege: The Social Tropes of Elizabethan Courtesy Literature* (Berkeley: University of California Press, 1984), p. x.

5. See Richard L. Kagan, *Students and Society in Early Modern Spain*
(Baltimore: Johns Hopkins University Press, 1974), and Janine Fayard, *Les
membres du Conseil de Castille a l'époque moderne, 1621–1746* (Geneva:
Droz, 1979).

6. Whigham, *Ambition and Privilege*, p. 5.

7. Cited ibid., p. 7.

8. Stephen Greenblatt, *Renaissance Self-Fashioning: From More to Shakespeare* (Chicago: University of Chicago Press, 1980), p. 162.

9. M. Morreale points out in her edition of Lucas Gracián's *Galateo español*
(Madrid: Consejo Superior de Investigaciones Científicas, 1968), p. 2, that its

first translator, Domingo de Becerra, remarked that "para notar una mala costumbre o crianza . . . se suele dezir como proverbio 'no manda esso el Galateo.'" Morreale adds that "una europa ansiosa de afinar el trato social y difundir la urbanidad aun fuera de la clase aristocrática, no podía menos que apreciar los avisos del librito italiano, tan agudamente seleccionados y aplicables a las más variadas circunstancias."

10. See Margherita Morreale, *Castiglione y Boscán: el ideal cortesano en el renacimiento español, Boletín de la Real Academia Española*, Anejo 1 (1969).

11. Alonso de Barros, *Filosofía cortesana moralizada*, ed. Trevor J. Dadson (Madrid: Comunidad de Madrid, 1987).

12. John Elliott, *The Count-Duke of Olivares: The Statesman in an Age of Decline* (New Haven: Yale University Press, 1986), p. 9.

13. Ruth Pike, *Enterprise and Adventure: The Genoese in Seville and the Opening of the New World* (Ithaca: Cornell University Press, 1966), pp. 3–5; Henri La Peyre, *Une famille de Marchands les Ruiz* (Paris: A. Colin, 1955).

14. Cabrera de Córdoba, *Relaciones de las cosas sucedidas en la corte de España* (Madrid: J. Martín Alegría, 1857), p. 3.

15. Antonio Feros, "Gobierno de Corte y Patronazgo Real en el reinado de Felipe III (1598–1618)" (thesis, Universidad Autónoma de Madrid, 1986), p. 40.

16. I will cite Margherita Morreale's edition, *Galateo español*. Her preliminary study has been helpful in sorting out early editions, especially regarding the early texts of the *Lazarillo castigado* and Lucas Gracián's treatise.

17. See Claudio Guillén, *Literature as System: Essays toward the Theory of Literary History* (Princeton: Princeton University Press, 1971), pp. 135–58.

18. For Velasco, see María del Carmen González Muñoz, ed., *Geografía y descripción universal de las Indias* (Madrid: M. Atlas, 1971), "Estudio preliminar."

19. J. M. Bujanda et al., *Index des livres interdits*, vol. 7 (1988): 89–97. "Le comité présidé par Arias Montano semble avoir réalisé un travail de vérification, de compilation et de sélection" (p. 89).

20. Marcos Jiménez de la Espada, ed., "La correspondencia del Doctor Benito Arias Montano con el Licenciado Juan de Ovando," *Boletín de la Real Academia de Historia* 19 (1912): 488.

21. The Index of Antwerp (1570) reproduces the list of Valdés (1559) with one important change in the section beginning with the letter "L": the *Lazarillo*, which was sandwiched between *Las lamentaciones de Pedro* and the *Lengua de Erasmo en Romance, y en Latín, y en qualquier lengua vulgar* in Valdés, is missing in the Antwerp index. No longer completely prohibited, had the *Lazarillo*

been withdrawn to be expurgated? This is difficult to ascertain because certain *comedias* of Torres Naharro remained. See Bujanda, pp. 696, 700.

22. Many of his autograph manuscripts remain in the Escorial library, including this one, L. I. 13. See J. Zarco Cuevas, *Catálogo de manuscritos castellanos en la Real Biblioteca de El Escorial*, 3 vols. (Madrid: El Escorial, 1924–29).

23. The royal privilege included in the Madrid 1573 edition of Cristóbal de Castillejo (BN R-1.485) was issued at San Lorenzo de El Escorial on August 5 for its circulation in Aragón, and includes a reference to the works of Torres Naharro and to the *Lazarillo*: "Por parte de vos Iuan Lopez de Velasco, nos ha sido hecha relación, que mandado y commission del Consejo de la Sancta Inquisicion haviades recopilado y corregido la *Propaladia* de Bartholome de Torres Naharro, y la vida de *Lazarillo de Tormes*, y las obras de Christobal de Castillejo, Secretario que fue del emperador don Hernando, . . . Y vos aveys suplicado, que atendido vuestro buen zelo que teneys del comun aprovechamiento y el trabajo que en esto abeys tenido fuessemos servido de dar licencia y facultad, para que vos y quien de vos tuviese poder para ello, y no otra persona alguna lo podays y puedan imprimir y vender . . . assi *todo junto en un volumen, como dividido en dos, o tres volumenes, o partes, de la manera que a vos os pareciere mas a convertir a la utilidad de los leyentes*" (my emphasis).

24. C. Pérez Pastor, *Bibliografía madrileña (Siglo XVI)* (Madrid: Tip. de los Huérfanos, 1891), p. 39. The work of Castillejo was apparently published separately.

25. Juan Berrillo, a Madrid bookseller, had received permission to publish both texts in one volume in April 1599, but a copy of this edition has never been located. Enrique Macaya Lahmann, *Bibliografía del Lazarillo de Tormes* (San José, Costa Rica: Ediciones del Convivio, 1935), notes that the edition of the *Lazarillo* now in the Hispanic Society of America is bound together with the "Coplas de Jorge Manrique, las de Mingo Revulgo y las Cartas de Refranes de Blasco de Garay" (p. 65).

26. Lucas Gracián died in July 1587; Juan López de Velasco had managed to retain his original permission to publish the *Lazarillo*, but the fact that the novel began appearing within a year of his death seems an odd coincidence. There remains some mystery about the various editions of the *Lazarillo* published at this time. See Enrique Macaya Lahmann, *Bibliografía del Lazarillo de Tormes*, who refers to an edition of 1599 printed by Luis Sánchez, which he was unable to locate for his study (p. 64).

27. In an entry for February 1601, Cabrera de Córdoba noted that "Mandan mudar la Audiencia y Chancillería, que allí [Valladolid] reside, a Medina del

Campo, y las ferias que hasta agora se han hecho en Medina, las mandan pasar a Burgos" (p. 95). The *Lazarillo* was also published in Valencia in 1601 (remember that the court made a slow return to Madrid from Valencia in late 1599) and in Alcalá de Henares in 1607.

28. The town council records of Madrid at this time are filled with references as to how the (bankrupt) city would fulfill its end of the agreement. The Duque de Cea, Lerma's son, was provided a house (formerly of Agustín Alvarez de Toledo) whose rent was to be paid by the city. Cea had built a "pasadizo" from the house to the Royal Palace "en conformidad del . . . ofrescimiento . . . para S. M. por razon de la buelta de la corte a esta villa" (Archivo Municipal de Madrid: Libros de Acuerdos, vol. 25, fol. 400r, 20 November 1606). Madrid had also agreed to pay the king the sixth part of rental houses, but found that it was "muy ynconbiniente para esta villa y sus vecinos" (fol. 418r, March 1607), and ordered that a committee be sent to Valladolid "a tratar deste servicio por razón de la buelta de la corte" (ibid.). The original agreement stipulated that the city would pay the king 250,000 ducats; the city managed to have the amount spread over ten years, and in addition, "los alquileres de las casas del Marques de Auñón y Agustín Albarez de Toledo en que vive y a de vivir el Sr. Duque de Cea" (fol. 451v, 5 May 1607).

29. See Claudia W. Sieber, "The Invention of a Capital: Philip II and the First Reform of Madrid" (Ph.D. diss., Johns Hopkins University, 1985).

30. See Donald McGrady, "A Pirated Edition of *Guzmán de Alfarache*: More Light on Mateo Alemán's Life," *Hispanic Review* 34 (1966): 326–28.

31. Raymond Willis, "Lazarillo and the Pardoner: The Artistic Necessity of the Fifth Tractado," *Hispanic Review* 8 (1959): 267–79.

32. I cite the Medina del Campo edition of 1603, housed in the Library of Congress, BJ 1981. G66 / 1603.

33. Francisco Rico, ed., *La vida de Lazarillo de Tormes* (Madrid: Cátedra, 1987), p. 82. All subsequent references are to this edition.

34. Benito Brancaforte, ed., *Guzmán de Alfarache*, 2 vols. (Madrid: Cátedra, 1979), p. 248. All references to the novel are to this edition.

35. See Pablo Jauralde's note in his edition of the *Buscón* (Madrid: Castalia, 1990), p. 18.

36. All references to the *Buscón* are to Pablo Jauralde, ed. (Madrid: Castalia, 1990).

37. See Molho's perceptive study, "Cinco lecciones sobre el 'Buscón,'" in *Semántica y poética (Góngora, Quevedo)* (Barcelona: Crítica, 1977), pp. 89–131.

38. See Carroll B. Johnson, "*El Buscón*: Don Pablos, don Diego y don Francisco," *Hispanófila* 51 (1974): 1–26; Agustín Redondo, "Del personaje de don

Diego Coronel a una nueva interpretación del *Buscón*," *Actas del Quinto Congreso Internacional de Hispanistas* (Bordeaux: U. de Bordeaux, 1974 [1977]); Idalia Cordero, *El 'Buscón' o la vergüenza de Pablos y la ira de don Francisco* (Madrid: Playor, 1987). See also Angel G. Loureiro, "Reivindicación de Pablos," *Revista de Filología Española* 67 (1987): 225–44, and Henry Ettinghausen, "Quevedo's Converso Pícaro," *Modern Language Notes* 102 (1987): 241–54.

39. Vicente Andosilla Salazar, *A don Pedro Manso de Zúñiga, Patriarca de las Indias y Presidente del Consejo Real de Castilla* (place and year unknown), fol. 4v. This reference comes from Antonio Feros, p. 84.

40. James O. Crosby, *En torno a la poesía de Quevedo* (Madrid: Castalia, 1967), p. 157. This poem was first included in Pedro Espinosa's *Flores de poetas ilustres* (Valladolid, 1605). The collection, however, received official permission to be published almost two years later.

41. The text is taken from José Manuel Blecua, ed., *Francisco de Quevedo: Obra poética* (Madrid: Castalia, 1970), 2:175–76.

42. See the *Buscón*, p. 228.

43. See the *Planimetría general de Madrid*, facs. ed. (Madrid: Tabapress, 1988), 1:315–16.

44. See Cordero, p. 14, who cites Maravall, "La aspiración social de *medro* en la novela picaresca," *Cuadernos hispanoamericanos* 312 (1976): 595: "Muchos, aunque procedan de baja cuna, si consiguen reunir dinero en cantidad bastante, quieran disponer de placeres, comodidad, ociosidad, lujo, ostentación, consiguiente, de respeto social y, en fin, de poder y mayor riqueza."

45. *Relaciones de las cosas sucedidas en la corte de España desde 1599 hasta 1614*, pp. 4–5.

46. See Elena Postigo Castellanos, *Honor y privilegio en la corona de Castilla. El Consejo de las Ordenes y los caballeros de hábito en el siglo XVII* (Madrid: Valladolid: Junta de Castilla y León, 1988), p. 135. The *Diccionario de Autoridades* (Madrid: 1732) contains a useful definition of the "hidalgo de privilegio": "El siendo hombre llano [that is, he who pays taxes], por algun servicio particular o accion gloriosa, el Rey le concedio los privilegios exenciones, y prerogativos que gozan los hijosdalgo de casa y solar conocido: o aquel que compró este mismo privilegio a los reyes."

47. For Quevedo's ancestry and his early connection to the court, see Pablo Jauralde, ed., *El Buscón* (Madrid: Castalia, 1990), pp. 10–11. Jauralde points out that "la relación, bastante sinuosa, de Quevedo con la nobleza de su tiempo constituye uno de los capítulos más apasionados de su ya apasionante biografía" (pp. 10–11).

8

Cervantes and the Paternity of the English Novel

ROBERT TER HORST

➤ ◄

Prose fiction in Golden Age Spain employs both the sequential equili-
brations of contemporary high poetry and the dynamic disequilibrium
of images in disproportionate succession. But imbalance characterizes
the most productive Cervantine and post-Cervantine narration. At the
same time lyric poetry authenticates its seriality by guaranteeing equivalences on the patrician model of the father and son. Though father and
son may be opposite, they must at the last be equal. This patriarchal
equation is also the matrix veiling female or pseudofemale content in
lyric, the male address to the woman encapsulated in the sonnet or girt
by pastoral. Thus, even when Garcilaso advances the beautiful young
woman with fearful celerity into wintry old age and death, or his rival
Góngora outdoes him by taking her down into complete annihilation,
the ultimate negative charge is the equal of the initial positive input. The
negative is, moreover, implicit, immanent, so that, despite the shock of
the transformation of blooming youth into ugliness and void, the poet
succeeds in effecting a total transferral.

Similarly, early prose fiction in Spain strives to bring a succession of
images into conformity as Lazarillo of Salamanca becomes Lázaro of
Toledo; Guzmán of Seville, Guzmán of the galleys; Don Juan de Cárcamo, Andrés Caballero and then Don Juan again. But the antipoetics
of narrative has from the beginning destabilized the formula linking father to son, so that two techniques of resolution come simultaneously
into play, one yearning to establish full equivalence, the other thriving

on disequilibrium. Cervantes is of course a master of both modes and with dual and opposite results. In his fiction the poetic resolution is a function of closure, of the ending of the narration. Where it occurs, as it does in the *Persiles* and in the greater number of the twelve *Novelas ejemplares*, the tendency is to discourage artistic propagation. Closure is cloture. But where imbalance persists to the final pages, continuance is encouraged. In the disturbed relationship between father and son that characterizes early Spanish narrative there is implicit a colonial figuration of the problem of inequality, for Spain was the first great modern empire. But this possibility is not developed, although it may be a much greater presence than our critical eyes have yet been able to discern. Still, the projection in Cervantes remains embryonic. The embryo of the imperial-colonial is the lineage I would posit for Cervantes' paternity, through Defoe first and then through Fielding and Scott, of the English novel.

In poetry the child is mother to the woman or father to the man. In the novel generation, parenthood is highly problematic, and transfer is darkly consummated if at all. Thus the novel is a terribly inefficient recension of metaphoric function, a ruin of its system. Don Quijote, for example, fails to conform fully to the series of figures in his chosen line of chivalric descent, instead parodying his progenitors just as Lázaro parodies Lazarillo. The discrepancy, in early prose fiction, between original and copy nonetheless does not banish the idea of the father or of the mother. Rather, the deficiencies of transfer from parent to child augment the desire for equivalence as an inverse function of its efficiency, or lack of such. And so the parent-child relationship, along with its figurative projections, likewise becomes a haunted ruin. It is no accident that Guzmán spends a considerable portion of his Italian exile/repatriation in Rome serving a surrogate father, the Cardinal, apparently a relatively young man for whom it is not licit to sire offspring but who may acknowledge (though Monseñor does not) any number of "nephews" and "nieces."

Transfer is a major function of the novel. Lázaro projects himself to Toledo, while Guzmán extends the range to Italy, whereas Cervantes in story ranges farther still, all the way from the eastern Mediterranean to England and Iceland. Yet even though Lázaro, Guzmán, and Don Quijote, not to mention Don Juan de Cárcamo, all have unstable connections with their sires, they are a curiously unprocreative lot. They beget no offspring. There is almost no young child in all of the *Quijote,* hardly one in the entire works of Cervantes, save for the mysterious infant thrust into the arms of Don Juan de Gamboa in *La señora Cornelia* or Luisico in *La fuerza de la sangre.*[1] Geographical metaphors of paternity are similarly scarce, despite the fact that Spain was Europe's greatest colonial power; that Seville, a key city in Alemán's book as well as in many Cervantine narrations, was the only port of embarcation for the Indies, East or West; that Cervantes tried to emigrate to the New World; and that Alemán by means of bribery succeeded in doing so. The early Spanish novel, then, owing to the perplexities of the nonpoetic lines of transmission that it proposes, does not manage to propagate itself either at home or away from home, despite its abundant sense of its own descent. Indeed, Cervantes' sole[2] migrant to the Spanish colonies in America, Felipo de Carrizales, departs for Peru at the age of forty-eight and returns a rich man to Spain twenty years later to marry a child bride, by whom he understandably has no issue. No issue, "Huis clos," is in fact a central metaphor of the *Tale of the Jealous Extremaduran,* which, synecdochically, can be understood to represent the dilemma of the enterprise of prose fiction in Golden Age Spain. The enterprise is a theoretically infinite endeavor[3] that nonetheless stops its own posterity because it does not discover an oblique or collateral path of transmission to replace the chain of equivalences that constitutes transfer by image in poetry, even though Cervantes shows the way in the Prologue to the Quijote,[4] when he declares that he is Don Quijote's stepfather rather than his direct progenitor.

Once it has come into being and, through hunger and desire, gained ontological status, one great problem of the early novel is, accordingly, how to replace the immediate legitimate descent found in poetry with a fresh scheme of propagation. In the seventeenth century, even poetry, even Shakespeare's poetry, can encounter obstacles to perpetuation, as in the early sonnets the poet appears to be urging a reluctant young man to marry and sire a child who would reproduce his own beauty in his offspring. There would seem to be, in these initial poems at least, an identification of biology with poetics, in that humans, along with lyric verse, must come to a foreordained end. Shakespeare's sonnets, concluding, unlike their Petrarchan model, in the rhymed couplet, have a heightened sense of ending which their appearance as a formal sonnet sequence tends to counteract by at least delaying the inevitable. The problematics of the first sequence of Shakespeare's sonnets is the question of continuity, of overcoming the conclusion, of drawing the new beginning from the epiphany of the end. These poems may be read as an extended meditation on the physics and metaphysics of a progression constituted by a multitude of terminations, where biological procreation is the companion of artistic projection, each the image of the other, a parallelism well exemplified by sonnet 3:

> Look in thy glass and tell the face thou viewest,
> Now is the time that face should form another,
> Whose fresh repair if now thou not renewest,
> Thou dost beguile the world, unbless some mother.
> For where is she so fair whose uneared womb
> Disdains the tillage of thy husbandry?
> Or who is he so fond will be the tomb
> Of his self-love to stop posterity?
> Thou art thy mother's glass, and she in thee
> Calls back the lovely April of her prime;
> So thou through windows of thine age shalt see,
> Despite of wrinkles, this thy golden time.
> >   But if thou live rememb'red not to be,
> >   Die single and thine image dies with thee.[5]

Stephen Booth rightly reminds readers that seventeenth-century mirror and window glass had far greater distortion and opacity than the modern product.[6] For the poet, it is of course time that makes youthful loveliness dim and misshapen, so that equivalence between parent and child is achieved only in the prime of each. But that ageless "golden time" is the focus of the poem, which propagates itself from the height of image to the height of image "Despite of wrinkles." What the sonnet demonstrates is that lyric poetry, though formally doomed and in spite of a powerful inward drive to self-gratification, contains in its power to command a succession of near-equivalent or equivalent images the in-

herent potential to extend itself past its own conclusion, and so to survive, to endure as part of a sequence, until that sequence shall end. The
problem of lyric is to surpass its ending. And this it attempts to do by
peering down the spyglass of legitimate descent, or up it in reverse, as in
sonnet 3. Lyric is patriarchal, even though in sonnet 3 woman is presented as the principal source of image, or, perhaps better, because she
is shown in her traditional role as the provider of matter for the male creative function; man ears her womb and tills her fertile soil to produce his
own image and likeness.

In contrast to the relatively clear lyric progression, prose fiction has a
troubled descent, especially down the road of the patrilineal. There
seems to be no question that Lázaro's father is his sire, even if both his
parents are transgressors, of whom the father is, however, the less for-
tunate in being caught early and sent off to Gelves to die. This is when
the distressed widow turns to Zaide, who presents his "stepson" with an
illegitimate and nonwhite half brother, the "negrito muy bonito" who,
thinking himself descended solely from his mother and his big brother,
sees his dark father as an ugly anomaly: "¡Madre, coco!"[7] As Cervantes
indicates in the Prologue to *Don Quijote*, the kinship of stepson to stepfather uniquely qualifies basic relationships in the novel, especially
when this form of surrogate patriarchy accompanies, as it always does
in the early novel through a real or ghostly presence, the legitimate line,
Lázaro growing up with his black brother. But Zaide and his son
promptly disappear from Lázaro's story and are never heard of again,
although they most likely represent his future succession. Guzmán's sib-
lings express the "confuso nacimiento" that is their common lot by living all together as "primos," cousins. Among them the principle of paternity is especially opaque, even though Guzmán singles out one man
as his presumptive father and directs his travels to Italy as his fatherland,
despite the weakness of the evidence linking him to Genoa. But, like
Zaide and his son, all of Guzmán's "cousins" fail to sustain their part of
the story in which Guzmán and his mother alone persist. There is no issue at all in *Don Quijote*, and Alonso Quijano's only living relative we
know of is his unmarried niece, leaving collateral heirs through the
female as the sole potential line of his continuance. But the possibility
is in no way developed or exploited. Yet two lineages might be said

to meet and end in him, the biological line of the Quijanos, the legitimate branch, descending directly to the rural member of the gentry whose true name the reader learns late and uncertainly; and the metaphysical ancestry that derives from multiple fictional and historical sires such as Amadís and Rodrigo de Vivar, the illegitimate branch, whose last representative is spuriously dubbed a knight and whose misbegotten career is ended by a clownish adversary. Still, this is a counterpoint only hinted at by Cervantes, who does, however, play off legitimate engendering against illegitimate in three of the *Exemplary Tales*: *La fuerza de la sangre* (The Constraints of Kinship), *La ilustre fregona* (The Noble Scullery Maid), and *La señora Cornelia*. Of the twelve narrations in that collection, these are among the least read and commented upon and yet they contain the enigma that future prose fiction will devote its major energies to solving, the mystery of the misbegotten. *Tom Jones* and *Bleak House* and their congeners already exist embryonically in these tales, which attack illegitimate offspring at different points in their lives.

La fuerza de la sangre pornographically focuses on the moment of the bastard's conception, while *La señora Cornelia* thrusts the child on the reader shortly after its birth. It is a foundling, like Tom in Squire Allworthy's bed. *La ilustre fregona*, in contrast, presents its natural child at the height of her youthful beauty as another diamond set in lead. Her parentage is at a Dickensian depth of abstruseness, and it takes a wealth of reverse narration to untangle it, so that it displays the basic mechanics of the plot, again, of *Tom Jones*, or of *Oliver Twist* or *David Copperfield*, in each of which forward motion has reversionary meaning. Advancement is the function of the illegitimate plot. It capitalizes on the energies of disobedience to parents and, above all, to the father, to set a new course of which the goal is gratification, sexual at base. So in *La ilustre fregona* Carriazo twice throws over parental authority to enjoy the pleasures of freedom, taking his companion Avendaño along on his second and last excursion. Their joint caper takes them to an inn in Toledo, where they encounter the beautiful scullery maid who unconsciously personifies the forces of legitimacy, of poetry. She puts a halt to their progress, and the action of the story stalls in the imperial city as the legitimate plot strives with the illegitimate one and ultimately masters it. This mastery is achieved with considerable difficulty, because Costanza, the *fregona*, conceived in the rape of a widowed lady, a great lady, owes her existence to primordial male lawlessness[8] and is a creature of that anarchy to which the story owes its own creative force. So, in Costanza, the hidden illegitimate processes that produced her meet the controls of legitimacy, for at a time when serving girls at inns were expected to be fairly free with their favors, Maritorneses, Costanza is a model of virtue and decorum. These constraints emanating from her strike sympathetic and effective chords in, especially, the wellborn males who come under her influence. She acts upon the Corregidor, the magistrate, so as to supplant the stopped sequence of lawlessness with the tale's terminal lawfulness, its legitimation, its marriages, its three legal offspring.

The basic narrative thrust in Cervantes, and in the early novel, derives from the illegal plot that frees the teller of it from the constraints of a foreordained ending. But since the illegal enterprise is thereby essentially infinite, the problem of prose narration becomes the opposite of poetry's need to transcend the conclusion in which it is trapped. Prose fiction is compelled to contrive some more or less acceptable halt, and both Alemán and Cervantes have recourse to the moral and aesthetic laws of poetry to put a stop to their telling, momentarily at least. Full stops in Cervantes frequently produce an abundance of legitimate issue, such as the three sons dutifully studying at Salamanca on the last page of *La ilustre fregona*, Cornelia's two new daughters at the end of her story, "the many children and distinguished posterity" left in Toledo by Leocadia and Rodolfo of *La fuerza de la sangre*, and the blessed bounty of succession accruing to Sigismunda and Persiles in the last line of their history. Yet even though, significantly, the poets praise these parents' unions,[9] their offspring are artistically sterile in that they have inherited their sires' lawfulness in full measure but none of their anomalousness. Poetry, then, completely recuperates anarchy, putting an end to all save aristocratically replicative narration, cloning of the sort aspired to but happily failed at by Don Quijote. I suspect that the poetically recuperative conclusion in Alemán and Cervantes is a countermeasure designed at a later stage to exert some control over the ceaseless streamings of unhindered narrativity. The paradox is that the inconclusive endings, such as those terminating *Don Quijote*, *Rinconete and Cortadillo*, *The Colloquial Dogs*, altogether lack representations of biological issue at the same time that they hold out the prospect of plentiful artistic succession, a prospect not realized in Spain, where, following Cervantes, prose fiction goes into eclipse until the advent of Pérez Galdós in the third quarter of the nineteenth century.

The novel's eclipse in the country of its origin, like Spain's decline in the seventeenth century, probably is not susceptible of a truly satisfactory explanation. It is hard to persuade on the basis of what appears to be lacking. Yet there does seem to be a connection between narrativity and dominance. Telling requires domination and subjection. It is a mode of the imperial such as that celebrated by the *Lazarillo*[10] with its mention of Charles V's victorious entry into Toledo and his summoning of the Cortes. Traditional history, with its despotic insistence on the supreme importance of a few rulers and military men, is very likely the most imperial form of prose narration. From its precarious and marginal position, the early novel, by deigning to deal, even parodically, with the obscure destinies of such as Lázaro and Guzmán, challenges the omnipotence of the historical. Yet it does so without the security of a home base. Lázaro shares the same city with the emperor, as Monipodio in *Rinconete and Cortadillo* nervously shares Seville with its legal authorities. In Alemán and Cervantes, Italy offers great promise as a new homeland for the Spaniard's anarchy, and Guzmán and a number of Cervantes' male protagonists colonize it.[11] Insofar as Rome represents Christendom's legitimacy and authority, no principal character in prose fiction is able to transplant himself or herself there. What is wanting, then, in the early Spanish novel is the idea of the colony and, above all, of the penal colony. Where imperial England allowed its dissidents to emigrate and transported many of its criminals, imperial Spain tried to keep new Christians and convicts out of its colonies. A British *Guzmán de Alfarache* would have sent Guzmán to Virginia or to Australia to work his renewal in an exile that was at the same time the seat and home of lawlessness. The colony establishes anarchy, just as hunger established the novel. A new paternity, etymological, surrogate, and nonlegitimate, arises when the fatherland propagates itself abroad. Through transfer of the rectilinear concept of itself to a lesser place and breed, its succession assumes a dissident, collateral, and secretive format which subversively enters into dialogue with the imperial portrait of the sire in the *patria*. This relationship between colony and country of origin corresponds to a new novelistic poetics of imperfect equivalence, a dynamic metonymy of covert process.

Cervantes' most accomplished narrations, those that immolate themselves to the gratification of a demonstrable ending, correspond, in the absence of a dynamic resulting from superiority as against inferiority, to a novelistic poetics of equivalence. Several of the *Exemplary Tales* are based on a contrastive simile between the Spanish and the non-Spanish, *El amante liberal*, *El licenciado Vidriera* (The Man of Transparent Degree), *La señora Cornelia*. Others colonize Spain itself by delving into the jurisdictions occupied by the underclass: the mobile domain of the gypsies in *La gitanilla*, the fixed abode in Seville of Monipodio's criminal band. Yet in all these stories, despite a host of differences, the ultimate goal is equivalence, the same sort of equivalence achieved in Lope's *Peribáñez* where Casilda, though set in peasant lead, is as good as the finest lady, Pedro the equal of the doughtiest noble warrior. The most comparative of the *Exemplary Tales* is *La española inglesa* (The Spanglish Woman), whose very title truncatedly reveals the process by which simile overcomes differences to achieve metaphor. If ever there was an occasion for Cervantes to develop maximum narrative force from unequal interplay, culture and history provide it in this confrontation of the Spanish Isabel with her counterpart in the English queen Elizabeth. Nonetheless, despite two wonderfully balanced sets of horrors in both England and Spain—the cruelty and capriciousness of the queen, the invidiousness and corruption of her court, these set against the unspeakable ills of an inquisitorial society in Spain—every major person's image in the tale emerges from her or his vicissitudes whole and equal in value to the richest foreign equivalent. This is the corroborative sense of that complex sequence of transactions by means of which Queen Elizabeth ensures that the fine of ten thousand ducats imposed on the lady Tansi flows entirely undiminished into Isabel's purse and, from there, into her father's strongbox in Seville after being transferred from England to France to Spain. Coevally, Isabel's father regains his full status and function as a merchant, and she her beauty lost in England. But this is as well a false coda before the final consummation, in which Ricaredo fetches up in Seville at the very moment that Isabel is about to take her vows in religion, with yet another letter of credit in his possession, one which is instantly validated for the full amount. The monetary accompaniment to the spiritual progress confirms that the voyage has been accomplished without diminution in value, with equivalent value.[12] Narratively speaking, *La española inglesa* is at the last a perfectly balanced sheet.

Yet it is imbalance that conditions the most promising kinds of Cervantine narration and its true successors. Charles Dickens grossed $228,000 on his second American tour, but in the aftermath of the Civil War the dollar was trading for gold at a 40 percent discount, so that when he exchanged his receipts for it he realized a profit of only £20,000, instead of the £38,000 that might have been his.[13] The loss symbolizes a terribly complex set of interactions between England and its former colony, but it is a fundamental feature of novelistic discourse, which, as I see it, is governed by a lack of equality that makes transmission possible. And even though Cervantine equivalence stops Cervantes' own domestic posterity in Spain, it is nonetheless to Spain that we owe the imperial and colonial idea in its primacy. As the successor to that idea, England assumes a hostile but filial stance with respect to the progenitor of a new and nonpoetic system of exchange. Thus Spain is the stepfather or stepmother to the novel in England, fostering its alien offspring with disapproval if at all. The novel is, then, an aspect of technological transfer between a culture on the wane and another on the rise. The British mastery of finance[14] is already visible in the queen's careful and accomplished handling of Isabel's letter of credit. Like it, the novel must make its way not through poetic scenes of love and harmony but through the European arena of conflict in the age of the Thirty Years' War. Most technological transfer is effected under adverse conditions, and once the new possessor of knowledge has wrested it by force or stealth from the old,[15] theirs is a fierce and bitter filiation, better concealed than confessed.

The Spanish paternity of the English novel accordingly does not come to light in Europe, among whose states the Cervantine notion of equality is the rule. There, Spain's projection of prose fiction is an etymological, a linguistic, and an unconscious process in which one can use the word *picayune* in perfect ignorance of its origin and the old Provenzal *picaion*, or *nice*, thinking it purely Saxon, even though it derives from the Latin *nescius*. Study after the event can, nonetheless, expose the manner of transmission, as the great German philologists did in the nineteenth century, in the case of their derivation of the romance group from classical and vulgar Latin, the parent long vaguely recognizable in the children but strictly and systematically connected through sources only by Diez and Meyer-Lübke. Etymology is a technique of anagnorisis, a detecting of parenthood.[16]

The anagnorisis that springs from an understanding of the etymology of the English novel almost necessarily expresses itself as a parody, for the offspring is a corruption and deformation of the sire and at the same time is made in his image and likeness. In his *Roderick Random* of 1748, Smollett has his hero discover his father, lost to him from birth, in Buenos Aires, where his parent is known as Don Rodrigo. The father's ascent to that fortune which, when he meets his son, he is in the process of transferring to England, is the result of wanderings akin to those of Ricaredo in *La española inglesa*. But Don Rodrigo has followed a different route, from England to France and then to Spain. From Spain he accompanied the newly designated viceroy to Peru, where he engaged in trade, removing from there to Buenos Aires for a sixteen-year sojourn. The shift from Europe to the Indies is, in this parodic novelistic process of recovery, decisive. Don Rodrigo, a man turned out of the house by his biological English father, has prospered because of the patronage of great Spanish nobles who have acted *in loco parentis* toward him. Their surrogate parenting mends not only Don Rodrigo's fortune but also his paternity of his son Roderick, whom now he fosters, in a real exchange of affection and wealth. This final exchange is, however, lateral and collateral, not successive and intergenerational. The novel's transportation to England is, likewise, the result of a concealed lateral shift which becomes discernible only in the colonial environment, in Defoe above all. But from out of the New World, Smollett's parodic recension of paternity clearly points to Spain as the guilty party, guilty for having provided in the viceroyalty of Peru that common though adversarial ground where Roderick meets Rodrigo and draws from him a fortune in the form of the technique and technology of surrogate parenthood. Transplanted to England, these will sustain and at last repatriate to the land of Galdós that self-perpetuating industry created through a misalliance of poetry with commerce which we call the novel. Cervantes' glorious shame is to have been, in hidden and ignoble collaboration with his compeers who conceived the *Lazarillo de Tormes* and the *Guzmán de Alfarache*, its unrecognized, illegitimate begetter.

Notes

1. Diana de Armas Wilson here reminds me also of the infant thrust into Auristela's arms in the *Persiles* 3.2.

2. Cristóbal de Lugo does, in *El rufián dichoso*, hop over to Mexico after he has become a *fraile*.

3. "Picaresque and adventure novels are by nature interminable." Wallace Martin, *Recent Theories of Narrative* (Ithaca: Cornell University Press, 1986), p. 84.

4. *Don Quijote de la Mancha*, ed. John Jay Allen (Madrid: Cátedra, 1977), p. 67: "Pero yo, que, aunque parezco padre, soy padrastro de Don Quijote."

5. *Shakespeare's Sonnets*, ed. Stephen Booth (New Haven: Yale University Press, 1977), p. 7.

6. Ibid., p. 139.

7. *Lazarillo de Tormes*, ed. Francisco Rico (Madrid: Cátedra, 1987), p. 17.

8. Alban K. Forcione beautifully explores anarchy as an ethic in *El casamiento engañoso* and *El coloquio de los perros* in *Cervantes and the Mystery of Lawlessness* (Princeton: Princeton University Press, 1984).

9. Miguel de Cervantes, *Novelas ejemplares*, vols. 1 and 2, ed. Harry Sieber (Madrid: Cátedra, 1981), 1:134: "Y de tal manera escribió el famoso licenciado Pozo, que en sus versos durará la fama de Preciosa mientras los siglos duraren"; and 2:198: "Dio ocasión la historia de *la fregona ilustre* a que los poetas del dorado Tajo ejercitasen sus plumas en solenizar y en alabar la sin par hermosura de Costanza."

10. *Lazarillo*, p. 135: "Esto fue el mesmo año que nuestro victorioso Emperador en esta insigne ciudad de Toledo entró y tuvo en ella Cortes, y se hicieron grandes regocijos, como Vuestra Merced habrá oído."

11. For example, Ricaredo in *La española inglesa*, who accomplishes a pilgrimage to Rome; Tomás Rodaja in *El licenciado Vidriera*, who joins Captain Valdivia as a gentleman follower on a grand military tour; Rodolfo in *La fuerza de la sangre*, who, completely forgetful of Leocadia, spends years pursuing pleasure in Italy; and, finally, that very errant pair, Don Antonio de Isunza and Don Juan de Gamboa, who strike out for Flanders but, finding truce there, end up studying in Bologna at the university.

♦

12. Carroll B. Johnson's rich "*La española inglesa* and the Practice of Literary Production," *Viator* 19 (1988): 379–416, uncovers a major economic subtext of that novella, the struggle in it between middle-class and aristocratic capitalism. It seems that we are only just beginning to grasp something of Cervantes' economics.

13. Edgar Johnson, *Charles Dickens II* (New York: Simon and Schuster, 1952), p. 1096.

14. P. J. Dickson's *The Financial Revolution in England* (London, 1967), is aptly summarized by James D. Tracy in his *A Financial Revolution in the Hapsburg Netherlands* (Berkeley: University of California Press, 1985) as believing that "it was this system of public borrowing, enabling England to spend on war out of all proportion to tax revenue, which best explains why Britain prevailed against a larger and wealthier France during the long series of wars from 1689 to 1815" (pp. 1–2). And British finance also shows itself to be much superior to Spain's in *La española inglesa*; this advantage was a major reason why England prevailed over its earlier rival.

15. Arnold Toynbee brilliantly examines technological transfer over a hostile frontier (*limes*) in vol. 8, *Heroic Ages* (London: Oxford University Press, 1954), of *A Study of History*, showing how a less developed culture can quickly master especially the weapons of a more advanced society. See particularly "The Barbarians' Exploitation of their Civilized Neighbors' Weapons" (pp. 16–19).

16. The seven romance languages used to be called "les langues filles" of Latin.

The "I" of the Beholder

Self and Other in Some
Golden Age Texts

RUTH EL SAFFAR

*I*n 1977, eons ago from the perspective of feminist studies, Joan Kelly pointed out something that should have been obvious but was not at all. The Renaissance that meant the recovery of Greek and Latin classics, the growth of towns, the expansion of international commerce, the beginnings of technology, the explosion of schooling, the discovery of new lands: that Renaissance was above all, from a psychological point of view, an extended rite of passage by which men escaped the bondage of servitude to woman, to nature, to the land, to home. That rite of passage, while it liberated men, worked by and large to the detriment of women.[1] The forces at work during the Renaissance had the effect of deepening the split within the masculine subject, and, as an effect of that split, of making that masculine subject capable of relating to the feminized other only through a pattern of dominance and control.

The sense of freedom and autonomy won by men who seemed to be taking their lives in their own hands, achieving success, as *Lazarillo de Tormes* would have it, "con fuerza y mano remando"[2] [rowing hard and well (Rudder, p. 4)], had an undeniable appeal. It also had a price. Until feminism, Americanism, and global ecology began to force reflection on the legacy of oppression and despoliation that are the shadow side of Europe's rebirth, few questioned the dazzling achievements of the military and the heroes of arms and letters who have crowded our textbooks and school curriculums, to say nothing of the cultural values of individual-

178

ism and autonomy on which their achievements were based. Not only had scholars tended to miss the fact that masculine growth and autonomy depended on a corresponding restriction of female activity, they also tended, before the 1980s, to minimize the impact on native populations of Western colonialism.[3]

Since the 1980s, writers have begun challenging the values that underlay the age of discovery, specifically values that gave a marked preference to reason over affect, the visual over the auditory, the sense of independence over that of relationship. Carolyn Merchant's *The Death of Nature*, like Brian Easlea's *Witchhunting, Magic, and the New Philosophy*, narrates the impact on women and nature of modern science and the growth of technology, as does Morris Berman's *The Reenchantment of the World* and his more recent *Coming to Our Senses*. These works, and later ones that focus specifically on the growth of the "new science" as a gendered phenomenon, such as Sandra Harding's *The Science Question in Feminism* and Evelyn Fox Keller's *Reflections on Gender and Science*,[4] mark a growing sense that the reason and empiricism that fostered a view of the world as an object to be mastered were the products of a particular form of cultural conditioning, conditioning that promoted not only the great age of scientific discovery but also that of capitalism and colonialism.

Luce Irigaray, appropriating Lacanian language in her analysis of rationality, challenges the assumptions on which the scientific revolution was based, that is, that the principles of logic are universal, absolute, and ahistorical. She calls such assumptions the product of the "male imaginary" that emerges out of a visual misunderstanding of sexual identity, one that reduces women to a category of sexual indefinition. The reasoning that emerges out of the presumption of sameness, of a sexual theory that can imagine the female body not as other but as defective based on a male norm, makes an absolute out of such principles as identity, noncontradiction, and binarism, and cannot tolerate the ambiguity, ambivalence, or multivalence that Irigaray sees as natural to the female imaginary.[5] Thus, polymorphous qualities of thought, like the "deformed" female body, become figures of abjection relegated in the dominant culture to the unconscious.[6]

The sense of lack, inferiority, and powerlessness inherent in the other as female extends from its origins in the male imaginary out into all forms of social, cultural, political, and economic expression under certain sociohistoric conditions. In sixteenth-century Spain a combination of factors such as the growth of cities and commerce, the separation of home and workplace, the introduction of institutionalized schooling, the strengthening of a centralized monarchy, and the widespread practice of paternal despotism created the atmosphere necessary for the formation of the divided, masculinized subject.[7] That divided subject, perforce alienated from body, passion, and all else associated with maternal care, is above all the product of specialized schooling and the introduction of the arts of reading and writing into the lives of young men aspiring to power in the new nation states that were developing in Western Europe. The literate subject and, more specifically, the Latin-trained scholar were forced at an early age to forgo the life of maternal and material comfort in order to adapt to the punitive, all-male environment that was the world of Renaissance schooling. It was the ability to cast aside desire for home and mother and, by extension, concern for feelings and the body that would determine the young man's capacity to take up power in the world.[8]

Augustine's *Confessions* reflect the struggle boys selected for education and hence for power have long experienced as they are chastised into submission to the hard lessons of schooling. The child in Augustine is by nature egotistical and lazy and must be disciplined into the wisdom of God-consciousness.[9] Renaissance pedagogy tended to follow the pessimistic view of childhood articulated by Augustine and to use that view as support for practices of flogging and brutality. For somewhat different but related reasons, Walter Ong has likened the learning of Latin to a Renaissance puberty rite.[10]

My point here is not to exalt a period prior to the Renaissance as one in which women were more highly regarded among philosophers and writers than they were in later centuries. In no century do women receive high marks in the discourses devoted to the exaltation of reason. On the contrary, woman regularly stands for the realm of emotion and indefinition from which philosophers would like to distinguish their work. As Jean Grimshaw points out, "the history of the views of male philosophers about women is a dreary one of misogyny which is easy to document."[11] I am saying that when the disciplines applied to schooling reach a significant portion of the population, and when the criteria for success and power are linked to education, then the conditions are in place that spread repressed hostility and the rejection of feeling, the body, the land, and the woman into all aspects of social organization. Then, whether or not one finds, as one *can* find, a fulsome expression of feminism in the writings of men and women in the Renaissance, the material circumstances mitigate against the experience of power and hence of freedom of expression among women.[12] The theoretical misogyny endemic to philosophy becomes generalized policy. Joan Kelly, Merry Wiesner, Jean-Louis Flandrin, and others have shown that women *lost* power in the Renaissance, as the bases of power came to be associated with money, schooling, and military, ecclesiastic, and government jobs.

The factors mentioned here are complex and interrelated. Literacy, urbanization, centralization of political power, the strengthening of the father's power and of the nuclear family, the growth of jobs in commerce and letters all form part of a picture that has ultimately to do with a separation of social structures from the rhythms of nature and the exigencies of the passions.[13] The sense of power of the Other seen as female and autonomous is clearly a factor in medieval literature, iconography, and medicine. David Herlihy's research reveals that between the tenth and twelfth centuries women occupied positions of prominence in economic, political, and familial settings. By the later Middle Ages, however, that power in all spheres was already in decline, as Shulamith Shahar's *The Fourth Estate* documents. Women come increasingly to represent the passions and the emotions that work to destabilize the social order. Resistance to female power, in the form of the fifteenth-century literature of misogyny, betrays a feeling that men struggled still with a sense of entrapment within the grip of mother and nature, that is, within the grip of forces greater than they which threatened to overwhelm them.

Earth mother cults continued to flourish in "pagan," that is, rural settings in the fifteenth and sixteenth centuries. Carlo Ginsberg's study of the *benandanti* shows how groups resembling witches' covens were understood in farming areas of Italy to be necessary to the growth of crops. Mother Nature was a reality in the nonurbanized areas to be propitiated and understood. One could not afford to cross her, and one could not assume, in her presence, much in the way of personal power.[14]

The anthropological and archaeological debates of the late nineteenth and early twentieth centuries about whether a matriarchal phase in human culture preceded patriarchy provided a backdrop for Freud's work on the origins of civilization, as Rosalind Coward has shown. Those debates reflect the cyclical shifts of power between Mother and Father imagoes in the human psyche. In the period between 1450 and 1550 a social-historical process was taking place that produced a tendency, wherever urban living and literacy had been developed, to dethrone the mother goddess automatically present, whatever the official religion, in rural settings. The 1486 *Malleus Maleficarum* marks the first extended, official attempt to wrest the successes of witchcraft from the powers of earth deities. The Dominican authors of the *Malleus* make the central point of the long treatise—which frequently slides from the question of what powers witches have and how to combat them to the more familiar misogynistic descriptions of women themselves—that witches are empowered by the devil. The devil figures in the *Malleus* as a notably masculine figure, God's rebellious son, the fallen angel of pride and willfulness. The insistence that the witches' power comes not from their own resources but from the devil further reinforces the male imaginary notion of the one sex. Women figure in the economy of a single sex as that which images man's weakness, gullibility, lasciviousness, and envy.[15]

The object of the authors of the *Malleus* is to demonstrate that it is the devil, working through female imperfection, that disrupts the affairs of men. The resistance to the notion of an earth goddess marks a paradigm shift away from the notions of animism and of the *lumen naturae* that found their way into European philosophy as late as in the writings of Paracelsus.[16] The Other that is Nature, the Mother, the passions, the animal world becomes progressively abjected, pushed into the unconscious, denied.[17] Lacking the discipline and intellect required to suppress that unconscious, women's relatively weaker egos are more easily flooded by the repressed material, which, when it surfaces into the collective, appears in negative form as the devil's work.[18]

♦

Textual Examples

In the writings on the woman question so popular in Spain in the fifteenth century, from the Archpriest of Talavera's 1430 *Corbacho* to Juan de Flores' *Grisel y Mirabella* at the end of the century, writers scoured the ancient and sacred texts for examples to support, alternately, the image of woman's faithfulness and devotion, and the story of her lust, loquacity, and depravity. Underlying the misogynist debates was the deeper struggle to realign the psychic deities to account for the realities of lives increasingly lived in nonagricultural settings. Patricia Grieve has noted the mix of redemptive and terrifying qualities attributed to women in the sentimental novels of the fifteenth century, a mix that makes it difficult for critics to distinguish misogynist from antimisogynist works.[19]

The object relations studies of the twentieth century, spearheaded by the pioneering work of Melanie Klein, have brought to our attention as never before the intense dramas of terror and desire that characterize the infant's early relations with the mother.[20] Writings influenced by the sense of contingency and helplessness vis-à-vis the mother will emphasize alternately the destructive and the satisfying aspects of that dependency. In the love poetry of the *cancioneros*, in the manuals of the witch hunters, in the sentimental romances, and in the discussions of the woman question can be seen the dynamics of fear and dependency that suggest a period prior to the Renaissance in which resistance to, but captivity still within, the figure of the Mother is the dominant collective experience.

Fernando de Rojas's *La Celestina* carries the sense of frustration over mother domination to the breaking point. Both in the prologue, where he presents the baby viper's splitting open the mother's side at birth as an act of revenge, and in the text itself, where his young male characters knife the mother Celestina to death, we find an uncannily prescient imaging of the new self emerging in the sixteenth century, a self formed out of the repudiated and mutilated body of the mother. The year 1500, when *La Celestina* appeared, makes a convenient marking place for the discussion of that new birth, the re-naissance that enabled the son to free himself from the mother and identify more fully with the father's world. That father's world, with its emphasis on centralized authority, and the enforcement of ecclesiastical law, commerce, schooling, and conquest, made more radical than in previous centuries in Western Europe the split between Mother and Father and therefore also between self and other. Those splits have important consequences for characters depicted in the literature of the sixteenth century, as I will show in the cases of *Lazarillo de Tormes* and the *Life* of Saint Teresa.

The sense, in the work of such early modern scientists as Francis Bacon and Descartes, that knowledge can be freed of the obscure and the maternal is less evident in the works of writers such as the author of *Lazarillo de Tormes* and Cervantes, as I have tried to show elsewhere.[21] To find systematic recognition of the loss underlying the achievements of reason so associated with Western Europe in the modern period, we really have to wait for the work of Freud and Jung in the twentieth century.[22] Freud and Jung, as well as Melanie Klein, tally the price of the deepening of the split between nature and reason on which modern science, economics, and social ordering are based.

Diego de San Pedro's 1492 *Cárcel de amor* presents an image of the masculine ego fragmented and caught in an idealization of the Mother imago. Such an idealization makes of the woman either a beautiful but untouchable object of desire or an enveloping mother in whom he is destined to be swallowed in death. Diego de San Pedro's work, against which Fernando de Rojas was reacting when he wrote *La Celestina* at the end of the fifteenth century, still preserves the mother as an image, albeit split off from the father, of power and importance. By the sixteenth century, however, the negative mother, so immanent in the misogynistic tracts of the previous century, becomes a figure of abjection. The mother as witch or prostitute, the mother as debased and despicable if not silenced, becomes the dominant figure for a feminine/natural world split off from the ego. To organize the ego into a subject capable both of witnessing and experiencing, of acting and reflecting, seems to require the slaying of that negative, devouring mother.

The devouring, pre-Oedipal mother already carries an other independent of the father, as both Erich Neumann and Julia Kristeva, in different ways, discuss.[23] Neumann points out that the "slaying of the mother and identification with the father-god go together" (p. 165), and my point here is that it is in the period of great separations—the period when the monarchies, the schools, and the impulses of global conquest were demanding the uses of men in great numbers—that genres associated with autobiography begin to proliferate.[24] "Self-fashioning," as Stephen Greenblatt would have it, was a Renaissance phenomenon. What I want to emphasize here is that the "I" that is born in the Renaissance is one that is born in pain and anger. Whether the birth comes because the father breaks up the mother/child dyad, as Freud and Lacan would stage the separation, or whether it is the child, seeking freedom, who forces the break, as Torok would say, or whether it is the son's need to overcome the fear of the all-powerful mother that precipitates the hero's journey into consciousness, as Jung would have put it, the fact remains that, born with the "I" is an Other who dwells as reject at the peripheries of the ego. That Other carries the demons of guilt, desire, rage, fear, grief, shame, and ecstasy that in its formation the "I" has expelled.

The task of the "I" is to maintain control over the forces that threaten to engulf it. The sixteenth century, which emphasized the importance of discipline in the schools and at home, and in which the widespread practice of wet-nursing destabilized the early mother-child bonding so essential to adult psychological health, produced evidence of especially troubled I-other relations.[25] Cultural insistence—through sermons, educational treatises, courtesy books, and drama—on the silence and obedience required of women reflects the collective effort to head off the conflicts with the outer (female) other whose dissent or self-expression might throw her husband, father, or other male superior into rage or disorientation. Women, as in the myth of Pandora, became the containers in which the toxic wastes of collective rage, fear, and desire were stored. Their release threatened the stability of the whole culture.[26]

Catherine Belsey, in *The Subject of Tragedy*, has pointed out the fascination that the character of "patient Griselda" held in seventeenth-century drama. Griselda fascinates as an image of the female other who evades definition by carrying to its absolute extreme the requirement of submission and obedience imposed on her by the rules of patriarchal marriage. Never being able to push her to her breaking point, or to the point of her rebellion, however, Griselda's husband fails to find the limit of that other whose patience and absolute obedience so confound him. Like such sixteenth-century Spanish invaders as Aguirre and De Soto in their confrontation with America, the effort of domination has the paradoxical effect of revealing the smallness of the self in the face of the Other's unfathomability.

Fascination with the definition and parameters of the Other also troubles Anselmo's marriage to Camila in Cervantes' interpolated novella "El curioso impertinente," found in *Don Quijote*, Part 1. In the "Curioso" Anselmo is reduced to an obsession he associates with the diseases of women as he worries over the possibility of his wife Camila's infidelity: How much can he trust her? Would she be faithful if another lover presented himself to her? What are the limits of her honesty? Beneath these anxieties hides the deeper question: "Who *is* this woman in whom I have entrusted my life and my honor?" As repressed Other, she belongs to the unconscious. As unconscious, she represents a force over which, ultimately, the husband has no control. Intuiting her ungovernability, Anselmo seeks to control Camila by stage-managing a feigned seduction, that is, by turning his worst fears about Camila and Anselmo's best friend Lotario into a script written and produced by him. Anselmo's mania for control makes of his wife an adulteress and his best friend a seducer. It is fear of the Other, and the consequent effort to contain it, that creates havoc in life and relationships, as Anselmo, at the end of his life, seems to have come to understand.[27]

Cervantes' work shows in many places how the marriage structure, based on a model of dominance and submission, produces in the one called upon to assert his control a terror and anxiety that only makes of his would-be paradise a torment. In *El celoso extremeño* anxiety itself generates a manifestation of what it seeks to avert. For all his efforts to forestall the possibility of her infidelity, the aging Carrizales' child wife still belongs to something other than he. It is his effort to control the otherness inherent to her that ultimately undoes not only him but all associated with him.

Calderón, in an even more powerful way, probes the terror that possesses the one whose gender role requires that he dominate and subdue another. So fragile is, for example, Gutierre's hold on his position of dominance over Mencia in *El médico de su honra* that her slightest engagement in conversation with a former lover initiates a series of moves and countermoves—all driven by fear—that culminate in her murder.

More often Calderón will present his heroes as seeking safe haven out of reach of the woman, as in *La vida es sueño* or *La devoción de la cruz*. When the mother is in a position of dominance, as in *Eco y Narciso* or *La hija del aire*, the male figures over whom she exerts power wither into inefficacy. Fear of mother power underlies the efforts at dominance and control so central to Golden Age drama in general, which is why the action so often focuses on the feminine figure least capable of defending herself, the young maiden. To win the battle that stifles her rebellion, as in, for example, Shakespeare's *The Taming of the Shrew*, is to offer the audience an image of order and reason winning out over chaos.[28] Cervantes' and Calderón's forays into the forbidden territory of what Kathryn Rabuzzi, in *The Sacred and the Feminine*, has called the "happily ever after" reveal the ongoing presence of a fear that leads to death. The "master" discovers to his chagrin his dependency on that which he had expected to rule.[29]

The otherness of the apparently submissive and obedient nun became no less a site of terror and a place inspiring efforts at education and control than that of the wife in sixteenth- and seventeenth-century Spain, as Electa Arenal and Stacey Schlau's *Untold Sisters* documents.[30] Further excavations of nuns' writings being carried out by Ronald Surtz, Darcey Donahue, Alison Weber, and Mary Giles reveal a tremendous amount of manuscript material having to do with visionary nuns' spiritual lives.[31] The autobiographies were generally ordered by confessors leery of the ecstatic and visionary experiences reported to be common among their subjects. While in the period between 1300 and 1500 women visionaries were generally honored and their ecstatic pronouncements accepted for the most part as the outpouring of God's word, in the sixteenth and seventeenth centuries churchmen and confessors began to pass women's visionary experiences under the strictest scrutiny.

Often, as was the case with Sor María de Santo Domingo—also referred to as "la beata de Piedrahita"—the issue of female authority came under attack when women began to assume power commonly allowed only men. While Cardinal Cisneros and King Ferdinand, following the late medieval tradition of supporting the genuineness of female ecstatic experiences, could say of Sor María that they had never seen living doctrine until they beheld her, her detractors argued, in a series of lawsuits brought against her, that her empowerment caused her to overstep gender role boundaries and threaten hard-won male prerogatives.[32] Although the trials failed to result in the condemnation of Sor María, subsequent efforts to challenge and limit the only voice of authority that women could achieve were more successful.

The stories of Isabel de la Cruz, María de Cazalla, and Francisca Hernández, to name only the best-known of the visionaries and heterodox religious women brought to trial in the second and third decades of the sixteenth century, are stories of the church's systematic and by and large successful effort to place under scrutiny expressions of ecstatic and visionary experience that in former periods were a source of true empowerment.[33] In the case of St. Teresa, whose visions only narrowly escaped condemnation, the question came down to one that had already been framed by the authors of the *Malleus*. The overriding suspicion, given the weakness and inferiority inherent in a femininity reduced to "less than" in the dominant male imaginary, was that Teresa's visions, even of Jesus, were the devil's work. To her great shame she was urged, in effect, to "give him the finger" should Jesus appear to her in a vision ("Mandabanme que, ya que no habia remedio de resistir, que siempre me santiguase cuando alguna vision viese, y diese higas, porque tuviese por cierto era demonio y con esto no vernia"[34] [As I was quite unable to resist it, they commanded me to make the sign of the cross whenever I had a vision, and to gesture insultingly { = closed fist with the thumb showing between the index and middle fingers} so as to convince myself that it came from the devil, whereupon it would not come again (Peers, p. 270; emended by Iarocci)]).

It is in that relationship between the observing ego of the confessors or inquisitors and the female hysterical body of the nun or witch that one gets a glimpse, once again, of the condition of a collective psyche—what Irigaray has called the male imaginary—caught in the unending effort to reject and condemn the very aspect of itself to which it is also drawn and on which it depends.[35]

Collectively, as schooling produced males trained into a culture and language radically divergent from the one into which they were born, men came to take on the "I" position in a split that was not only psychological but also cultural.[36] In that split women carried the role of other.

Other was also the category into which colonized natives, non-Christians, the uneducated, and those of lower social status fell, which is why, as Constance Jordan has pointed out, so many pro-feminist males in the Renaissance could write about and identify with the powerlessness endemic in the condition of being women.[37] The role of other, by definition lacking and inferior, was one into which no one wanted to be locked. In the rigid binarism of self and other that is the structure that results from the birth of a self that conceives itself as separate, competition for the position of "I," for the right to exercise one's autonomy and claim one's authority, becomes a struggle for survival.

Autobiographical Instances: Lazarillo *and St.* Teresa's Vida

Two texts I touch on in closing illustrate the stakes involved in winning the right to self-definition and therefore survival which mark a deep change in the structure of the psyche in early modern Spain. The two, *Lazarillo de Tormes* and St. Teresa's *Vida*, use the form of autobiography increasingly important in sixteenth-century letters as their stories dramatize the many-staged process of self-fashioning.[38] The stages represent wrenching experiences of death and rebirth as the emerging "I" makes successive breaks from the parental imagoes. For the Other who threatens to negate that "I" is not only—and in fact not even primarily—the Other of maternal care. It is also the Other—as Lacan would have it—of the father world, the Other of language and culture that promotes the initial separation of child from mother, that must be left.[39] Both Lázaro and Teresa trace psychic journeys that force the child out of the mother and into the father's world, only to have that father's world in its turn eject them. It is out of the exile of psychic orphanhood that the writerly "I," the "I" of autobiography that is also the "I" of psychoanalysis, is born.

Lázaro left his mother reluctantly. The forces of empire—the king's army, the *comendador*'s wealth—drive the boy out of the country and the mother and into the hands of a series of male masters. On these masters falls the task of introducing the boy into the Father's world, a world ostensibly barricaded against the seductions of women by codes of honor and celibacy. The fathers' lessons in scarcity, independence, and deception are ones administered by a violence and heartlessness that reflect sixteenth-century pedagogical patterns.

Lázaro learns from the blind man to be wary and exploitative as he gives up the expectation that his world could provide him warmth or nourishment. From the priest, Lázaro learns to refine his arts of survival, entering into competition with him for possession of the nourishment the father world continues to deny him. By chapter 3 with the squire, Lázaro begins to learn the clothing and gestures in which power masquerades. In the squire he finds a model by which to imitate the role of "having" in a culture obsessed with image. Chapters 4 to 7 allude to Lázaro's sexual and social initiation while further reinforcing the lessons his schooling has taught him: that the position of "having" in culture is won not by repressing the primary desires, but by appearing to have done so. At the "height of his good fortune" Lázaro serves and is served by the power structure through his capacity both to supply the repudiated objects of pleasure and to protect the image of denial on which the structure is built.

The picture of the male imaginary presented in Lázaro's autobiography reveals a hierarchized and differentiated masculine economy whose survival depends on the suppression and exploitation of an anonymous and depotentiated feminine world. Lázaro shows that his education into the games of power has not extinguished desire for or relationship to that feminine world. It has, however, provided a whole false structure whose object is to disguise its continued dependency on that which it has repudiated. Lázaro as a member of the social order makes his living decrying those who are not. His official job is to shore up the power of the royal hierarchy by marking the boundary between the "I" of power and the "other" of indefinition and powerlessness.

Lacan's distinction between "having" and "being" the phallus describes well the combination of antagonism and dependency that characterizes the structures of psyche and body politic made evident in *Lazarillo de Tormes*. Lacan makes clear that the phallus as a symbol of the lack inherent in the subject can never in fact be possessed by the subject. Thus Lacan images traditional gender roles as a game of illusion in which the woman is required to reflect the other of the man's desire.

Lázaro, not having been born into the structures of power, functions in relation to Vuestra Merced as a woman. The power he wields is that of refusal. He can, under pressure from Vuestra Merced, refuse his role as support of the power structure. Vuestra Merced's demand of an explanation for his "dishonor" frees Lázaro to withdraw his dissembling posture vis-à-vis the men in power whom he supplies with women and wine. By demonstrating in his letter to Vuestra Merced his power to expose the empty structure of denial on which the father's power is built, Lázaro establishes a self superior in its awareness, mobility, and flexibility to the fixed and parasitic forms that men of power have adopted. He inverts, in the process, the hierarchy of self and other which had initially defined his relation to Vuestra Merced. Like Griselda, Lázaro's act of obedience, his agreement to respond to Vuestra Merced's demand that he explain his relationship to the archpriest and his wife, finally gives him power by exposing his tormentor to the vastness of all he has denied. Lázaro's "I," an "I" forced on him by his threatened expulsion from the father's world, gives him a vantage point outside that father world that converts it from a structure that possesses him to one he is in a position to dismantle.

Lázaro shows in his autobiography that "I" is *not* a fixed position. It is not something conferred on one by entering the male hierarchy, by wearing gentleman's clothing, and having a job in the royal service. "I" is a position easily confused with the "safe harbor" of male authority because one first wins the use of it in that ambit. The real truth about the "I," however, is that it is defined and assumable only because of the other. "I" is where the other is not. The great period of individualism, of break-away from home, family, and tradition in Western Europe, is also the age of the telescope and the microscope, the age that gave centrality to the sun, that introduced gunpowder into warfare: an age that made distance an aspect of control. The distance that empowers makes invisible the Other to which the "I" remains bound.

In St. Teresa's autobiography once again we read the story of successive separations. Teresa's mother's pattern—marriage at age thirteen, nine children, withdrawal into fantasy, depression, and early death—offered little to inspire a young woman fired by the dream of heroism and martyrdom. The death of her mother in Teresa's early adolescence most likely only made definitive a separation made psychologically much earlier. Teresa played the classical father's daughter role, having enjoyed a special place of privilege in her father's affections. Stifling within the confines of her father's love surfaced fairly early, however, and came to a head when her desire to enter the convent won out against her father's opposition. Comparing her escape from his house and control with a death ("no creo sera mas el sentimiento cuando me muera, porque me parece cada hueso se me apartaba por si," 4.1.134) [I do not think my distress will be greater when I die, for it seemed to me as if every bone in my body were being wrenched asunder (Peers, p. 77; emended by Iarocci)], Teresa describes early in her autobiography what will become its principal theme, that is, the struggle to validate a self not authorized by paternal approval. For the truth is that, much like Lázaro, the "I" given to her by the ruling authority was a ventriloquized "I," the "I" prescribed and centered in the Other of Law.

The decisive battle in her struggle to locate a sense of her identity comes out of the visions of Jesus that begin to appear as her spiritual practice matures. The visions are as threatening to the confessors and church authorities in Teresa's life as are the rumors of the archpriest's mistress to the authorities of state in Lázaro's life, or as the suspicion of Mencía's adultery to Gutierre in Calderón's *El médico de su honra*. The "I" that represents authority can only rest untroubled when the Other of repressed desire is quiescent and submissive. For that Other—only apparently the nun, the rogue, or the wife—is in fact the whole world of the feelings and the body that the subject has been required to repress. At a time when the ego is rigidified into defensiveness and paranoia because of the intensity of the traumas of separation by which it was born, the unconscious is the receptacle of repressed pain, rage, shame, grief, and guilt that might at any moment burst open. The chaos that writers like Calderón imputed to the influence of seductive women was the chaos of an unconscious feared as powerful and unruly, and therefore in need of close surveillance.

By 1560, when Teresa began to get her visions, to tap into the unconscious was extremely dangerous business. Many women had already admitted having been in service to the devil when authorities challenged the source of their ecstatic pronouncements. The terror surrounding the

experience of Teresa's visions is clear in the *Vida*. In chapter 28 Teresa
reveals the fear with which both she and her confessor met the revela-
tions of Jesus that were a part of her ecstatic experience. She writes:

> [Mi confesor] pasolos [trabajos] harto grandes conmigo de muchas
> maneras. Supe que le decian que se guardase de mi, no le enganase
> el demonio con creerme algo de lo que me decia; trainle ejemplos
> de otras personas. Todo esto me fatigaba a mi. Temia que no habia
> de haber con quien me confesar, sino que todos habian de huir de
> mi. No hacia sino llorar. (28.14.343)
>
> [Very great trials befell my confessor on my account, and this in many
> ways. I knew they used to tell him that he must be on his guard against me,
> lest he should be deceived by the devil into believing what he {the devil} was
> telling me, and they gave him examples of what had happened to other
> people. All this worried me. I was afraid that there would be no one left to
> hear my confession, and that everyone would flee from me: I did nothing
> but weep.] (Peers, p. 266; emended by Iarocci)

The fear of being rejected by her confessor, and worse, of being left
without a confessor, was particularly acute in Teresa's case. She admired
and often loved the men who accompanied her on her spiritual journey,
and often expressed in her writings a sense of despair when they were
absent. The testing of her visions placed her in a role of opposition to
those with whom, as an adoring subordinate, she had heretofore identified herself. In their effort to subdue the dragon of the unconscious,
they insisted on their authority over her, and she, taking up, and perhaps
to some extent exaggerating the opposition, accepted her role as female
other, as weak in the face of their strength, ignorant in the face of their
knowledge.

We get a sense of the difficulty of her position in Teresa's description
of her efforts to persuade her confessors and the leaders of the church
that in receiving visions she was, in effect, one of them. She writes:

> Los siervos de Dios que no se asiguraban, trababanme mucho. Yo,
> como hablaba con descuido algunas cosas que ellos tomaban por
> diferente intencion. . . . y ansi lo que yo decia . . . sin mirar en ello,
> pareciales poca humildad. En viendome alguna falta, que verian

muchas, luego era todo condenado. Preguntabanme algunas cosas;
yo respondia con llaneza y descuido. Luego les parecia les queria
ensanar, y que me tenia por sabia. (28.17.344)
[Those of God's servants who were not convinced that all was well would
often come and talk to me. Some of the things I said to them I expressed
carelessly and they took them in the wrong sense . . . so what I would say
. . . without thinking about it seemed lacking in humility to them. When
they saw any faults in me, and they must have seen a great many, they condemned me outright. They would ask me certain questions, which I answered plainly, though carelessly; and they then thought that I was trying
to instruct them and that I considered myself a person of learning.]
(Peers, p. 267)

She goes on:

Duro esto harto tiempo, afligida por muchas partes. . . . Bastantes
cosas habia para quitarme el juicio, y algunas veces me via en ter-
minos que no sabia que hacer sino alzar los ojos a el Senor, porque
contradicion de buenos a una mujercilla ruin y flaca, como yo, y
temerosa, no parece nada ansi dicho, y con haber yo pasado en la
vida grandisimos trabajos, es este de los mayores. (28.18.344–45)
[This state of things went on for a long time and I was troubled on many
sides. . . . I had troubles enough to deprive me of my reason, and I sometimes found myself in such a position that I could do nothing but lift up my
eyes to the Lord. For though the opposition of good people to a weak and
lowly woman like myself, and a timid one at that, seems nothing when described in this way, it was one of the worst trials that I have ever known in
my life, and I have suffered some very severe ones.] (Peers, pp. 267–68)

Teresa writes of being afraid of losing her mind, of weeping so much
she thought she might go blind, of experiencing a sense of pain and loss
so acute as to be beyond description at this period in her life. Distinguishing her from so many long forgotten visionaries and witches sent
to trial and condemned, however, was the requirement that she write.
The act of transforming experience into image and word has the effect
of creating a container for the otherwise inchoate self. In the successive
acts of writing her life, Teresa was forced to gather together the fragments of a being, and to create a place of her own on which to stand.

Long before the decision of chapter 23 that made of her life a new life and of her book a new book, Teresa had already converted her interlocutor and confessor into her student, her "son." She instructs him in the levels of prayer, and talks authoritatively about the uses and value of mental prayer, of visions, of locutions. In chapter 23 Teresa lays hold of a source of authority once claimed by her confessors, an authority to which they have access only secondhand, but which she has encountered in the intimacy of her own experience. Now it is she, not they, who can claim authenticity, power, the right to teach, speak, write, and found. The conversion to a self not defined by the social world is announced there, when she writes, "Es otro libro nuevo de aqui adelante, digo otra vida nueva" (23.1.294) [From this point onward, I am speaking of another and new book—I mean, of another and new life (Peers, p. 219; emended by Iarocci)]. In chapter 23 she claims an identity that no longer relies on social convention. "La [vida] de hasta aqui era mia; la que he vivido desde que comence a declarar estas cosas de oracion, es que vivia Dios en mi" (23.1.294) [Until now, the life I was describing was my own; but the life I have been living since I began to expound these matters concerning prayer is the life which God has been living in me (Peers, pp. 219–20)].

It is from that newly claimed and grounded "I" that Teresa can invert her relation to the devil. Having a place on which to stand, Teresa can expose the devil as the devil-monger's own creation. When Teresa says, "Es sin duda que tengo ya mas miedo a los que tan grande le tienen al demonio que a el mesmo" (25.22.319) [I am without a doubt more fearful of those who are terrified by the devil than I am of the devil himself (Peers, pp. 243–44; emended by Iarocci)], she has managed, like Lázaro in the prologue, to invert the power relations between the socially constructed "I" and "other." Like Teresa, Lázaro survives on the side of the father only on condition of good behavior, his safety always precarious. Both are entirely too close to, too contaminated by, the world of desire, the rejected realm of the unconscious, thoroughly to be assimilated into the upper reaches of the social hierarchy. Both Teresa and Lázaro represent not the mirror the Other is forced to hold up to the dominant order in support of its illusion of substance, but the turbulence of a self that is truly Other.

As Luce Irigaray has pointed out, however, the male imaginary that has been exalted to the status of the symbolic cannot tolerate, or even contemplate, difference. The expulsion of Lázaro and the torment of Teresa came because of the reminder they brought to the portals of hegemonic power of the Other that hides under the surface of the mirror meant to suppress otherness. Their survival depends on their being able to convince their superiors that the desire which infuses life into the dead structures of paternal prohibition is not only destructive. God is the life-spring of religious life, as Teresa was able finally to convince at least enough of her superiors. Wine and women, as Lázaro seeks to convince his superiors, are also the life blood that gives the archpriest sustenance. As each manages to show how essential the connection to the underside of the social self is, how little in fact these rejections have managed truly to expel desire, they grow in power, and demonstrate the intricate and painful process by which a self emerges from successive rejections of the structures by which they were defined.

Notes

1. Kelly begins her memorable essay by saying: "To take the emancipation of women as a vantage point is to discover that events that further the historical development of men, liberating them from natural, social, or ideological constraints, have quite different, even opposite, effects upon women" ("Did Women Have a Renaissance?" in *Women, History, and Theory: The Essays of Joan Kelly*, ed. Catherine Stimpson [Chicago: University of Chicago Press, 1984], p. 19). Ruth Kelso's 1956 *Doctrine for the Lady of the Renaissance* (rpt. with a foreword by Katherine M. Rogers; Urbana: University of Illinois Press, 1978) anticipates many of Kelly's observations and stands as the single exception to the tendency among critics to assume an equality of the sexes that in fact is not a part of Renaissance social, political, or economic change.

2. Anonymous, *Lazarillo de Tormes*, ed. Francisco Rico (Madrid: Cátedra, 1987), p. 11.

3. A great number of books are now devoted to the topic of the effect on the land and peoples of the Americas of what was from their point of view an invasion. See especially Peter Hulme, *Colonial Encounters: Europe and the Native Caribbean, 1492–1979* (London: Methuen, 1986); Rolena Adorno, *Guama Poma: Writing and Resistance in Colonial Peru* (Austin: University of Texas Press, 1986); and Louise Burkhart, *The Slippery Earth: Nahua-Christian Moral*

Dialogue in Sixteenth-Century Mexico (Tucson: University of Arizona Press, 1989).

4. Carolyn Merchant, *The Death of Nature: Ecology and the Scientific Revolution* (London: Wildwood House, 1980); Brian Easlea, *Witchhunting, Magic, and the New Philosophy* (Sussex: Harvester Press, 1980); Morris Berman, *The Reenchantment of the World* (Ithaca: Cornell University Press, 1981); Morris Berman, *Coming to Our Senses: Body and Spirit in the Hidden History of the West* (New York: Simon and Schuster, 1989); Sandra Harding, *The Science Question in Feminism* (Ithaca: Cornell University Press, 1986); and Evelyn Fox Keller, *Reflections on Gender and Science* (New Haven: Yale University Press, 1985).

5. This summary of Irigaray's critique of rationality is indebted to Margaret Whitford's excellent article "Luce Irigaray's Critique of Rationality," in *Feminist Perspectives in Philosophy*, ed. Morwenna Griffiths and Margaret Whitford (Bloomington: Indiana University Press, 1988), 109–30. Irigaray's grounding of the imaginary in the body has of course opened her to criticism, especially on the issue of essentialism. For response to the concerns about essentialism expressed by such American writers on feminist theory as Elaine Showalter, Mary Jacobus, and Nancy K. Miller, see Diana Fuss, *Essentially Speaking: Feminism, Nature, and Difference* (New York: Routledge, 1989), ch. 4, and Margaret Whitford, *Luce Irigaray: Philosophy in the Feminine* (New York: Routledge, 1991), pp. 14–16.

6. As Margaret Whitford sums it up, Irigaray "begins with an analysis of an imaginary which is anal, that is to say, which interprets sexual difference as though there were only one sex, and that sex were male (woman as defective man). For our culture, identity, logic and rationality are symbolically male, and the female is either outside, the hole, or the unsymbolizable residue (or at most, the womb, the maternal function)" ("Luce Irigaray's Critique of Rationality," p. 121).

7. For a more elaborate discussion of the factors contributing to a shift in the formation of masculine identity in sixteenth-century Spain, see my "The Evolution of Psyche under Empire: Literary Reflections of Spain in the Sixteenth Century," in *Cultural and Historical Grounding for Hispanic and Luzo-Brazilian Feminist Literary Criticism*, ed. Hernan Vidal (Minneapolis: Institute for the Study of Ideologies and Literature, 1989), pp. 165–92.

8. Lawrence Stone notes about punitive practices in Renaissance schools that "the chief inducements to learning were thought to be the desire for pleasure and the aversion to pain. Despite the warnings of the reformers, the latter was rap-

idly twisted by lazy schoolmasters into an excuse for the massive brutality that was to prevail in grammar schools for many centuries" (*The Family, Sex, and Marriage in England, 1500–1806* [New York: Harper and Row, 1977], p. xii). Luis Vives, in his influential *Formación de la mujer cristiana*, makes of material absence and restraint a virtue. He asks mothers in the book: "¿Queréis ser amadas de veras? . . . Haced que no os amen cuando ignoran todavía que es amor. . . . De nadie sentía más aversión que de mi madre cuando yo era niño. Y ahora su memoria es para mí la mas sagrada, y todas las veces que me asalta su recuerdo . . . la abrazo y beso en espíritu con la más dulce de las gratitudes" (*Formación de la mujer cristiana. Obras completas*, ed. Lorenzo Riber [Madrid: Aguilar, 1947], 2.11.1144b).

9. Augustine says in the *Confessions*: "So as to this period of my life, which I cannot remember having lived . . . I am reluctant to count it as part of this present life of mine which I live in the world; for . . . it is just the same as the period of life which I spent in my mother's womb. But if I was shapen in my iniquity, and in sin did my mother conceive me . . . when . . . was I ever innocent?" (*Confessions*, trans. Rex Warner [New York: Penguin, 1963], p. 25).

10. See Walter Ong, *Interfaces of the Word: Studies in the Evolution of Consciousness and Culture* (Ithaca: Cornell University Press, 1977). Gerald Strauss notes the importance of Augustine in the development of pedagogical theory in the Renaissance. He says, "looking back from the literature written for children in that age [the sixteenth century], we can see Augustine looming as the apostle of unmitigated pessimism. Augustine shows that the young child, the infant even, displays the signs of human depravity, greed, envy, lust, the insistent will, and the *amor sui* which is the heart of sin. Without grace the infant remains in the 'thick darkness of ignorance,' incapable out of his own powers to surmount his animal-like condition" ("The State of Pedagogical Theory c. 1530: What Protestant Reformers Knew about Education," in *Schooling and Society*, ed. Lawrence Stone [Baltimore: Johns Hopkins University Press, 1976], pp. 72–73). "In the Reformation the Augustinian position was most often cited as an argument for the systematic use of severe restrictive and enforced conditioning of the young" (Strauss, p. 74). Strauss's observations help to explain Lawrence Stone's comment that "there can be no doubt . . . that more children were being beaten in the sixteenth and early seventeenth centuries, over a long age span, than ever before" (Stone, *The Family*, pp. 163–64).

11. Jean Grimshaw, *Feminist Philosophers: Women's Perspectives on Philosophical Traditions* (Brighton, Eng.: Wheatsheaf, 1986), pp. 36–37. Luce Irigaray goes much further than Grimshaw, arguing that philosophy by its very nature, at its origins, depends on the exclusion of woman (see for example, "Plato's

Hystera," in *Speculum of the Other Woman*, trans. Gillian C. Gill [Ithaca: Cornell University Press, 1985], pp. 243–64). As Margaret Whitford explains: "from her (Irigaray's) point of view, the philosophers, of whatever persuasion, are comfortably installed in the male imaginary, so comfortably that they are completely unaware of the sexuate character of 'universal' thought. So Irigaray has a twofold task. The first is to reveal the imaginary body of philosophy, to show the sexual dynamics at work in the theoretical constructions of philosophy. The second is to show how the body of the maternal-feminine has been left out of the ideal and intelligible realm while continuing to nourish it and supply its sensible, material conditions" (*Luce Irigaray*, p. 103).

12. In the Afterword to her *Renaissance Feminism*, Constance Jordan notes that "[Renaissance] feminists learned, among other things, that power is rarely if ever renounced because of appeals to principles. And in fact their protests became progressively more focused on the consequences of poverty and, in particular, of the economic deprivation of women. The privileges that law and custom allow are to a large degree purchased by wealth: this they knew and stated with increasing vehemence" (*Renaissance Feminism: Literary Texts and Political Models* [Ithaca: Cornell University Press, 1990], p. 309).

13. The separation of masculine authority from feminine sentiment can already be seen, for example, in the dramatically different discourses of the king and queen in Diego de San Pedro's *Cárcel de amor*, as well as Juan de Flores' *Grisel y Mirabella*. Patricia Grieve notes of the latter text something applicable to many of the sentimental romances of the late fifteenth century: "The King, consistently described as judicious, is contrasted with the mother, who is described at first in terms of her concern for her daughter. She is the voice of *voluntad* who opposes her husband's voice of *razón*" ("Mothers and Daughters in Fifteenth-Century Spanish Sentimental Romances: Implications for *Celestina*," *Bulletin of Hispanic Studies* 67 [1990]: 350).

14. Lynda Schmidt's article "How the Father's Daughter Found Her Mother" (in *To Be a Woman*, ed. Connie Zweig [Los Angeles: Jeremy P. Tarcher, 1990]), records a sense of one's contingency in the face of a natural world indifferent to one's weaknesses. The feeling is not unlike that expressed by Fernando de Rojas in the prologue to *La Celestina*, where he alludes to the "terremotos y torvellinos . . . los naufragios y encendios" which constantly assail us (*La Celestina*, ed. Dorothy Severin [Madrid: Cátedra, 1992], p. 78). Schmidt, raised on a ranch in the twentieth century, comments for her part that "it makes me nervous to think of a human mother having the power over me that nature did, yet it is my impression that that is what it is like for mothers' daughters. On the ranch we had to keep tuned to everything going on around us, or else we would be in danger for

our lives. We had to be alert for booby traps in the ground, such as gopher holes, that would trip us on our horses, breaking legs or heads. We had to swim in the ocean with constant caution against being crushed by great waves. . . . We had to watch for rattlers, scorpions, black-widow spiders, pay heed that we not fall off a suddenly turning cowpony, or be run over by an angry bull, or kicked by a frightened calf. We had to read the minds of animals and cowboys or be humiliated or injured. Is this what it is like to be a mother's daughter?" (p. 79).

15. The attack on the very notion of a female god figure is quite forthright in the *Malleus*. The authors take on St. Isidore on the question, for example, since Isidore referred to Fortune as a goddess. Kramer and Sprenger insist that "to believe that there is such a goddess, or that the harm done to bodies and creatures which is ascribed to witchcraft does not actually proceed from witchcraft, but from that same goddess of Fortune, is sheer idolatry; and also to assert that witches themselves were born for that very purpose that they might perform such deeds in the world is similarly alien to the Faith, and indeed to the general teachings of the Philosophers" (Heinrich Kramer and James Sprenger, *The Malleus Maleficarum*, trans. and ed. Montague Summers [New York: Dover Publications, 1971], p. 35a).

16. Writing about Paracelsus, Carl Jung notes that "his most secret, deepest passion, his whole creative yearning, belonged to the *lumen naturae*, the divine spark buried in the darkness. . . . The light from above made the darkness still darker, but the lumen naturae is the light of the darkness itself, which illuminates its own darkness, and this light the darkness comprehends" (*Alchemical Studies: Collected Works*, trans. R. F. C. Hull [Princeton: Princeton University Press, 1967], 13:160–61. Ernst Robert Curtius points out that the struggle by the Christian church to limit the powers of the goddess Physis or Natura persisted throughout the Middle Ages (*European Literature and the Latin Middle Ages*, trans. Willard R. Trask [New York: Pantheon Books, 1953], p. 107).

17. The problem of the difference between the "other" and the "Other" is one that has concerned me as I work on this paper. I use Other (upper case) to refer to either the unconscious of the abjected (m)Other or the realm of language and culture of the father world, while "other" (lower case) refers to the cultural role assigned to women in the male imaginary, the role of reflector and support for the illusion of having that grants male power. The distinction is not always easy to maintain, however, as the social role prescribed for women is connected to deeper layers of the unconscious where the feminine is associated with pre-Oedipal passions that have been subjected to banishment from consciousness. For more on this topic, see also note 39 below.

18. Part 1, Question 6 of the *Malleus Maleficarum* is devoted to the issue of

why women are more susceptible than men to the devil's wiles. Citing from all manner of sources, the authors set out to prove that women are lacking in faith and intelligence, and that they are more lustful, depraved, and deceitful than men. Quoting from St. John Chrysostom, for example, they exclaim: "What else is woman but a foe to friendship, an inescapable punishment, a necessary evil, a natural temptation, a desirable calamity, a domestic danger, a delectable detriment, an evil nature, painted with faint colours!" They go on to conclude: "Therefore if it be a sin to divorce her when she ought to be kept, it is indeed a necessary torture; for either we commit adultery by divorcing her, or we must endure daily strife" (p. 43a).

19. See her "Mothers and Daughters."

20. See, for a discussion of early infant feelings, Klein's "Our Adult World and Its Roots in Infancy," in *Envy and Gratitude and Other Works, 1949–1963* (New York: Delta, 1977). A good general resource for the work of Melanie Klein is Hanna Segal's *Introduction to the Work of Melanie Klein* (London: Hogarth Press, 1964).

21. See my "The Making of the Novel and the Evolution of Consciousness," *Oral Tradition* 2 (1987): 231–48.

22. For a discussion of the sense of loss that underscores twentieth-century psychology, see Peter Homans's *The Ability to Mourn: Disillusionment and the Social Origins of Psychoanalysis* (Chicago: University of Chicago Press, 1989). The mother and the mother world that Freud maintained one had to reject remained in the psyche as a mark of constant disconformity with the demands of civilization. Jung, breaking with Freud over this point, insisted that the only salvation for the Western world was a return to an awareness of that rejected material. In both seminal figures one senses the tremendous sense of loss that had been the effect of a psyche brought into connection with civilization through a splitting off of the maternal aspects of development.

23. Neumann says: "All reductive interpretations assert that being swallowed is identical with castration, with fear of the dragon and fear of the father, who prevents incest with the mother. That is to say, incest with the mother is in itself desirable, but is made terrible by this fear of the father. The mother is supposed to be a positive object of desire, and the father the real obstacle. This interpretation is erroneous, because incest and the fear of castration are already apparent at the stage when no father is operative, much less a jealous father" (*The Origins and History of Consciousness*, trans. R. F. C. Hull [Princeton: Princeton University Press, 1970], p. 155). Kristeva also alludes to the importance, in the pre-Oedipal situation, of an emptiness within the mother that is her desire for the father, and that it is that emptiness, that place of the virtual father of the

mother's desire, that forces the formation of the ego by revealing that the mother's desire is oriented not toward the child but toward an other. It is the creation of an ego in the place of that other that is coincident, in Neumann and in Kristeva, with the need to abject, to throw off, the otherwise all-powerful mother. Kristeva says: "The immediate transference toward the imaginary father, who is such a godsend that you have the impression that it is he who is transferred into you, withstands a process of rejection involving what may have been chaos and is about to become an *abject*. The maternal space can come into being as such, before becoming an object correlative to the Ego's desire, only as an *abject*" (*Tales of Love*, trans. Leon S. Roudiez [New York: Columbia University Press, 1987], p. 41). Maria Torok, also working out of a system that disputes Freud's giving primacy to the fear of the father in the Oedipal drama, argues that it is the desire to be free of the mother's regressive pull that causes the child to separate from the mother. She considers the child's evocation of the castrating father a strategy on the child's part to justify to the more terrifying mother the need to separate from her. See "The Significance of Penis Envy in Women," in *Female Sexuality: New Psychoanalytic Views*, ed. Janine Chasseguet-Smirgel (London: Maresfield Library, 1985), pp. 135–70.

24. I am thinking, of course, of the *relatos* of the explorers, the confessional and autobiographical tracts required of so many visionary nuns by their confessors, the trial records of the inquisitors, the picaresque novels, and the fascination with letter writing as a form of literary entertainment. For more on the question of first-person narrative and the development of the notion of the autonomous subject in early modern letters, see Antonio Gómez-Moriana, "Autobiografía y discurso ritual," *Zagadnienia Rodzajow Literackich* 27 (1984): 5–23, and Nicholas Spadaccini and Jenaro Talens, "Introduction: The Construction of the Self. Notes on Autobiography in Early Modern Spain," in *Autobiography in Early Modern Spain*, ed. Nicholas Spadaccini and Jenaro Talens (Minneapolis: Prisma Institute, 1988), pp. 9–40.

25. The importance of the mother-child bond is the subject of much study by object relations theorists. See, for example, Margaret Mahler, Fred Pine, and Anni Bergman, *The Psychological Birth of the Human Infant: Symbiosis and Individuation* (New York: Basic Books, 1975), as well as John Bowlby, *Attachment and Loss* (New York: Basic Books, 1969, 1973), 2 vols., and D. W. Winnicott, *Babies and Their Mothers*, ed. Clare Winnicott, Ray Shepherd, and Madeleine Davis (Reading, Mass.: Addison-Wesley, 1987), for extended discussions about and observations of the effects of damage to early bonding on later child and adult character formation. Lawrence Stone has pointed out that, due to the strengthening of the patriarchally ordered family and the increase in

the importance of schooling, "more children were being beaten in the sixteenth and early seventeenth century, over a longer age span, than ever before" (pp. 163–64). Stone also discusses the prevalence of the practice among families of reasonable income to send their infants to the countryside to be nursed by country women for a year or two. Philippe Ariès notes that in the same period the "coddling" attitude toward the rearing of children came under severe attack: "it is even better known to us by the critical reactions it provoked at the end of the sixteenth century and particularly in the seventeenth century" (*Centuries of Childhood: A Social History of Family Life*, trans. Robert Baldick [New York: Random House, 1962], p. 130).

26. Ruth Kelso points out that in the Renaissance "the first law of woman . . . was submission and obedience, exemplified in the beginning and for all time by our Mother Eve. . . . Education for the gentleman was a wide-flung subject, involving all that was called liberal and drawing on the best pedagogical advice of the time. Education for the lady looked to her proficiency in domestic affairs and what in moral and religious training would keep her safely concerned only with them" (*Doctrine for the Lady of the Renaissance*, pp. 3–4). In *La perfecta casada*, an enduring Spanish Renaissance classic devoted to the conduct of the married woman, Fray Luis de León emphasizes the idea of enclosure for women. He says in chapter 15: "Así como la naturaleza, como dijimos y diremos, hizo a las mujeres para que, encerradas guardasen la casa, así las obligo a que cerrasen la boca. . . . Porque el hablar nace del entender, y las palabras no son sino como imágenes o señales de lo que el ánimo concibe en sí mismo. Por donde así como a la mujer buena y honesta la naturaleza no la hizo para el estudio de las ciencias ni para los negocios de dificultades, sino para un solo oficio simple y doméstico, así las limitó el entender, y por consiguiente les tasó las palabras y las razones" (*Formación*, p. 320).

27. The paper found with Anselmo's dead body after the full force of the tragedy has impacted him says, "un necio e impertinente deseo me quita la vida. Si las nuevas de mi muerte llegaren a los oídos de Camila, sepa que yo la perdono, porque no estaba ella obligada a hacer milagros, ni yo tenía necesidad de querer que ella los hiciese; y pues yo fui el fabricador de mi deshonra, no hay para qué" (*Don Quixote de la Mancha*, ed. John Jay Allen [Madrid: Cátedra, 1977], 1.35.425). Anselmo apparently dies, as does Carrizales in *El celoso extremeño*, aware that his own mania has provoked the dishonor of his wife.

28. For an interesting study of the period of chaos that precedes marriage, and how that plot is played and replayed in Renaissance drama, see Frederick de Armas, *The Invisible Mistress: Aspects of Feminism and Fantasy in the Golden Age* (Charlottesville, Va.: Biblioteca Siglo de Oro, 1976).

29. Kathryn Rabuzzi, *The Sacred and the Feminine: Toward a Theology of Housework* (New York: Seabury Press, 1982).

30. Electa Arenal and Stacey Schlau, *Untold Sisters: Hispanic Nuns in Their Own Works* (Albuquerque: University of New Mexico Press, 1989).

31. A good resource for material on nuns' lives in sixteenth- and seventeenth-century Spain is the *Journal of Hispanic Philology* 13 (1989), guest edited by Alison Weber.

32. See Mary E. Giles, *The Book of Prayer of Sor María of Santo Domingo: A Study and Translation* (Albany: State University of New York Press, 1990), for a discussion of the case against Sor María.

33. Elizabeth Petroff notes that the visionary path was one of the few that offered women power in late medieval society. The tendency to distrust the visions and to associate them with aberrant female sexuality became a dominant aspect of Inquisitorial investigation only in the sixteenth century. See *Medieval Women's Visionary Literature* (New York: Oxford University Press, 1986), pp. 5–6.

34. All references to the *Libro de la vida* of Saint Teresa are by chapter, section, and page in the edition by Dámaso Chicharro (Madrid: Cátedra, 1987).

35. I find particularly helpful Judith Butler's formulation of the situation, filtered through the Lacanian notion of the symbolic order and Hegel. She says: "The Symbolic order creates cultural intelligibility through the mutually exclusive positions of 'having' the Phallus (the position of men) and 'being' the Phallus (the paradoxical position of women). The interdependency of these positions recalls the Hegelian structure of failed reciprocity between master and slave, in particular, the unexpected dependency of the master on the slave in order to establish his own identity through reflection" (*Gender Trouble: Feminism and the Subversion of Identity* [New York: Routledge, 1990], p. 44).

36. Walter Ong (*Interfaces of the Word: Studies in the Evolution of Consciousness and Culture* [Ithaca: Cornell University Press, 1977], p. 137) has emphasized the importance of schooling and the creation of the printing press in the development of an internalized sense of the self in the sixteenth century. The sense that the privatization that results from knowing how to read and write gives access to power is stressed by Roger Chartier, who notes that "there emerges a strange alliance between reading, that most private and hidden practice, and true, effective power, power far more effective than that of public office" ("The Practical Impact of Writing," in *A History of Private Life*, ed. Roger Chartier, trans. Arthur Goldhammer [Cambridge: Harvard University Press, 1989]).

37. *Renaissance Feminism*, p. 20.

38. Antonio Gómez-Moriana, in his interesting study of the nature of the au-

tobiographical subject in sixteenth-century Spain, also compares the seemingly differently based and conceived works of the saint and a fictional rogue. It is their condition of writing out the mandate of an authoritative Other who seeks to take power over their respective subjectivities that makes comparable the two first-person narratives.

39. Malcolm Bowie discusses the confusing proliferation of definitions given by Lacan to the concept of the Other: "How can the term remain useful as an operational device when it may be variously defined as a father, a place, a point, any dialectical partner, a horizon within the subject, a horizon beyond the subject, the unconscious, language, the signifier? The *nom-du-père*, the original Other, introduces a gap between desire and its object(s) which the subject is bounded by, and bound to, throughout his life and at all levels of experience" (*Freud, Proust, and Lacan: Theory as Fiction* [Cambridge: Cambridge University Press, 1987], p. 119). It is in this sense of gap that I have variously used the term "Other" here to signify the unconscious of the Mother world and the structuring demands of law and language associated with the Father. For a good discussion of Lacan's use of "Other" to refer both to the (m)Other as the source of unconscious discourse, and the father of culture and the symbolic order, see Ellie Ragland-Sullivan, *Jacques Lacan and the Philosophy of Psychoanalysis* (Urbana: University of Illinois Press, 1986), pp. 104–5.

III

Historical Contexts

10

History and Modernity in the Spanish Golden Age

Secularization and Literary Self-Assertion in *Don Quijote*

ANTHONY J. CASCARDI

Yo, que siempre trabajo y me desvelo
por parecer que tengo de poeta
la gracia que no quiso darme el Cielo.
Cervantes, *Viaje del Parnaso*

———◆◆———

In *The Theory of the Novel*, first published in 1919, Lukács wrote that "the first great novel of world literature stands at the beginning of the time when the Christian God began to forsake the world." "Cervantes," he says, "lived in the period of the last, great and desperate mysticism, the period of a fanatical attempt to renew the dying religion from within; a period of a new view of the world rising up in mystical forms; the last period of truly lived but already disoriented, tentative, sophisticated, occult aspirations." As Lukács went on to say, this was "the period of the demons let loose, a period of great confusion of values in the midst of an as yet unchanged value system. And Cervantes, the faithful Christian and naively loyal patriot, creatively exposed the deepest essence of this demonic problematic: the purest heroism is bound to become grotesque, the strongest faith is bound to become madness, when the ways leading to the transcendental home have become impassable."[1]

The thrust of these passages is to suggest that the beginnings of literary modernity in Cervantes' *Don Quijote* can be understood in terms of the process of secularization. And yet it also seems that the Lukácsean analysis of secularization as it bears on Cervantes' text raises at least as many problems as it resolves. For it is not altogether clear how the metaphysical language that we find in *The Theory of the Novel* can allow us to represent the connections between the increasingly secular (not to say prosaic) modes of consciousness encountered in the novel and the archaic sources of authority and belief out of which the culture of modernity emerges and which the novel continues to invoke. Although Lukács clearly intends such connections to be made, it seems that to formulate this issue in terms of the secularized idiom of modernity would lead to the writing of a suspiciously progressive, self-validating form of literary history, while to express it in the language of belief would be to embark on what would have to be described as a quixotic project to restore the cultural authority of the past. This difficulty shows up in the strangely lyrical metaphoricity of Lukács's language, which in phrases like "the demonization of the world" and "the waning of the gods" hovers mysteriously between the idiom of rationality and the idiom of belief. Yet one is hard pressed to describe the difficulties of *The Theory of the Novel* simply as a language problem, for what stands behind them is in fact central to the critical method employed throughout the work, which Lukács describes as "historico-philosophical" in nature and scope. As I take it, whereas a strictly philosophical approach to Cervantes would result in a suppression of the differences between the languages of rationality and of belief, a narrowly historical approach might well tempt us to conceive of the division between archaic modes of consciousness and the secular modern world as categorical, definite, and absolute.

The theoretical efforts of most recent critics of the novel, including some Hispanists and Cervantistas, have been to inscribe the process of secularization within the dynamics of a still more advanced or complex secular dialectic called historical materialism. Thus Jay M. Bernstein argued in *Lukács, Marxism, and the Dialectics of Form* that the Lukács of *Theory of the Novel* was already a historical-materialist, even though he may not have known it, and that the only way in which the language of metaphysical idealism that pervades *Theory of the Novel* can make sense is if we agree to transpose it into the discourse of historical materialism, thus interpreting the secularization process reflected in the quixotic tension between "soul" and "world" in terms of the critique of bourgeois culture developed in Lukács's later Marxist works like *History and Class Consciousness*. But if, in spite of Bernstein's claims, one believes that a mapping of the *Quijote* onto a materialist grid represents a betrayal of Lukács's original intentions in positioning Cervantes' work in relation to the secularization process, and if we nonetheless remain uncomfortable with the language of *Theory of the Novel*, which speaks of secularization, as in the passages cited above, in the unstable language of "demons" and "gods," then how are we to make sense of the role that Lukács ascribes to Cervantes as the inaugurator of the novel, as standing at the inception of literary modernity in the West?

In what follows here, I want to follow up Lukács's lead in arguing that the origins of literary modernity as reflected in Cervantes' work may indeed be understood in terms of the process of secularization. But at the same time I want to modify these claims so as to suggest that the attempt to represent the boundary between secularized and presecular modes of awareness yields what might best be described as a series of tropes, of which the literary-historical rhetoric of self-assertion is but one. Moreover, I hope in this connection to suggest that the process of secularization visible in a work like *Don Quijote* is not anything happening in culture external to literature, but that literary history itself, as an effort to negotiate between the authorities of the present and those of the past, is the best example of the "secularization" process whose consequences Lukács is hinting at in the passages cited above. As I hope also to explain in connection with Cervantes' text, the notion, or trope, of secularization provides a significant basis for resistance to the suspiciously progressive, self-validating, and self-assertive rhetoric of modernity. Indeed, when taken as a corrective to modernity's understanding of itself, the secularization process embodied in Cervantes' text can lead us to a more complex understanding of the dynamics of literary history, and eventually to the conclusion that the authority of literature in the modern age is not in fact self-sustaining but represents one consequence of the impossible and unfulfillable, not to say quixotic, desire to adapt a prior mode of cultural authority to the purposes and aims of the present age.

The question of secularization as it bears on the interpretation of Cervantes' text can best be understood in terms of a conflict between two versions of cultural history, which for simplicity I shall call the humanist and the modernist. Whereas modernism represents an attempt to generate a historical orientation for and from itself, humanism reads the past in order to distill a rhetoric of values and a canon to sustain its ideals. Unlike modernist self-assertion, humanism recognizes that it stands in essential need of the tradition as the value-field out of which it arises and to which it ultimately refers. But, to take the rhetoric of *translatio* as an example of the ways in which the humanist version of cultural history was expressed, it seems that humanism also implicitly recognizes the belatedness of its intentions as it strives to recuperate the values of the past. Humanism thus amounts to a demand placed upon cultural history that attempts to derive more from history than it can yield. But since the tradition is humanism's only resource against the potentially devastating sense of inadequacy that might follow from this fact, recourse to the tradition also becomes humanism's contradictory attempt to defend against the consequences of its failure to derive a more certain orientation from history than it can possibly provide.

If we consider the displacement of humanism by the self-assertive gestures of modernizing figures like Descartes and Hobbes, we can perhaps begin to understand how modernists attempted to reject the humanist rhetoric in order to secure the autonomy of their own age. The modernist exercise of freedom with respect to history commences for a figure like Descartes with the abandonment of all attachments to the past: "Regarding the opinions to which I had hitherto given credence, I thought that I could not do better than undertake to get rid of them, all at one go, in order to replace them afterwards with better ones, or with the same ones once I had squared them with the standards of reason."[2] Similarly, Hobbes claimed that political science was no older than his own work *De Cive*,[3] and in the *Discourse on Method* Descartes recommended razing the faltering edifice of received opinion for the purpose of building anew.[4]

History has been invoked by humanist writers as a fund of value, but
for Descartes history is no longer a reflection of preexisting norms and
no longer supplies examples worthy of imitation. This is confirmed in
the first part of the *Discourse on Method*, where Descartes classifies
works of history together with exemplary fables of the past; both may
present seductive ideals, but they fail to meet the criteria of autonomy
that the modern writer would invoke:

> Fables make us imagine many events as possible when they are not.
> And even the most accurate histories, while not altering or exag-
> gerating the importance of matters to make them more worthy of
> being read, at any rate almost always omit the baser and less nota-
> ble events; as a result, the other events appear in a false light, and
> those who regulate their conduct by examples drawn from these
> works are liable to fall into the excesses of the knights-errant in our
> tales of chivalry, and conceive plans beyond their powers.
>
> (*Discourse*, 1:113–14)

To be sure, the "overcoming" of history by philosophy does not
emerge full-blown with Descartes. It was itself provoked by a cultural
crisis evident in the efforts of Renaissance writers to assert themselves by
means of and against the example of the Ancients. Already for figures
like Petrarch, Machiavelli, Montaigne, and of course Cervantes, historical examples were the source of considerable unease, as writers came to
discover the anxieties that could follow from the irrecuperable distance
between the present and the past.[5] Hobbes attempts to address this anxiety when he criticizes "men that take their instruction from the authority of books, and not from their own meditation."[6] This is part of
Hobbes's wider program of "self-assertion," in which the accomplishments of reason are seen as self-justifying insofar as they reflect the successful actualization of human aims, intentions, and designs (Hobbes:
"Good successe is Power").[7]

The modernist response to humanism may at the same time be understood as a critique of the secularization thesis on which the humanist
understanding of cultural history depends. To think of culture not so
much as secular but as secularized is dangerous because it threatens the
integrity of this enlightened historiographical perspective of self-

understanding with respect to the present age. More specifically, to posit the origins of modernity in a process of secularization would be to embrace a fundamentally skeptical thesis with respect to the affirmative claim that the originating sources of value emanate from the subject in a process of radical self-assertion. For if modernity were shown to be secularized in some essential way, that is, if its specific forms of self-assertion were found to bear within them the hidden traces of preexisting modes of action and belief, then the claims of modern culture to have achieved an unprecedented level of autonomy would be drastically compromised.

Why is this so? Seen from the perspective of Enlightened modernity, the secularization theorem places at risk modernity's crucial distinction between the languages of imagination and belief on the one hand—however tenuous, secondary, or remotely connected to their origins these may be—and, on the other, a rational language of criticism, embodied not only in philosophy but, as we shall see in Cervantes, in hermeneutic efforts to decode (and recode) the past. Thus for a recent modernizing critic like Hans Blumenberg the idea of "secularization" as encountered in the Christian-humanist synthesis favored by a writer like Cervantes must be the source of a historical self-*mis*understanding from which we as moderns have been struggling to clear free.[8] For if the process of "secularization" somehow makes deoriginating figures out of all humanist transpositions of authority from one realm to the other, then any instance of the rhetoric of "secularization" would threaten to reveal a breach in the connections between the secular modes of consciousness represented in literary institutions like the novel and the archaic paradigms of authority informing these. Indeed, the greatest threat of secularization is that it may reveal a discontinuity in history itself. The specter of a rupture between one form of authority and another—as we attempt to "think back" from poetry to prophecy, or from genius to grace—threatens the humanist synthesis and leaves the imagination with few creative resources aside from its own somewhat desperate inventiveness.

So conceived, the secularization theorem is premised neither on the rejection of the images and authority of the tradition, nor on their reintegration within the sequential homogeneity of modern historical time, but rather on the failure of the secular fully to subsume the sacred. As the work of a writer like Cervantes makes clear, those forms of (mis)reading that are made available through the humanist tradition never become fully presumptive tropes of the original; they remain always haunted, mysteriously possessed and secretly energized by various "demonized" forms of the preceding culture. In the specific case of *Don Quijote,* which Lukács described as "demonic" in a similar respect, the transformation of an archaic heroic ethos into the substance of "quixotic" dreams whose basis lies neither in the world nor in history but in a tradition of texts may be seen as a result of the failure of secularization insofar as the power of that archaic ethos is never categorically and conclusively eclipsed, but survives in such a way as to possess Cervantes' hero as well as those other characters, like the Barber and the Priest, who seek to reorient Don Quijote to "orthodox" secular ways.

This is also to say that, for Cervantes at least, the origins of literary modernity must be located in the failure of the humanist paradigm of cultural history, as reflected in the still more general inability of secular culture fully to subsume its predecessors. As in the Prologue of *Don Quijote,* Part I, the humanist understanding of cultural transmission and continuity, or *translatio studii,* as fundamentally textual argues the failure of secularization, suggesting also that precisely where secularization fails is in relation to our desire, through literature, to imagine radically new ends for society and the self. As reflected in the Prologue, this "failure" appears as a disorder internal to the humanist desire to transpose and repossess the authority of the past. Thus the Prologue's "author" suggests that the modern writer is bound to fail in his attempt to recuperate the sources of value located in the culture of the past. When confronted with the demand that a great work of art should imitate and pay homage to preexisting forms, the "author" is counseled to buttress his modernizing efforts by reproducing the authoritative modes of discourse that historically have licensed literature—including references to canonized authors, learned allusions, marginal notes, and similar techniques—even if these are outmoded or "secularized" and no longer function as truly efficacious signs:

Vengamos ahora a la citación de los autores que los otros libros tienen, que en el vuestro os faltan. El remedio que esto tiene es muy fácil, porque no habéis de hacer otra cosa que buscar un libro que los acote todos, desde la A hasta la Z, como vos decís. Pues ese mismo abecedario pondréis vos en vuestro libro; que, puesto que a la clara se vea la mentira, por la poca necesidad que vos teníades de aprovecharos dellos, no importa nada; y quizá uno haya tan simple que crea que de todos os habéis aprovechado en la simple y sencilla historia vuestra; y cuando no sirva de otra cosa, por lo menos servirá aquel largo catálogo de autores a dar de improviso autoridad al libro. Y más, que no habrá quien se ponga a averiguar si los seguistes o no los seguistes, no yéndole nada en ello.[9]

[Let us come now to references to authors, which other books contain and yours lacks. The remedy for this is very simple; for you have nothing else to do but look for a book that quotes them all from A to Z as you say. Then you put this same alphabet into yours. For, granted that the very small need you have to employ them will make your deception transparent, it does not matter a bit; and perhaps there will even be someone silly enough to believe that you have made use of them all in your simple and straightforward story. And if it serves no other purpose, at least that long catalog of authors will be useful to lend authority to your book at the outset. Besides, nobody will take the trouble to examine whether you follow your authorities or not.]

The transformation of an imperfect or incomplete secularization process into the dynamics of modern literary history, with its attempt at radical self-assertion, may nonetheless offer a way to *deflect* the implications of inadequacy that the failure of the humanist effort to reappropriate the past might have for culture as a whole. One thinks, for instance, of the ambivalent terms in which Cervantes' *Galatea* is judged in chapter 6 of *Don Quijote*, Part 1: "Tiene algo de buena invención; propone algo, y no concluye nada: es menester esperar la segunda parte que promete; quizá con la emienda alcanzará del todo la misericordia que ahora se le niega" (1.6.120–21) [It is well conceived in some respects; it proposes something, but concludes nothing: it is necessary to wait for the second part; perhaps with this change it will gain the mercy that so far it has been denied]. A passage like this serves both as an admission of weakness and as a defense against it, but perhaps the most interesting fact about it is that Cervantes never completely conceals the devastating implications of the secularization theorem behind the rhetoric of self-assertion that this occasion of self-judgment invites; on the contrary, the conditions of failure, loss, and self-abasement maintain a continuing presence throughout his work. "¿Qué podría engendrar el estéril y mal cultivado ingenio mío," asks the Prologue's author, "sino la historia de un hijo seco, avellanado, antojadizo y lleno de pensamientos varios y nunca imaginados de otro alguno, bien como quien se engendró en una cárcel, donde toda incomodidad tiene su asiento y todo triste ruido su habitación?" (p. 50) [What could be expected of a sterile and uncultivated wit such as that which I possess if not an offspring that was dried up, shriveled, and eccentric: a story filled with thoughts that never occurred to anyone else, of a sort that might be engendered in a prison where every annoyance has its home and every sorry sound its habitation?].

The example of the landed gentleman whose brains have failed from reading too many of the chivalric novels is here transposed into the image of an author whose imagination fails him when called upon to invent an opening for his work, or to place it with respect to the traditions of the past, and who thus represents himself as unproductive, sterile, abandoned, and alone:

> Salgo ahora con todos mis años a cuestas, con una leyenda seca como un esparto, ajena de invención, menguada de estilo, pobre de conceptos, y falta de toda erudición y doctrina, sin acotaciones en las márgenes y sin anotaciones en el fin del libro, como vea que están otros libros, aunque sean fabulosos y profanos, tan llenos de sentencias de Aristóteles, de Platón y de toda la caterva de filósofos que admiran a los leyentes y tienen a sus autores por hombres leídos, eruditos y elocuentes. (p. 52)
> [I now appear, burdened by my years, with a tale that is as dry as a weed, bereft of any imagination, meager in style, impoverished in content, and wholly lacking in learning and wisdom, without marginal citations or notes at the end of the book, when other works of this sort, even though they may be fabulous and profane, are so packed with maxims from Aristotle and Plato and the whole learned crowd of philosophers that they fill

the reader with admiration and lead him to regard the author as a well-read, learned, and eloquent individual.]

The author can only defend against his deficiencies by taking the humanist notion of reading—or of *translatio*, as a form of "misreading"—not just as confirming evidence that no proper work remains for the modern writer to accomplish, but as an anti-idealist and indeed ironic basis for the creation of an equally anti-authorial stance. Indeed, it is through the author's self-projection and doubling as his own "friend," who intervenes in the Prologue in order to take up the imaginative slack created by the writer's secondariness with respect to the past, that Cervantes finds a way to fend off the potentially disturbing inferiority, indeed the haunting nothingness, that the modern writer's creative labor threatens to reveal:

> Muchas veces tomé la pluma para escribille [el prólogo], y muchas la dejé, por no saber lo que escribiría, y estando uno suspenso, con el papel delante, la pluma en la oreja, el codo en el bufete y la mano en la mejilla, pensando lo que diría entró a deshora un amigo mío, gracioso y bien entendido, el cual, viéndome tan imaginativo, me preguntó la causa, y no encubriéndosela yo, le dije que pensaba en el prólogo que había de hacer a la historia de Don Quijote, y que me tenía de suerte que ni quería hacerle, ni menos sacar a luz las hazañas de tan noble caballero. (pp. 51–52)
>
> [Many times I took up my pen and many times I laid it down again, not knowing what to write. On one occasion when I was thus in suspense, paper before me, pen over my ear, elbow on the table, and chin in hand, a very clever friend of mine came in. Seeing me lost in thought, he inquired as to the reason, and I made no effort to conceal from him the fact that my mind was on the preface which I had to write for the story of Don Quijote, and that it was giving me so much trouble that I had just about decided not to write any at all and to abandon entirely the idea of publishing the exploits of so noble a knight.]

To raise the question of secularization in relation to the *Quijote* is thus not to ask in a literal way about the relationship between Cervantes as a writer and the Christian God, as Lukács thought, or even to inquire into the historical relationship between the genesis of the *Quijote* and the social situation of the *conversos* in Spain, as critic Américo Castro sought to do. Rather, it is to pose some fundamental questions relating to the transmission of literary and cultural authority in the early modern age, where the battle between the old and the new begins from the humanist question of how to honor the past while claiming contemporaneity, and proceeds from there to the fully modernist dilemma of how to defend literature against the failure of the project of historical self-assertion. Nowhere in Cervantes are the implications of these issues for the work of the imagination more richly explored than in the scene of "absorptive" reading that opens the work. Here the deficit of the poetic imagination hinted at in the author's struggles with the Prologue to Part 1 is transformed into the experience of the principal character's seduction by, and fall into, the text. Although characters like the Barber and the Priest may over the course of the novel attempt to invent strategies to reorient Don Quijote to their orthodox ways, Cervantes seems to suggest that nothing in the world can prevent this fall. Indeed, the experience of reading under the conditions of modernity is conveyed not so much in our experience of a fall, but rather, as our foremost theoretician of poetic falls, Harold Bloom, has said, in the disorienting awareness that *we are falling*.[10] What "causes" Alonso Quijano to become overwhelmed by the texts he reads may be interpreted as a function of his inability to defend himself against the power of poetic imagination conveyed by them. Thus while Cervantes objectifies and concretizes the modern reader's engagement of the literary tradition through Don Quijote's encounter with the chivalric books, the possibility of an imaginative "fall" into the text remains nonetheless a constant trap, a sign of the vulnerability of the imagination, or of a weakness of the particular power of resistance on which the reader's capacity for self-assertion rests.

Moreover, this fall signals a failure that flies in the face of Cervantes' own historical self-assertions, which elsewhere he relates to the glories of the Spanish Empire and, more specifically, to the heroism of self-sacrifice exemplified while fighting under the imperial flag of Don Juan of Austria at Lepanto, "la más memorable y alta ocasión que vieron los pasados siglos, ni esperan ver los venideros, militando debajo de las vencedoras banderas de hijo del rayo de la guerra, Carlo Quinto, de feliz memoria"[11] [the most memorable and exalted occasion that past centuries have seen or that future ones can expect to see, fighting under the victorious flag of the son of the lightning bolt of war, Charles V, may he rest in peace]. These and similar assertions represent one side of the ceaselessly contradictory self-estimations, characterized by equal measures of praise and self-deprecation, that we find scattered throughout Cervantes' texts. While Cervantes may for instance boast in the Prologue to the *Novelas ejemplares* that he is the first to write novels in Spanish, or that his *Persiles* will compete with Heliodorus, he also doubts his literary authority and prestige, not only in the Prologue to the *Quijote* but also in the preface to the *Ocho comedias y entremeses*, which records the damaging effect of Lope's success on his own theatrical (mis)fortunes.[12]

For a critic like Américo Castro, Cervantes' most problematic self-estimations are best explained in terms of Cervantes' existential retreat into the depths of self-reflection in the face of adverse social circumstances. For example, the assertion made in the Prologue to Part 1 that *Don Quijote* was engendered in jail (a claim echoed in chapter 21 in relation to Ginés de Pasamonte's picaresque autobiography, which is said similarly to have been composed in jail) would have to be seen as a direct reflection of Cervantes' social situation as a *converso* in Spain, and not as an example of his playful and ironic self-reflection on his own creative powers and his place in relation to the literary traditions of the past. For instance, in explaining the genesis of the *Quijote*'s "first author," *Cide Hamete*, Castro writes that "the *Quijote* forces one to imagine a long period of retreat on Cervantes' part, a withdrawal into the innermost part of his self, of forced and inconsolable solitude. All possible paths in the surrounding material, moral, and literary worlds were closed to him."[13] Similarly, Castro interprets the claim that the *Quijote* was engendered in jail as an expression of the creative anguish of Cervantes' soul ("it is evident to me that the *Quijote* had to have been conceived in the deepest reclusion of Cervantes' soul, precisely 'where every unhappiness finds its home' ").[14]

And yet precisely because Cervantes sees the consequences of all history—including literary history—as bound up with the compensatory ambition of imaginative literature as a source of hope, he instructs us to read the existential problems of failure and loss in relation to the writer's defenses against his own feared historical fate. What is particularly problematic in Cervantes' way of imagining this dilemma is that in attacking the pretensions of greatness, he also calls into question this "saving power" of literature, which represents its most fundamental compensatory myth. Indeed the poetic *tu quoque* defends the modern writer only by reviving the very dangerous question addressed by poets like Garcilaso and, before him, by Petrarch and the authors of pastoral and elegiac verse: of what use is poetry in the face of loss and death? In Garcilaso's Eclogue 1 the shepherd Salicio in essence grants that poetry may be unable to compensate against loss. But his companion Nemoroso attempts to sublimate loss according to a vision in which the fruit of transcendence is a new pastoral-poetic space:

> busquemos otro llano
> busquemos otros montes y otros ríos,
> otros valles floridos y sombríos
> donde descanse y siempre pueda verte
> ante los ojos míos,
> sin miedo y sobresalto de perderte

[let us seek out other mountains and other rivers, / other valleys full of flowers and shade, / where I can rest and always see you / before my eyes, / without the fear of losing you]

Finally, in Eclogue 3 Garcilaso goes on to suggest that it is the very artificiality, indeed the imaginary quality of poetry, that makes it available as the language of secular faith in a world of loss: "mas con la lengua muerta y fría en la boca / pienso mover la voz a tí debida" [even with my tongue dead and cold in my mouth I intend to stir the voice which I owe to you].

Some of these same issues are raised in relation to the Marcela and Grisóstomo episode of *Don Quijote*, Part 1. In the Marcela and Grisóstomo episode, however, Cervantes transforms the existential problem of loss into an even farther-reaching investigation of literature's power and limits, for Grisóstomo's passing prompts those who survive him to wonder: what is the effective power of poetry in the face of death? For

Grisóstomo and those who survive his death, literature offers the promise of a means through which the poet can be remembered and thus saved from loss. Indeed, Vivaldo says that his friend's writing will live on, and he implores Ambrosio not to burn Grisóstomo's papers.[15] Grisóstomo, a *pastor culto*, was the son of a rich nobleman and also a student at Salamanca, who returned from his studies "wise and learned." But his principal fame was as a poet; his name means "silver tongued." (Moreover, Grisóstomo, like his friend Ambrosio, bears a saintly name; they recall St. John Chrysostom and St. Ambrose.) Indeed, what lies at stake in the episode is whether poetry can serve a redemptive function in a secular world.

As the narrator of the episode clearly understands, the power of literature as posited by the pastoral myth lies in its ability to transcend loss by means of a sublimation of forces at work in the natural world; the question is whether poetry can any longer be successful in such an attempt, or whether its quasi-magical inscriptions will in fact be transformed into records of that same loss:

> No está muy lejos de aquí un sitio donde hay casi dos docenas de altas hayas, y no hay ninguna que en su lisa corteza no tenga grabada en el mesmo árbol, como si más claramente dijera su amante que Marcela la lleva y la merece de toda la hermosura humana. Aquí sospira un pastor; allí se queja otro; acullá se oyen amorosas canciones; acá, desesperadas endechas. Cuál hay que pasa todas las horas de la noche sentado al pie de alguna encina o peñasco, y allí, sin plegar los llorosos ojos, embebecido y transportado en sus pensamientos, le halló el sol a la mañana, y cuál hay que, sin dar vado ni tregua a sus sospiros, en mitad del ardor de la más enfadosa siesta del verano, tendido sobre la ardiente arena, envía sus quejas al piadoso cielo. (1.12.166–67)
> [Not far from here is a place where there are a couple of dozen tall beeches, and there is not a one of them on whose smooth bark Marcela's name has not been engraved; and above some of these inscriptions you will find a crown, as if by this her lover meant to indicate that she deserved to wear the garland of beauty above all the women on earth. Here a shepherd sighs and there another voices his lament. Now are to be heard amorous ballads, and again despairing songs. One will spend all the hours of the night seated

at the foot of some oak or rock without once closing his tearful eyes, and morning sun will find him there, stupefied and lost in thought. Another, without giving truce or respite to his sighs, will lie stretched upon the burning sands in the full heat of the most exhausting summer noontide, sending up his complaint to merciful Heaven.]

As this and similar passages suggest, the pastoral poet's love of nature is inseparable from a deep preoccupation with suffering and loss. But beyond this, it is the imaginative desire to test and move beyond the limiting condition imposed by loss that characterizes the poetic stance in which the power of imaginative desire seems to outweigh any of the ties that may bind the poet to the natural and social worlds. After all, Grisóstomo lives on as spirit and as voice.

Let us consider in this light Cardenio's sonnet in *Don Quijote* 1. 23. Although Cardenio is mad with jealousy and wild with rage at Fernando's deception and Luscinda's apparent betrayal, his sonnet presents him as one who is nonetheless able to achieve good form, as exemplified in the poem's well-balanced and harmonious shape:

> O le falta al Amor conocimiento,
> o le sobra crueldad, o no es mi pena
> igual a la ocasión que me condena
> al género más duro de tormento.
> Pero si Amor es dios, es argumento
> que nada ignora, y es razón muy buena
> que un dios no sea cruel. Pues ¿quién ordena
> el terrible dolor que adoro y siento?
> Si digo que sois vos, Fili, no acierto;
> que tanto mal en tanto bien no cabe,
> ni me viene del cielo esta rüina.
> Presto habré de morir, que es lo más cierto;
> que al mal de quien la causa no sabe
> milagro es acertar la medicina.
> (1.23.282)

[Either Love, it would seem, lacks intelligence, / Or else it is over-cruel, or my poor heart / Is all unequal to its painful part, / Condemned to the direst torment there can be. / If love is God, it is certain He / Knows all—

that takes no caustic art—/ And He's not cruel. Where, then, does my
grief start, / That grief I cherish so persistently? / To say that it is thou,
Phyllis, would be wrong; / In the same body, nor is Heaven to blame. /
One thing I know: I am not here for long; / He's a sick man who cannot
decide / The nature of his ill or whence it came.]

For Grisóstomo, by contrast, suffering cannot so easily be relieved by
the wit and other refinements of verse. For him, loss represents the absolute limit of imagination and expression; his poetry tests itself against
this limit, and since it cannot pass beyond it, is turned destructively
against nature and itself. Indeed, when viewed in contrast to Cardenio
and in light of the pastoral setting of the episode, Grisóstomo's *canción
desesperada* raises some fundamental doubts about the power of poetry
in relation to the disintegrative forces of history, loss, and death.
Whereas the pastoralism of the scene might suggest the image of poetry
as a defense against the potentially disorienting consequences of loss, it
seems that poetry is bound to be a record of the irrecuperability of that
loss: something remains untransformed. Indeed, the *canción desesperada* fails not only to defend against or transform loss; it fails also to fulfill the civilizing and sublimating functions so often imagined for pastoral verse; Grisóstomo's *canción* is a denaturing complaint that serves
principally to reinforce the idea of nature as the site of irreducible strife:

> Escucha, pues, y presta atento oído,
> no al concertado son, sino al rüido
> que de lo hondo de mi amargo pecho,
> llevado de un forzoso desvarío,
> por gusto mío sale y tu despecho.
> El rugir del león, del lobo fiero
> el temeroso aullido, el silbo horrendo
> de escamosa serpiente, el espantable
> baladro de algún monstruo, el agorero
> graznar de la corneja, y el estruendo
> del viento contrastado en mar instable;
> del ya vencido toro el implacable
> bramido, y de la viuda tortolilla
> el sentible arullar; el triste canto

del enviado búho, con el llanto
de toda la infernal negra cuadrilla,
salgan con la doliente ánima fuera,
mezclados en un son, de tal manera,
que se confundan los sentidos todos,
pues la pena cruel que en mí se halla
para contalle pide nuevos modos.

(1.14.181)

[Then listen, and lend thy attentive ear, / Not well consorted tunes but howling to hear, / That from my bitter bosom's depth takes flight, / And, by constrained raving borne away, / Issues forth for mine ease and thy despite. / The lion's raving, and the dreadful cries / Of ravening wolf, and hissing terrible / Of scaly serpent; and the fearful yell / Of some grim monster; and the ominous crow's / Foreboding, sinister caw; the horrible / Sound on the tossing sea of the blustering gale; / The implacable bellow of the new-conquered bull; / The lonely widowed turtle's sobbing moan, / Most mournful, and the dreary night descant / Of the envious owl, commingled with the plaint / Of all the infernal black battalion; / Let all together cry from my aching soul / United in one sound of such sad dole / That all the senses may confounded be, / For my fierce torment needs a manner new / Wherein I may recount my misery.]

In the literary tradition that extends in Golden Age Spain from Garcilaso forward, nature is supposed to have the power to transform occasions of conflict and loss into experiences of an inestimable, if painful, beauty. Indeed, Cervantes seems to recognize that the economy of nature in the pastoral is doubly aesthetic, in the sense that it is determined by the irreducible experiences of pleasure and pain which poetry is in turn charged to transform. And yet for a poet like Grisóstomo, schooled in the Renaissance tradition and committed to the idea of poetry as the sublimation of loss and the reconciliation of strife, there remains the central fact of poetry's failure to defend successfully against death—a failure here so intensified that the fascination with loss turns the power of poetry against itself. Grisóstomo is, in this respect, Cervantes' challenge to the received myth of the pastoral and to the efficacy of poetry as a source of sublimation and a substitute for transcendence in a secularized world.[16]

Anthony J. Cascardi

◆

For her part, Marcela appears unswervingly confident in her ability to resist and transcend Grisóstomo's irreversible "fall" into the realm of suffering and loss. She validates her self-chosen solitude under the guise of the poetic ideal of a fusion with the natural world. But this ideal is one that in turn debars her from the social modes of reconciliation on which the pastoral's claims to redemption in a secular world were based:

> Yo nací libre, y para poder vivir libre escogí la soledad de los campos; los árboles destas montañas son mi compañía; las claras aguas destos arroyos son mis espejos; con los árboles y con las aguas comunico mis pensamientos y hermosura. Fuego soy apartado y espada puesta lejos. A los que he enamorado con la vista he desengañado con las palabras; y si los deseos se sustentan con esperanzas, no habiendo yo dado alguna a Grisóstomo, ni a otro alguno, en fin, de ninguno dellos, bien se puede decir que antes le mató su porfía que mi crueldad. (1.14.186–87)
> [I was born free, and to live free I chose the solitude of the fields. The trees on these mountains are my companions; the clear waters of these streams my mirrors; to the trees and the waters I disclose my thoughts and my beauty. I am the distant fire of the far-off sword. Those whom I have attracted with my eyes I have undeceived with my words; if desires are nourished by hope, as I never gave any to Chrysostom or to any other, it may not justly be said that any man's end was my doing, since it was his persistence rather than my cruelties that killed him.]

Finally, Marcela's rejection of the erotic melancholy characteristic of the pastoral seems to suggest in her a mode of imagination that is directed equally against the idea of nature for or in itself, and against the idea of sublimating loss through recourse to the culturing, socializing, and beautifying powers of a poeticized world.

Indeed, the Marcela and Grisóstomo episode would suggest that the procedures of literary sublimation can only confirm the failure of the poetic imagination to absorb the shock created by the discovery that nature is the locus of suffering, loss, and death. Moreover, a character like Marcela reveals that if the discourse of the sublime is seen as effort to compensate for loss, then it is inherently problematic, if only because it seeks to establish itself as the superhuman authority upon whose very absence its own power is based. It is thus perhaps no surprise to find that the instabilities inherent in the discourse of the sublime are so easily transformed into the bases of the modern subject's self-assertion, if only because that assertion rests on the subject's paradoxical rejection of the idea of an identity based on subjection to an alien power or will: "Tengo riquezas propias, y no codicio las ajenas," says Marcela; "tengo libre condición, y no gusto de sujetarme; ni quiero ni aborrezco a nadie" (1.14.187–88) [I have my own riches, and do not covet those of others; I have a taste for freedom and no wish for subjection].[17]

If there is no way to avoid the problem of loss, which makes itself evident as the "ground" in which the procedures of sublimation take root, and if there is likewise no hope to escape the "fall" into the entanglements of literary history that Cervantes represents at the beginning of *Don Quijote*, Part 1, there are nonetheless means to defend, even if unsuccessfully, against some of the more radical consequences of these events, and the self-conscious elaboration of these defenses goes a long way toward explaining Cervantes' stance with respect to the problematic status of literature in the modern age. Foremost among the defensive strategies we witness in *Don Quijote* are the procedures of textualization, which offer the means by which the modern poetic imagination, conscious of literature's loss of its effective power, attempts to convert its disturbing deficiencies into something seemingly positive, objective, and real. In the case of the *Quijote*, it seems that by objectifying the conditions of imaginative failure and loss Cervantes attempts to secure his identity as a modern writer or, what amounts to the same thing, to gain a critical perspective on history, by projecting a concrete object, the text, as a defense against the overwhelming prestige and authority of the past. But as we have already begun to see, the difficulty with an attempt to stabilize the author's identity through the fortifying objectification of the writer's weakened imagination as the author's friend is that this defense may not necessarily be able to defend against itself. Indeed, we do not know and cannot decide whether the formation of the quixotic text represents a solution to the problem of a failed poetic imagination overwhelmed by the power and authority of the past, or a redoubling of that same problem for the modern writer, whose encounters with the tradition are necessarily mediated through texts. Indeed, it could well be said that Cervantes' accomplishment is to have shown how the same literary "defense" against tradition that may enable the self-assertion of the modern writer cannot produce anything other than figures, personae, tropes, and of course texts, all of which threaten to disorient and overwhelm the reader, who in their presence cannot help be overwhelmed by his own weakness with respect to the past.

To be sure, Cervantes has predecessors in this ambiguous strategy of textualization as defense. Already in a work like the *Lazarillo de Tormes* the process of textualization (which here assumes the form of letter writing) is taken as the sign of a coveted maturity, autonomy, and independence, which form the bases of the writer's self-assertion. In the *Lazarillo*, the passage from the fundamentally oral discourse of folktale and proverb to the genre of the written letter addressed to "Vuestra Merced" protects and guarantees the author's critical stance precisely when his identity and autonomy are most vulnerable. By allowing Lázaro to speak of the conditions of his own degradation ironically and in a double voice, writing helps insure the integrity of his self-consciousness and conceals his self-abasement and humiliation. For a critic like Francisco Rico, however, these aspects of the *Lazarillo*'s epistolary and autobiographical form are angled toward the successful formation of a rigorously personal and humanistic point of view, and this is in turn the basis of the "realism" of the work, its claim to literary and novelistic "modernity": "Relativism, whether in epistemology or axiology, is also a form of humanism. . . . Is it not in their attention to the individual that a Cervantes or a Fielding marks out the modern novel? In recognizing subjectivity as a measure of things there is the upsurge of a novelistic impulse, which the anonymous author of the *Lazarillo* could hardly resist. If the *I* is the touchstone of reality, then what could be more realistic than autobiography?"[18] And yet it seems that the *Lazarillo* contains a more subtle play between autobiographical self-assertion and the experience of self-abasement than this reading can allow. For the *Lazarillo* seems to suggest that the writer's precious achievement of a textual identity can occur only through his simultaneous absorption into the world of social masks: had Lázaro been content simply to expose society's deceits, and to assert himself as the critic of a corrupt world, he might well never have lived to write his story or tell his "truth."

The text's failure to stabilize identity thus brings with it the need, or the hope, for strategies to reorient the critical authority transmitted through it. The various critical procedures imagined in Cervantes' text, beginning with the "escrutinio de los libros" in chapter 6 of Part 1, represent just one such attempt. For, once the text enters the public domain, or accedes to the roster of canonized works, the expectation is that it may itself be criticized and judged not only according to the desires and needs of its author but according to objective and rational principles as well. Unlike the private imaginings of the author, the text can be construed as a public object that stands open to the pressures of critical judgment. And, unlike the normative judgment of the masses—"el antiguo legislador que llaman vulgo" [the ancient lawgiver they call the public], as Cervantes puts it in the Prologue—who in the modern context are increasingly empowered to determine whether an author will succeed or fail[19]—the establishment of a critical discourse promises a "disengaged" assessment of the text.

This is to say that the development of modern literary history is inconceivable without the parallel emergence of a "science" of interpretation and judgment, such as the Barber and the Priest initiate in chapter 6 and as the Canon and the Priest pursue in chapters 47 and 48 of Part 1. Yet, if these examples are to be taken as any measure of such a project's potential success, it would seem that the discourse of criticism remains inextricably entwined with the ambitions and vulnerabilities of literature itself, and is a sign and symptom of literary modernity rather than a solution to the problems it presents. Indeed, since there is nothing to ensure that the critical text will not in turn become the site of yet another imaginary scene of self-projection against loss, literature cannot be entirely redeemed, nor the imagination's disconcerting fall from power and grace reversed, by recourse to a literary-critical discourse. Thus the Canon admits that he has himself attempted to write a novel of chivalry, and Don Quijote responds to his criticisms with the very powerful story of the Knight of the Lake (1.50), which leaves the Canon thoroughly astonished and amazed.

One might at best suggest that the process of textualization constitutes a defense against history and loss that calls for interpretation, or more exactly that such a defense initiates a circle of interpretation that can succeed neither in unlocking the "kernel" of the efficacious literary sign nor in fully repressing the power of what was "originally" imagined. In this case, the secularization process manifests itself in the form of a constant alternation between the equally strong powers of an imaginative remembering and those of a defensive forgetfulness. And, just as in the case of repression it is in failure that the underlying structure of desire is brought into view, so too with secularization it is in the experience of its failure that literary history is suddenly revealed as something interpretable. This, at least, is the significance I would attribute to the episode of the leaden box that occurs at the very end of *Don Quijote*, Part 2. The discovery of this box serves as a convenient reminder of the process of secularization insofar as it is found in the rubble of a monastery in the course of renovation (1.52). Moreover, the box contains parchments whose original gothic letters have not altogether been displaced by the Spanish verses that have been superimposed upon them, thus suggesting that the process of secularization they model has been left significantly incomplete. And while some of these verses can be read, and are found to contain the epitaphs of Don Quijote, Sancho Panza, Dulcinea, and Rocinante, "los demás, por estar carcomida la letra, se entregaron a un académico para que por conjeturas los declarase" (1.52.607) [the rest, as the characters were worm-eaten, were entrusted to a university scholar to decipher]. They have, in other words, become the imaginary, if not also the anticipatory, objects of the very "sciences" of interpretation whose relationship to the formation of modern culture we are now attempting to decipher.[20]

As I hope to have suggested, the notion that literature might somehow afford an opportunity for the modern writer's self-assertion must be qualified in Cervantes' case so as to reflect the failure of modern writing either to appropriate or fully to supersede the authority of the past. And yet we have also seen that these apparent "failures" in turn allow Cervantes to circumvent and ironize the rhetoric of self-assertion characteristic of the modern age. In conclusion, I would suggest that the defeat of the myth of the writer's fame at the hands of literary history in turn opens up a new kind of poetic endeavor whose mechanisms are those of

♦

compensation and defense, all of which are premised in some measure on the failure of the modern imagination in its desire to compete with the past. Cervantes' response to literary history, which defines his particular stance as a modern writer, is thus to write within the circle of repression and defense, and so rather than redefine literature *tout court*, to redirect its imaginative energies and residual power and, in the process, to create a new form by questioning the values and authority of all those who would inherit the past. In this way, the modern writer's stance of lateness or inadequacy represents a way of making space within the tradition that is at least as powerful, and certainly more complex, than what the rhetoric of self-assertion was able to afford.

Notes

Epigraph: "I, who always strive to seem as though I have the poetic talent that Heaven did not wish to grant me."

1. Georg Lukács, *Theory of the Novel*, trans. Anna Bostock (Cambridge: MIT Press, 1971), pp. 103–4.

2. *Discourse on Method*, in *The Philosophical Writings of Descartes*, trans. John Cottingham, Robert Stoothoff, and Dugald Murdoch (Cambridge: Cambridge University Press, 1985), 2:117.

3. Hobbes, *English Works*, ed. William Molesworth (London: John Bohn, 1839), 1:ix.

4. Admittedly, we never see people pulling down all the houses of a city for the sole purpose of rebuilding them in a different style to make the streets more attractive; but we do see many individuals having their houses pulled down in order to rebuild them, some even being forced to do so when the houses are in danger of falling down and their foundations are insecure (*Discourse*, 1:117).

5. Karlheinz Stierle provides an illuminating discussion of Montaigne in "L'Histoire comme example, l'example comme histoire," *Poétique* 10 (1972): 176–98. See also Marcel Gutwirth, *Michel de Montaigne ou le pari d'exemplarité* (Montréal: Presses de l'Université de Montréal, 1977), and Michael Wood, "Montaigne and the Mirror of Example," *Philosophy and Literature* 13 (1989): 1–15.

6. See Gary Shapiro, "Reading and Writing in the Text of Hobbes' *Leviathan*," *Journal of the History of Philosophy* 18 (1980): 152. This does not, of course, explain the paradox of the instructive powers that Hobbes claims for his own book.

7. Hobbes, *Leviathan*, ed. C. B. Macpherson (Harmondsworth: Penguin, 1968), 1.10.151.

8. Hans Blumenberg, *The Legitimacy of the Modern Age*, trans. Robert M. Wallace (Cambridge: MIT Press, 1985).

9. I follow the edition of Luis Murillo (Madrid: Castalia, 1986), p. 57. The translations are my own.

10. Harold Bloom, *Anxiety of Influence* (New York: Oxford University Press, 1973), p. 20.

11. "Prólogo," *Novelas ejemplares*, ed. Juan Bautista Avalle-Arce (Madrid: Castalia, 1982), 1:63. Cervantes evokes this same rhetoric in the Prologue to Part 2 of *Don Quijote*, where he speaks of the injury to his hand having been sustained "en la más alta ocasión que vieron los siglos pasados, los presentes, ni esperan ver los venideros." He continues: "Si mis heridas no resplandecen en los ojos de quien las mira, son estimadas, a lo menos, en la estimación de los que saben dónde se cobraron; que el soldado más bien parece muerto en la batalla que libre en la fuga" (p. 33).

12. "No hallé pájaros en los nidos de antaño," he says describing his experience upon returning to works some of which were composed decades ago; "quiero decir que no hallé autor que me las pidiese, puesto que sabían que las tenía, y así las arrinconé en un cofre y las consagré y condené al perpetuo silencio. En esta sazón me dijo un librero que él me las comprara si un autor de título no le hubiera dicho que de mi prosa se podía esperar mucho, pero que del verso nada." In *Obras completas*, ed. Angel Valbuena Prat (Madrid: Aguilar, 1970), 1:210b.

13. Américo Castro, "El cómo y el por qué de Cide Hamete Benengeli," in *Hacia Cervantes* (Madrid: Taurus, 1967), p. 412.

14. Castro, "Los prólogos al *Quijote*," in *Hacia Cervantes*, p. 264.

15. The problem of fame, together with the need to be remembered, was an issue of constant concern to Cervantes. In chapter 37 of *Don Quijote*, Part 1, the Captive mentions a certain Spanish soldier named "Saavedra, el cual, con haber hecho cosas que qudarán en la memoria de aquellas gentes por muchos años" (p. 486).

16. Castro's estimation of the Cervantine pastoral is radically different, on several accounts. First, Castro claims that Cervantes is relatively uncritical of the pastoral ("Cervantes no ironiza lo pastoril ni lo toma en broma en el *Quijote*, aunque bien fácil le hubiera sido proyectar cualquier penumbra sobre Marcela—un alma de armiño, presuntuosa de su albura. No cabía hacerlo, sin embargo, porque la maravillosa muchacha descansaba sobre una última intuición de lo humano, en la cual se basa todo el *Quijote*: 'Yo nací libre, y para vivir libre

escogí la soledad de los campos,'" *Hacia Cervantes*, p. 282). Second, and in line with the preceding, Castro associates the pastoral with the revelation of a distinctly "human" intimacy, rather than with a specifically literary problematic: "En el relato pastoril es donde, por primera vez, se muestra el personaje literario como una singularidad estrictamente humana, como expresión de un 'dentro de sí'" (p. 276). Castro recognizes the pastoral's status as a secularized discourse ("lo pastoril es una hijuela laica de la mística religiosa, y opera con el amor humano como Santa Teresa con el divino"), but then subordinates this claim to the assertion that both are examples of an increasingly humanistic mode of discourse ("con un intento similar de traer a expresión las más hondas vivencias, de aquellas que en ciertos casos se han resuelto en armoniosa composición poética," p. 276).

17. Cf. Castro, who interprets the pastoral as the direct exposition of a personal conscience in Cervantes: "La narración pastoril . . . llega a ser posible cuando el individuo, en busca de conciencia personal, rotas todas las amarras, se lanza a remar en su propio bote, sin más pertrecho que el de su sola existencia, 'monda y desnuda'" (*Hacia Cervantes*, p. 277).

18. Francisco Rico, *La novela picaresca y el punto de vista* (Barcelona: Seix Barral, 1976), p. 50.

19. Cervantes addresses this position in the Prologue to Part 1, explaining to the (common) reader that he will not bend to "la corriente del uso, ni suplicarte casi con las lágrimas en los ojos, como otros hacen, lector carísimo, que perdones o disimules las faltas que en este mi libro vieres, pues ni eres su pariente ni su amigo, y tienes tu alma en tu cuerpo y tu libre albedrío como el más pintado y estás en tu casa, donde eres señor della, como el rey de sus alcabalas" (p. 51).

20. The episode is also a direct reference to the discovery among the moriscos of Granada of the so-called "libros plúmbeos," of the interpretation of their inscriptions, and of the (false) relics and martyrs to which they attested. See Miguel José Hagerty, ed., *Los libros plúmbeos de Sacromonte* (Madrid: Editorial Nacional, 1980).

11

"The Matter of America"

Cervantes Romances Inca Garcilaso de la Vega

DIANA DE ARMAS WILSON

Si fuera de cuatro jornadas, la cuarta acababa en América.
Don Quijote, 1.48

———————◆◆———————

The title of my essay—adapted from Jean Bodel's late-twelfth-century categories ("The Matter of Britain/France/Rome") to describe the conventional subject matter of romances—points toward New World poetics. The essay itself seeks out something that, like Edmundo O'Gorman's America, may not be discoverable but must be invented: namely, Cervantes' last words on the messianic vision of Spain's American empire. Given that Cervantes was curtly refused that "oficio en las Indias" for which he had at least twice applied,[1] his words will not, of course, depend upon the authority of firsthand witnessing, an authority often bound up with European dreams of conquest.[2] They will depend, instead, upon the less suspect act of reading, of exploiting continuation of the textual family of the chronicles. It has become an extended family, thanks to colonial literary studies, including not only *crónicas* but also eyewitness accounts, journal entries, letters, official reports, notarial records, royal proclamations, papal bulls, memoranda, questionnaires, inventories, charters, essays, theological debates, and legal depositions.[3] Key members of this textual family were adopted into Inca Garcilaso de la Vega's *Comentarios reales* (1609), a text that may have provided Cervantes a virtual thesaurus of New World cultural authorities, including various triumphal narratives of conquest. My essay aims to explore some ways in which Cervantes romances America in the *Persiles*, a text that opens with a sustained parody—indeed, a grotesque mimicry—of the symbolic acts of empire.

Setting aside all the ornamental references in Cervantes to America—such as the mention of "el cacao" in *La Gitanilla* or "el tabaco" in *Viaje del Parnaso* (chap. 8)—I begin my quest with Porras Barrenechea's definition of *Don Quijote* as "una sátira benévola del conquistador de ínsulas o Indias"⁴ [a benevolent satire of the conqueror of {enchanted} isles or the Indies]. Although the term "sátira," with its suggestions of malicious or even savage indignation, may seem overdetermined here, the adjective "benévola" mollifies it into parody. The discourse of conquest being parodied in *Don Quijote* is recontextualized in the *Persiles* to discredit its object more openly. Where the parody in *Don Quijote* tilts toward the *libros de caballerías* (the discourse of "ínsulas"), the parody in the *Persiles* takes as its object the chronicles (the discourse of "Indias"). This last discourse, it bears stressing, occasionally recalls that of the books of chivalry. Perhaps the hoariest example of this discursive drift is Bernald Díaz del Castillo's chivalric description of the enchanting first sight of Mexico City: "Y decíamos que parecía a las cosas de encantamiento que cuentan en el libro de Amadís, por las grandes torres y cues y edificios que tenían dentro en el agua"⁵ [and due to the large towers and temples and buildings in the water, we said that it seemed like the enchanted things that are described in the book on Amadís]. A less enchanting imitation of chivalric discourse may be found in Bernardo de Vargas Machuca's *Milicia y descripción de Indias*, which gave Spaniards the standard formula for taking possession of an Indian village. The conqueror, dressed in full armor and sword in hand, is urged to pronounce, in high dudgeon ("arrebatándose de cólera"), the following quixotic speech: "Si hay alguna persona que lo pretenda contradecir, salga conmigo al campo, donde lo podrá batallar, el cual se lo aseguro, porque en su defensa ofrezco de morir ahora y en cualquier tiempo"⁶ [Should there be anybody planning to hold the contrary, let him take the field with me, where he may battle it out; this I assure him, and I offer to die defending it, now or at any time]. This unwitting parody of a parody of the *libros de caballerías* shows the age's propensity for literary continuation.

Whereas *Don Quijote* shares with the *crónicas* the rhetoric of chivalry, the *Persiles*, emerging from the same cultural matrix as the *crónicas*, shares with them an insistent use of the Christian marvelous. Where Cervantes fictionalizes a Christian pilgrimage—a *peregrinaje* animated by all kinds of signs and apparitions, punctuated by periodic wonders, and exalted by numberless trials and ordeals—some of the *crónicas*— for example, Columbus's famous 1493 letter—structure their narratives as if they were chronicling a pilgrimage. Where Cervantes shows us "the imagination at play," to borrow Stephen Greenblatt's useful distinction, the chronicles exhibit a less disinterested "imagination at work."[7] The fertile and antic imagination at play in the *Persiles*, although resolutely wanting in humor, intensifies the ridicule begun in *Don Quijote*. The aging Cervantes, like James Joyce, seems to have believed that a writer's first obligation was to ridicule, not flatter, national vanity.

In light of the striking reticence of Spanish authors in incorporating America into their texts, a phenomenon noted by J. H. Elliott,[8] Cervantes' dark use of "the matter of America" to launch the *Persiles* is intriguing. Various questions spring to mind. If the chroniclers saw America through the haze of the *libros de caballerías*, the common cultural referent of his age, how did Cervantes—who avowedly wrote to *topple* the books of chivalry—see America? If, moreover, the *libros de caballería* "related to the way Europeans wrote about Amerindians," as Rolena Adorno claims, how "European" was Cervantes in writing about the Amerindians?[9] Did he (or didn't he) see them through the haze of Inca Garcilaso de la Vega's *Comentarios reales* (1609), a European publication by a trilingual humanist who identified—indeed, who legitimized—himself through his non-European origins? How would Cervantes have responded to the fluidity of identity behind Inca Garcilaso's American writing?

"The Matter of America" in Don Quijote

No Amerindians are represented in *Don Quijote*,[10] where "the matter of America" is confined to the spatial or economic. "Por evitar la prolijidad" (to use a formula dear to Cervantes), I shall spare readers the tedium of an annotated catalog of American references in *Don Quijote*, save to recall that the text mentions "las Indias" some half-dozen times (1.8, 1.29, 1.39, 1.42, 2.54, and 2.66); "el Nuevo Mundo" once (2.8);

"América" once (the only use of the term in Cervantes) (1.48); "Nueva España" once (1.43); "Méjico" once (1.42); "Pirú" once (1.42); and "Potosí" twice (2.40 and 2.71). Apart from the Priest's testimony to having seen a play in which every act took place on a different continent (1.48), a remark from which I have taken my epigraph, the common denominator of most of the references in *Don Quijote* is that America is the place to become rich and famous.[11] None approaches the darkness of the representation of America in the opening paragraph of *El celoso extremeño* (ca. 1605), where Cervantes, describing "el pasarse a las Indias," paints the New World with rhetorical grimness: "refugio y amparo de los desesperados de España, iglesia de los alzados, salvoconducto de los homicidas, pala y cubierta de los jugadores . . . , añagaza general de mujeres libres, engaño común de muchos y remedio particular de pocos" [refuge and shelter for Spain's desperate men, haven for the bankrupt, safe-conduct for the cut-throats, asylum for the gamblers . . . , general lure for women of easy virtue, the common delusion of many, and the singular remedy of a few (Thacker, p. 9; emended by Iarocci)].

The most personal entry in the catalog of Americana in *Don Quijote* occurs in the one reference to "el cortesísimo Cortés" (2.8), exalted by Don Quijote for "burning the ships behind him" in his exemplary desire for fame.[12] An indirect allusion to America crops up during the scrutiny of Don Quijote's library, where Ercilla's *La Araucana* is counted among "las más ricas prendas de poesía que tiene España" (1.6).[13] Another gesture to the New World occurs when the Duke's men verbally abuse Don Quijote and Sancho, calling them "trogloditas," "bárbaros," and "antropófagos" (2.68), a suggestive little catalog that Cervantes iterates and expands, in his interlude *El rufián viudo*, to include "un caimán, un caribe, un come-vivos"[14] [an alligator, a carib, a hooligan]. These man-eating references move us closer to the Americanized world of cannibalizing barbarians found in the *Persiles*.

"The Matter of America" in the Persiles

Cervantes, who memorably thematized a celebration of the unsaid, does not mention the Amerindians in the *Persiles*, but they are at the center of its opening narrative.[15] A text inscrutable to traditional hermeneutic readings, the Isla Bárbara chapters invite readers into an "inaugural scene" of slavery and cannibalism that one *Persiles* editor describes as the book's "repellent long beginning." The Barbaric Isle narrative has been critically marginalized by the guardians of the Cervantine canon who, wishing to see Cervantes as the producer of artistic discourses, found "repellent" the sexual or political implications that his discourses produced.[16] Cervantes did not take any pains to explain and justify his opening representation in the *Persiles* (through a preface, a dedication, or a narrator). As Don Quijote himself said of Part 1 of *Don Quijote*, "tendrá necesidad de comentario para entenderlo" [it will need commentary in order to be understood].

Elsewhere I have addressed the Barbaric Isle as an all-male fantasy island.[17] In accord with Eduardo González's prescient psychoanalytic observation that the initial presence on the island is male,[18] I was more interested, in my earlier writing, in the kind of consciousness that gendered acts of conquest. But even then I could see that the territorial concept of the female body used by Cervantes was grounding a colonial discursive practice that needed closer attention. In Feliciana de la Voz's interpolated story of the loss of her maidenhead, for example, the reference to a "don Francisco Pizarro" gestures to the son of the "real life" magistrate of Trujillo in 1607,[19] a descendant of the conqueror (to use Sir Walter Ralegh's striking phrase) "of the maidenhead of Peru." The woman/land trope, in short, is much in evidence in Cervantes' last romance. But it is the land that becomes the ground and site of some extraordinary notions of transculturation.

The *Persiles* opens with a sustained six-chapter parody that manifests an astonishing cultural hybridity: an American prologue to a pan-European romance avowedly written to compete with that Renaissance blockbuster of a Greek novel, Heliodorus's *Aethiopica*. The object of Cervantes' parody is the symbolic acts of a tribe of "gente bárbara" awaiting the coming of their messiah, the birth of a world conqueror— literally, a conquistador "del mundo." The hatching grounds for this conqueror are inarguably American: the inhabitants of Isla Bárbara dress themselves in, and serve their food on, animal hides ("pieles de animales") (pp. 94, 65); they eat a diet of fish, dried fruits, and unleavened bread; they drink water in vessels made out of tree bark (p. 71); they sail about in wooden rafts like the Incas' ("balsas . . . de cinco o de siete palos largos, atados unos con otros"), rather than in "piraguas" or "canoas" like the Florida Indians);[20] they fight with bows and flintstone-headed arrows (p. 53); and they communicate with outsiders either "por señas" (p. 53) or through "la intérprete" (p. 69)—a kind of Polish-speaking Doña Marina. Isla Bárbara even includes a Spanish castaway (Antonio) who, upon encountering a barbarian maiden (Ricla), begins an exchange with her, in *señas* and with much confusion, that ends in a cross-cultural marriage (p. 82). In addition, Cervantes' fictional barbarians, whom his European pilgrims encounter sometime in the recognizable 1560s, practice cannibalism—what Columbus called "[el] escándalo de los indios," and José Piedra, more recently, the "Europeans' worst banqueting fear."[21]

The American material that launches the *Persiles* is indeed a startling representation of the "other," an analytic category traditionally classified, in Golden Age discourse, by Moors and Jews, Spain's recognized minorities. That these peoples could handily be assimilated to Amerindians, however, is instanced by López de Gómara's description of the (rumored) lifestyle of Indians in the province of Esmeraldas: "Viven como sodomitas, hablan como moros y parecen judíos"[22] [they live like sodomites, they talk like Moors, and they look like Jews]. The category of the "other," in short, had been traditionally occupied by everything *but* the European subject.[23]

In the *Persiles*, however, the category of the "other" is pried open to include that subject. Or put another way, in Cervantes the "other" loses some of his otherness by being drawn within a European community. Cervantes' Americanized barbarians are, in fact, spectacularly Eurocentric. They are otherness domesticated. The text displaces the locus of alterity to Europe, to some unspecified island in the North Sea, near the Baltics, on a European *mapa mentis* reserved for "others." The subtitle for the *Persiles*, "Historia Setentrional," together with its Old World setting, may have been suggested by a cited passage in the *Comentarios reales* about the northern Amerindians, who lived "en las partes septentrionales, *que corresponden a las regiones septentrionales del mundo viejo*" (1.2.6, emphasis added) [in the northern areas, *which correspond to the northern regions of the Old World*]. The Inca's correspondence between Old and New World northern regions, in short, may have provided the germ for the setting (and not only the setting) of Cervantes' "historia setentrional."

Inca Garcilaso in the Persiles

The bibliographical evidence that would guarantee Cervantes' reading of Inca Garcilaso remains teasingly circumstantial: Cervantes' talking dog Berganza, recalling events circa 1589, refers to one of the Inca's relatives, the Marqués de Priego; and Cervantes himself, in his official capacity as purveyor to the king in 1591, manages to override a 1587 plea from the Council of Montilla, begging the king for exemption from tributes, signed by Inca Garcilaso.[24] Numerous scholars, however—including Schevill and Bonilla, Jorge Campos, William Entwistle, John Grier Varner, and Alban Forcione[25]—have suggested the presence of Garcilaso in the threshold chapters of the *Persiles*, a presence that has not been investigated with any great rigor. On the other hand, Juan Bautista Avalle-Arce, who dates Part 1 of the *Persiles* (Isla Bárbara episode) between 1599 and 1605, and who has investigated Inca Garcilaso enough to produce an "Antología vivida" of his work, denies Inca Garcilaso's influence on the *Persiles*: "No creo que los *Comentarios* sean piedra de toque irrefutable e infalible"[26] [I do not believe that the *Comentarios* are an infallible, irrefutable touchstone].

Like Sor Juana, Inca Garcilaso has had to work overtime in colonial literary studies: "Ha tenido que representar todas las sensibilidades posibles en tanto mestizo y americano"[27] [As a mestizo and as an American, he has had to represent all possible sensitivities]. In my own study—in which Cervantes, in the manner of Borges, creates his own precursors—the Inca represents the *sensibilidad* of a precursor. Inverting the long-standing tendency of imposing European models on American texts, I wish to consider the Inca, even to impose him, as an American model for a European text. Cervantes' "American" scene signals not only to Garcilaso but, through him, to all the conquest chronicles internalized in Garcilaso. We might envision the first six chapters of the *Persiles* as "an absorption of and a reply to" Inca Garcilaso's long history of absorption and replies.[28] Together with *his* own precursors, I believe, Inca Garcilaso helped to reorient (in all senses of that verb) Cervantes' notions of empire.

The connection between the two writers begins, somewhat obliquely, through the Prologue to Part 1 of the *Quijote*, where an invented "amigo" reminds the apprehensive Cervantes that there is only one authority for writing about love: "Si tratáredes de amores, con dos onzas que sepáis de la lengua toscana, toparéis con León Hebreo" [If you are on the subject of love and have two pennyworth of Italian, you will come across León Hebreo]. Although Cervantes himself may have used the Tuscan original, by 1590 there was available to him the third, and the finest,[29] of the Spanish translations of León Hebreo's difficult Neoplatonic text *La Traducción del Indio de los Tres Diálogos de amor de León Hebreo, hecha . . . por Garcilaso Inca de la Vega*. The Italian text of a Portuguese Jew expelled from Spain, in other words, had been reintegrated back into the Spanish language by an American Indian translator. Although Inca Garcilaso proudly offered this translation, his first literary work, to Philip II, not everybody at the time celebrated this multicultural literary event. The humanist Francisco Murillo, for instance, fumed about the presumption of an Antarctic Indian in translating an Italian text for Spaniards: "Qué tiene que ver con hacerse intérprete entre italianos y españoles, y ya que presumió serlo por qué no tomó libro cualquiera y no el que los italianos más estimaban y los españoles menos conocían?"[30] [What does he have to do with becoming an interpreter for Italians and Spaniards? And since he did presume to be such an interpreter, why didn't he take any old book instead of the one the Italians most esteemed and the one the Spaniards knew the least?].

In his second endeavor as a cultural go-between, Inca Garcilaso served as an interpreter between Indians and Spaniards. His "texto de cultura" or cultural ethnohistory of Peru, the *Comentarios reales* (1609),[31] brilliantly recuperates the customs, ceremonies, and rites of the Incas: how they constructed a suspension bridge ("puente de mimbre") over the Apurímac (1.3.7); how they operated the House of Virgins (*escogidas*) in Cuzco (1.4.1–4); how they thought rainbows caused tooth decay (1.3.21). Sometimes remembrance of things past gives way to present colonial concerns: how cocaine contracts enrich

Spaniards (2.8.15); or how the different varieties of American man are categorized by Spaniards as *criollos, cholos, mestizos,* and so forth (2.9.31).

Such cultural descriptions are strategically interwoven with a long history of "guerras y conquistas" (1.2.20), a text documenting whole lifetimes of militaristic expansion forced on the Incas by a royal ancestor cult that promoted "split inheritance."[32] The *Comentarios reales* earned its author the title of the "Herodotus of the Incas"—an odd honorific, given that Herodotus, unlike the Inca, tried to describe events that he had *not* witnessed, and men whose language he did *not* understand.[33] Garcilaso himself saw the *Comentarios* as an act of translation, not just of Quechua signs but of the whole Andean culture that used them. The text, a vast labor of reparations, is constituted by a number of complex and contradictory maneuvers that aim to reconstruct, within a new historical discourse, the American subject—largely the *royal* American subject—prior to conquest.

Closer to our comparative aims, the *Comentarios* is a cannibalizing text, one that incorporates the writing of multiple peninsular predecessors.[34] To read the Inca is to entertain his reading, his absorption of, and replies to texts that take us back to Peter Martyr and Thomas More,[35] and forward, through a whole catalog of chronicles, of what Mary Campbell has called "guilty texts." In Garcilaso, we find roughly eighty-six references to *cronistas* such as Pedro Cieza de León, Agustín de Zárate, Padre José de Acosta, the Viceroy Francisco de Toledo, and, perhaps most indignantly, to López de Gómara.[36] Inca Garcilaso's most cherished source, however, is that "insigne varón" Padre Blas Valera (1545–1598), a fellow mestizo and Jesuit who wrote, "en elegantísimo (or "galano") latín" (1.1.6), an unfinished history of Peru. Father Blas Valera's "papeles rotos" (1.1.11), devastated during the 1596 sack of Cádiz by the Count of Essex, found their way, courtesy of another Jesuit named Maldonado de Saavedra, into Inca Garcilaso's hands (1.1.6). These tattered papers provided him with a treasury of citations from the Jesuit's own extensive reading, which included Peter Martyr's *Decades* (*De Orbe Novo*) and Fray Bartolomé de las Casas.[37]

Garcilaso's use of his multiple sources is complicated, however, by his eloquent silences,[38] by his cautious strategies of representation, and by his various—often simultaneous—subject positions: as an Inca, he reproduces the imperial ideology of the Incas; as a Christian, he reproduces the religious ideology of the Spaniards; as a mestizo, he regularly subverts both ideologies. Sometimes he reproduces the discourse of Petrarchan models, as in his description of the songs composed by the Colla Indians: "cantares . . . de pasiones amorosas, ya de placer, ya de pesar, de favores o disfavores de la dama" (1.2.26) [songs . . . of amorous passion, now pleasurable, now painful, songs of the lady's favor and disfavor]. His *Comentarios reales*, in short, are the product of a colonized subject: a hybrid construction with a variety of subject positions and contradictory discourses, often the markers of irony.[39] Such writing practices, which tend to dissolve authority or to problematize subjectivity, could not have been lost on Cervantes, acquainted as he was with irony, the trope that can shield a text from official censure.

Inca Garcilaso's approach to cultural authority bears comparison with that of Cervantes, whose attitude may be summed up in the Prologue to *Don Quijote*, Part 1: "lo que yo me sé decir sin ellos" [what I can say without authorities]. As Robert Alter succinctly reminds us, "the novel begins out of an erosion of belief in the authority of the written word and it begins with Cervantes."[40] Where Cervantes excludes, Inca Garcilaso tends to outdo the reigning authorities. He avails himself of the "outdoing topos" to supplement, as well as to rectify, the peninsular historians of Peru, whose representations, to his mind, have distorted its language and culture: "como propio hijo, podré decir mejor que otro que no lo sea" [as a true son, I will be able to speak better than any who is not] (1586 dedication to his León Hebreo translation). In a 1589 letter to Philip II, his second dedication to the *Diálogos de amor*, the Inca speaks of his words as "escritas con alguna más certidumbre y propiedad de lo que hasta ahora se han escrito" [written somewhat more accurately and with more certainty than what has been written until now]. When a politically touchy subject comes up, however, Garcilaso, aiming for gravity and veracity, alludes to a prior textual tradition. He calls in the Spaniards to confirm such issues as the Inca resurrection of the body: "porque cosa tan ajena de gentiles . . . parecía invención mía, no habiéndola escrito algún español" (1.2.7) [a thing so foreign to non-Christians might seem to be of my own invention, had it not been written by some Spaniard]. One touchy subject for which the Inca does not consult authorities, however—the issue of cannibalism— is exploited by Cervantes in the opening chapters to the *Persiles*.

A Comparison of Cannibals

In the opening book of the *Comentarios*, Garcilaso feels obliged to remind us that "toda comparación es odiosa" (1.1.19), a judgment that, as all *cervantistas* recall, Don Quijote also makes in the Cueva de Montesinos (2.23). Although comparisons on the parallel theme of human sacrifice and cannibalism may seem especially odious, these practices interested Renaissance Europe to the point of obsession. To what degree accusations of such practices were leveled against the Amerindians by way of justifying their subjugation and enslavement is a polemic eloquently addressed by Anthony Pagden, W. Arens, and Michael Palencia-Roth, among others.[41] Garcilaso deflects the accusation away from the Incas, resolutely distancing them from human sacrifice, a practice he claims they abominated almost as much as sodomy: according to Garcilaso, the Incas legislated a great "pesquisa de los sodomitas" among the coastal fisherfolk, who were burned alive for "cosa tan abominable" (1.3.13).[42] Although the Incas did offer sacrifices, Garcilaso insists that these were confined to their birds and rabbits, their prettiest woolen clothing, and even their coca leaves ("la yerba *cuca*," the subject of 2.8.15), but never people: "no sacrificaron carne ni sangre humana" (2.4.17 and 1.2.8).

As for cannibalism, Garcilaso writes that it also was an abomination for the Incas. Although he is careful to displace the practice onto a personification—"como la crueldad no sepa hartarse, antes tenga tanta más hambre y más sed cuanta más sangre y carne humana coma y beba" (2.9.37) [as cruelty cannot be satisfied, the more human blood and flesh it eats and drinks, the hungrier and thirstier it becomes]—he represents the Incas at least imaginatively capable of revenge cannibalism. At the funeral of a son of Atahualpa (regarded, by Garcilaso's kin, as the traitor who destroyed their empire), an old Inca bites the hem of his garment (a sign of great *ira*), and then rhetorically asks for the corpse in order to eat him raw: "Dénmelo así muerto, como está, que yo me lo comeré crudo, sin pimiento" (2.9.39) [Give it to me dead, the way it is, and I will eat it raw, without seasoning].

As models of Amerindians who did practice cannibalism, however, Garcilaso offered the pre-Incas as candidates, the cultures from "la primera edad," to whose horrific lifestyle Garcilaso dedicated no fewer than six chapters. Before the arrival of Manco Cápac, the first Inca ruler (1.1.9), men lived and indeed dressed like animals: "cubríanse con pieles de animales" (1.1.13). Apart from their sumptuary norms, they were "barbarísimos fuera de todo encarecimento" (1.1.14) [barbaric beyond belief]. The barbarity becomes a refrain—"hacían sacrificios muy bárbaros" (1.1.20)—and is linked with the pre-Incas' inability to transcend: "porque no levantaron los pensamientos a cosas invisibles" (1.1.9) [for they did not lift their thoughts to invisible things]. The amplification of the invisible is connected here, in the style of Freud, to an "advance in civilization,"[43] while the inability to transcend is intertwined, in turn, with the urge to cannibalize. Garcilaso describes the pre-Incas as "amicísimos de carne humana" (1.1.12), a condition that recalls Aristotle's Anthropophagi, those Black Sea tribes of the Achaeans and Heniochi who were said to "delight in human flesh" (*Pol.* 1338 b 19 and *NE* 1148 b 19ff.).

Although Garcilaso leaves us the impression that, before the messianic eruption of Manco Cápac into the pre-Incan dark ages, the whole Andean world lived in a dire state of savagery, recent studies in archeology and ethnohistory contest such claims. Geoffrey Conrad and Arthur Demarest, for instance, regard this debasement of the pre-Incas as part of "Cuzco's imperial propaganda," as well as "the most flagrant fiction."[44] I shall not seek the motives that may have impelled Inca Garcilaso to accuse the pre-Incas of cannibalism. Although Roberto González-Echevarría suggests that Garcilaso's own personal recognition and enfranchisement depended on his establishing the nobility of the Incas, which in turn depended on the corresponding "barbarism" of earlier cultures,[45] these and similar issues of social defensiveness are, I think, best left to Max Hernández's splendid new psychobiography of Inca Garcilaso.[46] The search for any "objective" formulation of the truth of human sacrifice among the pre-Incas seems fruitless here. What concerns us is the textual portrait of pan-Andean barbarism that Garcilaso may have offered Cervantes.

In the *Persiles*, the barbarians have been persuaded—"o ya del demonio, o ya de un antiguo hechicero" [either by the devil or by an ancient sorcerer]—to practice both ritual sacrifice and cannibalism. Inaugurating Cervantes' "Historia setentrional," these barbarians structurally recall the Chancas, rivals of the Incas, who lived in "el *septentrión* del Cuzco" and who had been persuaded by demons that human sacrifice was the right thing to do: "estaban *persuadidos de los demonios*, sus dioses" (1.4.15; emphasis added). The sacrifices performed by Cervantes' barbarians are linked to a prophecy that their tribe is destined to produce a world conqueror. In order to identify the father of their future world conqueror, the barbarians have devised a foolproof test: the pulverized hearts of sacrificed males must be swallowed, by all potential fathers, without wincing ("sin torcer el rostro") (p. 57). P. Blas Valera's description of the pre-Incas' testing of a potential victim, who would be cannibalized "si al tiempo que atormentaban al triste hizo alguna señal de sentimiento *con el rostro*" (1.1.11; emphasis added) [if while they were torturing the poor wretch *his face* showed some sign of emotion] may be the subtext for the barbarians' taste-test. As for the pulverized hearts, Inca Garcilaso speaks of the pre-Incan predilection for organ meats—"quemaban . . . el corazón y los pulmones hasta consumirlos" (1.1.11) [they would burn . . . the heart and lungs until they were consumed]—a diet that links them to Cervantes' barbarians, who are also ritual heart-consumers.

But Cervantes' "bebida de polvos" also seems to have various points of ideological contact with the Inca "cult of the royal mummies." It is not inconceivable that Cervantes may have heard the story, which Father Bernabé Cobo would publish in 1653, of a certain idol in Cuzco, a statue of the sun god whose hollow stomach was "filled with a paste made of gold dust mixed with the ashes or powder of the Inca kings' hearts."[47]

Rewriting Barbary

What is Cervantes up to with this macabre narrative, a far cry from the "survival" cannibalism he represented in *Numancia*, where the besieged

Numantines—"barbarians" fighting for their liberty against an aggressor Roman empire—are given orders to kill and dole out the dismembered bodies of Roman prisoners?[48] The cannibalism that opens the *Persiles* suggests, I would argue, a powerful Cervantine critique of the European conquest of America—of what Stephen Greenblatt calls "the greatest experiment in political, economic, and cultural cannibalism in the history of the Western world."[49] The late Cervantes, I think, could be ranked among that visionary company of Spaniards—Antonio de Montesinos, Francisco de Vitoria, Bartolomé de Las Casas—who were actively generating an internal critique of their own empire's colonial abuses. The great messianic event in Cervantes' text, we recall, is the vision the barbarians have of their forthcoming messiah as a man who will conquer the world. This may be a veiled critique of Carlos V, who was envisioned by Cortés as "monarch of the world"—a vision of "universal monarchy" that J. E. Elliott informs us was shared by eminent figures in the imperial entourage if not by the Spanish humanists. Francisco de Vitoria, for instance, devoted a whole section of *De Indis* (1.2.2) "to refuting the thesis that the Emperor could be lord of the whole world."[50] In Garcilaso's own version of Fray Vicente de Valverde's speech to Atahualpa at Cajamarca, the friar praises Carlos V for his potency in the arms race and for his diligence in sending out the military "para conquistar el mundo."[51]

But Cervantes' critique does not merely side with the vanquished in the American wars of conquest. His empire-building barbarians have a strikingly mixed lineage: they are a conflation of the Spaniards, with their advertised aims for world conquest, and of the Incas, whose own messianic imperialism was overthrown by the Spaniards. Cervantes' text would seem to ridicule all imperialist policies tied to providentialist historical schemes—whether by the expansionist Incas or by the conquistadores who destroyed them in order to construct their own "feudal paradise."[52] In six short chapters, Cervantes gives us the barbaric realities of universal empire. By parodying the despotism of an imperial culture, he instances the similarity as well as the barbarity of *all* imperial "civilizing" missions—whether the Inca mission in Tawantinsuyu or, later, the Spanish mission there.

Figured forth as oxymora, Cervantes' European-based "Amerindians" overwhelm the operating taxonomy. The discursive strategy of their ambiguous representation is to suggest that Spanish and Inca imperial practices were disturbingly similar, that each empire had its fair share of imperial atrocities, its cult of sacrificial rituals, and its religious rationale for conquest. The echoes, affinities, and uncanny structural parallels between the bellicose and despotic Incas and the Spaniards who supplanted them were not lost on Cervantes, who perceived the hidden network of resemblances between their ostensibly opposite cultures. Cervantes seems to have read the heroic past of the subject Incas, those master empire builders of the New World, as a laundered version of the Spanish imperial present. Such a reading distinguishes him from the chronicles of the "toledanos"—the Spaniards campaigning for "the extirpation of idolatries" in Peru—whose official view of the Incas as tyrants comfortably allowed them to see themselves as liberators. Cervantes' text in no way legitimizes the "liberation" of the Indians from the tyrannical Incas so that they could be free to enjoy the "suave yugo" of the Spanish crown.[53] Where such chronicles posit absolute difference between European and American cultures, Cervantes, Mercutio-like, intuited points of deep resemblance: "A pox on both your empires."

Because the savagery of Cervantes' displaced "Amerindians" is not the least bit noble—given their total preoccupation "con la ira y la venganza" (p. 69)—they seem a far cry from the sentimentally appealing "bon sauvage" we find in Montaigne, whose cultural relativism had profound consequences for the topos of the Noble Savage. "On Cannibals," with its apology for the Brazilian Indians and its corresponding condemnation of contemporary Europeans, recast the pieties of a Western historiographical tradition. Like Montaigne, Cervantes wished to move out of what José Rabasa rightly deplores as "the semantic field from which the 'West' defines the 'rest' and posits itself as a universal cultural model."[54] Unlike Montaigne, however, Cervantes fashioned a cultural critique dependent not upon an inversion but a subversion of binary oppositions. The discourse of empire, Cervantes' cannibals imply, cannot be reduced to binaries.

Recent studies exhibit this resistance to reiterating, through an idealization of Amerindian cultures, the logic that informed the earlier European Saint / American Savage dichotomy. The contemporary historian Simon Schama, for example, deplores the "conveniently emasculated" version of Amerindian history that, by its exquisite care "not to commit any act of vulgar Eurocentricity," whitewashes American cultures of their vices and robs them of their human complexities. Schama himself describes the Spanish conquest of the Aztec empire in a bluntly nonpartisan way: "One bellicose and sacrificial culture faced another, one despotism of tribute and service was annihilated by another."[55] Closer to our Cervantine subtext, Sabine MacCormack's new study of *Religion in the Andes* examines "the resentment of some Indians toward the imperial Incas, who imposed on them a centralized view of the cosmos and the social order and bade them make large offerings to alien dieties."[56] We need not whitewash the imperial Incas of their own human complexity, in short, in order to deplore what the Spaniards did to them.

Although Inca Garcilaso's *Comentarios reales* largely addresses events before this encounter, his text also destabilizes the opposition between civilized European and dull-witted barbarian. The Inca offered the European readership of his age, Cervantes included, a number of fresh candidates for the barbaric. The peoples the Incas had to absorb into the empire he calls "bárbaros en la lengua *como los castellanos*," deftly assimilating the pre-Inca barbarians to the Spaniards (1.5.21); the Spaniards themselves, he reminds Spaniards, were often laughed at by the Indians for their linguistic "barbarismos" (1.4.11).[57] The very name *Perú* (which only the Spaniards use, the Indians keeping to Tawantinsuyu), Inca Garcilaso regards as "bárbaro" (1.1.6), along with *Lima*, which he shows to be a Spanish corruption of "Rímac" (2.6.30). Inca Garcilaso's corrective philology, in short, was part of his own civilized "conquest of the word" (the theme of an important essay by María Antonia Garcés).[58] It is the kind of conquest still evident in Pedro Basadre's moving description of the encounter between two kinds of "barbarians":

> Por su ignorancia del cristianismo, de la escritura, del dinero, del hierro, de la rueda, de la pólvora, de la monogamía, de muchas plantas y animales, los indios aparecieron *como bárbaros entre los españoles*. Por su destrucción de andenes, caminos, terrazas, tem-

plos, ciudades, graneros y tributos; por su rapiña, su crueldad, su lascivia y hasta su superioridad guerrera, los españoles aparecieron *como bárbaros entre los indios.*[59]

[Because they were unaware of Christianity, writing, money, the wheel, gunpowder, monogamy, and many plants and animals, *among the Spaniards the Indians seemed like barbarians.* Because they destroyed footpaths, roads, terraces, temples, cities, granaries, and tributes; because of their violent robbery, their cruelty, their lust, and even their superiority at war, *among the Indians the Spaniards seemed like barbarians.*]

Our postcolonial age has become increasingly aware of the instability of that ancient dualism of civilization/barbary. Who determines what is barbarous and what is civilized? "Only one of the two parties to the agreement," Todorov answers, "between whom subsists no equality or reciprocity."[60] By marrying a civilized male Spaniard to a Christianized female barbarian—perhaps unconsciously rewriting the tragic history of Inca Garcilaso's own parents—Cervantes yokes the two parties together in a total linguistic reciprocity that becomes paradigmatic for all the other couplings in the text: "Háme enseñado su lengua y yo a él la mía" (p. 82) [He has taught me his language and I have taught him mine]. Cervantes knew, as the Walter Benjamin epigram puts it, that "there is not a document of civilization which is not at the same time a document of barbarism."[61] Personifying the civilization/barbary dualism, Cervantes' exemplary couple also instances Todorov's experience of alterity: "the discovery *self* makes of the *other*."[62] This experience is addressed throughout the *Persiles*, where all characters who attempt to comprehend the *other* are inevitably forced into reappraising themselves. In its disquieting opening narrative, the *Persiles* bids farewell to the categorical rigor implicit in the civilization/barbary binary. That reorientation may be the richest of Inca Garcilaso's American legacies to Cervantes.

Notes

Epigraph: "If it had four acts, the fourth would end in America."

1. A document in Cervantes' own hand, found this century in the archives at Simancas, testifies to his 1582 application to the Council of the Indies for a post in America. When he reapplied in 1590, he was rejected: "[que] busque por acá

en qué se le haga merced," the secretary of the council jotted in the margins of this second petition. For the whole text of Cervantes' 1590 application, see José Toribio Medina, "Cervantes americanista: Lo que dijo de los hombres y cosas de América," in *Estudios cervantinos* (Santiago de Chile: Fondo Histórico y Bibliográfico José Toribio Medina, 1958), pp. 535–36.

2. That the "conquest of America" is both a loaded term and a Eurocentric idea bears repeating: what Europe saw as a "conquest" the Amerindians saw as "an invasion and occupation." See Rolena Adorno's "Colonial Spanish American Literary Studies: 1982–1992," *Revista Internacional de Bibliografía* 38 (1988): 170.

3. In the textual family today known as the *Crónica de Indias*, Walter Mignolo includes "cartas relatorias, relaciones, la crónica y la historia" (see "Cartas, crónicas y relaciones del descubrimiento y la conquista," in *Historia de la literatura hispanoamericana*, vol. 1: *Epoca colonial* [Madrid: Cátedra, 1982]).

4. Raúl Porras Barrenechea, "Cervantes, La Camacha y Montilla," in *El Inca Garcilaso en Montilla, 1561–1614* (Lima: Editorial San Marcos, 1955), p. 238.

5. Bernal Díaz del Castillo, *Historia verdadera de la conquista del la Nueva Espanña*, ed. Joaquín Ramírez Cabañas (Mexico City: Porrúa, 1967), p. 147.

6. See Gonzalo Menéndez Pidal, *Imagen del mundo hacia 1570* (Madrid: Consejo de la Hispanidad, 1944), p. 12; cited by Daniel P. Testa in "Parodia y mitificación del Nuevo Mundo en el *Quijote*," *Cuadernos Hispanoamericanos* 430 (April 1986): 67–68.

7. See Stephen Greenblatt, *Marvelous Possessions: The Wonder of the New World* (Chicago: University of Chicago Press, 1991), p. 80.

8. Elliott informs us that "one of the most striking features of sixteenth-century intellectual history [was] the apparent slowness of Europe in making the mental adjustments required to incorporate America within its field of vision." There seemed to be no "overwhelming interest" on the part of the "European reading public" for American matters. Not only were Spanish authors "strangely reticent about the New World," but the most resounding silence appears in the memoirs of Charles V himself. Elliott also notes "the marked neglect of American affairs in the discussions of the Council of Trent." See *The Old World and the New, 1492–1650* (Cambridge: Cambridge University Press, 1970), pp. 8, 12–14, and 81.

9. See Rolena Adorno, "Literary Production and Suppression: Reading and Writing about Amerindians in Colonial Spanish America," *Dispositio* 11 (1986): 28–29, 1–25.

10. Miguel de Cervantes, *El ingenioso hidalgo Don Quijote de la Mancha*, ed. Luis Andrés Murillo, 2 vols. (Madrid: Clásicos Castalia, 1978). All citations

are taken from this edition and will be parenthetically documented, by volume and chapter numbers, within the text.

11. In 1.8, Don Quijote meets a Biscayan (*vizcaína*) lady whose husband is about to sail from Seville to the Indies, where a lofty position awaits him. In 1.29, the Priest mentions a relative who has sent to Seville over 60,000 "pesos ensayados" (whose percentage of silver and gold had been determined). In 1.39, the Captive's second brother decides to go to the Indies to invest his "hacienda" or portion of his father's legacy. In 1.42, the Captive's third brother, the licenciado Juan Pérez de Viedma, is represented as going as an "oidor a las Indias, en la Audiencia de Méjico," while Judge Viedma himself, supposedly the youngest of the Viedma brothers, claims that his younger brother "está en el Pirú, tan rico, que con lo que ha enviado a mi padre y a mí ha satisfecho bien la parte que él le llevó." In 2.71, Don Quijote tells Sancho that, for a job as important as disenchanting Dulcinea, "las minas del Potosí fueran poco para pagarte."

12. The motif of "burning the ships behind him" first crystallized in Cortés's Second Letter, which appeared in various sixteenth-century printings and translations after its initial printing in 1522. Of the *Corpus cortesianum* (1519–1526), only the first and fifth letters were unavailable to Cervantes. The "Gran Hernando Cortés" is also mentioned in *El licenciado Vidriera*, where Mexico City—"espanto del mundo nuevo"—is favorably compared to Venice; see *Novelas ejemplares* (Buenos Aires: Espasa-Calpe, 1967), p. 106.

13. An earlier allusion to don Alonso de Ercilla y Zúñiga occurs in the fourth stanza of Cervantes' *Canto de Calíope*. See *La Galatea*, ed. Juan Bautista Avalle-Arce (Madrid: Espasa-Calpe, 1968), 2:191.

14. The insults in *Don Quijote* are: "—¡Caminad, trogloditas! / Callad, bárbaros! /¡Pagad, antropófagos!" (2.68). The line from *El rufián viudo* is part of a speech by Trampagos that begins, "Fuera yo un Polifemo, un antropófago, / Un troglodita, un Bárbaro Zoílo, / Un caimán, un caribe, un come-vivos" (Miguel de Cervantes, *Entremeses*, ed. Eugenio Asensio [Madrid: Clásicos Castalia, 1970], p. 83, ll. 134–36).

15. The Amerindian is always at the center of colonial writing, Rolena Adorno claims, even when he or she is not mentioned ("Literary Production," p. 20).

16. See the Espasa-Calpe edition (Buenos Aires, 1952) of *Los trabajos de Persiles y Sigismunda* for its anonymous editor's warning about its "repellant" beginnings. On the *Persiles* as a victim of institutional neglect, see Rafael Osuna, "El olvido del *Persiles*," a prescriptive essay that laments its "forgetting" (*Boletín de la Real Academia Española* 48 [1968]: 55–75).

17. See "Cervantes on Cannibals," in *Allegories of Love: Cervantes's "Per-*

siles and Sigismunda" (Princeton: Princeton University Press, 1991), pp. 109–29.

18. Eduardo González, "Erase una vez una isla obstinada," in *La persona y el relato: Proyecto de lectura psicoanlítica* (Madrid: José Porrúa Turanzas, 1985), p. 126.

19. Related to Cervantes by marriage, Don Francisco Pizarro and Don Juan de Orellana were brothers and the sons of a Don Fernando de Orellana, the *regidor* of Trujillo in 1607. See Avalle-Arce's footnote in *Persiles*, p. 288. See also Astrana's *Vida*, 6.519 and 7.431–32, as well as his Appendix 27, pp. 746–50, for unedited documents on the Pizarros et al. Stelio Cro argues that these names show Cervantes' familiarity "con las cosas de Indias" ("Cervantes, el *Persiles*, y la historiografía Indiana," *Anales de literatura hispanoamericana* 4 [Madrid: Universidad Complutense, 1975]: 5–25).

20. See Inca Garcilaso de la Vega, *Comentarios reales*, ed. Aurelio Miró Quesada (Venezuela: Biblioteca Ayacucho, 1976), vol. 1, book 3, chap. 16, p. 155. All further citations from the *Comentarios* will be from this two-volume edition and appear parenthetically in the text by volume, book, and chapter numbers.

21. Cristóbal Colón, *Textos y documentos completos: Relaciones de viajes, cartas y memoriales*, edición de Consuelo Varela (Madrid: Alianza Editorial, 1982), p. 117; José Piedra, "The Banquet," paper delivered at the MLA Convention, San Francisco, 30 December 1992.

22. See Porras Barrenechea, *El Inca Garcilaso en Montilla*, p. 230. Garcilaso responds to this racism, in the margins of his edition of Gómara's text, "pues ni son judíos ni moros sino gentiles." See also the opinion of Luis E. Varcárcel that "nuestro Garcilaso era un indio, era un hombre de color, un infiel, a la misma altura que un morisco o un judío"; cited by Juan Durán Luzio in "Sobre Tomás Moro en el Inca Garcilaso," *Revista Iberoamericana* 42 (1970): 351.

23. See Rolena Adorno, "Nuevas perspectivas en los estudios literarios coloniales hispanoamericanos," *Revista de crítica literaria latinoamericana* 14, no. 28 (1988): 19.

24. Although references to the great lyricist Garcilaso de la Vega abound in Cervantes, there is no extant mention of his descendant Inca Garcilaso by Cervantes and vice versa. Records thus far show no definite contact between them, although the chances of no contact are unlikely. In the *Coloquio*, Berganza recalls how his master, the "alguacil" (constable), showed three sword sheaths to the "Asistente" (Lieutenant Governor) of Seville "que, si mal no me acuerdo lo era entonces el licenciado Sarmiento de Valladares," a real-life official who was in office between February 1589 and the end of that year. It is soon after that ep-

isode that Berganza arrives in Montilla, "villa del famoso y gran cristiano Marqués de Priego," who is a relative of Inca Garcilaso. Documents show that Inca Garcilaso left Montilla in November of 1591, when he sold his house and moved to Córdoba. Cervantes arrived in Montilla, foraging for the king, the very next month, remaining there from early December of 1591 until mid-1592. See Porras Barrenechea, *El Inca Garcilaso en Montilla, 1561–1614*, pp. 237–39. See also Rodríguez Marín, *Novelas ejemplares*, 2: 271 and 283.

25. Schevill and Bonilla claimed—in their 1914 edition of the *Persiles* and on the strength of some rather spotty parallels—that Cervantes "leyó con detenimiento" the *Comentarios reales*, and that he began the *Persiles* only after their 1608–9 publication. Garcilaso "parece haber sido la fuente más accesible a Cervantes y más cercana al *Persiles*, pues la primera parte de su historia salió a luz en 1609." See "Introducción," *Persiles y Sigismunda*, 2 vols. (Madrid: Imprenta Bernardo Rodríguez, 1914), 1:ix and xxviin.

Jorge Campos writes of Cervantes' "lectura innegable" of the *Comentarios reales*, adding that "en Cervantes estaba presente siempre el mundo español del otro lado del océano," in "Presencia de América en la obra de Cervantes," *Revista de Indias* 8 (1947): 371–404.

William Entwistle announced Cervantes' depiction of a tribe of barbarians who "practice the rites and wear the clothing of Garcilaso de la Vega el Inca's American aborigines." See "Ocean of Story," in *Cervantes: A Collection of Critical Essays* (Englewood Cliffs, N.J.: Prentice-Hall, 1969), p. 164.

John Grier Varner sees Cervantes as having "ostensibly utilized a description of the premarital sexual initiations found in Garcilaso's history of the Incas." Varner is alluding to Cervantes' *lex primae noctis* episode of Transila (Fitzmaurice, 1.12–14). The passage from Garcilaso reads: "En otras provincias corrompían la virgen que se había de casar los parientes más cercanos del novio y sus mayores amigos" (1.1.14).

Alban Forcione mentions Inca Garcilaso (once) as among "the historians of the Indies [who] were a source of much of Cervantes's marvelous subject matter." Elsewhere Forcione links the persecution of Cervantes' hero "not only with the American Indians but also with the powers of hell," a conventionally European linkage, given that Spaniards viewed the Andean networks of the sacred as the fruits of diabolic delusion. Alban Forcione, *Cervantes, Aristotle, and the "Persiles"* (Princeton: Princeton University Press, 1970), p. 272n; and *Cervantes' Christian Romance: A Study of "Persiles and Sigismunda"* (Princeton: Princeton University Press, 1972), p. 38n.

26. Avalle-Arce sees the writing of *Don Quijote* as interpolated between Part 1 of the *Persiles* (written between 1599 and 1605) and Part 2 (written between

1612 and 1616). Avalle-Arce's objections are in the "Introducción" to *Los trabajos de Persiles y Sigismunda*, ed. Juan Bautista Avalle-Arce (Madrid: Clásicos Castalia, 1969), pp. 14–15n. Avalle-Arce's anthology is entitled *El Inca Garcilaso en sus "Comentarios"* (Madrid: Gredos, 1964). Max Singleton, who dates the composition of the *Persiles* before 1609 (date of the publication of the *Comentarios reales*), also denies any influence.

27. See Adorno, "Nuevas perspectivas," p. 21.

28. See Julia Kristeva on Bakhtin's notion of writing "as a reading of the anterior literary corpus and the text as an absorption of and reply to another text," in "Word, Dialogue, and Novel," in *Desire in Language: A Semiotic Approach to Literature and Art*, ed. Leon S. Roudiez, trans. Thomas Gora, Alice Jardine, and Leon S. Roudiez (New York: Columbia University Press, 1980), p. 69.

29. Unlike the 1568 and 1584 Spanish translations, Inca Garcilaso's was regarded by the contemporary rhetorician Francisco de Castro as an improvement on the original Italian: "luce mejor en español." See Francisco de Castro, S.J., *De Arte Rhetorica* (Córdoba, 1611), cited by José Durand in "En torno a la prosa del Inca Garcilaso: a propósito de un artículo de Roberto González Echevarría," *Nuevo Texto Crítico* 102 (1989): 217–18. Menéndez Pelayo later afirmed that the Inca's translation "resulta mucho más amena de estilo que las otras dos que tenemos en castellano" (see P. Carmelo Saenz de Santa María, ed., "Producción Literaria," in *Obras completas del Inca Garcilaso de la Vega*, vol. 1, *Biblioteca de Autores Españoles* (Madrid: Atlas, 1965), p. xlii.

30. Garcilaso himself cites Murillo's speech in the Prologue to the *Historia general del Perú*, in *Obras completas del Inca Garcilaso de la Vega*, vol. 3, ed. P. Carmelo Saenz de Santa María, S.J. (Madrid: Atlas, 1960), p. 14. On this speech, see John Grier Varner, *El Inca: The Life and Times of Garcilaso de la Vega* (Austin: University of Texas Press, 1968), p. 300.

31. See Julio Ortega, "Garcilaso y el modelo de la nueva cultura," in *Socialismo y participación* 53 (1991): 61. Alberto Escobar considers the *Comentarios reales*, in the modern anthropological sense, as an "etnohistoria." See "Lenguaje e historia en los *Comentarios reales*," in *Patio de Letras* (Lima: Caballos de Troya, 1965), pp. 18–20.

32. In fully developed patterns of "split inheritance," one principal heir receives the position, rights, and duties of the deceased Inca. The dead man's personal possessions and sources of income, however, are assigned, corporately, to his other descendants, who serve as his "trustees." The emergence of the "cult of the royal mummies," then, was indirectly tied to the growth of empire, in that a new ruler, denied his predecessor's wealth, was forced into conquests as a way of accumulating his own. See Geoffrey W. Conrad and Arthur Demarest, *Reli-

Diana de Armas Wilson

♦

gion and Empire: The Dynamics of Aztec and Inca Expansionism (Cambridge: Cambridge University Press, 1984), pp. 91–94.

33. "El Heródoto de los Incas"—Pedro Henríquez Ureña's phrase for Inca Garcilaso (see rear of bookjacket of volume 1 of the Ayacucho edition of *Comentarios reales*)—might be reconsidered in the light of Arnaldo Momigliano's reminder that Herodotus was considered, throughout antiquity, as both "the father of history and a liar" ("fabulosus"). Regarded as excessively pro-Barbarian (*philobarbaros*) by Plutarch, among others, Herodotus was, however, vindicated by the sixteenth century, which began to appreciate his "comparative method of ethnography" (see especially Henricus Stephanus's 1566 *Apologia pro Herodoto*). The methods and reliability of Herodotus as a historian were subjected to an animated debate in the sixteenth century. See A. D. Momigliano, "The Place of Herodotus in the History of Historiography," *History* 43 (1958): 1–6. See also Stephen Greenblatt's remarks on Herodotus in *Marvelous Possessions*, pp. 122–28.

34. Over thirty citations from Pedro de Cieza de León, *Crónica del Perú*; just under thirty citations from Padre José de Acosta, *Historia natural y moral de las Indias*; fifteen citations from Francisco López de Gómara, *Historia general de las Indias*; eleven citations from Agustín de Zárate, *Historia del descubrimiento y conquista del Perú* (see *Los cronistas del Perú* [Lima: Grace, 1962], pp. 169ff.; cited by José Durand, *La transformación social del conquistador* [Mexico City: Porrúa, 1953]; p. 214).

35. According to Menéndez y Pelayo, "los comentarios reales no son texto histórico; son una novela utópica, como la de Tomás Moro" (*Orígenes de la novela* [Madrid: Bailly, 1905–1915], 1: 392). See also Juan Durán Luzio, "Sobre Tomás Moro en el Inca Garcilaso," *Revista Iberoamericana* 41 (1970):349, and Margarita Zamora, "'Nowhere' Is Somewhere: The *Comentarios reales* and the Utopian Model," in *Language, Authority, and Indigenous History in the "Comentarios reales de los Incas"* (Cambridge: Cambridge University Press, 1988), pp. 129–65.

36. On Gómara's history as "el germen . . . de los *Comentarios*," see Miró Quesada's prologue, p. xxi. The Inca's marginal notes to an edition of Gómara's *Historia* (in the Biblioteca Nacional in Lima) include a personal defense of his father's tarnished military reputation at the Battle of Huarina. Gómara claims that Captain Garcilaso de la Vega gave a horse to the rebel Gonzalo Pizarro in the heat of battle. The indignant Inca's marginal comment: "Esta mentira me ha quitado el comer."

37. Inca Garcilaso was unjustly accused of plagiarism of Blas Valera ("plagio contra él"), an accusation definitively refuted (see Miró Quesada's prologue).

38. See José Durand, "Los silencios del Inca Garcilaso," *Mundo Nuevo* 5 (Paris: Instituto Latinoamericano de Relaciones Internacionales, 1966): 66–72.

39. For Rolena Adorno, colonial literary production "was constituted by the subtle, complex, and contradictory maneuvers—both internal and external to discourse itself—whose full understanding lies yet before us." See "Literary Production and Suppression," p. 19. Elsewhere Adorno uses the Bakhtinian notion of "polivocalidad" to consider "dialogic" practices a perfect model for a colonial society. The paradigm that typically operates within colonial discourse is a simultaneity of various subject positions demanded by the diverse facets of the project of colonialism. See "Nuevas perspectivas," p. 14.

40. Robert B. Alter, "Mirror of Knighthood, World of Mirrors," in *Don Quixote*, The Ormsby Translation, ed. Joseph R. Jones and Kenneth Douglas (New York: W. W. Norton, 1981), p. 956.

41. Pagden thinks it very likely that "except for survival cannibalism and acts of extreme revenge," the Amerindians—"many of whom did practise human sacrifice"—did *not* eat people: "I, at least, have not found a single eye-witness account of a cannibal feast nor, indeed, a single description which does not rely on elements taken from classical accounts of anthropophagy" (*Fall of Natural Man* [Cambridge: Cambridge University Press, 1982], pp. 80, 83, and 217n). W. Arens sees cannibalism as having been invented to justify the Conquest. See *The Man-Eating Myth: Anthropology and Anthropophagy* (New York: Oxford University Press, 1979). See also Michael Palencia-Roth's "Cannibalism and the New Man of Latin America in the 15th- and 16th-Century European Imagination," *Comparative Civilizations Review* 12 (Spring 1985): 1–27.

42. On sodomy as "the sexual practice most consistently attributed to the Amerindian"—as instanced by Cieza de León's *Primera parte de la crónica del Perú* (Seville, 1553)—see Rolena Adorno, "Literary Production and Suppression," p. 7.

43. In *Moses and Monotheism*, Freud includes the "victory of intellectuality over sensuality," and of the father over the mother, in this advance. See Sigmund Freud, *The Standard Edition of the Complete Psychological Works of Sigmund Freud*, 24 vols., trans. James Strachey (London: Hogarth, 1953–74), 23: 114.

44. Conrad and Demarest, *Religion and Empire*, p. 86. The authors note that Cieza de León, for one, was perceptive enough to realize "that the claim of pan-Andean barbarism was intended to glorify the Incas and legitimate their rule" (p. 138, n. 2).

45. Roberto González-Echevarría, "The Law of the Letter: Garcilaso's *Commentaries* and the Origins of Latin American Narrative," *Yale Journal of Criticism* 1 (1987): 122.

258

Diana de Armas Wilson

♦

46. Max Hernández, *Memoria del bien perdido: conflicto, identidad y nostalgia en el Inca Garcilaso de la Vega* (Madrid: Editorial Siruela / Quinto Centenario, 1992). Hernández's title echoes a line from the *Comentarios reales*, concerning the laments of his mother's family that Garcilaso overheard during his childhood: "Y con la memoria del bien perdido siempre acababan su conversación en lágrimas y llanto diciendo: 'Trocósenos el reinar el vassallaje'" (1.15).

47. Cited by Conrad and Demarest, *Religion and Empire*, p. 115. A Jesuit who arrived in Lima in 1600, Father Cobo used, as his two primary sources, Inca Garcilaso and the *toledano* Corregidor of Cuzco, Polo de Ondegardo. Although the story of the idol may be apocryphal, archeological evidence corroborates Cobo's claim that the Incas did occasionally practice human sacrifice. See Bernabé Cobo, *Historia del Nuevo Mundo*, ed. Marcos Jiménez de la Espada, 4 vols. (Seville: Sociedad de Bibliófilos Andaluces, 1890–95), 3: 325. See also *Inca Religion and Customs by Father Bernabé Cobo*, trans. and ed. Roland Hamilton (Austin: University of Texas Press, 1990).

48. According to Willard F. King, the cannibalized aggressor Romans are "obviously . . . playing the role of the expansionist Castilian empire" of Cervantes' day; see "Cervantes' *Numancia* and Imperial Spain," *Modern Language Notes* 94 (1979): 206, 208. See also Carroll B. Johnson, "La *Numancia* and the Structure of Cervantine Ambiguity," *Ideologies and Literature* 3 (1980): 75–94.

49. See Greenblatt, *Marvelous Possessions*, p. 136.

50. Elliott, *Old World and the New*, pp. 84–85.

51. *Historia general del Perú: Obras completas del Inca Garcilaso de la Vega*, ed. P. Carmelo Saenz de Santa María, S.J., vol. 3 (Madrid: Ediciones Atlas, 1960), p. 50.

52. Elliott, *Old World and the New*, p. 28.

53. See Franklin Pease, "Garcilaso Andino," p. 43.

54. See José Rabasa's cogent insights on inversions in "Utopian Ethnology in Las Casas," in *1492–1992: Re/discovering Colonial Writing*, Special Issue of *Hispanic Issues* 4, ed. René Jara and Nicholas Spadaccini (Minneapolis: The Prisma Institute, 1989): 265.

55. Simon Schama, "They All Laughed at Christopher Columbus," *New Republic*, 6 and 13 January 1992, p. 32.

56. See J. Jorge Klor de Alva's review of Sabine MacCormack's *Religion in the Andes: Vision and Imagination in Early Colonial Perú* (Princeton: Princeton University Press, 1992), in the *New York Times Book Review*, 29 March 1992, p. 20.

57. Emphasis added. The Spaniards misconstrue the American reality: "como corrompen los españoles todos los vocablos que toman del lenguaje de los indios" (1.4); "los españoles corrompen todos los más [nombres] que toman en la boca" (2.5.71).

58. María Antonia Garcés argues that the model of a "conquest" Garcilaso offers his readers is that of Manco Capac, the first Inca, who subjugates his own barbaric vassals through the *word*. See "Lecciones del Nuevo Mundo: la ética de la palabra en el Inca Garcilaso de la Vega," *Texto: Contexto* 17 (Bogota: Universidad de los Andes, 1991): 125–50.

59. Jorge Basadre, *Perú: problema y posibilidad* (Lima: Cotesca, 1984), p. 13; cited by Max Hernández, *Memoria del bien perdido*, p. 29.

60. Tzvetan Todorov, *The Conquest of America*, trans. Richard Howard (New York: Harper and Row, 1984), p. 150.

61. Walter Benjamin, "Theses on the Philosophy of History," in *Illuminations*, ed. Hannah Arendt, trans. Harry Zohn (New York: Schocken Books, 1968), p. 256.

62. Todorov, *Conquest*, p. 3.

CHAPTER

12

The Discourse of Empire in the Renaissance

WALTER COHEN

———◆ ◆———

I hope here to provide an overview, in a certain sense a map, of the discourse of empire in the Renaissance, to argue for the utility of making that map (at least for literary critics), and to locate Hispanic discourse on it. Yet emphasis specifically on the *discourse* of empire in the narrowly linguistic sense employed here may feel like bad faith or at least preciosity, in the face of the central fact about European imperialism in the New World during this period. For Tzvetan Todorov "the sixteenth century perpetrated the greatest genocide in human history."[1] At the level of deliberate design the term remains debatable; at the level of demographic destruction it does not. In the latter sense there are few if any parallels in world history—not the Black Death of the fourteenth century, for instance. Even the sequence of mass bloodlettings that has marked our own century, though it may exceed the earlier period in absolute death toll, probably has less to account for in the way of complete elimination of entire peoples.

The agents of destruction included oppression, enslavement, social dislocation, murder, war, and especially disease. In the interior of Colombia the evidence pertains to tributaries rather than inhabitants, who presumably were far more numerous. One tribe, the Quimbaya, numbered 15,000 when the Spanish first arrived in 1539; by 1628 only 69 remained. The tribe had effectively ceased to exist by 1600. The Pamplona went from 60,000 or more in 1532, when Spanish explorers appeared on the scene, to 10,000 at the turn of the century and from there to below 2,400 in the late eighteenth century. And the Tunja, for whom there seem to be no figures at the time of conquest in 1537, were at

168,000 in 1564, 45,000 in 1636, and 25,000 in 1755.[2] Judging from the astonishing drop in population that routinely occurred elsewhere in the very first years following contact, the preconquest figure must have been much higher. West central Mexico experienced a decline from 295,000 people in 1548 to 38,000 in 1650.[3] For the Bahamas the statistics are even starker: in 1492, as many as half a million; in 1542, 0. Here, however, massive deportations to Hispaniola for forced labor greatly contributed to the extermination.[4] The Yucatan witnessed a fall from 800,000 in 1528 to 185,000 in 1600. But once again the earlier number is misleadingly low, since it does not refer to the entire territory of the Maya and since it follows, rather than precedes, initial contact with the Spanish, including a devastating epidemic of smallpox.[5] The indigenous population of Spanish Peru collapsed from 5 million people when Pizarro arrived in the 1530s to less than three hundred thousand 250 years later. But the Inca empire may have had as many as 30 million subjects on the eve of colonization.[6] Hispaniola went from 8 million in 1492–93 to less than half that number in 1496 and from there to 250 in 1540. Effective extinction may be dated to 1535.[7] And in central Mexico the 25 million people who awaited Cortés in 1519 had barely 1 million descendants in 1610.[8] Although these figures are not strictly commensurate, a conservative estimate of the population decline in these areas alone—as opposed to all of Spanish America or all of the Americas—would be 40 million. Note generally that much and sometimes most of this decline occurred in the first few years following contact and in particular, as we have seen, that such was the case with Hispaniola, which Columbus reached on his first voyage. If the human disaster there may in some measure be treated as a tragic result of European expansion, no such generous interpretation is possible for the subsequent behavior of the Spaniards. Before they reached the mainland, they had the consequences of conquest before their eyes. But, as the policy of deporting the native population of the Bahamas reveals, Spanish consciousness registered the death of millions of Indians only as a labor shortage.

As we all know, however, this shortage was ultimately made good not by shuffling the native deck but by introducing a wild card—the African slave. And after reviewing the data on the indigenous population, one turns to the level of violence associated with slavery almost in relief, at least initially. Roughly 9.5 million African slaves were imported to the New World between the late fifteenth and the late nineteenth centuries, though less than 20 percent came before 1700. In the entire period of the slave trade, perhaps "only" 1.5 million Africans died in transit. But Philip Curtin, from whom these relatively low figures derive, also argues, "The cost of the slave trade in human life was many times the number of slaves landed in the Americas. For every slave landed alive, other people died in warfare, along the bush paths leading to the coast, awaiting shipment, or in the crowded and unsanitary conditions of the middle passage. Once in the New World, still others died on entering a new disease environment." And though the absolute numbers were far smaller, death *rates* for the Europeans involved in the slave trade were astonishingly high as well—higher, for instance, in transit for the sailors who brought the slaves to the Americas than for the slaves themselves. If this boomerang effect seems like poetic justice—as Abraham Lincoln felt in tallying up the moral and mortal ledgers of the Civil War—it is nonetheless worth emphasizing that most of the European fatalities did not plague the two groups who most clearly benefited from slavery, the merchants and the planters.[9] Finally, the fate of the descendants—of the African slaves and more strikingly still of the indigenous population—does not allow even the ambiguous consolation that the suffering of the parents was an unavoidable, if unpleasant, prelude to the joy of the children.

This quantification of human misery is bound to be numbing—as it is, unwittingly, in Las Casas's *Devastation of the Indies*. Its scale exceeds by many orders of magnitude most people's capacity to imagine destruction, much less to respond empathetically to it. One can hardly avoid concluding that this trail of devastation is the first and most important matter to evoke in discussing not only European expansion in the Renaissance but indeed the Renaissance itself. I consider the conclusion correct. And from there it is fairly easy to conclude that the trail of devastation is the *only* important matter to evoke in such discussions. I consider *this* conclusion incorrect. Yet in what follows, which is concerned with discourse in a relatively narrow sense and hence only indirectly with European violence toward Americans and Africans, my hope is that the weightiness of the demographic data will put productive pressure on the account of the discourse.

I

As this essay like so many others testifies, imperialism is a popular topic in American academic literary criticism these days, and nowhere more so than in Renaissance studies, where Stephen Greenblatt's essays of the late 1970s on the topic, many of them collected in *Renaissance Self-Fashioning*,[10] have redefined the field. More recently Todorov's *Conquest of America* has won prestige and prominence for the Spanish side of things. This relatively recent interest belongs to the more general, vaguely leftist turn in criticism, a turn with which I identify. Yet in any interdisciplinary perspective, there is little room for self-congratulation. If empire is currently "hot," one can hardly avoid asking why it was previously "cold." Historians have long considered Europe's global expansion beginning in the late fifteenth century *the*, or at least *a*, turning point of modern world history. Indeed, many of the Renaissance chroniclers of discovery, conquest, and colonization felt the same way. My sources for the data on the European destruction of Amerindian and African peoples all appeared in the 1960s and early 1970s. By contrast, the virtual exclusion of empire from literary criticism during the first thirty postwar years would seem to tell its own story.

Yet, however important, political obtuseness does not in itself adequately explain the belatedness of literary criticism's discovery of America. The essays on empire in *Renaissance Self-Fashioning* have a curiously oblique, almost perverse relationship to their subject. Thus Greenblatt devotes more attention to the topic in the chapter on Marlowe than in the one on More, analyzes Book Two rather than the openly colonialist Book Five of Spenser's *Faerie Queene*, chooses *Othello* rather than the more obvious *Tempest*,[11] and, in what may have been the next essay he wrote, abandons even the racial relevance of *Othello* to investigate the connection between New World imperialism and Shakespeare's second *Henriad*.[12] Todorov abandons literature itself in order to consider the conquest of America. One might infer that literary critics so rarely entered the New World because the New World so rarely entered literature.[13] *Utopia* and *The Tempest* are and are not about America; the same is true of the relevant writings by Rabelais and Montaigne. The poetry of Donne and of Góngora reacts to the issue by rejecting it. The outstanding imperial epic of the era, Camões's *Lusiads*, celebrates the opening of a trade route to India. And although Cervantes and Lope de Vega resister the impact of the Indies in the American sense—which actually forms the subject of one of the latter's plays, to which I'll return—their most celebrated creations camp contentedly in the Castilian countryside. The historian J. H. Elliott has argued that the Old World simply found the New World too alien to understand. He concludes: "If America nurtured Europe's ambitions, it also kept its dreams alive. And perhaps dreams were always more important than realities in the relationship of the Old World and the New."[14] But if that reality proved elusive for the enormous array of historians and ethnographers, who at least pretended to factuality, it virtually vanished for frankly fictionalizing writers. Although this fact/fiction divide was not yet the unbridgeable epistemological gulf it sometimes seems to be in subsequent centuries, it already counted as an analytical category. And unlike classical antiquity or even the contemporary Islamic world, the colonial relationship does not seem to have possessed sufficient social density to sustain literary invention until far later, in the age of the second great European land grab.

The tenuous, tangential attachment of literature to empire calls into question the importance of a literary critical account of colonialism. The question has been answered in various, mutually compatible ways—by focusing on those literary texts, including several already mentioned, that seem to bear directly on European expansion; by adapting the tools of literary criticism to nonliterary works in order to elucidate the cultural contours of colonialism (Todorov); and by uncovering the imperial imbrication of ostensibly *un*imperial aesthetic artifacts (Greenblatt). For good scholarly and linguistic reasons, this research has proceeded along national or, in the unusual case of Peter Hulme's *Colonial Encounters*, regional lines.[15] Yet it seems to me that a comparative and international perspective of the sort frequently offered by historians has its value in these more restricted inquiries as well. My own procedure will be to move from the general to the specific.

II

The demographic destruction with which I began places the very notion of the Renaissance in a harsh and unflattering light. Leaving aside other historiographical problems with the term, we might ask whether it is bearable to retain the Renaissance as a totalizing and periodizing category, or even as an account of the crucial movement in the arts, high culture, and education. It is easy to just say no, to argue that the continuation of this venerable practice is intolerable, that the word is too positively loaded to be acceptable, that we must replace it with something at least neutral rather than self-congratulatory. From this perspective the historians' admittedly tendentious preferred phrase, "the early modern period," has the advantage of leaving open the question of whether the age witnessed a celebrated re-nativity from which Europeans have grown up into attractive adults or whether, to take the opposite extreme, the birth was a monstrous one that meant the beginning of the end for the rest of the world. Such a neutral response seems to me plausible, perhaps even correct.

But there is another way to think about things. One might argue that the idea of the Renaissance encompasses more than just a narrow elite movement whose expansion into a totalizing category has obscured the misery of the majority of Europeans of the time, not to mention the experience that is my primary concern here. It is easy for the term to function in this fraudulent fashion. But the Renaissance may also be viewed as genuinely hegemonic in the early modern period, as the cultural dominant in a society where culture may still have been dominant.[16] On this argument it shapes developments not just in the elite arts but throughout European civilization and beyond. The recovery of classical antiquity, without which the category of the Renaissance has no meaning, is connected in interrelated fashion with the rise of towns, of absolute private property, and of a new form of subjectivity eventually known as individualism; with the cultivation of Latin and especially Greek letters; and, most important for my purposes, with what Perry Anderson calls "the double moment of an equally unexampled expansion of space, and recovery of time. It is at this point, with the rediscovery of the Ancient World, and the discovery of the New World, that the European state-system acquired its full singularity. A ubiquitous global power was eventually to be the outcome of this singularity, and the end of it."[17]

Beyond the obvious uncertainties that grand historical narratives inspire, this model overestimates the narrowly Greco-Roman and hence proto-European character of even Europe's *self*-understanding of the antiquity it was recovering.[18] Nonetheless, one can hardly miss the consciously classicizing side of the discourse of empire. Ercilla and Camões model themselves on Vergil; More gets his style from Cicero, his structure from the Platonic dialogues, and his theme from *The Republic*; Rabelais looks not only to More but also to Stoicism and Epicureanism for the philosophy of his humanist giant and to Plato, though this time to *The Symposium*, for his form; Sepúlveda turns to Aristotle; Shakespeare observes the classical, ostensibly Aristotelian three unities in only one other play besides *The Tempest*; Grotius defends Dutch maritime marauding through classical allusion; Peter Martyr, like so many of his successors, finds antiquity in America, complete with Amazons, giants, cannibals, and a revival of the Golden Age—a Golden Age that the Inca Garcilaso de la Vega locates in preconquest Peru. Columbus, it is true, tends to see things through a medieval Christian lens, but it is Vespucci, who knows how to fake both a voyage of discovery and a classical education, to whom the discursive day, after all, belongs.

Vespucci's fraudulent first voyage not only helps him win the European-wide competition to name every last bit of the presumably nameless New World, however; it also helps inspire *Utopia*.[19] More's work in turn provides the blueprint for Vasco de Quiroga's social and political reorganization of the indigenous population of New Spain in the 1530s.[20] This strange interplay of lies, fiction, and fact is echoed in France shortly thereafter. The report of Cartier's second voyage leaves its mark on the fourth book of *Gargantua and Pantagruel*, in which the characters set off on a voyage in search of the northwest passage that sends up nonfictional travel and discovery narratives.[21] Rabelais's irreverence then seems to weigh heavily on André Thevet, who fearing the ridicule his reports of Canada will elicit, contrasts the truth of his eyewitness accounts with the falsehoods of writers who do not see for themselves, publishes a map of Newfoundland that includes an imaginary territory called Thevet Island, and never visits Canada.[22] One might look at the other side of a point made earlier and conclude that the field of humanistic letters has not yet undergone the process of fragmentation and specialization now taken for granted, that the generic boundary between fact and fiction, though recognized as such, has not yet acquired foundational status.[23] It is certainly reasonable to register the generative character of the specifically discursive, often classicizing dimension of the imperial project.

Unlike the early modern model, then, this explanatory schema insists on the centrality of the Renaissance. Yet in so doing it aims not to disguise but to define the discourse of empire and, more broadly, the imperial enterprise as a whole. It tells us that there *was* a Renaissance and that in America it meant in part what the demographic record reveals. Walter Benjamin's ubiquitously useful aphorism is particularly appropriate here: "There is no document of civilization which is not at the same time a document of barbarism."[24] Furthermore, an important task emerges for the literary or at least cultural critic concerned with imperialism in the age of the Renaissance. A student of the early modern period, as opposed to a student of the Renaissance, is unlikely to ask, much less answer, the questions raised by viewing the Renaissance as culturally hegemonic. And indeed Anderson, though himself a historian, draws his inspiration from the work of the art historian Erwin Panofsky.[25]

This line of inquiry helps clarify the way in which the discourse of empire in the Renaissance contributes to European culture's ongoing enterprise of defining and redefining its putative essence. It is customary— and to my mind often correct—to conceptualize this issue in terms of the relationship between self and other—between colonizer and colonized, Christian and heathen, rational mind and irrational body, differentiated individuals and homogeneous collective, civilization and barbarism, master and slave, superior race and inferior race, and so on. Yet any such formulation distorts matters in at least two ways. First, the discourse of empire cannot be reduced to the endless proliferation of self-congratulatory binary oppositions—a point to which I'll return at some length. And second, that proliferation had begun long before the conquest of America—which inflected and intensified rather than invented a certain outlook—and it continues to the present day. We may get at

this long historical process by asking, in various guises, a disarmingly
simple question: "What is European literature?" or "What is European
culture?" or "What is Europe?" or "What is Western civilization?" My
answer will be concerned less with the elucidation of essences that en-
grossed great Hegelian literary historians and theorists of this century
like Auerbach, Bakhtin, Curtius, and Lukács, whom I revere, than with
the breaking of boundaries that has preoccupied more recent, more
Nietzschean aestheticizing philosophers like Adorno and Derrida,
about whom I feel considerably more ambivalent. I can only note self-
consciously in passing the prominence of geographically marginal, often
Jewish thinkers on my list of the leading analysts of the European intellectual tradition.

At any rate, the obvious answer to the question "What is European
literature?" is "literature written in Europe" or perhaps "literature written by Europeans." Even if we ignore the problematic status of the category of literature—as I plan to do—both definitions, separately or together, immediately founder on their striking irrelevance to the Homeric
poems, the Jewish and Christian Bibles, and Augustine—to mention
only a few prominent instances. A move forward in time to the Middle
Ages yields the instructive examples of pagan poetry from Iceland (European), Islamic literature from Spain (not European), and Christian
writing from the Byzantine Empire (status uncertain, but unquestion-
ably less European than earlier pagan literature in Greek). Neither ge-
ography nor religion, neither nationality nor ethnicity, neither expressive genres nor thematic preoccupations, neither linguistic continuity
nor cultural heritage defines the pattern of inclusions and exclusions
constitutive of European literature. Any stable combination of these
manifestly powerful forces fails just as clearly as an overarching explanation. Yet a demystifying claim of this sort, however necessary it may
be to dispel "natural" defenses of the Western canon, fails to do justice
to the history of European literature. For I think a coherent, if cumber-
some, logic, at the level of self-definition, does shape its formation. This
logic emerges in the Middle Ages, the first period for which the notion
of Europe makes any sense. European literature, then, may be defined as
the literature of medieval Latin Christendom's self-constitution as such,
of its chosen predecessors, of its successors, of those successors' chosen

269

The Discourse of Empire in the Renaissance

◆

predecessors, of the cultures deeply influenced by those successors, of their chosen predecessors, and so on.

This formulation aims to grasp the process by which medieval western Europe admitted biblical Hebrew, biblical Greek, and with some ambivalence classical Latin to its ancestry, paid little more than lip service to classical Greek, largely ignored Byzantine Greek and medieval Hebrew, and rejected medieval Arabic, to which it was deeply indebted. Similarly, it helps make sense of the Renaissance recovery of Latin and especially Greek antiquity at precisely the time when Greece itself was under Islamic rule. It is relevant to the early-nineteenth-century rejection of the previously orthodox belief in the Egyptian origins of European civilization just when the decipherment of the hieroglyphs was beginning to make it possible to study the texts.[26] And it bears on the expansion of western European culture eastward as far as Russia and—following the international success of the nineteenth-century Russian novel—the incorporation into European literature for the first time of the entire body of Russian literature from the Middle Ages to the present. The definition has the added advantage of also accounting for the expansion, well beyond the geographical confines of Europe, of Western civilization or of what we might call, for the sake of consistency and in order to steal the name of a current anthology, the literature of the Western world.[27] But with this last move obvious problems arise. In the first edition of the anthology in question, from 1984, the literature of the Western world includes the work of Latin American and African-American writers. The second edition, published four years later, adds white South African literature to the fold. But why stop there? Why exclude the white literature of other settler colonies (like Australia and New Zealand); why exclude any literature written in European languages from the settler colonies, from Africa, India, Oceania, the Philippines, Vietnam, the Middle East; why exclude contemporary literature composed in the language of the Old Testament; and, finally, why exclude any literature in any language from any country that adapts Western forms and themes?

I ask these rhetorical questions not to advocate this extension or even, primarily, to indicate one of the ambiguous consequences of European global imperialism beginning in the Renaissance. My point is that the potential for this outcome is intrinsic to the original logic of the definition, with its far-flung but almost curiously selective choice of precursors and its contrastingly generous recognition of successors. As Europe and its leading settler colony pursue a relentlessly expansionist agenda, that potential is increasingly realized. Since this process has no internal limit, since only external forces can check it, the telos of the definition must be the equation of Western literature with world literature or, to put it another way, the appropriation of the latter by the former. One cannot really afford to choose between the extreme alternatives this process poses: to accept the logic as indicative of a certain reality (palatable or not), or to reject it as hopelessly self-contradictory and therefore to begin rethinking the categories of European and Western literature. Either way, however, the problem does not arise from the belated recognition that European literature is a constructed, rather than a natural category; that it produces its own predecessors as well as being produced by them; or that it operates by a series of somewhat arbitrary inclusions and exclusions. There is nothing wrong with any of this, at the very least because there are no other possible scenarios. There can be no natural cultures, only constructed and self-constructed ones. The problem begins when that act of self-construction is taken to be natural, organic, teleological, or essential; when that supposed essence is felt to be a badge of superiority, rather than merely comfort, satisfaction, meaning, or pride; and when that superiority is backed up by guns. Beginning in 1492 this was Europe's "privileged" relationship—first to the New World, then to the whole world.

But of course the self-constitution of European literature does not rely on external exclusions alone. The discourse of empire provides an unusually heightened example of the characteristic and cross-cultural elision of women. This is a form of writing that focuses on men at sea (Columbus, Rabelais, Camões) and men at war (Díaz del Castillo, Ercilla)—on men, that is, engaged in their own *Odysseys* and *Iliads*. On the rare occasions when they discuss the meaning of their experience, they do so in philosophical retirement with other men (More). Rabelais's company of male voyagers hopes to find a woman in every port; Díaz del Castillo reports that his fellow soldiers cared for little but gold and girls—two valuable commodities frequently juxtaposed as the conquest of Mexico nears completion. Ercilla is thus hardly alone when, in a simultaneous repudiation of Ariosto and return to Vergil, he begins *La Araucana* (The Araucaniad) by saying:

> No las damas, amor, no gentilezas
> de caballeros canto enamorados . . .
> mas el valor, los hechos, las proezas
> de aquellos españoles esforzados.

[Not of ladies, love, or graces / Do I sing, nor knights enamored . . . / But the valiant acts and prowess / Of those never-daunted Spaniards.][28]

Yet women have a curious tendency to intrude upon the proceedings. In Utopia women disturb the rationalist logic of the society by providing an irreducible locus of the bodily and of individualized affective bonds.[29] Utopia is a patriarchal state possessed of only a founding father, King Utopus, who as a single parent raises his national family in difficult circumstances. The figure of the mother returns, however, in the womblike shape of the island itself, which, after a rape of the earth, gives birth to her unique inhabitants.[30] This female framing function reappears in different form in *Gargantua and Pantagruel,* where the company of men undertake their voyage to visit the oracle of the Holy Bottle so as to find out whether or not Panurge should marry. Long before the barrage of casually belittling comments about women in the *Historia verdadera de la conquista de la Nueva España*, Díaz del Castillo offers high praise for the woman subsequently anathemized as la Malinche: Doña Marina— indigenous aristocrat, Christian convert, mistress of Cortés, wife of one of his company, and, most important, interpreter par excellence. When we recall the importance of the psychological and rhetorical savvy that Cortés repeatedly deploys to manipulate friend and foe alike among the native population, it is worth weighing the significance of the following conclusion: "He querido declarar esto porque sin ir doña Marina no podíamos entender la lengua de la Nueva España y México" [I have made a point of telling this story, because without Doña Marina we could not have understood the language of New Spain and Mexico].[31] And in Camões's *Lusiads* Portuguese mastery of the sea and the worldly honor won by Vasco da Gama and his crew are astonishingly allegorized by the Island of Love, an imaginary territory created by Venus with the aid of

Cupid, where the triumphant mariners cheerfully indulge their pent-up lust in a mad dash for carefree and, in the event, indescribably great intercourse with compliant neoclassical nymphs, who may stand in for presumably available indigenous females.[32] Thus, whether unacknowledged origin, indispensable assistant, or desired destination, woman drives the masculinist discourse of empire even in her absence. Moreover, the complexity of this relationship precludes any homologies between the female and the native.

III

This ambiguity, even dissonance, enables us to turn from the validating exclusionary logic of the discourse of empire back to a point made earlier in passing—that this discourse cannot be reduced to the self-congratulatory. Part of its interest in fact derives from the indications it gives of the imaginative and sympathetic capacities of Europeans. A map of the continent's international division of labor in the imperial enterprise will help locate the specificity of those capacities, especially in Spain. That division depends on each country's prior experience and on the new lands and people with which it comes in contact. Although any retrospective account of European expansion in this period can hardly avoid emphasizing the English and Spanish, things might have seemed different at first. Perhaps the three most impressive voyages—Columbus's first crossing of the Atlantic, da Gama's trip to India, and Magellan's circumnavigation—are led by an Italian and two Portuguese. Italians have an even more prominent position in the early publicizing of the discoveries: Columbus, Peter Martyr, and Vespucci write of the New World, Pigafetta of Magellan's journey. Italy's initiative arises from its aesthetic, maritime, and commercial domination of the western Mediterranean, a domination that, ironically, it helps to render irrelevant by its contribution to the opening of the Atlantic. Its fiscal involvement in America continues, however, through the relations between its financiers and the Spanish crown. Something similar occurs in Germany, where a banking interest is eventually superseded by the task of ideological consolidation epitomized by de Bry's *Great Voyages*.[33] On the Atlantic coast, of course, five countries—Portugal, Spain, France, Holland, and England—combine overseas trade with formal colonialism in varying proportions. Whereas the Spanish, fresh from the Reconquest, specialize from the start in territorial acquisition, the smaller powers concentrate on commerce. The writings of Grotius on war and on the freedom of the seas may be taken as exemplary of the latter interest. But it is two other small nations, Portugal and to a lesser extent England, that eventually dominate the slave trade.[34]

Partly because of this diversity, a critical discourse of empire comes in many forms. In France a demystifying tradition represented in very different ways by Rabelais and Montaigne provides scant rhetorical or philosophical support for an expansionist enterprise. In England utopian works such as More's original text, Bacon's *New Atlantis*, and, ambiguously, Shakespeare's *Tempest*, though more complicit with colonialism, respond to the dual forces of overseas discovery and domestic social upheaval by imagining radical alternatives to the prevailing European order. In Italy, where Campanella's *City of the Sun* ignores the Atlantic and Pacific for a more narrowly Mediterranean focus than even *The Tempest*'s, utopian radicalism partly involves the replacement of European models by Egyptian ones.[35] And in Portugal, Camões's *Lusiads* combines imperial jingoism about the past with an unstable mixture of self-contradiction, negativity, and disillusionment about the present.

Although neither the demystifying nor the utopian option seems to have been open to Spain, the distinctiveness of its response is worth pursuing. Lope de Vega's *Arauco domado* presents an orthodox defense of the Spanish conquest of Chile. The very confidence with which a hegemonic position is deployed, however, allows for the representation of words and actions that, to a modern eye at least, call that position into question. Because of the barrage of criticism leveled at the conquistadores and because of Lope's own hostility to a money economy in general and to New World money in particular, the ideology of empire cannot have the contradictorily capacious embrace of God and Mammon characteristic of, for example, Camões's position. Predictably, then, religion provides a rationale for the reconquest of the rebellious natives. The leader of the expedition, Don García de Mendoza, repudiates the pecuniary motives that have driven other Spanish military leaders in America. Committed to the spread of the faith, he engages in acts of religious humility and, following his battlefield triumph, persuades Caupolicán, the defeated Araucanian leader, to convert to Christianity just before undergoing a gruesome execution. Similarly, Don García's second reason for the war is, amazingly, the restoration of legitimate government to Chile. This government is the Habsburg monarchy, which conquered the land, lost power following a successful rebellion, and now wants its property back. Lope feels no need to justify the initial expropriation: he cheerfully grants the Araucanians the opportunity to argue that, since they were born free, they have the right to remain free. And this is not all they say. Their complaints about Spanish greed are apparently neutralized by the indication, noted above, that at least one Spaniard, Don García, is not interested in such frivolous ends. The characterization of the rebels produces the same double result. On the one hand, the play's evocation of their military prowess recalls the sophisticated imperial ideology often attributed to the *Aeneid*, in which you build up your foe in order to glorify your own victory while adopting a generous and tolerant stance toward the defeated. On the other, both the neoclassical pastoralism of Araucanian life and especially the representation of romantic relationships in their culture, but not among the Spaniards, threaten to shift human sympathy away from the virtuous invaders. The introduction of women here again disrupts imperial discourse. *Arauco domado* offers at once both the utopian vision and the barbaric reality of universal empire.

Lope's play ultimately derives from Ercilla's *La Araucana*, to which it owes its relatively uncondescending treatment of Spain's antagonists. Although, like Díaz del Castillo, Ercilla served in the military campaign he memorializes and witnessed the bravery of his foes, his self-conscious ambivalence goes well beyond anything found in the chronicler of the fall of Mexico. In the Prologue he writes,

> Y si alguno le pareciere que me muestro algo inclinado a la parte de los araucanos, tratando sus cosas y valentías más estendidamente de lo que para bárbaros se requiere, si queremos mirar su crianza, costumbres, modos de guerra y ejercicio della, veremos que mu-

chos no les han hecho ventaja, y que son pocos los que con tan gran
constancia y firmeza han defendido su tierra contra tan fieros ene-
migos como son los españoles. (1:121–22)
[And should it seem to some that I show myself somewhat inclined toward
the side of the Araucanians, treating of their affairs and prowesses more extensively than is required for barbarians, we might look at their upbring-
ing, their customs, their methods of warfare and the exercise thereof, and
we should see that many have not outstripped them, and that few are those
who with such constancy and firmness have defended their land against
such fierce enemies as are the Spaniards.] (p. 27)

And, unlike Lope, he comes out against the execution of Caupolicán at
the climax of his poem.

> Hecho la confesión como lo escribo,
> con más rigor y priesa que advertencia,
> luego a empalar y asaetearle vivo
> fue condenado en pública sentencia.
> . . . .
> que si yo a la sazón allí estuviera,
> la cruda esecución se suspendiera.
>   (2:352, 356)

[After the eloquent confession, / With more rigorous haste than
foresight / They condemned the chief in public / To be impaled and shot
with arrows. . . . / Had I been there at that season, / I had stayed the
execution.] (pp. 302, 304)[36]

For a modern reader, however, both the grandeur and the pathos of the
scene are damaged by Caupolicán's class-conscious and apparently rac-
ist outrage when he discovers that his executioner is to be an African
slave.

This passage, notwithstanding *The Araucaniad*, goes to considerable
lengths to present a victim's-eye-view of Castilian expansion—primarily through its female characters. The Spanish ladies are little more than
scenery; by contrast, the native women are obtrusively deployed to lament the deaths of their husbands or lovers at the hands of the Spanish,
and thereby to elicit pathos for the indigenous population. Ercilla then
offers ancient authority for his strategy by invoking Dido, "que Virgilio

Marón sin miramiento / falsó su historia y castidad preciada / por dar a sus ficciones ornamento" (2: 339: canto 33, stanza 54, ll. 3–5) [falsified by Vergil Maro. / Precious chastity he libeled / To enhance and stuff his fictions (p. 297)]. Yet Ercilla seems irritated with Vergil for ideological rather than literary reasons. From his sixteenth-century perspective, the account in the *Aeneid* might have looked like the just and destined defeat of irrational, dark-skinned Afro-Asiatics by European imperialists. In *The Araucaniad* Dido lives a century before Aeneas: the Phoenician founding of an African city takes chronological precedence over the Trojan founding of an eventually European one. Aeneas and Rome thus play no part in the drama of Dido, who kills herself to protect both her nascent state and her vows of fidelity to her murdered, Phoenician husband. Once again the virtuous suffering woman does double duty as the representative of a non-European, noble civilization subjugated by Western weaponry.[37]

Ercilla's dual allegiances may stand as a model for a number of Spanish texts, including ones that ostensibly have nothing to do with the discourse of empire. In Góngora's *Soledad primera* a shipwrecked youth wandering through a mountainous countryside is addressed by an old man who recalls a comparable figure in *The Lusiads*:

> ¿Cuál tigre, la más fiera
> que clima infamó hircano,
> dió el primer alimento
> al que—ya deste o aquel mar—primero
> surcó, labrador fiero,
> el campo undoso en mal nacido pino?

[What fiercest tiger or wild boar / disgracing even the Hyrcanian shore / was fosterparent to that farmer dark, / the first to furrow in an evil hour / the spumy country in ill-destined bark?][38]

This attack on seafaring—for that is what it is—continues for 135 lines and includes denunciations of greed and of "metales homicidas" ("homicidal metals," pp. 50–51)—gold and silver—as well as more or less hostile references to the invention of the compass, Columbus, the conquistadores, Magellan, the Isthmus of Panama, the Cape of Good Hope, the Pacific, the East and the East Indies in particular, and the Moluccas.

It ends by presenting psychological motivation—the loss of the speaker's goods and son at sea. The passage contrasts the fabulous and unnatural wealth of the Spanish overseas empire with the natural abundance to be found at home. Yet it is not hard to hear the crow of colonialist pride in the following account of the conquest of the Caribbean:

> A pesar luego de áspides volantes
> —sombra del sol y tósigo del viento—
> de caribes flechados, sus banderas
> siempre gloriosas, siempre tremolantes,
> rompieron los que armó de plumas ciento
> lestrigones el istmo, aladas fieras.

[The flying vipers from the Carib bow /—shading the sun and poison to the wind—/ have not the ever-waving banners harmed, / that glorious still, routed the fierce winged foe / the isthmus with a hundred feathers armed.]   (pp. 48–49)

Though these may be the banners of greed, they are "glorious still." More important, the moral concern never extends to the victims, as opposed to the agents, of the Spanish Empire. And finally, Góngora presents the critique of empire in a poetic discourse designed to evoke the richness of a nature that participates in the timeless Neoplatonic harmony of the cosmos. Against the poet's apparent intent, the object of opprobrium, not relegated to a lower stylistic register, dances to the music of the spheres.

Todorov has persuasively made a similar claim about Francisco de Vitoria—that an anti-imperialist subjectivity produces an imperialist objectivity of far greater plausibility and sophistication than any of the arguments previously presented by open apologists of empire.[39] And though to a limited extent the same holds true for Las Casas, one would not want to belittle someone who could write of the conquest of Mexico, in an entirely typical tirade,

> Mas han muerto los españoles dentro de los doze años dichos . . .
> a cuchillo y a lançadas y quemandolos bivos, mugeres y niños y moços y viejos: de quatro cuentos de animas: mientras que duraron

(como dicho es) lo que ellos llaman conquistas: siendo ynvasiones
violentas de crueles tiranos.

[The Spaniards have killed more Indians here in twelve years by the sword,
by fire, and enslavement than anywhere else in the Indies. They have killed
young and old, men, women, and children, some four million souls during
what they call the Conquests, which were the violent invasions of cruel
tyrants.][40]

The moral bitterness and irony here might bring to mind a more recent
critic of imperial policy: I am thinking of Noam Chomsky, and I mean
the comparison to redound to the credit of both writers.

But I want to conclude with two figures who internalize the imperial
experience in a rather different way. Gonzalo Guerrero, a Spaniard who
settles with an indigenous tribe in the Yucatan, is familiar from various
Spanish narratives and, for all practical purposes, from *Dances with
Wolves*. When asked by another Spaniard to return with him, Guerrero
replies:

> Yo soy casado y tengo tres hijos, y tiénenme por cacique y capitán
> cuando hay guerras; idos con Dios, que yo tengo labrada la cara y
> horadadas las orejas. ¡Qué dirán de mí desde que me vean esos es-
> pañoles ir de esta manera! Y ya veis estos mis hijitos cuán bonicos
> son. (1: 98)
> [I am married and have three children, and they look on me as a *Cacique*
> here, and a captain in time of war. Go, and God's blessing be with you. But
> my face is tattooed and my ears are pierced. What would the Spaniards say
> if they saw me like this? And look how handsome these children of mine
> are!] (p. 60)

Even more instructive is Cortés's response when he learns that Guerrero's change of allegiance has extended to orchestrating an attack on
Spanish invaders: "En verdad que le querría haber a las manos, porque
jamás será bueno" (1: 104) [I wish I could get my hands on him. For it
will never do to leave him here (p. 65)]. It is the threat of Guerrero's example, however unlikely to be repeated, that Cortés finds unbearable.

The second figure, Fernando de Alva Ixtlilxochitl, is a descendant of
the royal house of Texcoco in Mexico who writes a history of the conquest to demonstrate the importance of the indigenous allies, and of his

ancestor in particular, to Cortés's victory. The narrative is pervaded by sadness, not least because those allies cannot imagine that the answer to the rhetorical question "What can be worse than the Aztecs?" is "The Spanish." But Alva Ixtlilxochitl attributes his ancestor's behavior primarily to a commitment to the propagation of Christianity. We recognize here the regular role of religion: not only does it inspire the conquerors; it softens up the conquered. But there is a further twist. "The Spaniards treated the friars very badly because they defended the Indians, so much so that they did everything but throw the friars out of Mexico."[41] This partisanship only increases the authority of the clergy among the native population, an authority they employ to prevent rebellion. One has now entered the totally administered societies of some contemporary theory, in which criticism of the system is routinely recycled so as to strengthen that system. The more anti-imperialist the friars are, the greater their influence on the indigenous peoples, and (short of a call to arms) hence the greater their service to the Spanish Empire. Yet this cannot be the last word on Alva Ixtlilxochitl. The very existence of such writers—of native intellectuals who can record the history of their people from something approaching that people's point of view—expands the boundaries of the discourse of empire in quite extraordinary fashion.

It is this expansion I have sought to evoke, describe, and analyze. The conquest of America continued the Reconquest of Spain from the forces of Islam. Both Reconquest and conquest involved interaction as well as confrontation. In a sense the Spanish were unlucky: not only did they get here first; they also stumbled rather quickly upon one of the most densely populated and socially complex civilizations of the Americas. They accordingly became the leading colonialists and killers of their age—perhaps of any age. But in a sense the Spanish were also lucky: they developed the most distinguished discourse of empire, and not just in the apologetic sense. By the very (dialectical) logic of their past and their present, they generated the most powerful critiques of empire in the Renaissance. If this not quite counterhegemonic discourse falls short of a fully anti-imperialist ideology, it may be the closest approximation to one that was intellectually, psychologically, and politically possible at the time.[42] And if it does not counterbalance the violence of the forces

that made it both possible and necessary—and obviously it does not—
it alerts us to the ironies of history we inevitably confront whenever we
selectively seek to define our own predecessors by recovering a dissident
tradition as part of the ongoing process of cultural self-constitution.

Notes

1. Tzvetan Todorov, *The Conquest of America: The Question of the Other*,
trans. Richard Howard (New York: Harper Torchbooks, 1987), p. 5.

2. Sherburne F. Cook and Woodrow Borah, "The Historical Demography of
Interior Tribes of Colombia in the Studies of Juan Friede and German Colmena-
res," in *Essays in Population History: Mexico and the Caribbean*, 2 vols. (Berkeley: University of California Press, 1971 and 1974), 1:411–29, esp. 413, 420–
22, and 426.

3. Ibid., 1:300–375, esp. 310.

4. Ibid., 1:403.

5. Ibid., 1:1–179, esp. 1–2, 38–40, and 114.

6. Eric R. Wolf, *Europe and the People without History* (Berkeley: University
of California Press, 1982), p. 134.

7. Cook and Borah, *Essays in Population History*, 1:376–410, esp. 376,
401, 407–8.

8. Woodrow Borah and Sherburne F. Cook, *The Aboriginal Population of
Central Mexico on the Eve of the Spanish Conquest*, Ibero-Americana series, 45
(Berkeley: University of California Press, 1963), and *The Indian Population of
Central Mexico on the Eve of the Spanish Conquest*, Ibero-Americana series, 44
(Berkeley: University of California Press, 1960).

9. Philip D. Curtin, *The Atlantic Slave Trade: A Census* (Madison: University of Wisconsin Press, 1969), pp. 268 and 275–86. The quoted passage comes
from p. 275.

10. Stephen Greenblatt, *Renaissance Self-Fashioning: From More to Shakespeare* (Chicago: University of Chicago Press, 1980), esp. chs. 4–6.

11. Greenblatt does have a brief discussion of *The Tempest* in an essay from
the late 1970s, "Learning to Curse: Aspects of Linguistic Colonialism in the Sixteenth Century," recently collected in *Learning to Curse: Essays in Early Modern Culture* (New York: Routledge, 1990), pp. 16–39. For *The Tempest* see pp.
23–26.

12. Greenblatt, "Invisible Bullets" (1981), in *Shakespearean Negotiations:
The Circulation of Social Energy in Renaissance England* (Berkeley: University
of California Press, 1988), pp. 21–65.

13. Not surprisingly, I am indebted to Greenblatt for the second half of this formulation.

14. J. H. Elliott, *The Old World and the New, 1492–1650* (Cambridge: Cambridge University Press, 1970), p. 104.

15. Peter Hulme, *Colonial Encounters: Europe and the Native Caribbean, 1492–1797* (London: Methuen, 1986).

16. I have phrased this so as to suggest a parallelism with Fredric Jameson's recent controversial claim that postmodernism occupies a similar position in contemporary America and, increasingly, other parts of the world. See his *Postmodernism, or, The Cultural Logic of Late Capitalism* (Durham, N.C.: Duke University Press, 1991).

17. Perry Anderson, *Lineages of the Absolutist State* (London: NLB, 1974), pp. 420–28. The quoted passage appears on p. 422.

18. See Martin Bernal, *Black Athena: The Afroasiatic Roots of Classical Civilization*, vol. 1: *The Fabrication of Ancient Greece, 1785–1985* (New Brunswick, N.J.: Rutgers University Press, 1987), esp. pp. 151–69.

19. Richard Halpern, *The Poetics of Primitive Accumulation: English Renaissance Culture and the Genealogy of Capital* (Ithaca: Cornell University Press, 1991), pp. 165–67. Hythlodaeus, More's fictional reporter of Utopia, joins Vespucci on his last three voyages, one of which definitely occurred and the other two of which may well have occurred.

20. James Holstun, *A Rational Millennium: Puritan Utopias of Seventeenth-Century England and America* (New York: Oxford University Press, 1987), pp. 3–18.

21. Marius Barbeau, *Pantagruel in Canada* (Ottawa: National Museums of Canada, 1984).

22. *André Thevet's North America: A Sixteenth-Century View*, trans. Roger Schlesinger and Arthur P. Stabler (Kingston: McGill-Queen's University Press, 1986).

23. See Lennard J. Davis, *Factual Fictions: The Origins of the English Novel* (New York: Columbia University Press, 1983), esp. pp. 42–70, and Michael McKeon, *The Origins of the English Novel, 1600–1740* (Baltimore: Johns Hopkins University Press, 1987), pp. 25–128.

24. Walter Benjamin, "Theses on the Philosophy of History," in *Illuminations*, trans. Harry Zohn (New York: Schocken, 1969), p. 256.

25. Anderson, *Lineages of the Absolutist State*, pp. 148–49, n. 11, and Erwin Panofsky, *Renaissance and Renascences in Western Art* (New York: Harper and Row, 1969).

26. Bernal, *Black Athena*, 1: 250–57.

27. Brian Wilkie and James Hurt, eds., *The Literature of the Western World*, 2 vols. (New York: Macmillan, 1984, 1988).

28. Spanish text: Alonso de Ercilla, *La Araucana*, ed. Marcos A. Morínigo and Isaías Lerner, 2 vols. (Madrid: Editorial Castalia, 1979), canto 1, stanza 1, ll. 1–6; English text: Alonso de Ercilla y Zúñiga, *The Araucaniad*, trans. Charles Maxwell Lancaster and Paul Thomas Manchester (Nashville, Tenn.: Vanderbilt University Press, 1945), p. 33. Subsequent references to both versions are noted in the text.

29. Susan Bruce, "This World Uncertain Is: Selves, Sex, and Skepticisms in the Makings of Utopia" (Ph.D. diss., Cornell University, 1990), pp. 23–34 and 41–47.

30. Louis Marin, *Utopics: The Semiological Play of Textual Spaces*, trans. Robert A. Vollrath (Atlantic Highlands, N.J.: Humanities Press, 1984), pp. 103–9.

31. Spanish text: Bernal Díaz del Castillo, *Historia verdadera de la conquista de la Nueva España*, ed. Joaquín Ramírez Cabañas, 4th ed. (Mexico City: Editorial Porrúa, 1955), 1:124; English text: Bernal Díaz, *The Conquest of New Spain*, trans. J. M. Cohen (Harmondsworth, Middlesex: Penguin, 1963), p. 87. Subsequent references are noted in the text. For the strongest claims about the discursive dimension of Cortés's victory, see Todorov, *The Conquest of America*, pp. 98–123. For more on Doña Marina, see Cordelia Candelaria, "La Malinche, Feminist Prototype," *Frontiers* 5, no. 2 (1980): 67–72, and for a discussion of the recent revaluations of this figure, Norma Alarcón, "Traddutora, Traditora: A Paradigmatic Figure of Chicana Feminism," *Cultural Critique* 13 (1989): 57–87.

32. For the Island of Love as symbolizing Portuguese mastery of the sea, see William C. Atkinson, Introduction to *The Lusiads*, by Luis Vaz de Camões (Camoens), trans. Atkinson (London: Penguin, 1952), p. 25.

33. See Germán Arciniegas, *Germans in the Conquest of America: A Sixteenth Century Venture*, trans. Ángel Flores (New York: Macmillan, 1943), and Bernadette Bucher, *Icon and Conquest: A Structural Analysis of the Illustrations of de Bry's Great Voyages*, trans. Basia Miller Gulati (Chicago: University of Chicago Press, 1981).

34. Curtin, *The Atlantic Slave Trade*, p. 268 and passim.

35. Bernal, *Black Athena*, 1:176.

36. Consider the complicit narrator's similar comment, following the brutal beating of the titular figure in Aphra Behn's *Oroonoko or, The Royal Slave* (1688; New York: Norton, 1973), p. 68: "While we were away, they acted this Cruelty; for I suppose I had Authority and Interest enough there, had I sus-

pected any such thing, to have prevented it." She is again conveniently away when Oroonoko is cut into pieces and burnt at the stake (pp. 76–77). But pathos, and indeed specifically female pathos, is supplied by the presence of related but more ineffectual women: "My Mother and Sister were by him all the while, but not suffer'd to save him" (p. 77).

37. I owe much of the material in this paragraph to comments by David Quint, of the Comparative Literature Department, Yale University.

38. Luis de Góngora, *The Solitudes*, trans. Edward Meryon Wilson; rev. ed. Willis Barnstone (New York: Las Américas, 1965), *Soledad primera / The First Solitude*, pp. 46–47. Subsequent references are noted in the text.

39. Todorov, *The Conquest of America*, p. 149–50.

40. Bartolomé de Las Casas, *Brevísima relación de la destrucción de las Indias* (Barcelona: Fontamara, 1974), p. 58; English translation: Bartolomé de Las Casas, *The Devastation of the Indies: A Brief Account*, trans. Herma Briffault (New York: Seabury, 1974), p. 68.

41. Fernando de Alva Ixtlilxochitl, *Ally of Cortes*, trans. Douglass K. Ballentine (El Paso: Texas Western Press, 1969), p. 82.

42. Todorov, *The Conquest of America*, pp. 125–254, provides a sympathetic but incisive account of this writing. See also the essays in René Jara and Nicholas Spadaccini, eds., *1492–1992: Re/Discovering Colonial Writing* (Minneapolis: Prisma Institute, 1989).

13

The Role of Discontinuity in the Formation of National Culture

JOAN RAMÓN RESINA

*F*rom the viewpoint of traditional historiography, the Spanish Renaissance was primarily the accomplished integration of state and territory. Ferdinand II of Aragon and Isabella I of Castile completed the assemblage of the political and territorial fragments from the national body, thus reestablishing or giving second birth to a community legitimated by its alleged existence prior to the disruptive dissemination of power and cultural definitions. This scattering of national essence is understood to have been facilitated and sustained by the collapse of homogeneous space and the appearance of multiple, heterogeneous spaces on the map. The Reconquest (a term signifying the reproduction of an event, hence the resumption of a process where it had been interrupted) was conceived of as the erasure of difference by the rolling back of the solid-color sheet of identity. Thus Spanish culture could be likened to a palimpsest on which the new scripture effaced a previous one, which, now rendered invisible, remained nonetheless as a deactivated text at once assimilated and disowned by its supporting medium. Continuity with a legitimating source of identity as power (power supplied with meaning) was thus predicated on discontinuity, obliteration, and fracture.

This, obvious enough for those Hispanic cultures—Moorish, Jewish—whose interruption was not altogether closural in time but could (arguably) be conceived of as submitting to a *translatio* or relay in space, had different and far severer implications for those other cultures that, remaining in their "niche," found the integrating or homogenizing process decisively obstructive for *their* continuity. Deprived of the possibility of qualifying "space," they were simultaneously rendered incapable of qualifying time, that is, of entering into the historical process that from the Renaissance on turned European culture into the competing arena for the creation and definition of national cultures, all of which were predicated on continuity. The creation of "continuity" in time, which must be seen as its "extension" in space, was accomplished by means of discontinuities, by the abolition of discrete historical narratives under the progressive homogenization of space, a process that can also be described as its progressive organization or, in economic terminology, "rationalization." This entails the maximization of certain areas (core areas) and the redistribution of others as a periphery that will henceforth be redefined in terms of the core, as an appendage to it. The formation of the European nation states reveals the political aspect of this process, and needs no illustration; what is less generally acknowledged is that a cultural reorganization was the necessary correlation to the peripheralization by which the core was constituted. The invention of a tradition coextensive with the totality of previously heteronomic spaces was simultaneously the positing of a strong or "creative" center for this tradition and of its weaker, merely receptive margins, and this operation was indispensable insofar as culture was charged with endowing the new political structure with meaning.

A corollary to the preceding is that, while core and periphery share the same cultural space (albeit in an opposition of relative strength in which they are mutually defining and reinforcing), this relation requires the abrogation of the heterogeneous space which previously sustained a different and possibly rival core. With this premise I think it may be fruitful to turn to a problem of literary historiography that has hitherto found only descriptive treatments, however poignant and even correct some of these observations may have been. This comment is in no way a disparaging one, and I hasten to add that in matters of historiographic erudition I depend fully on the authority of those scholars whose work I will try to complement by raising their empirical knowledge to general considerations of a theoretical nature. The problem in question is that of the so-called decadence of Catalan literature in the sixteenth century.

Decadence does not seem the right word; *disappearance* would be more accurate, considering the suddenness with which this literature ceased to grow out of itself after a century that can be characterized only as brilliant: Ausias March, Francesc Eiximenis, Joan Roís de Corella, *Tirant lo blanc.* Certainly, a number of poets and prose writers continued to write in Catalan, but the very few worth mentioning do not support Arthur Terry's assertion that "the decline of literature is one of standards, not of quantity."[1] It is in fact both, and, even where writing proceeds, its literary status is often questionable.[2] In continuing to call this phenomenon "decadence" it is important to note that I do so for the sake of the terminological consensus, insofar as the word has been accepted as a period marker encompassing the historical segment from the beginning of the sixteenth to the middle of the nineteenth century. This term is, however, not without problems, not the least of which is the implication of a protracted, and therefore continued, existence spanning empty time before its reanimation in the promised land of national reconstitution in recent (modern) times. A sort of desert-crossing during which the Ark of the Covenant of founding traditions would have maintained the cultural identity of the nation is not to be thought of.[3] As I will be arguing, the decadence of Catalan literature in the early sixteenth century precluded the formation of a Catalan national culture (and hence of a Catalan national identity) at the time when other European cultures were developing into national cultures. Once again, the principle at work in the Catalan case is discontinuity.

If we think of this phenomenon in terms of a "gap" (and not just a suspension) between a medieval formation and the modern, romantic constitution of a national culture, we will not only avoid the conceptual trap of predicating an absurd continuity between discrete phenomena (however effectively such continuities serve the legitimating purposes of political societies), but we will, I think, throw some light on the principle of discontinuity at work in all cultural traditions, including those that have not been afflicted by a cessation as abrupt and historically decisive as that of Catalan literature in the sixteenth century. I have in mind culture's servitude to time, its need to advance to new positions by sacrificing earlier ones, its diachronic dimension rather than its allegedly synthetic power to remain true to itself, permeated by an essence in all its manifestations. The extent to which a literature can be said to present continuity is no more than that by which its objects (texts) reiterate previous ones, rephrase them, so to speak, and in doing so obliterate them. In this sense *Don Quijote* repeats the *Amadís*, and this repetition ensures that the latter will no longer be read. This repetition, which does away with the traditional notion of influence (an image of continuity), is not closer to the concept of intertextuality, at least not as this is commonly understood, namely, as retention of a text by another. Instead, repetition is a distancing undertaking; it reinstates but only in order to expel. A trace is a mark of absence. Where the trace is, the object is not. Thus a literature reasserts itself (it does not "evolve") by creating a void. "Void" is merely another name for "tradition." A literature's canon thus signals the positions or loci where the literature no longer is. And vice versa, its future positions, the places to which it will advance in its current "evolution," are by no means determined by its present deployment. As a concept the void is undetermined and affords no determination. At each moment the next move is open to a plurality of possibilities, including cessation, the creation of a void that remains fascinated with itself.

This sketches the situation of Catalan literature in the sixteenth century, inasmuch as the move from its strong positions in the previous century does not lead to other comparable positions, not even in terms of the redefinition of cultural spaces described above. The homogenization of political space leading to the invention of a Spanish national culture by the peripheralization of previously heterogeneous cultures does not entail a transposition in literary production, whereby Catalan literature might have been expected to use its voiding power in the capture of new positions in the transformed, homogenized space of the new (Spanish) national culture. This process is visible in Valencia, where literary practice in the Catalan language is abandoned in favor of the Spanish language with results amounting to a respectable movement: Joan Timoneda, Gil Polo, Guillem de Castro, and others who at times felt compelled to justify their substitution of the new national language for the previous one by referring to the homogenizing aspect of their choice (in effect an appeal to pragmatics and to the force of the political fait accompli). When Gaspar Escolano published his *Decada primera de la historia de la insigne y Coronada Ciudad y Reyno de Valencia* in 1610, he supported his choice with an argument which, although common-place enough today, in that early date still reveals the very tensions undermining its conceptual structure: "Si en el phrasis Castellano me conocieres estrangero, pasa por ello, que mi pretensión no ha sido ser imitado sino solamente entendido de muchos, en lengua vniversal, que lo es la Castellana"[4] [If some of the phrasing in Castilian betrays me as a foreigner, overlook it, for I intended, not to be imitated, but only to be understood by many, in a universal language, and Castilian is such a language]. The "lengua universal" is not such, inasmuch as it defines the quality of "estrangero" or, more precisely, of peripheral dependence. Cultures subsumed in this false universality (false because it is an empirical one) find themselves incapable of introducing their "semantics" into the political and cultural area of the state-core except through a communicative apparatus which modifies as it translates, while asserting, like all translating processes, the difference, the discontinuity, of that which is trans-lated (transferred or removed) in the very act of rendering its sameness.

If Valencian authors accepted the rules of the new "universalizing" dispensation, an altogether different situation developed in Catalonia, the core area of the Aragonese kingdom. While Catalan continued to be routinely employed by the administration, it ceased to exist as a literary language; but unlike what happened in Valencia, there arose no substitute literature in Spanish to replace what had been lost.[5] Jordi Rubió described this phenomenon as a passive resistance, as a refusal to "play the game": "Catalunya ni s'adapta a la nova influència, ni té prou força o prou voluntad per a continuar la seva tradició, modernitzant-la. Veu mutilat el seu antic domini lingüístic i diríeu que abandona el joc"[6] [Catalonia does not adapt to the new influence, nor does it have enough strength or will to continue its own tradition by modernizing it. It sees its previous linguistic dominance mutilated, and one would say that it abandons the game]. Martí de Riquer agrees with Rubió: "Existeix, segurament, entre els catalans una certa desconfiança en l'ús de la llengua pròpia, però per l'altra banda també ha d'existir temor o repugnància en l'ús del castellà, car, altrament, hauríem de concloure que des del segle XVI al XVIII els catalans han estat negats per a la literatura de certa categoria"[7] [It is surely true that there is a certain uneasiness, among Catalans, in the use of their own language, but there must also be fear or repugnance in the use of Castilian, for on the other hand one ought to conclude that from the sixteenth through the eighteenth centuries, Catalans have been denied producing literature of a certain prestige]. This unwillingness to merge into the new worldview of the nation state, to "play the game" according to rules set elsewhere, denotes a difference and a deferral: a different worldview, another blueprint for the creation of the void, and an indefinite deferral of the motion required by the new, unfulfilled positions.

Such an explanation, which could be charged with being somewhat fanciful, appears less so when one considers the lack of correlation between the withdrawal of literary production and the other parameters usually assumed to gauge a culture's strength: Catalonia's economy recovered from the severe losses incurred during the war against John II (1458–1479). Likewise, its population grew during the sixteenth century. Its bourgeoisie was wealthy, and employment opportunities attracted foreign artisans and artists, as well as workers, many of whom immigrated from France.[8] Indeed, to some extent Catalonia's economy proved more resilient than Castile's to the general downturn in the course of the seventeenth century, a circumstance that acquires its full meaning only when we keep in mind the restraint enforced on the Catalan economy by the prohibition of direct commerce with the American colonies. Le Roy Ladurie has pointed out that the regression experienced by northern Italy and Castile was limited in southern France and Catalonia to a slowing down and absence of marked growth, not yet reaching the turnaround of its neighboring areas.[9]

Why did Catalonia, in the midst of economic stability and relative well-being, refuse to re-create its literary culture and to ensure the linguistic modernization required for a strong position in the emerging world of nation states? Evidence of a readiness to effect such a renewal is strong. Within the Iberian peninsula Catalonia displayed a precocious attention to the classics. Rubió observes that during the monarchy of Alfonso the Magnanimous (1416–1458) the Catalan language had long since begun to adapt itself to the new literary orientation.[10] The first attempt to adapt the Petrarchan style to a Hispanic language was Bernat

Metge's translation of Petrarch's *Griselidis* in 1388. Humanism was likewise an early flower in Catalonia, growing in the royal chancellery out of Latin epistolography in the learned environment fostered by John I, the first of the peninsular classicist kings, as Rubió i Lluch described him.[11] However, when the time for consolidation came, a time that was to prove decisive for the formation of modern literatures, Catalan suffered a retraction on all fronts. It was not just an absence of the linguistic dialectics between Latin and the *vulgare eloquentia* that elsewhere permitted humanist debate to dignify vernacular languages by promoting them to the status of literary languages. It was also the disappearance of Catalan production in the area least dispensable: entertainment literature, the genre with the widest audience, was as badly served as any other, in spite of demand and the possibilities for reaching a public larger than ever before, through the active printing industry which had been established in Barcelona and Valencia at an early date.

Arguably, a flagging concern with the "literature of pleasure" can be already sensed in the fifteenth century. Catalan song compilations (*cançoners*) from the time of Ferdinand II included songs in Spanish by Castilian poets. This trend, originating in the bilingual nature of the court of a Castilian dynasty since its establishment in 1412 with Ferdinand I, was accentuated by the definitive preeminence given to Castilian culture from 1474 on through the unification of the Aragonese and Castilian crowns under a double Castilian dynasty with Ferdinand II and Isabella I, and through the definitive removal of the court from Catalan-speaking territory. Martí de Riquer has noted that the popular classes, while not renouncing their language, tended to accept Castilian songs, which they sang in a more or less distorted Spanish.[12] Music certainly played an important role in furthering this acceptance, just as in the second half of the twentieth century English and American songs have been mimicked all over the world by people who often had no formal knowledge of the English language. But if music was an agent, it was not the reason for the acceptance of foreign creations. French songs, which were also popularized in Catalonia from early on, were sung in Catalan.[13] The prestige of the court has to be admitted as a strong seduction, coupled with the growing scarcity and dwindling inventiveness of the Catalan poets. The situation of writers and public must have been mutually reinforcing. To the abandonment of the field by the authors, the public responded by accepting imported products (in entertainment, more than in other social areas, the *horror vacui* is determining for the direction of cultures), which in turn undermined the writers' confidence in the efficacy of their language. In Valencia this situation was more acute, given the early bilingualism and the quick progress of Castilian expression. Joan Fuster has characterized the literary climate there in a way that allows no doubt as to the early and irreversible Castilianization of Valencian culture, which after *Tirant lo blanc* (1490) produced no other work in Catalan that could be considered "entertainment." "Llegir per distraure's," says Fuster, "un valencià, ho havia de fer en castellà, i en castellà ho feia"[14] [A Valencian had to do his pleasure reading in Castilian, and in Castilian he read].

This development is strongly reminiscent of what in our own day has been called cultural imperialism, a less than satisfactory term, but one that refers to the displacement of local cultures and the subduing of diversity by the products of an allegedly homogenizing and hegemonic foreign culture. Perhaps the most telling expression is the one employed by John Tomlinson in a widely different context, when he speaks of "transported ordinariness."[15] The political Castilianization of the Catalan lands under the Trastámara dynasty would not have had a lasting social impact without the changed practices of the popular classes assimilated to a culture that triumphed by default. And these practices did not take place in the political sphere, where the explanatory accent is usually placed, but in the more diffuse and pervasive one of daily life—a life that, in the sixteenth century, was essentially religious in its self-representation and therefore in its dependence on the identity provided by the imagined community. And this community, an ideologically universalizing one, that of Christian humanity, came to be progressively mediated by another such universal, albeit a more restrictive one, that of the Castilian language on its way to becoming the Spanish language. By far the majority of books printed and read in Barcelona and Valencia in the sixteenth and seventeenth centuries were devotional, a fact attesting to the primacy of religion in constituting the consciousness in this period. And the vast majority of these books were in Spanish. Josep-Sebastià Pons pointed out that Spanish in these centuries was for Catalans the language of theology, mysticism, and asceticism,[16] and Fuster added, with particular relevance to everyday life in Valencia, that it was also the language of sermons, novenas, and the entire vestry.[17] It is here, on the self-understanding provided by the formation of the subject as a member of a community, that questions of identity (and of colonized identity) hinge.

Whereas in the Middle Ages religion can be thought of as the dominant form of cultural identification—which may be a reason for the loose character of the state in general and the weak articulation of the Catalan-Aragonese state in particular—the strenuous emphasis on religious identity marked by outward conformity in the sixteenth and seventeenth centuries points to the very opposite, to the dissolution of religious bonds and their substitution as the primary form of identification in early modernity—yet one more gap, and one that will be filled with an alternative form of conformity. Language, in this respect, though apparently a mere vehicle for the substance of the bond (religio), becomes itself the bond. An aid and, as it were, a channel for the law, language turns out to be Law. Particular legislation, including that based on a metaphysics of eternity, devolved into provisionality, while domination by language proved to be permanent. The coercive nature of language and the violence inherent in its expansion was self-evident to Antonio Nebrija, who in the year of the discovery of America looked forward to the universalization of Spanish, remarking that "siempre la lengua fue compañera del imperio," and adding that after military subjugation "muchos pueblos bárbaros e naciones de peregrinas lenguas . . . tenían necesidad de recibir las leies quel vencedor pone al vencido e con ellas nuestra lengua"[18] [language was always the companion to the empire . . . many barbarous peoples and nations with odd languages needed to receive the laws that the victor imposes on the vanquished, and with those laws they needed our language].

Two things can be observed in this short and telling assertion. First, that the opposition between linguistic diversity and linguistic unity is formulated in spatial terms. By having recourse to the concept of foreignness (peregrinas lenguas), Nebrija expresses a distance, whose corresponding term of proximity is the possessive "nuestra." Possession and proximity are identified, thus pointing to the constitution of peripheral space (or space brought into the center's compass) out of previously heterogeneous remoteness. In such a conception we see the political expression of a metaphor dear to Renaissance rhetoricians, one that it is tempting to relate to the reconstitution of the world based on the voyages of circumnavigation. This metaphor is that of the circle and the center it supposes, and we may assume with Renato Barilli that its appeal had to do with its supporting an atemporal model. The metaphor, we may add, proved useful not just for the defense of poetry as a superior art, which is the context where the rhetorical use of the image seems to have emerged, but for the spatialization and metaphysical legitimation of the concept of empire, which, to borrow Barilli's words about the circle metaphor, isolates "a *locus* or a moment that can comprehend and merge with itself all possible human concerns: practical, theoretical, emotional, and doctrinal" (emphasis added).[19]

The second observation is the conflation of a grammatical opposition, that of singular and plural, in the identification of "vencedor" with the collective subject implied by "nuestra lengua." Here again the spatial metaphor of circle and center supports Nebrija's rhetoric. "Vencedor" can only refer to the monarch, who as the single power authorized to wage war is, however, no longer distinguishable from the totality of subjects identified with the nation. This trait of the modern nation state was already quite apparent in late-fifteenth-century Spain, as can be surmised from Ferdinand's lapse from political power in Castile after Isabella's death. Because he was perceived as an Aragonese monarch, his Castilian extraction notwithstanding, he was deemed incapable of the complete integration with his Castilian subjects that the nation state demanded. Integration was now dependent on birth, even when, as with Charles V, a foreigner, Castilian nationality was bestowed on the king by the maternal body. Only under Charles V was Spain's political unity truly realized. His was the first integrated Spanish monarchy, and it is certainly not irrelevant for understanding subsequent Spanish history that the state thus created was from its very inception more than a nation state: Spain came into being as an empire.

From the beginning, however, one of the emperor's difficulties was the entrenched suspicion of his policy as insensitive to Castilian interests, and the demand that the emperor be in fact a Spanish king. The war of the Castilian communities against the emperor was undertaken as a patriotic struggle, as an attempt at a national uprising. It is relevant to point out, in view of what will be discussed later, that such an uprising had never occurred in Catalonia.[20] When in 1412 the Count of Urgell, a candidate for the succession to the crown of Aragon, took arms against the Castilian forces that entered Catalonia with the first Trastámara king, no national sentiment moved Catalans to join the count in what was perceived as a dynastic struggle. Charles V, on the other hand, had to contend with Castilian demands for a national monarchy, and with a growing intolerance for the medieval concept of the state. In the Middle Ages the state had been based on the power of the king and on his reputation as an able protector of his vassals, that is, as a source of power rather than a recipient of power from the nation. The interrelation of king and nation later came to be represented by the growing intermediary role of an administrative body. The Renaissance state bureaucracy emerged as an ally of the king against the nobility, but it was an ally that set limits on the king's designs.[21]

The growing nationalization of the state provides an objection to Riquer's opposition between the Castilianization of Catalan culture under the Trastámara dynasty and the non-Germanization of Spanish culture under the Habsburgs.[22] In fact, Riquer's own explanation for the decline of Catalan literature, namely the bilingualism of the Catalan-Aragonese state, which would, according to him, have facilitated the Catalan adaptation to the communicative demands of a nonbilingual Spanish state, is hardly satisfactory as an explanation, however faithful it is as a description of events. The question of why the Catalan-speaking people, the majority in the Catalan-Aragonese state, should have renounced their language without significant resistance is not disposed of by reference to Castilian monolingualism. More significant would seem to be the status of language in the Catalan-Aragonese state. And in this regard, an answer is not lacking. Mention has already been made of the absence among Catalan humanists of any preoccupation with the defense of the vernacular as a vehicle for culture. For them Latin continued to be the superior language. The speedy dismissal of the Aragonese language and its complete and irreversible absorption into Castilian shows that in the non-Catalan-speaking part of the kingdom language was even less tied to political identity. Where the question of political identity begins to hinge on linguistic difference, as in Valencia from the sixteenth century on, it is to be remarked that the deliberate distancing from the common language (Catalan) in the name of an allegedly modernized speech (Valencian) is inseparable from an unhesitant relinquishing of the autochthonous language in favor of the language of the new nation state.[23]

The point to retain is that the Catalan-Aragonese state had no use for the rhetorical image of the circle, of a totality presupposing a center. The court was itinerent; the monarch ruled over a coalition of political entities largely independent of each other; the state was not a national state. It did not envision itself as a circle, but as a series of openended linkages modeled on the feudal structure, which allowed for the incorporation of political units without their assimilation into a homogenized space and a national essence. Linguistic pluralism was a concomitant to this political structure, including not only Catalan and Aragonese (and eventually Castilian) but also Provençal and, after the conquest of Naples, Italian.

Even allowing for the indifference that may be reasonably attributed to their exclusion from the American enterprise, for a traditionally seafaring people like the Catalans, the utter lack of interest in the voyages of circumnavigation and in the American conquest seems inexplicable except by positing an incompatibility of political and social models between hegemonic Castile and a progressively reluctant and withdrawn Catalonia. The fact has been remarked, and the question asked: "Poques coses podien haver colpit, en l'esfera religiosa, política i humana, la revitalizació de la voluntat que portava el Renaixement, com la descoberta d'Amèrica. ¿Com és que ni a les botigues dels llibreters, ni a les biblioteques de la nostra burgesia no veiem llibres que hi facin referència?"[24] [Few things could have impacted the religious, political, and human domain and the renewal of will that the Renaissance brought as did the discovery of America. How is it that neither in the book stalls nor in the libraries of our middle class do we see books that make reference to it?].

The beginning of an answer may lie in the retention by Catalans of a pre-Renaissance worldview, the political and cultural model on which

Catalonia had risen to the level of a political power and to hegemony in the Mediterranean. A simulacrum of continuity is essayed in the midst of the abruptest discontinuity. Rubió observes a lack of suppleness in the activities that the new direction of history demanded. With characteristic perspicacity, he notes that the persistence of the gothic style among artists and even in typography seems a gesture of rebellious resistance to adaptation.[25] In literature the significant novelty of *Tirant lo blanc* had no sequel, and narrative lived on material recycled from medieval texts. Two of the most frequently reprinted works, *Història de Partinobles* (1588) and *Història de Pierres de Provença* (1616), both of which were reissued until the eighteenth century, preserve the medieval spirit of the works from which they derive.[26] This spirit is also in evidence at the universities, which remained insensitive to the developments that were transforming the curricula of prestigious Castilian universities like Salamanca and Alcalá.[27]

The disappearance of heterogeneous space, associated with Barcelona's passing as a political center of gravity, dictated an attempted compensation through the prolongation of time, a vain resistance to a historical development that was not to be slowed down or deflected. But such a suspension over the void could not command creativity. It was not by empowering the old forms with a surplus of time that new developments could have arisen in Catalan literature to match the creative impulse of Castilian letters in this century. This realization must have been at the heart of the literary withdrawal that characterizes the period. A reiteration of the old as a refusal "to play the game" imposed by the new world-system would not lead to formal development, while participation in the new, homogenized cultural scene could only afford an epigonal role in the creative process led by those who set the rules and defined the needs. This secondary role, accepted by Valencian authors, was refused by Catalans, and confirmed by the few who, like Boscà, did not know how to refuse.

Franco Moretti, on whose spatial model for European literature I depend for my conception of qualitative space, has noted that in literature "a form needs time in order to reproduce itself: but in order to be born it is space that it needs most. The space of neighbouring, but different, and rival national cultures: where the exploration of formal possibilities

may be allowed, and in fact encouraged as a sort of patriotic duty."[28]
The disappearance of this kind of space precluded the effective voiding
of Catalan literature, which remained attached to its previous positions,
fascinated by the void it could not overcome in order to reposition itself
beyond it. This literature could not give birth to new forms, because it
no longer possessed a space to shape its authors' imagination. The lack
of a real, geographical space gave epigonal Catalan literature the utopian quality it has displayed ever since. Half a century after the Pact of
Caspe (1412), in the reigns of John II and Ferdinand II, Catalan humanists were already fleeing to the never-never land of classical culture,
whose spiritual capital, Rome, promised the only sort of universality
that immediate political interests could not belie.[29] A multiplicity of
spaces, inseparable from the multiplicity of languages that Bakhtin saw
as the condition for the formation of the novel, made up the structure of
the old Catalan-Aragonese federation. In these conditions Catalan literature thrived in its three politically autonomous areas: in Catalonia,
and in the kingdoms of Majorca and Valencia. Gaps in space allowed for
cultural continuity of a dialogical sort, one that recognized and worked
with the variations to arise on the other side of the political divide. Thus,
as late as 1521, when as a commercial operation the choice of Spanish
would have been far more astute, the Majorcan Joan Bonllavi adapted
Llull's *Blanquerna* to the Valencian idiom in an effort to obtain a readership among those whose language had supposedly become too distant
from Llull's medieval Catalan.

The development of Spanish literature also benefited from cultural
dialogue. Contrary to the opinion prevailing among Spanish scholars,
Spanish culture was abetted, not hindered, by significant cultural gaps
and linguistic plurality. In this respect, Américo Castro's emphasis on
the role of converted Jews in Spanish literature of the Golden Age is well
founded, irrespective of the often thin evidence on which he based his
identifications of Jewish ascendancy for particular authors. The *Quijote* was possible at a time when there was still memory of cultural and
linguistic coexistence, although that memory was fading fast. The lack
of continuation of the novel in Spain, another gap for which no convincing explanation has been proffered, can be understood in the context of the homogenization (political, ideological, ethnic, and linguis-

tic), in short, of the breaking down of difference within Spanish society. True, monoglossia, as Bahktin noticed, is never absolute; in a language there are always traces of its past and what Bahktin called "a potential for other-languagedness," but such traces were frantically covered by a society afraid of its own past, and the potential for other-languagedness was dissipated by strict adherence to the ideal of a unified culture.

On the eve of Spanish literature's own decadence, the last explosion of form in Góngora's poetry bore an abstract linguistic character, just as much as his genial detractor's. Even Quevedo's derision of the humanist exaggerations in Góngora's syntax and lexical constructs, achieved by projection of this form against the backdrop of the national language, strives for a normative, authoritative language, although with full consciousness of semantic mobility, of the quicksilver instability of words, a condition making it the more necessary to catch the trickster *concepto* at its protean carnival of pluralistic games. As Bahktin put it, parody's linguistic confrontation is "an intra-linguistic one, one that nourishes itself on the stratification of the literary language into generic languages and languages of various specific intentions."[30] *Conceptista* parody lay open the strata of the literary language of its day, exposing a variety of intentions to the ridiculing light of an implicit normative language. This was the key to its effectiveness. On the other hand it remained intralinguistic, oblivious of the multiplicity of social (not merely literary) discourses and even languages that the novel had to heed. The novel's very structure as a voyage set the conditions for interaction at various levels of social and ethnic discourse, and—a fact that has not been given sufficient weight—the *direction* of travel was of paramount importance, inasmuch as Don Quijote's route was outward bound, like that of the Spanish imperial armies, certainly, but unlike theirs, an exploration that posited no center (Don Quijote's village is not even located) and thus no centralization of language. In contrast, the direction of the hero in the early English novel is centripetal; *Robinson Crusoe* entails no contradiction, nor does *Moll Flanders*.

Full linguistic centralization, the crystalization of linguistic and ideological unity, was achieved not in the novel (which was blighted by this development and simply disappeared) but in drama, tellingly called "teatro nacional" in Spanish literary historiography. If, as Moretti assumes, the national variants of baroque tragedy came into existence as a result of competitive pressures between rival nations, then it must be added that the energies required for the selection and fruition of a single national variant were accumulated at the cost of suppressing or—if suppression seems too strong a term—neglecting other avenues of formal experimentation *within* the space of these nations. I have in mind the incipient Valencian bourgeois theater that at the end of the fifteenth and beginning of the sixteenth century was a sign of dialogical vitality inside Spain. In the *Cortesano* Lluís del Milà makes a character say: "Senyora Dona Violante, amagau lo valencià, que castellans van per la terra que per burlar la nostra llengua nos furten les paraules y porten-les a Castellà per a fer farses amb elles, que només són de València, parlant amb reverència"[31] [Lady Doña Violante, hide the Valencian language because Castilians go through the land, mocking our language, stealing the words, taking them to Castile to make farces. Only native Valencians can speak with reverence for the language]. This statement testifies to a competitive dynamism that *used* the coexistence of languages and their different temporal signification in the formation of Castilian drama prior to the attainment of its definitive form as "national theater." Whatever was left in the early sixteenth century of a cultural border between Valencia and Castile could be transformed into a temporal value, insofar as the dialogue between languages was also one between hitherto independent social developments.[32] The sterility following the attainment of a full-fledged national drama was the price to be paid for its success in shaping the generic channel for—to borrow Bakhtin's expression—all "forces of verbal-ideological life."

Whereas the decadence of Catalan literature in the sixteenth century was related to a loss of space, the decadence of Spanish literature less than two centuries later resulted, paradoxically, from acquiring too much space—all of it, in fact, within the bounds of the peninsular territory. Recourse to the "gap" category allows us to perceive the importance of fractures, whether geographical, political, linguistic, or social, for the creation and modification of forms. The growth and stabilization of Castilian hegemony can be shown to have depended on the deepening of preexisting rifts and the creation of new fractures, which traced the lines of force of the new situation. One need only recall the origin of the

Castilian political unit as a split satellite from the Leonese kingdom, which it was later to assimilate into its own space. But in the period that concerns us, the role of fracturing and divergence in the development of new organisms can be advantageously shown within the territorial borders of the Catalan-speaking lands as inseparable from the extension and consolidation of Castilian hegemony as the Spanish national state. For it is in this period that we find the origin of the deliberate linguistic fragmentation that is a concomitant of the political dissolution of the Catalan-Aragonese federation. The philologically absurd notion of a distinct Valencian language, nourished today by the same political outlook and with the same purpose as in the sixteenth century (though with the decisive difference that four and a half centuries later the project is no longer creative), appeared precisely at the time when the autochthonous language was abandoned in favor of Spanish.[33] In view of the generative role that I assign to gaps in the formation of new paradigms, it may be asked why the ideological rift posing as linguistic otherness between the Catalan-speaking lands did not serve as a stimulus for new differentiations and creative interaction as in the past. The answer is, of course, that these gaps were not produced by the inner dynamics of Catalan culture, as the ideological explanation would have it.[34] They were not an event that would later prove conducive to Valencia's comparatively superior adaptation to the unitary culture, but were an aspect, one might even say a strategy, of the establishment of homogeneity by means of the void effected on the autochthonous culture.

One final word in conclusion. In the fifteenth and sixteenth centuries European nation states came into existence through the integration of neighboring territories into an ideological space that rendered them politically and culturally homogeneous. This is, in essence, accepted knowledge, what one may call the official story. That this process entailed a centralization that was tantamount to the canonization of certain cultural strains and the peripheralization of others is, perhaps, part of the officious story. What seems to have escaped either sort of historians is the gap formation, the disunification and breaking of identities accompanying the gravitational movement into the orbit of the new centers of influence. This suggests some reflections on the process of European unification, a process that cannot be achieved and therefore—

if I may be allowed momentarily to fall into a sermonizing mood—
should not be willed apart from the rifts and inevitable breakdown of
the tension-filled unities corresponding to the present political spaces. A
consolation for nostalgia may be found in the thought that, the myth of
remote continuity notwithstanding, the modern nation state is as fleeting a structure as any other product of the social life of human beings.

Notes

1. Arthur Terry, *Catalan Literature* (London: Ernest Benn, 1972), p. 61.
2. "El que baixa vertiginosament és la intenció literària i, quan aquesta
existeix, el to." Martí de Riquer, in Martí de Riquer, Antoni Comas, and Joa-
quim Molas, *Història de la Literatura Catalana (Part Antiga)*, vol. 4 (Barcelona:
Ariel, 1964), p. 435.
3. Even where Catalan sentiment runs highest, as in Cristòfol Despuig's in-
censed protest against the Castilian monopoly of Spanishness, the national sentiment in evidence is Spanish, not Catalan. Cristòfol Despuig, *Los col.loquis de
la insigne ciutat de Tortosa*, ed. F. Fita (Barcelona, 1877), p. 57.
4. Cited in Joan Fuster, "Notes sobre el 'llemosí' a la València del segle XVI,"
in *Llibres i problemes del Renaixement* (Barcelona: Publicacions de l'Abadia de
Montserrat, 1989), p. 58.
5. Rather than posing a contradiction, a figure like Joan Boscà has confir-
matory value. He was attached to the imperial court, and it was this circumstance that proved decisive for the development of Spanish poetry by setting the
scene for the literary conversation with Andrea Navagero in Granada in 1526.
6. Jordi Rubió i Balaguer, "Sobre les causes d'una decadència," in *Obres de
Jordi Rubió i Balaguer*, vol. 8 (Barcelona: Publicacions de l'Abadia de Montserrat, 1990), p. 138.
7. Riquer, p. 440.
8. Jordi Rubió i Balaguer, "L'ambient literari de la Catalunya del segle XVI,"
in *Obres*, 8:117.
9. Emmanuel Le Roy Ladurie, *Les paysans du Languedoc*, 2 vols. (Paris:
S.E.V.P.E.N., 1966), 2:636–37.
10. Jordi Rubió i Balaguer, "Humanisme i decadència?" in *Obres*, 8:353.
11. Rubió calls him a hellenist, but "classicist" is obviously meant, as the
king seems to have read the "ystoriis Grecorum" in Latin translations. Jordi Rubió i Balaguer, "Sobre els orígens de l'humanisme a Catalunya," in *Obres*, 8:31–
32.
12. Riquer, p. 438.

13. Ibid., p. 438.

14. Fuster, p. 50.

15. John Tomlinson, *Cultural Imperialism* (Baltimore: Johns Hopkins University Press, 1991), 1.

16. Josep-Sebastià Pons, *La littérature catalane en Rousillon au XVIIe et au XVIIIe siècles* (Toulouse, 1929), pp. 3ff. Cited by Fuster, p. 51.

17. Fuster, p. 51.

18. Cited in Rubió, "Humanisme i decadència?", p. 358.

19. Renato Barilli, *Rhetoric*, trans. Giuliana Menozzi (Minneapolis: University of Minnesota Press, 1989), p. 55.

20. The stirring of a national sentiment can be seen, however, in the ten-year war against John II (1462–1472). But it was kept in check by subsequent developments. It is also interesting to note that, having removed themselves from the king's authority, Catalans did not reestablish a Catalan dynasty, but offered the crown to Henry IV, king of Castile.

21. "And it was the bureaucracy which emerged now as a distinctive social grouping with special characteristics and interests, the principal ally of the prince, and yet one which, as we shall see, was to remain ambivalent. And it was the various parliamentary bodies the sovereigns created as mechanisms to assist them in the legislating of taxes, bodies composed largely of nobles, which the kings tried to use against the nobility and the nobility against the king." Immanuel Wallerstein, *The Modern World-System I. Capitalist Agriculture and the Origins of the European World-Economy in the Sixteenth Century* (New York: Academic Press, 1974), p. 31.

22. "No res menys, el que més ens podria allunyar de creure que l'entronització dels Trastàmares fou una de les causes de la nostra decadència literària és que tal cosa, així enunciada, diu molt poc a favor de la nostra cultura medieval, car sempre, a tot arreu, quan una dinastia forastera ha regnat sobre un país és aquest qui ha assimilat aquella i no aquella aquest. Exagerant els termes del problema hauríem de suposar una germanització de les lletres a Espanya en començar a regnar els Habsburgs i que els espanyols s'haguessin posat a escriure en francès a conseqüència de l'entronització dels Borbons amb felip V." Riquer, p. 436.

23. On this question, see Fuster.

24. Rubió, "Humanisme i Renaixement [Segle XVI]," in *Obres*, 8:225.

25. Rubió, "Sobre les causes d'una decadència," p. 138.

26. Jaume Vidal Alcover, *Síntesi d'història de la literatura catalana* (Barcelona: La Magrana, 1980), 1:241–42.

27. Riquer, p. 441.

28. Franco Moretti, "Modern European Literature," (paper), p. 7.

29. Rubió, "Humanisme i decadència?", p. 359.

30. Mikhail Bahktin, *The Dialogic Imagination*, trans. Caryl Emerson and Michael Holquist (Austin: University of Texas Press, 1981), p. 76.

31. *El Cortesano*, Colección de libros españoles raros o curiosos (Madrid, 1874), p. 371. Cited by Rubió, "Sobre el primer teatre valencià," in *Obres*, 8:154.

32. "València, a la primera meitat del segle XVI, molt abans de Rueda, i seguint una tradició que venia de lluny, havia trobat la força de crear un art teatral, que es manifestava en diàlegs sobre temes urbans, vivificats de l'esperit satíric popular." Rubió, "Sobre el primer teatre valencià," p. 155.

33. For an intelligent discussion of this phenomenon, see Fuster, pp. 53–54.

34. This explanation posited a fictitious language, "Llemosí," allegedly introduced by James I in Valencia, and a further differentiation between the regional variants after the unification of the Castilian and Aragonese crowns, which resulted in the dissolution of the political unity among the members of the Catalan-Aragonese state. See Fuster, pp. 53–54.

14

Cosmological Time and
the Impossibility of Closure

A Structural Element in
Spanish Golden Age Narratives

HANS ULRICH GUMBRECHT

———◆ ◆———

For quite some time now we have been discussing the question of whether Western culture finds itself in the middle of a transition from an age called "modernity" into a "postmodern" stage, but the most important product of this discussion may well be a by-product. It could lie in the only recently acquired and by no means fully exploited possibility of historicizing "historical time"—and, with it, any form of time—as segments of historically specific social constructions of reality. Having some distance on modernity was a necessary condition for the insight that "historical time," as the specific time-construction out of which modernity had emerged, could claim neither metahistorical nor transcultural validity. However, once we see time-constructions in their historical and cultural relativity, we can observe how they shape—and are shaped by—different forms and ranges of experience and action.[1] This is the philosophical background that makes possible a historical investigation concerning relations of interdependence between time-structures and structures of power and authority. As we assume that texts in general (and narrative texts in particular)[2] react to the time-constructions established in their environment both by reflecting them and by developing alternatives to them, we may hope, in addition, that

304

analyzing the techniques by which texts produce effects and impressions of timeliness will contribute to our understanding of historically specific forms of actions and usages of power.

In this essay, I try to make evident the existence of a relationship between a general frame or condition for everyday action and for the exercise of power in the Spanish Empire after 1550 and a highly recurrent structural element in Golden Age narratives. What I want to highlight as a general condition for the politics of the empire and for any kind of everyday interaction within its limits is the tension between a Subject-centered worldview and the superimposition of a Christian cosmology that eliminated the spaces of subjective choice, action, and interpretation. As early as during the reign of the Reyes Católicos, such a Subject-centered style of behavior had probably reached a higher level of complexity in Spain than in any other European society.[3] Following the Tridentinum, however, the new claim of the Spanish crown to carry out a divine mission in world history found its articulation in the reinstitutionalization of a theologically based "order of things." Although the tension between these two principles may have been the decisive condition for the emergence of Golden Age culture and literature, it was never explicitly thematized (and perhaps never even perceived in its totality) by contemporary texts. One of its more indirect materializations was an authentic obsession concerning the impossibility of narrative closure that haunted Spanish authors since the middle of the sixteenth century.

The most famous literary context in which such an obsession with closure found its articulation is certainly the conversation between Don Quijote and Ginés de Pasamonte, which precedes the "liberation" of the prisoners held in chains by the Santa Hermandad. In this context, it is important to notice that the short autobiographical narratives previously presented to Don Quijote by Pasamonte's companions are introduced as emerging out of what must be seen as the most typical institution for the production of narratives constituting Subject-identity, namely, the institution of legal accusation and legal defense.[4] This seems to be the reason why none of the protagonists (nor, may we assume, any contemporary reader) was surprised by the prisoners' capacity to offer well-shaped (although, of course, treacherous) narratives of individual identity. Ginés de Pasamonte, however, is a different prisoner. Not only does he appear as "by far the most dangerous" among this group of criminals; he is, at the same time, the only one whose behavior toward Don Quijote is arrogant and condescending, and who, instead of presenting his identity, refers him to an autobiography which, as Pasamonte claims, will outshine even the most popular picaresque novels:

> Señor caballero, si tiene algo que darnos, dénoslo ya y vaya con Dios; que ya enfada con tanto querer saber vidas ajenas; y si la mía quiere saber, sepa que soy Ginés de Pasamonte, cuya vida está escrita por estos pulgares.
> —Dice verdad—dijo el comisario—; que él mismo ha escrito su historia, que no hay más, y deja empeñado el libro en la cárcel en doscientos reales.[5]
> ["Sir knight, if you have anything to bestow, pray let us have it, and the Lord be with you, for you only tire us with inquiring about other people's affairs; if you want to be informed of my history, know, I am that Ginés de Pasamonate whose life has been written by these ten fingers."
> "He speaks the truth," said the commissary; "for, he has actually written his own history, as well as could be desired, and pawned the manuscript in jail for two hundred reales."] (Smollett, p. 162; emended by Iarocci)

The following exchange between Ginés and Don Quijote has traditionally (and, I assume, correctly) been read as evidence for Cervantes' prejudice against the picaresque genre. It culminates in pointing to the logical incompatibility between the two central claims of the autobiographical discourse, namely, the claim of representing the totality of an individual life and the claim of being narrated by the central protagonist:

> —¿Y cómo se intitula el libro?—preguntó Don Quijote.
> —La vida de Ginés de Pasamonte—respondió él mismo.
> —¿Y está acabado?—preguntó Don Quijote.
> —¿Cómo puede estar acabado—respondió él—si aun no está acabada mi vida? Lo que está escrito es desde mi nacimiento hasta el punto que esta última vez me han echado en galeras . . .
> —. . . y no me pesa mucho de ir a ellas, porque allí tendré lugar

de acabar mi libro, que me quedan muchas cosas que decir, y en las galeras de España hay más sosiego de aquel que sería menester, aunque no es menester mucho más de lo que yo tengo de escribir, porque me lo sé de coro.

—Hábil pareces—dijo Don Quijote.

["And what is the title of your book?" asked Don Quijote. "The Life of Ginés de Pasamonte," replied the other. "And is it finished?" asked Don Quijote. "How can it be finished," he answered, "when my life is not yet concluded? What I have written is from my birth to the last time I was sent to the gallies . . . and it does not pain me a great deal to go to them now, for there I shall have time to finish my book, and set down a great many things I have to say, there being spare time enough in the gallies of Spain, for that purpose which does not require much leisure, as I know every circumstance by heart." "You seem like an ingenious fellow," said Don Quijote.] (Smollett, p. 162; emended by Iarocci)

The problem whose discussion brings Don Quijote's and Pasamonte's conversation to an end is of course inherent in any kind of autobiographical discourse. In other words, its existence does not depend on any conditions specific to Spanish Golden Age culture. And yet it is remarkable that this concern is frequently thematized in Spanish texts between 1550 and 1650, whereas otherwise it is a convention characterizing autobiographical texts as a genre to bracket the logical impossibility of their closure. Our observation leads to the hypothesis that, beyond Cervantes' probable intention to criticize the picaresque genre from a poetological point of view, there must be a larger and historically specific condition that deletes the brackets around the issue of narrative closure. I will try to argue that it lies in an interference between two different time-constructions depending on the interference between a Subject-centered and a cosmological worldview. The unfolding of this argument, however, makes it necessary to discuss, with more conceptual depth, some notions concerning the phenomenology of time and the historicization of time-constructions and the relation between time-constructions and different forms of narrative in order to understand, finally, the obsession with closure that characterizes Spanish Golden Age literature.

I

Husserl's description of time as "form of experience" presupposes a four-leveled model for the understanding of human experience and action.[6] Its basic level refers to the multiplicity of sensuous perceptions simultaneously registered by the human body at any given moment. Under the notion of "lived experience" ("Erleben"), the second level thematizes the reduction of such complexity by the mind's focusing on one of those perceptions at each single moment and thus establishing a sequence of objects of experience. The actual "production of experience" ("Erfahrung," "Erfahrungsbildung"), as a third level, lies in the interpretation of such objects of experience through elements of knowledge that the mind has inductively acquired in previous acts of experience production or which have been provided in the context of socialization processes. Finally, it is through the combination of different elements of experience that motivations for actions are constituted. Such "motivations" are images of future situations to whose realization actions are designed to contribute. What becomes apparent in this concept of "motivation" is equally valid for the levels of "experience" and "lived experience": each moment constituting the present of the mind is embedded between the impact of its immediate past and the anticipation of its immediate future. Husserl calls these two dimensions "Retention" and "Protention." The horizon of Retention provides a background against which the specificity of each present experience can be identified, whereas Protention functions as an expectation of either the similarity or the difference between each present and its immediately following experience. Together, Retention and Protention produce our impression of consciousness as a time-flow ("Bewusstseinsstrom").

Although Husserl insists on the short temporal range of both Retention and Protention, I think that it is possible to combine his thought with a typology by which the historian Reinhart Koselleck has tried to characterize different forms in the experience of history.[7] Parallel to the binarism "Protention/Retention," Koselleck's basic distinction sets apart the past as "space of experience" from the future as "horizon of expectation." "Space of experience" and "horizon of expectation" can be either in a relation of symmetry or in a relation of asymmetry. Under the condition of symmetry, present and future are expected to be similar to the past, and past experience thereby receives an absolute authority as a model for present and future actions. In addition, symmetry between the space of experience and the horizon of expectation makes any drawing of sharp distinctions between the past, the present, and the future superfluous. It constitutes a time of continuity.

What, in contrast, we call "historical time," the general assumption of an asymmetry between the space of experience and the horizon of expectation, weakens the authority of the past, or at least makes much more complex the conditions under which "learning from history" is assumed to be possible.[8] Historical time requires the identification of "periods" within which certain conditions of experience and action were/are valid, and it is therefore constantly confronted with the necessity of drawing lines of closure. This task establishes a double relationship between historical time and the notion of "Subjectivity." The retrospective of a Subject-position is necessary for the shaping of the past into different "historical periods." At the same time, the Subject's retrospective is concerned with the identification of other Subjects as points of convergence for styles of experience and action that remain stable against the effects of time. Historical time thus brings forth both a Subject-position as prerequisite for the structuring of the past and Subject-configurations as the result of such structuring.

II

What we call "paratactical narrative" corresponds to the time-construction of continuity (or of symmetry between past and future). Mostly remaining on the phenomenological level of "lived experience," paratactical narratives present a series of objects of experience that are barely connected by the expectation of an ongoing sequentiality (". . . and then . . . and then"). The position of an auctorial voice, of a narrator, or of an author remains void because no structuring of the objects of experience presented by the narrative into time periods or subject figures takes place. Like any other kind of text, paratactical narratives come to an end, but as they are never actively brought to an end, they are always open for continuation. One might go so far as to say that, applied to paratactical texts, the distinction between "finished" and "unfinished" texts (which, especially among medievalists, has opened so many endless discussions) appears to be inadequate.

"Hypotactical narratives," in contrast, are based on the assumption of an asymmetry between past and future, and therefore alternate between a level of lived experience and a level on which lived experience is interpreted and structured. With their concern for distinguishing "stages" as parts of a "development," the discourses of the bildungsroman or of philosophy of history, as they dominated in Western culture during the second half of the eighteenth and during the nineteenth century, are perhaps the most obvious examples of this relationship between a social time-construction and a type of narrative. The structuring interventions of the auctorial voice (or of the narrator) take place from a position of Protention because they presuppose an awareness of the outcome to which the narrative will lead. While the role of the narrator, as a function of Subjectivity, marks the inevitable position of closure and of fulfillment for hypotactical narratives, it shapes, at the same time, protagonists as Subject-figures who do not share its status of omniscience.

At this point in our argument, it is certainly no longer surprising to associate what we have described as "time of continuity" with the time-construction of medieval cosmology.[9] The very meaning of the medieval phrase "media aetas" comprehends the totality of "historical time" in the modern sense as a continuity between the two events of the creation and of the end of the world. Despite all the speculations of high and late medieval millenarism about the date of doomsday, it was the primary understanding that no "development" would interrupt the continuity of media aetas and, thus, announce the end of the world. Tropes such as "translatio studii" and "figura" presuppose and underline the assumption of a sameness of times: the transfer of knowledge between different places on the medieval world map would not affect its content (translatio), and the identification of similarities between events belonging to different times, especially to those of the Old Testament and the New Testament, would rely on a premise of continuity (figura). Within this construction of cosmological time, any experience of change was attributed to the "fickleness" ("mutabilitas") of the world—and implied an imperative to come back to the original order of creation. While concepts such as "event" or "development" had no place within medieval cosmology, the negative connotation that was automatically related with any experience of change transformed long-standing institutional continuity into a value of legitimation and authority. In contrast, there was hardly a place within these relevance-structures for the individual human life as a form. While medieval documents normally inform us about the year in which a king was crowned or in which a church dignitary took over an important office, we almost regularly ignore the birth dates of even the most important historical protagonists. For hagiographical texts, the most important relevance perspective lies in the absolute avoidance of sins—that is, in the absence of events. In a world of cosmological time, the concern with continuity prevails over the interest in development and Subjectivity.

Since the emergence, however, of a historical worldview, which we usually trace back to the efforts of the Renaissance of positioning itself as present in relation to classical antiquity and to the Middle Ages as periods of the past, time has been perceived as an agent of never-ending change. In this sense, the social history and the literary history of early European modernity confirm the philosophical argument about the relatedness between an asymmetry of past and future on the one side and, on the other side, the emergence of functions of Subjectivity and the concern with narrative closure. From its beginning, Renaissance historiography was concerned with the attribution of protagonists, phenomena, and events as a device of determining their relevance for the present. The beginning of this practice coincides with the beginning of an attrition of the present as a space (or a duration) which will culminate in the nineteenth-century definition of the present as a mere point of transition. Finally, the continuity of institutions does not only progressively lose its connotation of legitimacy; it is transformed into an attribute that will end up entailing, within the construction of historical time, the necessity of problematization for whatever maintains a continuity over a larger timespan. Under conditions of historical time, authority and continuity enter a process of mutual dissociation.

III

If we apply the concepts and criteria laid out in the previous sections to texts, institutions, and cultural artifacts in the medieval reign of Castile, we find—long before the age of the Reyes Católicos—evidence for the emergence of time-constructions and textual forms built around structures of Subjectivity. The most plausible explanation for their existence seems to lie in the fact that, on the Iberian peninsula, Christian cosmology had always been confronted with Jewish and with Islamic culture, so that the experience of cultural difference must have brought forth an awareness of the necessity to mediate and even to choose between different worldviews. As early as the fourteenth century, the chronicles of Pero López de Ayala were conceived as biographies. They yield portraits of considerable "psychological depth" for several Castilian rulers, and they are characterized by continuous interventions and commentaries from a third-person narrator. Interestingly, an important part of these commentaries is dedicated to Ayala's effort to shed a positive light on the murder of King Pedro I by his half-brother and successor Enrique de Trastámara—which means that he tried to legitimize a case of flagrant genealogical discontinuity. Fernán Pérez de Guzmán's *Generaciones y semblanzas* and Fernando de Pulgar's *Claros varones de Castilla* make it evident that, during the following century, a main focus on individual protagonists was already fully accepted as a normal form of historiographical representation. In some of the portraits drawn by Pérez de Guzmán and by Pulgar, certain topoi coming from the earlier tradition based on the perspective of genealogy can be easily distinguished from details concerned with the narrative constitution of individuality. The short text that Pérez de Guzmán dedicated to Dona Catalina de Lancaster, the wife of King Enrique III, combines information about her status and some of the standard positive attributes applied to any member of any royal family in medieval historiography, with some less favorable details (italicized in the following quotation) which begin to evoke an individual portrait:

> La reina dona Catalina, muger deste rey don Enrique, fue fija de don Iohan de Lencastre, fijo ligitimo del rey Aduarte de Inguelterra, el cual duque caso con dona Costanca, fija del rey don Pedro de Castilla e de dona Maria de Padilla.

Fue esta reina alta de cuerpo e muy gruesa, blanca e colorada e rubia. En el talle e meneo del cuerpo tanto parecia onbre como muger. Fue muy onesta e guardada en su presona e fama, liberal e manifica, pero muy sometida a priuados e muy regida dellos, lo cual, por la mayor parte, es bicio comun de los reyes. No era bien regida en su presona; ouo una grande dolencia de perlesia, de la cual non quedo bien suelta de lengua nin libre de cuerpo. Murió en Valladolid en hedad de cincuenta anos, ano de mill e cuatrocientos e dies e ocho anos.[10]

[Queen Catalina, wife of this King Henry, was the daughter of John, duke of Lancaster, legitimate son of King Edward of England; the duke married Costanza, daughter of Peter of Castile and Maria of Padilla. This queen was tall, very corpulent, fair skinned, of a rosy complexion, and blond. Her build and demeanor could just as easily have been those of a man or a woman. She was honest and careful with both her person and her reputation; she was generous and magnanimous, but she would submit to the will of her favorites and was under their power, which on the whole is a common fault among monarchs. Her physical condition was not good; she suffered a great bout of paralysis, from which neither tongue nor body were ever completely freed. She died in Valladolid at fifty years of age in the year fourteen hundred and eighteen.]

In general, fifteenth-century historiographers seem to assume that there is a problematic relationship between individuality and authority. Their most extensive portraits do not refer to successful politicians but to those who, as the authors argue, had lost their authority through an excess of individuality. One of them was Juan II of Castile, who, according to Fernán Pérez de Guzmán, had handed over all political power to his privado Alvaro de Luna: "E porque la condicion suya fue estrana e marauillosa, es nescesario de alargar la relacion della"[11] [And because his position was extraordinary and awesome, it is necessary to prolong the accounting of it]. Exactly the same relation between individuality, loss of authority, and narrative structure provokes Celestina's long autobiographical confession in the *Tragicomedia de Calisto y Melibea*. Here, the servant Sempronio tries to blackmail the go-between, who had controlled every kind of business in the underworld, by threatening that he will reveal her true identity in public. Celestina replies with the insistence on a perspective that emphasizes the normality of her life form:

> SEMPRONIO—. . . Danos las dos partes por cuenta de quanto de Calisto has recebido, no quieras que se descubra quién tú eres. A los otros, a los otros, con esos halagos, vieja.
> CELESTINA—¿Quién só yo, Sempronio? ¿Quitásteme de la putería? Calla tu lengua, no amengues mis canas, que soy vna vieja qual Dios me hizo, no pero que todas. Viuo de mi oficio, como cada cual oficial del suyo, muy limpiamente.[12]
> [Sempronio: . . . Give us two parts of that which you have received from Calisto, lest you wish to be discovered for what you are; come, come old woman, exercise your wits upon some other. Celestina: Why, what am I, Sempronio? Did you bring me out of whoring? Bridle your tongue, and do not belittle my gray hairs, for I am an old woman of God's making, no worse than all other women are. I live quite honestly, by my occupation, as other women do.] (Mabbe; emended by Iarocci)

The amazing impression of modernity that the fictional autobiography of Lazarillo de Tormes, first published in 1554, continues conveying to readers of the late twentieth century can be seen as a culminating point in the particularly early emergence of Subjectivity and biographical narrative within Castilian culture. The structurally necessary distinction between the level of the first-person narrator and that of the first-person protagonist, however, seems to be strengthened—and, semiotically speaking, overdetermined—by the fact that, while the protagonist exploits the spaces of Subjective action and Subjective world-interpretation, the narrator clearly adapts his discourse to the religious cosmology that was newly institutionalized in the Spanish Empire around the middle of the sixteenth century. We can therefore characterize the historical place of the picaresque genre on the level of its narrative construction as the convergence and tension between the two world-views that constituted Spanish Golden Age culture. However, regarding our main question, the relation between narrative closure and narrative continuation, this very structure explains why picaresque novels oscillate between closure (as modern tales of individuality) and a desire for continuation (as participating in a medieval kind of cosmology and its time-construction). Typically enough, the text of the first Lazarillo edition ends with a sentence that sums up what is described as the most successful stage in the protagonist's life, whereas the 1555 edition explicitly announces a continuation of the narrative: "Pues en este tiempo estaua en mi prosperidad y en la cumbre de toda buena fortuna. De lo que de aqui adelante me suscediere auisaré a Vuestra Merced"[13] [And at this time I was prosperous and at the height of all good fortune. I will inform Your Grace about what happens to me from this point forward].

If a textual demonstration is still necessary, the ending of the first Lazarillo edition proves that there are narrative techniques by which the logical problem of closing an autobiography can be overcome. Therefore, the fact that Golden Age texts in general—and picaresque novels in particular—are characterized by an oscillation between such gestures of closure and an opening of the narrative for continuation must go back to a historically specific condition. I have argued for the identification of the overlapping between two different social constructions of time as the driving force behind the Golden Age's obsession with closure and continuation. Although, obviously, its manifestations were not restricted to a single genre, I will now focus on the final passages of some further picaresque novels in order to show that a true narrative morphology emerged out of the concern of balancing closure and openness for continuation.

The most frequently used variant can be described as a double turning point. In the final episode of his autobiography the fictional protagonist reaches a situation of economic safety (normally together with a minimum of social respectability) from which he can look back to his former life. This final episode, however, surprisingly ends with a sentence that reopens the narrative, either by simply alluding to a continuation of the story or by announcing a second turn in the protagonist's fate, a turn back to the instability of picaresque existence. At the end of the second part in Mateo Alemán's *Guzmán de Alfarache*, the protagonist achieves his return to freedom by giving away the secret of a conspiracy among his fellow galley slaves. But the announcement of a third part of the novel (which Alemán probably never wrote) relativizes the status of this episode as a concluding element: "Aquí di punto y fin a estas desgracias. Rematé la cuenta con mi mala vida. La que después gasté todo el restante della verás en la tercera y última parte, si el cielo me la diere antes de la eterna que todos esperamos"[14] [This is where I put an end to these misfortunes. I cleared the slate on my evil life. You will see how I spent the rest of my life in the third and final part, if heaven allows it before bestowing on me the eternal life that we all await].

Of course such a reopening of an already closed autobiography definitely undermines the belief in a central Subject-function, that is, the conviction that it is possible to create and to achieve one's own social status. In the final paragraphs of *La Pícara Justina*, this very same motif becomes the object of open irony. From one marriage to the next, in the past and in the future, Justina's life is a long sequence of such "turning points," which in her case always consist of the restitution of the protagonist's virginity. In the final paragraph of *El Buscón*, Quevedo lets Pablos once more escape the police before the hero finally travels to America. But the obligatory announcement of a second part of the novel (which Quevedo probably never planned to write) goes together with what may be the only entirely serious sentence in the whole book. The narrator knows that his fate and his social status will not change because he is not sincerely trying to change his lifestyle:

La justicia no se descuidaba de buscarnos; rondábanos la puerta, pero, con todo, de media noche abajo, rondábamos disfrazados. Yo que vi que duraba mucho este negocio, y más la fortuna en perseguirme, no de escarmentado—que no soy tan cuerdo—, sino de cansado, como obstinado pecador, determiné, consultándolo primero con la Grajal, de pasarme a Indias con ella, a ver si, mudando mundo y tierra, mejoraría mi suerte. Y fueme peor, como v.m. verá en la segunda parte, pues nunca mejora su estado quien muda solamente de lugar, y no de vida y costumbres.[15]

[The law sought us without rest; they awaited for us at the door, but in spite of this, after midnight we would wander about in disguise. As I saw that this state of things was lasting a long time and that my fate persisted in pursuing me, after talking it over with Grajal I decided—not because I had learned my lesson (for I am not that sensible), but because I was tired—to go to the Indies with her in order to see if, by changing lands and surroundings, my luck would improve. But things took a turn for the worse, as you will see in the second part, for he who moves from one

place to another without changing his habits and his lifestyle never im-
proves his lot.]

We encounter a different version of the balance between closure and
opening at the end of H. de Luna's Lazarillo continuation. Here, the narrator pretends to follow a manuscript that he found in a Toledan ar-
chive. But he adds, with obvious irony, that the text of this manuscript
corresponds exactly to some tales his great-grandmother and his aunts
used to tell at the fireside. The end of Luna's continuation, where, referring again to his great-grandmother as main witness, the narrator says
farewell to his readers, seems to fully confirm the frame-narrative. Even
this closure, however, is destabilized by the fact that, in his preface, Luna
had already announced a further part of the novel containing Lázaro's
death and testament.

A third and final form of ending that we find in picaresque novels for-
goes both the announcement of a continuation and the final turning
point within the autobiographical narrative. In *Marcos Obregón* and
Estebanillo González, the first-person narrator arrives at the insight
that, although he is approaching his old age, the course of his life—his
fortune—will never decisively change. This attitude ultimately provides
the motivation and the necessary distance for writing the story of his
own life:

> Ya cansado de tantos golpes de fortuna, por mar y por tierra, y
> viendo lo poco que me había durado la mocedad, determiné de ase-
> gurar la vida y prevenir la muerte, que es el paradero de todas las
> cosas; que si ésta es buena, corrige y suelda todos los descuidos
> cometidos en la juventud. Escribíle en lenguaje fácil y claro, por no
> poner en cuidado al lector para entendello.[16]
> [Having tired of fortune's blows on land and on sea, and seeing how little
> my youth had lasted, I decided to secure my life and to prepare for death,
> to which all things come to rest; for if this *Life* is good, it mends and cor-
> rects all youthful lapses. I wrote it in a clear, easy language so as not to
> trouble the reader's understanding.]

Published in 1618 and in 1648, both *Marcos Obregón* and *Estebanillo
González* represent a relatively late stage in the history of the picaresque
genre. Can we therefore read them as symptoms of a final solution con-

cerning the narrative tension between closure and continuation that we had interpreted as a product of the interference between two different time-constructions? The answer to this question is ambiguous. Moving the first-person narrator's position closer to the end of the first-person protagonist's life certainly assures the possibility of narrative closure. On the other hand, by giving away the possibility of telling the protagonists' lives as a trajectory, and of conveying a form and an identity to them, these fictional autobiographies remain dependent on the pre-Subjective category of fate. Perhaps it is adequate to say that, during the course of the seventeenth century, the oscillation, characteristic of Golden Age culture, between a Subject-centered and a cosmological worldview was progressively replaced by a specific figure of Subjectivity. Reading the most frequently quoted Spanish autobiography written during the eighteenth century, Torres Villarroel's *Vida*, we may speculate that this was a Subjectivity that, in spite of reaching a high degree of reflexivity, never assumed a position of agency.[17] It may have been the only form of Subjectivity for which a time frame of continuity left sufficient space.

IV

In using notions from that chapter of Western history to which we often refer as "the rise of Subjectivity," it was impossible to fully avoid a halo of connotations which attribute strong positive values to anything related to "Subjectivity" and cast a negative light on all phenomena that are seen as interfering with its development. This very discourse made it an obligation to address the problem of Spain's "historical delay." If, however, there is anything serious behind the impression that we find ourselves moving out of the space of modernity, it is our growing hesitation to rely on self-reflexivity, and to claim a position of agency. It may be an overdramatization of the present situation to speak of a "death of the Subject," but we have certainly adopted a more ambiguous view on Subjectivity.

In this context, the question arises whether certain transformations that have characterized the Western novel since the time of high modernism cannot be seen as a reversal or, at least, as a dissolution of those structures that, especially in England and in France, the genre had progressively acquired during the seventeenth and the eighteenth centuries. There seems to be a desire to go back from the complexity of the hypotactical narrative to the elementary level of "lived experience." While the narrator becomes more and more "unreliable," the Subject figurations drawn by his discourse appear increasingly fuzzy (until the point where, in the nouveau roman, their names are being replaced by pronouns). Narrative closure becomes a problem again, and a lack of clear distinctions between different episodes and stages within the plot produces effects of simultaneity and paradox.

Even outside the sphere of purely textual experience, the premise is no longer unquestioned that we are still surrounded by the fast-moving historical time. Have we not become reluctant to identify "decisive changes" and "ground-breaking innovations"? Are we not increasingly uncertain as to where to locate thresholds between present and future? Has our present not become broader during the second half of the twentieth century? Although these questions are meant to be, on the one hand, rhetorical questions, it is, on the other hand, not entirely clear how we can answer them. While, in tandem with our impression of a weakening Subject, we begin to speculate about the end of historical time, we have no concepts, no philosophies, and no laws which would not constantly affirm the reality of the Subject and of historical time. The "postmodern condition" has not only sharpened our awareness of interferences between different time-constructions in the past—it is itself such an interference.

Notes

1. See Edmund Husserl, *Vorlesungen zur Phaenomenologie des inneren Zeitbewusstseins* (Halle: M. Niemeyer, 1928), p. 11.

2. While *narrative* texts often mimic the effects of time-structures in their environment, there is no evident reason to think that *literary* texts in general have a specific relation to everyday time-structures.

3. See chapter 21 of Machiavelli's *Principe*, where the personality and the achievements of Fernando de Aragón are analyzed from this very perspective. I have broadly documented and discussed the thesis of such an early development

of Subjectivity in my book *Eine Geschichte der spanishcen Literatur* (Frankfurt: Suhrkamp, 1990), esp. pp. 221ff. This book may also serve as a background reference for some of the perspectives presented here.

4. See Manfred Fuhrmann, "Rechtfertigung durch Identität—Über eine Wurzel des Autobiographischen," in Odo Marquand and Karlheinz Stierle, eds., *Identität: Poetik und Hermeneutik VIII* (Munich: W. Fink, 1979), pp. 685–90.

5. Quoted after the edition of Miguel de Cervantes Saavedra, *Obras completas*, ed. Angel Valbuena Prat (Madrid: Aguilar, 1970), 2:1115.

6. For a more detailed presentation of this theory, see my article "Sobre os interesses cognitivos, terminología básica e métodos de uma ciência da literatura fundada na teoria da açao," in Luiz Costa Lima, ed., *A literatura e o leitor: Textos de estética de recepçao* (Rio de Janeiro: Paz e Terra, 1979), pp. 189–211, and the chapters on narrative theory in my book *Making Sense in Life and Literature* (Minneapolis: University of Minnesota Press, 1992), pp. 33–75.

7. Reinhart Koselleck, " 'Erfahrungsraum' und 'Erwartungshorizont'—zwei historische Kategorien," in *Vergangene Zukunft: Zur Semantik geschichtlicher Zeiten* (Frankfurt: Suhrkamp, 1989), pp. 249–75.

8. Within Western culture these conditions were discussed for the first time in the *Querelle des Anciens et des Modernes.* The "philosophy of history," from Voltaire via Hegel up to Marx, can be seen as an effort to maintain the claim concerning the value of history for orientation in the present.

9. My remarks concerning medieval constructions of time are based on the results of a collective volume on medieval historiography that I published with my colleagues Ursula Link-Heer and Peter-Michael Spangenberg: *La littérature historiographique des origines à 1500* (Heidelberg: C. Winter, 1986), esp. 1:17–25.

10. Fernán Pérez de Guzmán, *Generaciones y semblanzas*, ed. J. Domínguez Bordoña (Madrid: Clásicos Castellanos, 1965), p. 19.

11. Ibid., p. 118.

12. Fernando de Rojas, *La Celestina*, ed. Julio Cejador y Frauca (Madrid: Clásicos Castellanos, 1968), p. 101.

13. *La vida de Lazarillo de Tormes y sus fortunas y adversidades*, ed. Julio Cejador y Frauca (Madrid: Clásicos Castellanos, 1969), p. 243.

14. Mateo Alemán, *Guzmán de Alfarache*, ed. Samuel Gil y Gaya (Madrid: Clásicos Castellanos, 1967), p. 177.

15. Francisco de Quevedo, *La vida del Buscón llamado Don Pablos*, ed. Fernando Lázaro Carreter (Salamanca: Consejo Superior de Investigaciones Científicas, 1965), p. 280.

16. Vicente Espinel, *Vida de Marcos de Obregón*, ed. Samuel Gil y Gaya (Madrid: Clásicos Castellanos, 1970), 2:308.

17. See my article "Vida, ascendencia, nacimiento, crianza y aventuras de el Doctor Don Diego Torres Villarroel, Cathedratico de Prima de Mathemáticas en la Universidad de Salamanca," in Volker Roloff and Harald Wentzlaff-Eggebert, eds., *Der spanische Roman* (Düsseldorf: Schwann Bagel, 1986), pp. 145–70.

Notes on Contributors

Marina S. Brownlee is the Class of 1963 College of Women Professor of Romance Languages at the University of Pennsylvania. She is the author of *The Poetics of Literary Theory: Lope's "Novelas a Marcia Leonarda" and Their Cervantine Context*, *The Status of the Reading Subject in the "Libro de buen amor,"* and *The Severed Word: Ovid's "Heroides" and the "Novela Sentimental."*

Anthony J. Cascardi is professor of Spanish, comparative literature, and rhetoric at the University of California, Berkeley, and general editor of the Penn State Series in Literature and Philosophy. Among his publications are *The Limits of Illusion: A Critical Study of Calderón*, *The Bounds of Reason: Cervantes, Dostoevsky, Flaubert*, and *The Subject of Modernity*.

Walter Cohen, professor of comparative literature and dean of the Graduate School at Cornell University, is the author of *Drama of a Nation: Public Theater in Renaissance England and Spain*.

The late Ruth El Saffar was professor of Spanish at the University of Illinois, Chicago. Among her published works are *Novel to Romance: A Study of Cervantes' "Novelas ejemplares,"* *Distance and Control in "Don Quijote,"* and *Beyond Fiction: The Recovery of the Feminine in the Novels of Cervantes*.

Edward H. Friedman is professor of Spanish and comparative literature at Indiana University. His work on Spanish literature includes *The Unifying Concept: Approaches to Cervantes' "Comedias"* and *The Antiheroine's Voice: Narrative Discourse and Transformations of the Pica-*

resque. He is currently the editor of the *Indiana Journal of Hispanic Literatures.*

Mary Malcolm Gaylord is professor and chair of the Department of Romance Languages and Literatures at Harvard University. She is the author of *The Historical Prose of Fernando de Herrera,* as well as many articles on Spanish Golden Age poetry, poetics, drama, and prose fiction.

Hans Ulrich Gumbrecht is the Albert Guérard Professor of Literature at Stanford University and a member of the departments of comparative literature, French and Italian, and Spanish and Portuguese. His extensive publications include *Eine Geschichte der spanischen Literatur* and *Making Sense in Life and Literature.* He is also a regular contributor to the *Frankfurter Allgemeine Zeitung.*

José M. Regueiro teaches medieval and Golden Age theater and lyric at the University of Pennsylvania, and has written on the concept of theatrical space. He is the author of *Semantica español.*

Joan Ramón Resina is professor of Spanish at the State University of New York at Stonybrook. His book publications include *La búsqueda del grial, Un sueño de piedra, Ensayos sobre la literatura del modernismo europeo,* and *Los usos del clásico.*

Lía Schwartz Lerner is professor of Spanish and comparative literature at Dartmouth College. She has published extensively on satire, love poetry, and the interplay of ideological forces in early modern Spain, and is the author of *Metáfora y sátira en la obra de Quevedo* and *Quevedo: discurso y representación.*

Harry Sieber is professor of Spanish at the Johns Hopkins University and general editor of *Modern Language Notes.* His published books are *The Picaresque* and *Language and Society in "La vida de Lazarillo de Tormes."*

Paul Julian Smith is professor of Spanish and head of the Department of Spanish and Portuguese at Cambridge University. Among his books are

The Body Hispanic: Gender and Sexuality in Spanish and Spanish American Literature, Laws of Desire: Questions of Homosexuality in Spanish Writing and Film, and *Desire Unlimited: The Cinema of Pedro Almodóvar.*

Robert ter Horst is professor of Spanish and comparative literature at the University of Rochester. He is the author of *Calderón: The Secular Plays,* as well as many articles on a variety of topics relating to the Golden Age.

Diana de Armas Wilson teaches Renaissance studies at the University of Denver. She has written on a variety of literary and theoretical issues pertaining to early modern Spain, including her book entitled *Allegories of Love: Cervantes' "Persiles and Sigismunda."*

LIBRARY OF CONGRESS CATALOGING-IN-PUBLICATION DATA

Cultural authority in Golden Age Spain / edited by Marina S. Brownlee
and Hans Ulrich Gumbrecht.
    p.   cm. — (Parallax)
    Includes bibliographical references.
    ISBN 0-8018-4936-5 (alk. paper). — ISBN 0-8018-4937-3 (pbk. : alk. paper)
    1. Spanish literature—Classical period, 1500–1700—History and criticism.
2. Politics and literature—Spain—History—16th century. 3. Politics and
literature—Spain—History—17th century. 4. Literature and society—
Spain—History—16th century. 5. Literature and society—Spain—History—
17th century. I. Brownlee, Marina Scordilis. II. Gumbrecht, Hans Ulrich.
III. Series: Parallax (Baltimore, Md.)
PQ6606.C8 1995
860.9'358—dc20   94-35505
                                              CIP